THE ANCIENT WORLD

TO A.D. 300

THE ANCIENT WORLD

TO A.D. 300

SECOND EDITION

EDITED BY

PAUL J. ALEXANDER

The University of Michigan

The Macmillan Company, New York
Collier-Macmillan Limited, London

First Printing

Library of Congress catalog card number: 68-10120

THE MACMILLAN COMPANY, NEW YORK
COLLIER-MACMILLAN CANADA, LTD., TORONTO, ONTARIO

PRINTED IN THE UNITED STATES OF AMERICA

PREFACE

As in the first edition and in accordance with the program for the series, this volume is designed to illustrate ideas and institutions of the ancient world that were basic for the development of Western Civilization. The selections are taken primarily from ancient texts. When the evidence for ancient civilizations is archaeological or when, for other reasons, the material by itself does not tell a clear story, discussions of this evidence by modern authors are reprinted.

Selection of materials is of necessity a difficult matter, especially when the thought and experience of several great civilizations of the past has to be considered in the narrow compass of a volume of modest size. The principal aim of this volume is to present ideas, as well as political, social, and economic institutions, of the ancient world which played a role in the evolution of Western Civilization in medieval and modern times. An attempt has been made to choose, wherever possible, passages that perform this function in a dramatic, eloquent, and authoritative fashion. Limitations of space, however, forbid the inclusion of texts which are important exclusively or primarily for their literary form. In many instances it would have been desirable to elaborate on a key concept by adding supplementary materials, but here again considerations of space intervened. Furthermore, remarkable texts, such as the comedies of Aristophanes, are not represented in this volume because in undergraduate courses, for which this series is designed, they do not yield their full profit without detailed commentary. It is hoped that readers will make up for these and other omissions by further study of the ancient authors.

The arrangement of the materials in this volume is chronological. Within each part, political, social, and economic materials are normally placed ahead of excerpts illustrating intellectual developments. In this as well as in other matters, however, strict and formal consistency may be the enemy of a natural unfolding and a clear exposition. In such cases the cause of consistency has been sacrificed without compunction.

For this second edition one reading has been eliminated and a number of new pieces added, particularly to the early sections. In addition, the entire text has been revised.

Acknowledgments: I wish to express again my sincere thanks to a number of persons who aided in the preparation of the first edition. Mrs. Irene Winner revised the style of Parts II to VI with remarkable imagination and understanding. Mrs. Jacqueline Brown performed a similar service for the rest of the manuscript. My wife typed several drafts, never lost her patience, and gave me most valuable advice. My son Lawrence helped me in selecting the materials and typed parts of the manuscript. Mrs. Linda Eggert, the secretary of the Department of History at The University of Michigan, kindly typed a number of selections. For the second edition of this book I have profited from the advice of three colleagues who used the book in their classes and offered their criticisms to the publisher. I do not know their names, but I wish to assure them that their remarks have been given most careful consideration. Two able teaching fellows in my own department, Messrs. Thomas McKibben and Timothy Gregory, also made valuable suggestions for additional readings.

P. J. A.

CONTENTS

I / THE ANCIENT NEAR EAST

MESOPOTAMIA AND SYRIA

1 / THE SARGON CHRONICLE

The text of this chronicle is preserved on tablets written in the Neo-Babylonian period. It records outstanding events that occurred under the Babylonian kings, Sargon of Agade (circa *2400* B.C.) *and his successors of whom the most important was Hammurabi* (circa *1700* B.C.). *It is reproduced here as an example of Oriental historiography.*[1]

Sargon, king of Agade, rose to power in the era of Ishtar and had neither rival nor opponent. He spread his terror-inspiring glamor over all the countries. He crossed the Sea in the East and he, himself, conquered the country in the West, in its full extent in the eleventh year of his rule. He established there a central government. He erected his stelae in the West. Their booty (i.e. the booty of the countries in the Eastern and Western Seas) he ferried over on rafts. He made his court officials live (around his residence, thus covering an area) of five double-miles, and held sway over the totality of the countries, without exception.

He marched against the country of Kazalla and turned Kazalla into

[1] Reprinted from *Ancient Near Eastern Texts Relating to the Old Testament* by James B. Pritchard by permission of Princeton University Press. Copyright 1950, 1955, by Princeton University Press. Second Edition, 1955.

James B. Pritchard, *Ancient Near Eastern Texts,* 2nd ed. (Princeton, New Jersey: Princeton University Press, 1955), p. 266 ff.

ruin-hills and heaps (of rubble). He (even) destroyed there every possible perching place for a bird.

Afterwards, in his old age, all the countries revolted against him and they besieged him in Agade. But Sargon made an armed sortie and defeated them, knocked them over, and crushed their vast army.

Later on, Subaru rose with its multitudes, but it bowed to his military might. Sargon made sedentary this nomadic society. Their possessions he brought into Agade. He took away earth from the foundation-pits of Babylon and he built upon it another Babylon beside the town of Agade. On account of the sacrilege he thus committed, the great lord Marduk became enraged and destroyed his people by hunger. From the East to the West he alienated them from him and inflicted upon him as punishment that he could not rest in his grave. . . .

Hammurabi, king of Babylon, called up his army and marched against Rim-Sin, king of Ur. He personally conquered Ur and Larsa, he took their possessions to Babylon. The . . . of . . . he threw down, the booty of . . . he carried away. . . .

2 / THE CODE OF HAMMURABI

King Hammurabi of Babylon (1728–1686 B.C., see No. 1) published a law code during the second year of his reign. It survives, written on a diorite stela now preserved in the Louvre in Paris. On top of the stela a bas-relief shows the King receiving the order to write the code from the sun-god Shamash. The code shows a highly differentiated society with social classes ranging from aristocrats to slaves. The Babylonian word translated here as "seignior" may mean either a noble or a free man. Considerable differences in the legal status of the social classes exist. State authority is strong and commands greater respect than the individual. Military obligations are based on feudal landholdings; both are firmly protected by the law. Irrigation, the basis of Babylonian agriculture and wealth, is carefully regulated. In criminal law the principle of "an eye for an eye" prevails.[2]

[2] Reprinted from *Ancient Near Eastern Texts Relating to the Old Testament* by James B. Pritchard by permission of Princeton University Press. Copyright, 1950, 1955, by Princeton University Press. Second Edition, 1955.

James B. Pritchard, *Ancient Near Eastern Texts*, 2nd ed. (Princeton, New Jersey: Princeton University Press, 1955), pp. 164–80.

If a seignior has purchased or he received for safekeeping either silver or gold or a male slave or a female slave or an ox or a sheep or an ass or any sort of thing from the hand of a seignior's son or a seignior's slave without witnesses and contracts, since that seignior is a thief, he shall be put to death.

If a seignior stole either an ox or a sheep or an ass or a pig or a boat, if it belonged to the church or if it belonged to the state, he shall make thirtyfold restitution; if it belonged to a private citizen, he shall make good tenfold. If the thief does not have sufficient to make restitution, he shall be put to death. . . .

If a seignior has helped either a male slave of the state or a female slave of the state or a male slave of a private citizen or a female slave of a private citizen to escape through the city-gate, he shall be put to death.

If a seignior has harbored in his house either a fugitive male or female slave belonging to the state or to a private citizen and has not brought him forth at the summons of the police, the householder shall be put to death. . . .

If either a private soldier or a commissary, whose despatch on a campaign of the king was ordered, did not go or he hired a substitute and has sent him in his place, that soldier or commissary shall be put to death, while the one who was hired by him shall take over his estate.

In the case of either a private soldier or a commissary who was carried off while in the armed service of the king, if after his disappearance they gave his field and orchard to another and he has looked after his feudal obligations—if he has returned and reached his city, they shall restore his field and orchard to him and he shall himself look after his feudal obligations.

In the case of either a private soldier or a commissary, who was carried off while in the armed service of the king, if his son is able to look after the feudal obligations, the field and orchard shall be given to him and he shall look after the feudal obligations of his father. . . .

If a seignior, upon opening his canal for irrigation, became so lazy that he has left the water ravage a field adjoining his, he shall measure out grain on the basis of those adjoining his. . . .

If outlaws have congregated in the establishment of a woman wine seller and she has not arrested those outlaws and did not take them to the palace, that wine seller shall be put to death. . . .

If an obligation came due against a seignior and he sold the services of his wife, his son, or his daughter, or he has been bound over to service, they shall work in the house of their purchaser or obligee for three years, with their freedom reestablished in the fourth year. . . .

If a seignior pointed the finger at a nun or the wife of another seignior, but has proved nothing, they shall drag that seignior into the presence of the judges and also cut off half his hair.

If a seignior acquired a wife, but did not draw up the contracts for her, that woman is no wife.

If the wife of a seignior has been caught while lying with another man, they shall bind them and throw them into the water. If the husband of the woman wishes to spare his wife, then the king in turn may spare his subject. . . .

If a seignior wishes to divorce his wife who did not bear him children, he shall give her money to the full amount of her marriage-price and he shall also make good to her the dowry which she brought from her father's house and then he may divorce her.

If there was no marriage-price, he shall give her one mina of silver as the divorce-settlement.

If he is a peasant, he shall give her one-third mina of silver. . . .

If a woman so hated her husband that she has declared, "You may not have me," her record shall be investigated at her city council, and if she was careful and was not at fault, even though her husband has been going out and disparaging her greatly, that woman, without incurring any blame at all, may take her dowry and go off to her father's house.

If she was not careful, but was a gadabout, thus neglecting her house and humiliating her husband, they shall throw that woman in the water. . . .

When a seignior's first wife bore him children and his female slave also bore him children, if the father during his lifetime has ever said "My children!" to the children whom the slave bore him, thus having counted them with the children of the first wife, after the father has gone to his fate, the children of the first wife and the children of the slave shall share equally in the goods of the parental estate, with the first-born, the son of the first wife, receiving a preferential share.

However, if the father during his lifetime has never said "My children!" to the children whom the slave bore him, after the father has gone to his fate, the children of the slave may not share in the goods of the paternal estate along with the children of the first wife; freedom for the slave and her children shall be effected, with the children of the first wife having no claim at all against the children of the slave for service; the first wife shall take her dowry and the marriage-gift which her husband, upon giving it to her, wrote down on a tablet for her, and living in the home of her husband, she shall have the usufruct of it as long as she lives, without ever selling it, since her heritage belongs to her children. . . .

If a member of the artisan class took a son as a foster child and has taught him his handicraft, he may never be reclaimed.

If he has not taught him his handicraft, that foster child may return to his father's house. . . .

If a son has struck his father, they shall cut off his hand.

If a seignior has destroyed the eye of a member of the aristocracy, they shall destroy his eye.

If he has broken another seignior's bone, they shall break his bone.

If he has destroyed the eye of a commoner or broken the bone of a commoner, he shall pay one mina of silver.

If he has destroyed the eye of a seignior's slave or broken the bone of a seignior's slave, he shall pay one-half his value.

If a seignior has knocked out a tooth of a seignior of his own rank, they shall knock out his tooth.

If he has knocked out a commoner's tooth, he shall pay one-third mina of silver. . . .

3 / CONQUESTS OF ASSYRIAN KINGS

In 732 B.C. King Sargon II of Assyria (721–705 B.C.) captured the capital of the Northern Hebrew Kingdom, Samaria. The King recorded his military achievement in an inscription (A).[3] *In 701 Sennacherib of Assyria (704–681 B.C.) undertook a campaign against several princes of Phoenicia and Palestine. The official Assyrian record of his campaigns, preserved on a prism, is reproduced here (B).*[4] *For a Judean record of the same campaign, see No. 16.*

A. ASSYRIAN CAPTURE OF SAMARIA

At the beginning of my rule, in the first year of my reign . . . Samerinai (the people of Samaria) . . . of Shamash who causes me to attain victory . . . 27,290 people, who lived therein, I carried away; 50 chariots for my royal equipment, I selected from among them. . . .

[3] D. D. Luckenbill, *Ancient Records of Assyria and Babylonia* II (Chicago: The University of Chicago Press, 1926–1927), p. 2.

[4] Reprinted from *Ancient Near Eastern Texts Relating to the Old Testament* by James B. Pritchard by permission of Princeton University Press. Copyright, 1950, 1955, by Princeton University Press. Second Edition, 1955.

James B. Pritchard, *Ancient Near Eastern Texts*, 2nd ed. (Princeton, New Jersey: Princeton University Press, 1955), p. 287 ff.

The city I rebuilt, I made it greater than it was before; people of the lands my hand had conquered I settled therein. My official I placed over them as governor. Tribute, tax, I imposed upon them as upon the Assyrians. . . .

B. ASSYRIAN CAPTURE OF JERUSALEM

In my third campaign I marched against Hatti. Luli, king of Sidon, whom the terror-inspiring glamor of my lordship had overwhelmed, fled far overseas and perished. The awe-inspiring splendor of the "Weapon" of Ashur, my lord, overwhelmed his strong cities such as Great Sidon, Little Sidon, Bit-Zitti, Zaribtu, Mahalliba, Ushu (i.e. the mainland settlement of Tyre), Akzib and Akko, all his fortress cities, walled and well provided with feed and water for his garrisons, and they bowed in submission to my feet. I installed Ethba'al (Tuba'lu) upon the throne to be their king and imposed upon him tribute due to me as his overlord to be paid annually without interruption.

As to all the kings of Amurru—Menahem from Samsimuruna, Tuba'lu from Sidon, Abdili'ti from Arvad, Urumilki from Byblos, Mitinti from Ashdod, Buduili from Beth-Ammon, Kammusunadbi from Moab and Airammu from Edom, they brought sumptuous gifts and—fourfold—their heavy *tâmartu*-presents to me and kissed my feet. Sidqia, however, king of Ashkelon, who did not bow to my yoke, I deported and sent to Assyria, his family-gods, himself, his wife, his children, his brothers, all the male descendants of his family. I set Sharruludari, son of Rukibtu, their former king, over the inhabitants of Ashkelon and imposed upon him the payment of tribute and of *katrû*-presents due to me as overlord—and he now pulls the straps of my yoke!

In the continuation of my campaign I besieged Beth-Dagon, Joppa, Banai-Barqa, Azuru, cities belonging to Sidqia who did not bow to my feet quickly enough; I conquered them and carried their spoils away. The officials, the patricians and the common people of Ekron—who had thrown Padi, their king, into fetters because he was loyal to his solemn oath sworn by the god Ashur, and had handed him over to [king] Hezekiah, the Jew—and he (Hezekiah) held him in prison, unlawfully, as if he (Padi) be an enemy—had become afraid and had called for help upon the kings of Egypt and the bowmen, the chariot-corps and the cavalry of the king of Ethiopia, an army beyond counting—and they had come to their assistance. In the plain of Eltekeh, their battle lines were drawn up against me and they sharpened their weapons. Upon a trust-inspiring oracle given by Ashur, my lord, I fought with them and inflicted a defeat upon them. In the mêlée of the battle, I personally captured alive the Egyptian charioteers with their princes and also the charioteers of the king of Ethiopia. I besieged Eltekeh and

Timnah, conquered them and carried their spoils away. I assaulted Ekron and killed the officials and patricians who had committed the crime and hung their bodies on poles surrounding the city. The common citizens who were guilty of minor crimes, I considered prisoners of war. The rest of them, those who were not accused of crimes and misbehavior, I released. I made Padi, their king, come from Jerusalem and set him as their lord on the throne, imposing upon him the tribute due to me as overlord.

As to Hezekiah, the Jew, he did not submit to my yoke, I laid siege to 46 of his strong cities, walled forts and to the countless small villages in their vicinity, and conquered them by means of well-stamped earth-ramps, and battering-rams brought thus near to the walls combined with the attack by foot soldiers, using mines, breeches as well as sapper work. I drove out of them 200,150 people, young and old, male and female, horses, mules, donkeys, camels, big and small cattle beyond counting, and considered them booty. Himself I made a prisoner in Jerusalem, his royal residence, like a bird in a cage. I surrounded him with earthwork in order to molest those who were leaving his city's gate. His towns which I had plundered, I took away from his country and gave them over to Mitinti, king of Ashdod, Padi, king of Ekron, and Sillibel, king of Gaza. Thus I reduced his country, but I still increased the tribute and the *katrû*-presents due to me as his overlord which I imposed later upon him beyond the former tribute, to be delivered annually. Hezekiah himself, whom the terror-inspiring spendor of my lordship had overwhelmed and whose irregular and elite troops which he had brought into Jerusalem, his royal residence, in order to strengthen it, had deserted him, did send me, later, to Nineveh, my lordly city, together with 30 talents of gold, 800 talents of silver, precious stones, antimony, large cuts of red stone, couches inlaid with ivory, *nîmedu*-chairs inlaid with ivory, elephant-hides, ebony-wood, boxwood, and all kinds of valuable treasures, his own daughters, concubines, male and female musicians. In order to deliver the tribute and to do obeisance as a slave he sent his personal messenger.

4 / THE AKKADIAN CREATION EPIC

The extant texts of this epic poem date from the first millennium B.C., *but the composition itself seems to belong to the early part of the second millennium* B.C. *It was recited each year on the fourth day of the New Year's festival; the turning of the year was supposed to re-enact the transition from primeval chaos to cosmic order. Apsu and Tiamat, the two primordial forces, represent fresh water and the sea. The creation of the world is preceded by a conflict between these two older gods and their divine progeny. The younger gods under the leadership of Ea, or Nudimmud, the god of earth and water, slay Apsu, but Tiamat organizes a rebellion and appoints Kingu commander in chief. This time the younger gods are led to victory under Marduk, Ea's son. He kills Tiamat and creates the world out of Tiamat's corpse. Finally Kingu is executed, and man is created from his body to serve the gods.*[5]

When on high the heaven had not been named,
Firm ground below had not been called by name,
Naught but primordial Apsu, their begetter,
And Mummu-Tiamat, she who bore them all,
Their waters commingling as a single body;
No reed hut had been matted, no marsh land had appeared,
When no gods whatever had been brought into being,
Uncalled by name, their destinies undetermined—
Then it was that the gods were formed within them.
Lahmu and Lahamu were brought forth, by name they were called.
Before they had grown in age and stature,
Anshar and Kishar were formed, surpassing the others.
They prolonged the days, added on the years.
Anu was their heir, of his fathers the rival;
Yea, Anshar's first-born, Anu, was his equal.
Anu begot in his image Nudimmud.
This Nudimmud was of his fathers the master;
Of broad wisdom, understanding, mighty in strength,
Mightier by far than his grandfather, Anshar.
He had no rival among the gods, his brothers.
The divine brothers banded together,
They disturbed Tiamat as they surged back and forth,
Yea, they troubled the mood of Tiamat
By their hilarity in the Abode of Heaven.
Apsu could not lessen their clamor
And Tiamat was speechless at their ways.

[5] Reprinted from *Ancient Near Eastern Texts Relating to the Old Testament* by James B. Pritchard by permission of Princeton University Press. Copyright, 1950, 1955, by Princeton University Press. Second Edition, 1955.

James B. Pritchard, *Ancient Near Eastern Texts,* 2nd ed. (Princeton, New Jersey: Princeton University Press, 1955), pp. 60–62, 67, 68.

Their doings were loathsome unto . . .
Unsavory were their ways: they were overbearing.
Then Apsu, the begetter of the great gods,
Cried out, addressing Mummu, his vizier:
"O Mummu, my vizier, who rejoicest my spirit,
Come hither and let us go to Tiamat!"
They went and sat down before Tiamat,
Exchanging counsel about the gods, their first-born.
Apsu, opening his mouth,
Said unto resplendent Tiamat:
"Their ways are verily loathsome unto me.
By day I find no relief, nor repose by night.
I will destroy, I will wreck their ways,
That quiet may be restored. Let us have rest!"
As soon as Tiamat heard this,
She was wroth and called out to her husband.
She cried out aggrieved, as she raged all alone,
Injecting woe into her mood:
"What? Should we destroy that which we have built?
Their ways indeed are most troublesome, but let us attend kindly!"
Then answered Mummu, giving counsel to Apsu;
Ill-wishing and ungracious was Mummu's advice:
"Do destroy, my father, the mutinous ways.
Then shalt thou have relief by day and rest by night!"
When Apsu heard this, his face grew radiant
Because of the evil he planned against the gods, his sons.
As for Mummu, by the neck he embraced him
As that one sat down on his knees to kiss him.
Now whatever they had plotted between them,
Was repeated unto the gods, their first-born.
When the gods heard this, they were astir,
Then lapsed into silence and remained speechless.
Surpassing in wisdom, accomplished, resourceful,
Ea, the all-wise, saw through their scheme.
A master design against it he devised and set up,
Made artful his spell against it, surpassing and holy.
He recited it and made it subsist in the deep,
As he poured sleep upon him. Sound asleep he lay.
When Apsu he had made prone, drenched with sleep,
Mummu, the adviser, was powerless to stir.
He loosened his band, tore off his tiara,
Removed his halo and put it on himself.
Having fettered Apsu, he slew him.
Mummu he bound and left behind lock.

Having thus upon Apsu established his dwelling,
He laid hold on Mummu, holding his by the nose-rope.
After Ea had vanquished and trodden down his foes,
Had secured his triumph over his enemies,
In his sacred chamber in profound peace had rested,
He named it "Apsu," for shrines he assigned it.
In that same place his cult hut he founded.
Ea and Damkina, his wife, dwelled there in splendor.
In the chamber of fates, the abode of destinies,
A god was engendered, most able and wisest of gods.
In the heart of Apsu was Marduk created,
In the heart of holy Apsu was Marduk created.
He who begot him was Ea, his father;
She who bore him was Damkina, his mother.
The breast of goddesses he did suck.
The nurse that nursed him filled him with awesomeness.
Alluring was his figure, sparkling the lift of his eyes.
Lordly was his gait, commanding from of old.
When Ea saw him, the father who begot him,
He exulted and glowed, his heart filled with gladness.
He rendered him perfect and endowed him with a double godhead.

[Tiamat then prepares for war against some of the gods and appoints her first-born son Kingu chief of her host. None of the gods is able to fight Kingu until Marduk is appointed chief of the gods. Marduk kills Tiamat and creates the natural order.]

When he had vanquished and subdued his adversaries,
Had . . . the vainglorious foe,
Had wholly established Anshar's triumph over the foe,
Nudimmud's desire had achieved, valiant Marduk
Strenghtened his hold on the vanquished gods,
And turned back to Tiamat whom he had bound.
The lord trod on the legs of Tiamat,
With his unsparing mace he crushed her skull.
When the arteries of her blood he had severed,
The North Wind bore it to places undisclosed.
On seeing this, his fathers were joyful and jubilant,
They brought gifts of homage, they to him.
Then the lord paused to view her dead body,
That he might divide the monster and do artful works.
He split her like a shellfish into two parts:
Half of her he set up and ceiled it as sky,
Pulled down the bar and posted guards.

He bade them to allow not her waters to escape.
He crossed the heavens and surveyed the regions.
He squared Apsu's quarter, the abode of Nudimmud,
As the lord measured the dimensions of Apsu.
The Great Abode, its likeness, he fixed as Esharra,
The Great Abode, Esharra, which he made as the firmament.
Anu, Enlil, and Ea he made occupy their places.
He constructed stations for the great gods,
Fixing their astral likenesses as constellations.
He determined the year by designating the zones:
He set up three constellations for each of the twelve months. . . .

When Marduk hears the words of the gods,
His heart prompts him to fashion artful works.
Opening his mouth, he addresses Ea
To impart the plan he had conceived in his heart:
"Blood I will mass and cause bones to be.
I will establish a savage, 'man' shall be his name.
Verily, savage-man I will create.
He shall be charged with the service of the gods
That they might be at ease!
The ways of the gods I will artfully alter.
Though alike revered, into two groups they shall be divided."
Ea answered him, speaking a word to him,
Giving him another plan for the relief of the gods:
"Let but one of their brothers be handed over;
He alone shall perish that mankind may be fashioned."

5 / THE EPIC OF GILGAMESH

This great poem has survived in several languages—in the original Akkadian, in Sumerian, and in Assyrian Hittite—and the original dates from the beginning of the second millennium B.C., *at least. Its hero Gilgamesh was fashioned by several gods and endowed with superhuman size. He became king of the city of Uruk and there befriended Enkidu, like himself created by a deity. He rejected the advances of the goddess Ishtar, and in retaliation the gods slew his friend Enkidu. Upon the death of his friend, Gilgamesh was disconsolate and afraid of dying. He set out to find Utnapishtim, a Mesopotamian counterpart to Noah who had escaped the Flood, and, after many adventures and hardships, found him. Utnapishtim told him of the Flood, of his escape, and of his acquisition of immortality. Utnapishtim then revealed to Gilgamesh where he would find the plant of life. Gilgamesh plucked the plant, but later lost it and thus failed. Man's quest for immortality was frustrated.*[6]

Gilgamesh said to him, to Utnapishtim the Faraway:
"As I look upon thee, Utnapishtim,
Thy features are not strange; even as I art thou.
Thou are not strange at all; even as I art thou.
My heart had regarded thee as resolved to do battle,
Yet thou liest indolent upon thy back!
Tell me, how joinedst thou the Assembly of the gods,
In thy quest of life?"

Utnapishtim said to him, to Gilgamesh:
"I will reveal to thee, Gilgamesh, a hidden matter
And a secret of the gods will I tell thee:
Shurippak—a city which thou knowest,
And which on Euphrates' banks is situate—
That city was ancient, as were the gods within it,
When their heart led the great gods to produce the flood.
There were Anu, their father,
Valiant Enlil, their counsel,
Ninurta, their assistant,
Ennuge, their irrigator.
Ninigiku-Ea was also present with them;
Their words he repeats to the reed-hut:
'Reed-hut, reed-hut! Wall! Wall!
Reed-hut, hearken! Wall, reflect!
Man of Shuruppak, son of Ubar-Tutu,
Tear down this house, build a ship!
Give up possessions, seek thou life.
Forswear worldly goods and keep the soul alive!
Aboard the ship take thou the seed of all living things.
The ship that thou shalt build,

[6] Reprinted from *Ancient Near Eastern Texts Relating to the Old Testament* by James B. Pritchard by permission of Princeton University Press. Copyright, 1950, 1955, by Princeton University Press. Second Edition, 1955.

James B. Pritchard, *Ancient Near Eastern Texts*, 2nd ed. (Princeton, New Jersey: Princeton University Press, 1955), pp. 93–5, 96–7.

Her dimensions shall be to measure.
Equal shall be her width and her length.
Like the Apsu thou shalt ceil her.' . . .

[Utnapishtim then builds the ship, and the earth is flooded.]

"When the seventh day arrived,
I sent forth and set free a dove.
This dove went forth, but came back;
Since no resting place for it was visible, she turned round.
Then I sent forth and set free a swallow.
The swallow went forth, but came back;
Since no resting-place for it was visible, she turned round.
Then I sent forth and set free a raven.
The raven went forth and, seeing that the waters had diminished,
He eats, circles, caws and turns not round.
Then I let out all to the four winds
And offered a sacrifice.
I poured out a libation on the top of the mountain.
Seven and seven cult-vessels I set up,
Upon their pot-stands I heaped cane, cedarwood, and myrtle.
The gods smelled the savor,
The gods smelled the sweet savor,
The gods crowded like flies about the sacrificer.
When at length as the great goddess arrived,
She lifted up the great jewels which Anu had fashioned to her liking:
"Ye gods here, as surely as this lapis
Upon my neck I shall not forget,
I shall be mindful of these days, forgetting them never.
Let the gods come to the offering;
But let not Enlil come to the offering,
For he, unreasoning, brought on the deluge
And my people consigned to destruction.'
When at length as Enlil arrived,
And saw the ship, Enlil was wroth,
He was filled with wrath over the Igigi gods:
'Has some living soul escaped?
No man was to survive the destruction!'
Ninurta opened his mouth to speak,
Saying to valiant Enlil:
'Who, other than Ea, can devise plans?
It is Ea alone who knows every matter.'
Ea opened his mouth to speak,
Saying to valiant Enlil:

'Thou wisest of gods, thou hero,
How couldst thou, unreasoning, bring on the deluge?
On the sinner impose his sin,
On the transgressor impose his transgression!
Yet be lenient, lest he be cut off,
Be patient, lest he be dislodged!
Instead of thy bringing on the deluge,
Would that a lion had risen up to diminish mankind!
Instead of thy bringing on the deluge,
Would that a wolf had risen up to diminish mankind!
Instead of thy bringing on the deluge,
Would that a famine had risen up to lay low mankind!
Instead of thy bringing on the deluge,
Would that pestilence had risen up to smite down mankind!
It was not I who disclosed the secret of the great gods.
I let Atrahasis see a dream and he perceived the secret of the gods.
Now then take counsel in regard to him!'
Thereupon Enlil went aboard the ship.
Holding me by the hand, he took me aboard.
He took my wife aboard and made her kneel by my side.
Standing between us, he touched our foreheads to bless us:
'Hitherto Utnapishtim has been but human.
Henceforth Utnapishtim and his wife shall be like unto us gods.
Utnapishtim shall reside far away, at the mouth of the rivers!'
Thus they took me and made me reside far away,
At the mouth of the rivers!
But now, who will for thy sake call the gods to Assembly
That the life which thou seekest thou mayest find?
Up, lie not down to sleep
For six days and seven nights." . . .

Gilgamesh says to him, to Utnapishtim the Faraway:
"What then shall I do, Utnapishtim,
Whither shall I go,
Now that the Bereaver has laid hold on my members?
In my bedchamber lurks death,
And wherever I set my foot, there is death!"

Utnapishtim says to him, to Urshanabi, the boatman:
"Urshanabi, may the landing-place not rejoice in thee,
May the place of crossing renounce thee!
To him who wanders on its shore, deny thou its shore!
The man thou hast led hither, whose body is covered with grime,

The grace of whose members skins have distorted,
Take him, Urshanabi, and bring him to the washing-place.
Let him wash off his grime in water clean as snow,
Let him cast off his skins, let the sea carry them away,
That the fairness of his body may be seen.
Let him renew the band round his head,
Let him put on a cloak to clothe his nakedness,
That he may arrive in his city,
That he may achieve his journey.
Let not (his) cloak have a moldy cast,
Let it be wholly new."
Urshanabi took him and brought him to the washing-place.
He washed off his grime in water clean as snow.
He cast off his skins, the sea carried them away,
That the fairness of his body might be seen.
He renewed the band round his head,
He put on a cloak to clothe his nakedness,
That he might arrive in his city,
That he might achieve his journey.
The cloak had not a moldy cast, but was wholly new.
Gilgamesh and Urshanabi boarded the boat,
They launched the boat on the waves and they sailed away.

His spouse says to him, to Utnapishtim the Faraway:
"Gilgamesh has come hither, toiling and straining.
What wilt thou give him that he may return to his land?"
At that he, Gilgamesh, raised up his pole,
To bring the boat nigh to the shore.
Utnapishtim says to him, to Gilgamesh:
"Gilgamesh, thou hast come hither, toiling and straining.
What shall I give thee that thou mayest return to thy land?
I will disclose, O Gilgamesh, a hidden thing,
And a secret of the gods I will tell thee:
This plant, like the buckthorn is its . . .
Its thorns will prick thy hands just as does the rose.
If thy hands obtain the plant, thou wilt find new life."
No sooner had Gilgamesh heard this,
That he opened the water-pipe,
He tied heavy stones to his feet.
They pulled him down into the deep and he saw the plant.
He took the plant, though it pricked his hands.
He cut the heavy stones from his feet.
The sea cast him up upon its shore.

Gilgamesh says to him, to Urshanabi, the boatman:
"Urshanabi, this plant is a plant apart,
Whereby a man may regain his life's breath.
I will take it to ramparted Uruk,
Will cause . . . to eat the plant . . . !
Its name shall be 'Man Becomes Young in Old Age.'
I myself shall eat it
And thus return to the state of my youth."
After twenty leagues they broke off a morsel,
After thirty further leagues they prepared for the night.
Gilgamesh saw a well whose water was cool.
He went down into it to bathe in the water.
A serpent snuffed the fragrance of the plant;
It came up from the water and carried off the plant.
Going back it shed its slough.

Thereupon Gilgamesh sits down and weeps,
His tears running down over his face.
He took the hand of Urshanabi, the boatman:
"For whom, Urshanabi, have my hands toiled?
For whom is being spent the blood of my heart?
I have not obtained a boon for myself.
For the earth-lion have I effected a boon!
And now the tide will bear it twenty leagues away!
When I opened the water-pipe and . . . the gear,
I found that which has been placed as a sign for me:
I shall withdraw,
And leave the boat on the shore." . . .

6 / UGARIT: GODS, WAR, AND PEACE

In the early 1930's French archaeologists uncovered at Ugarit (or Ras Shamra) in Canaan a number of tablets containing mythological poems. They were composed around the middle of the second millennium B.C. *and tell of quarrels within a family of gods. The chief god is El; also very important are Baal, god of rain and fertility, and his sister, the warrior goddess Anath. In the following excerpt Baal wishes that El have a palace built for him. In order to achieve his purpose, he prevails upon Anath to put an end to warfare on earth and to attack El instead. The passage exemplifies Oriental notions about the relations of gods and men (see also No. 4) and about the aimless frenzy of war. Furthermore, it illustrates the religious atmosphere attacked by the prophets of Israel (see No. 15).*[7]

Now Anath doth battle in the plain,
  Fighting between the two towns;
Smiting the Westland's peoples,
  Smashing the folk of the Sunrise.
Under her, heads like sheaves;
  Over her, hands like locusts,
  Like a grasshopper-mass heroes' hands.
She binds the heads to her back,
  Fastens the hands in her girdle.
She plunges knee-deep in knights' blood,
  Hip-deep in the gore of heroes.
With darts she drives . . . ,
  With the . . . of her bow . . .
Now Anath goes to her house,
  The goddess proceeds to her palace.
Not sated with battling in the plain,
  With her fighting between the two towns,
She pictures the chairs as heroes,
  Pretending a table is warriors,
  And that the footstools are troops.
Much battle she does and beholds,
  Her fighting contemplates Anath:
Her liver swells with laughter,
  Her heart fills up with joy,
  Anath's liver exults:
For she plunges knee-deep in knights' blood,
  Hip-deep in the gore of heroes.
Then, sated with battling in the house,
  Fighting between the two tables,
. . .s the knights' blood,
  Pours the fatness of dew in a bowl.
Maiden Anath washes her hands,

[7] Reprinted from *Ancient Near Eastern Texts Relating to the Old Testament* by James B. Pritchard by permission of the Princeton University Press. Copyright, 1950, 1955, by Princeton University Press. Second Edition, 1955.

James B. Pritchard, *Ancient Near Eastern Texts,* 2nd ed. (Princeton, New Jersey: Princeton University Press, 1955), p. 136 ff.

Yabamat Liimmim her fingers;
She washes her hands of knights' blood,
Her fingers of gore of heroes.
. . . to chairs,
Table also to table,
Footstools turn back into footstools.
She draws some water and bathes;
Sky-dew, fatness of earth,
Spray of the Rider of Clouds;
Dew that the heavens do shed,
Spray that is shed by the stars. . . .

[Baal then addresses his messengers, Gapn and Ugar:]

So then, O lads, enter ye;
At Anath's feet bow and fall down,
Prostrate you, do her honor.
And say unto Maiden Anath,
Declare unto Yabamat Liimmim:
'Message of Puissant Baal,
Word of the Powerful Hero:
Take war away from the earth,
Banish all strife from the soil;
Pour peace into earth's very bowels,
Much amity into earth's bosom.
Hasten! Hurry! Rush!
To me thy feet shall trot,
To me shall sprint thy legs.
For
I've a word I fain would tell thee,
A speech I would utter to thee:
Speech of tree and whisper of stone,
Converse of heaven with earth,
E'ven of the deeps with the stars;
Yea, a thunderbolt unknown to heaven,
A word not known to men,
Nor sensed by the masses on earth.
Come, pray, and I will reveal it
In the midst of my mount Godly Zaphon:
In the sanctuary, mount of my portion,
In the pleasance, the hill I possess.'

No sooner espies she the gods,
Than Anath's feet do stumble.
Behind, her loins do break;

Above, her face doth sweat:
Bent are the joints of her loins,
Weakened those of her back.
She lifts up her voice and cries:
"Why come Gapn and Ugar?
What enemy's risen 'gainst Baal,
What foe 'gainst the Rider of Clouds?. . ."
Answer the lads twain make:
"No enemy's risen 'gainst Baal,
No foe 'gainst the Rider of Clouds!
Message of Puissant Baal,
Word of the Powerful Hero:
Take war away from the earth,
Banish all strife from the soil, etc., etc."
Answers the Maiden Anath,
Replies Yabamat Liimmim:
"I'll take war away from the earth,
Banish all strife from the soil,
Pour peace into earth's very bowels,
Much amity into earth's bosom.
Let Baal . . .
Let him . . .
I'll take war away from the earth, etc.
Yet another word will I say:
Go, go attendants divine.
Ye are slow and I am swift.
From my Mount to the godhead afar,
Enibaba to the distant divinity,
Is two mathpads under earth's furrows,
Three underneath the hollows."—
There, she is off on her way
To Baal of the Summit of Zaphon.
From a thousand fields, ten thousand acres,
His sister's approach Baal sees.
The advance of his own father's-daughter.
He dismisses his wives from her presence.
He places an ox before her,
A fatted one in front of her.
She draws some water and bathes
Sky-dew, fatness of earth;
Dew that the heavens do shed,
Spray that is shed by the stars.
She rubs herself with ambergris
From a sperm-whale. . . .

EGYPT

7 / MILITARY CAMPAIGNS UNDER THE OLD KINGDOM

Early in the third millennium B.C. *the two kingdoms of Upper and Lower Egypt were united. During the Old Kingdom (2700–2200* B.C.*) Egypt was a powerful and prosperous state. The following text was inscribed on the tomb of a high court official and military commander, Uni, during the Old Kingdom. He lived under the Sixth Dynasty around 2350* B.C. *On command of the Pharaoh Pepi I he conducted several campaigns against "Asiatic Sand-dwellers," that is, nomads. These rebels may have resided in the Delta of the River Nile.*[8]

His majesty made war on the Asiatic Sand-dwellers and his majesty made an army of many ten thousands: in the entire South, southward to Elephantine and northward to Aphroditopolis; in the Northland on both sides entire in the stronghold, and in the midst of the strongholds, among the Irthet negroes, the Mazoi negroes, the Yam negroes, among the Wawat negroes, among the Kau negroes, and in the land of Temeh.

His majesty sent me at the head of his army while the counts, while the wearers of the royal seal, while the sole companions of the palace, while the nomarchs and commanders of strongholds belonging to the South and the Northland; the companions, the caravan-conductors, the superior prophets belonging to the South and the Northland, the overseers of the crown-possessions, were each at the head of a troop of the South or the Northland, of the strongholds and the cities which they commanded, and of the negroes of these countries. I was the one who made for them the plan while my office was that of superior custodian of the domain of Pharaoh of. . . . Not one thereof . . . with his neighbor; not one thereof plundered dough or sandals from the wayfarers;

[8] Reprinted from *Ancient Records of Egypt,* Vol. I, by J. H. Breasted by permission of the University of Chicago Press. Copyright 1906 by University of Chicago Press.

J. H. Breasted, *Ancient Records of Egypt,* Vol. I (Chicago, Illinois: University of Chicago Press, 1906–1907), p. 142 ff.

not one thereof took bread from any city; not one thereof took any goat from any people. I despatched them from the Northern Isle, the Gate of Ihotep, the bend of Horus, Nibmat. While I was of this rank . . . everything, I inspected the number of these troops, although never had any servant inspected.

This army returned in safety, after it had hacked up the land of the Sand-dwellers; this army returned in safety, after it had overturned its strongholds; this army returned in safety, after it had cut down its figs and its vines; this army returned in safety, after it had thrown fire in all its troops; this army returned in safety, after it had slain troops therein, in many ten thousands; this army returned in safety, after it had carried away therefrom a great multitude as living captives. His majesty praised me on account of it above everything.

His majesty sent me to despatch this army five times, in order to traverse the land of the Sand-dwellers at each of their rebellions, with these troops. I did so that his majesty praised me on account of it.

8 / THE EXPULSION OF THE HYKSOS

Early in the third millennium B.C. *the two kingdoms of Upper and Lower Egypt were united. During the Old Kingdom (2700–2200* B.C.*) and again under the Middle Kingdom (2100–1788* B.C.*) Egypt was a powerful and prosperous state. In the eighteenth century* B.C., *a period of great political unrest, Egypt was occupied by the Hyksos, or Shepherd Kings* (circa *1725–1575* B.C.), *consisting of peoples from Palestine and Syria. They established their capital at Avaris in the Nile Delta. The national struggle against this foreign domination began about 1600* B.C. *and ended in the expulsion of the Hyksos, a key event in Egyptian history. The best source is a biographical account by a captain of a Nile vessel, Ah-mose. He participated in the campaigns of liberation under the Pharaohs Ahmose I* (circa *1570–1545* B.C.), *whom he calls Neb-pehti-Re, and Thutmose I* (circa *1525–1495* B.C.). *The town of Sharuhen mentioned in the text lay in the southwest of Canaan.*[9]

[9] Reprinted from *Ancient Near Eastern Texts Relating to the Old Testament* by James B. Pritchard by permission of Princeton University Press. Copyright, 1950, 1955, by Princeton University Press. Second Edition, 1955.

James B. Pritchard, *Ancient Near Eastern Texts*, 2nd ed. (Princeton, New Jersey: Princeton University Press, 1955), p. 233 ff.

The commander of a crew, Ah-mose, son of Eben, the triumphant, says:

I speak to you, all mankind, that I may let you know the favors which have come to me. I have been awarded gold seven times in the presence of the entire land, and male and female slaves in like manner, and I have been vested with very many fields. The reputation of a valiant man is from what he has done, not being destroyed in this land forever.

He speaks thus:

I had my upbringing in the town of el-Kab, my father being a soldier of the King of Upper and Lower Egypt: Seqnen-Re, the triumphant, his name being Bebe, the son of the woman Ro-onet. Then I served as soldier in his place in the ship, "The Wild Bull," in the time of the Lord of the Two Lands: Neb-pehti-Re, the triumphant, when I was still a boy, before I had taken a wife, but while I was still sleeping in a net hammock.

But after I had set up a household, then I was taken on the ship, "Northern," because I was valiant. Thus I used to accompany the Sovereign—life, prosperity, health!—on foot, following his excursions in his chariot. When the town of Avaris was besieged, then I showed valor on foot in the presence of his majesty. Thereupon I was appointed to the ship, "Appearing in Memphis." Then there was fighting on the water in the canal Pa-Djedku of Avaris. Thereupon I made a capture, and I carried away a hand. It was reported to the king's herald. Then the Gold of Valor was given to me. Thereupon there was fighting again in this place. Then I made a capture again there and brought away a hand. Then the Gold of Valor was given to me over again.

Then there was fighting in the Egypt which is south of this town. Thereupon I carried off a man as living prisoner. I went down into the water—now he was taken captive on the side of the town—and crossed over the water carrying him. Report was made to the king's herald. Thereupon I was awarded gold another time.

Then Avaris was despoiled. Then I carried off spoil from there: one man, three women, a total of four persons. Then his majesty gave them to me to be slaves.

Then Sharuhen was besieged for three years. Then his majesty despoiled it. Thereupon I carried off spoil from there: two women and a hand. Then the Gold of Valor was given to me, and my spoil was given to me to be slaves. . . .

9 / THE PEOPLES OF THE SEA

After the expulsion of the Hyksos (No. 8), the Pharaohs of the eighteenth dynasty, especially Amenhotep III (1398–1361 B.C.), administered an Egyptian empire that included Palestine, Phoenicia, and parts of Syria and Nubia. Amenhotep IV (1369–1353 B.C.) was a religious reformer (No. 11), and under him the outlying provinces of the empire were neglected. The Egyptian empire was restored by the rulers of the nineteenth and twentieth dynasties. Ramses III (1198–1167 B.C.?), in the eighth year of his reign, was faced with the onslaught of migrating peoples who attacked the Egyptian dominions both by land and by sea. He recorded his victory over these hordes in an inscription accompanied by reliefs on the walls of a temple at Thebes. Of the names of peoples and places mentioned in the text, Hatti refers to the Hittites, Carchemish is a city on the Euphrates, Kode the coast of Cilicia, Alashiya is Cyprus, the Denye(n) may be the Danaans or Greeks, and Djahi is the Phoenician coast.[10]

Year 8 under the majesty of Ramses III. . . .

The foreign countries made a conspiracy in their islands. All at once the lands were removed and scattered in the fray. No land could stand before their arms, from Hatti, Kode, Carchemish, Arzawa, and Alashiya on, being cut off at one time. A camp was set up in one place in Amor. They desolated its people, and its land was like that which has never come into being. They were coming forward toward Egypt, while the flame was prepared before them. Their confederation was the Philistines, Tjeker, Shekelesh, Denyen, and Weshesh, lands united. They laid their hands upon the lands as far as the circuit of the earth, their hearts confident and trusting: "Our plans will succeed!"

Now the heart of this god, the Lord of the Gods, was prepared and ready to ensnare them like birds . . . I organized my frontier in Djahi, prepared before them:—princes, commanders of garrisons, and *maryanu*. I have the river-mouths prepared like a strong wall, with

[10] Reprinted from *Ancient Near Eastern Texts Relating to the Old Testament* by James B. Pritchard by permission of Princeton University Press. Copyright, 1950, 1955, by Princeton University Press. Second Edition, 1955.

James B. Pritchard, *Ancient Near Eastern Texts*, 2nd ed. (Princeton, New Jersey: Princeton University Press, 1955), p. 262 ff.

warships, galleys and coasters, fully equipped, for they were manned completely from bow to stern with valiant warriors carrying their weapons. The troops consisted of every picked man of Egypt. They were like lions roaring upon the mountain tops. The chariotry consisted of runners, of picked men, of every good and capable chariot-warrior. The horses were quivering in every part of their bodies, prepared to crush the foreign countries under their hoofs. I was the valiant Montu, standing fast at their head, so that they might gaze upon the capturing of my hands. . . .

Those who reached my frontier, their seed is not, their heart and their soul are finished forever and ever. Those who came forward together on the sea, the full flame was in front of them at the river-mouths, while a stockade of lances surrounded them on the shore. They were dragged in, enclosed, and prostrated on the beach, killed, and made into heaps from tail to head. Their ships and their goods were as if fallen into the water.

I have made the lands turn back from even mentioning Egypt; for when they pronounce my name in their land, then they are burned up. Since I sat upon the throne of Har-akhti and the Great-of-Magic was fixed upon my head like Re, I have not let foreign countries behold the frontier of Egypt, to boast thereof to the Nine Bows. I have taken away their land, their frontiers being added to mine. Their princes and their tribespeople are mine with praise, for I am on the ways of the plans of the All-Lord, my august, divine father, the Lord of the Gods.

10 / THE THEOLOGY OF MEMPHIS

The following text is preserved in an inscription, the Shabaka Stone, now kept in the British Museum. The text as it exists was composed around 700 B.C., *but it derives from an original written in the early third millennium* B.C., *not long after Upper and Lower Egypt were united and the capital of the united kingdom established at Memphis* (circa 2900–2700 B.C.). *The unification of Egypt is here represented as having been brought about by Geb, the earth-god, attended by the Ennead (or nine gods). Geb first reconciled a quarrel between his grandsons, Horus of Lower Egypt and Seth of Upper Egypt, and made each of them king of his respective part. Later he revised this first verdict and gave Horus the entire earth, especially the two Great Sorceresses, the crowns of Upper and Lower Egypt. Horus resided at Wall Nome, i.e., Memphis, and the god of Memphis, Ptah, then with mind ("heart") and speech ("tongue") brought forth Atum, the creator god. The god of Memphis became responsible for the divine and political orders.*[11]

The Ennead gathered themselves to him [Geb], and he judged Horus and Seth. He prevented them from quarreling further, and he made Seth the King of Upper Egypt in the land of Upper Egypt, at the place where he was born, Su. Then Geb made Horus the King of Lower Egypt in the land of Lower Egypt, at the place where his father was drowned, Pezshet-Tawi. Thus Horus stood in one place, and Seth stood in another place, and they were reconciled about the Two Lands. . . .

Words spoken by Geb to Seth: "Go to the place in which thou wert born." Seth—Upper Egypt.

Words spoken by Geb to Horus: "Go to the place in which thy father was drowned." Horus—Lower Egypt.

Words spoken by Geb to Horus and Seth: "I have judged you." Lower and Upper Egypt.

But then it became ill in the heart of Geb that the portion of Horus was only equal to the portion of Seth. So Geb gave his entire inheritance to Horus, that is, the son of his son, his first-born. . . . Thus Horus stood over the entire land. Thus this land was united, proclaimed with the great name: "Ta-tenen, South-of-His-Wall, the Lord of Eternity." The two Great Sorceresses grew upon his head. So it was that Horus appeared as King of Upper and Lower Egypt, who united the Two Lands in Wall Nome, in the place in which the Two Lands are united.

It happened that reed and papyrus were set at the great double door of the House of Ptah. That means Horus and Seth, who were reconciled and united, so that they associated and their quarreling ceased in the place which they reached, being joined in the House of Ptah, "the Balance of the Two Lands," in which Upper and Lower Egypt have been weighed. . . .

The gods who came into being as Ptah:—

Ptah who is upon the Great Throne . . . ;

Ptah-Nun, the father who begot Atum;

Ptah-Naunet, the mother who bore Atum;

[11] Reprinted from *Ancient Near Eastern Texts Relating to the Old Testament* by James B. Pritchard by permission of Princeton University Press. Copyright, 1950, 1955, by Princeton University Press. Second Edition, 1955.

James B. Pritchard, *Ancient Near Eastern Texts*, 2nd ed. (Princeton, New Jersey: Princeton University Press, 1955), p. 4 ff.

Ptah the Great, that is, the heart and tongue of the Ennead;
Ptah . . . who gave birth to the gods; . . .

There came into being as the heart and there came into being as the tongue something in the form of Atum. The mighty Great One is Ptah, who transmitted life to all gods, as well as to their *ka's*, through this heart, by which Horus became Ptah, and through this tongue by which Thoth became Ptah.

Thus it happened that the heart and tongue gained control over every other member of the body, by teaching that he is in every body and in every mouth of all gods, all men, all cattle, all creeping things, and everything that lives, by thinking and commanding everything that he wishes. . . .

And so Ptah was satisfied, after he had made everything, as well as all the divine order. He had formed the gods, he had made cities, he had founded nomes, he had put the gods in their shrines, he had established their offerings, he had founded their shrines, he had made their bodies like that with which their hearts were satisfied. So the gods entered into their bodies of every kind of wood, of every kind of stone, of every kind of clay, or anything which might grow upon him, in which they had taken form. So all the gods, as well as their *ka's* gathered themselves to him, content and associated with the Lord of the Two Lands.

11 / A RELIGIOUS REFORMER

The Pharaoh Amenhotep IV (1369–1353 B.C.*?) attempted a thoroughgoing religious reform in Egypt. He and his family worshipped the Aton, the sun disc, as the source of life. He built a new capital at Tell el-Amarna and changed his name to Akh-en-Aton ("He Who Is Serviceable to the Aton"). The hymn printed below was found inscribed in a rock tomb at Tell el-Amarna, and reveals the Pharoh's belief in the universality of his god. It is debatable whether his faith was monotheistic, but the hymn shows a striking resemblance to Psalm 104.*[12]

[12] Reprinted from *Ancient Near Eastern Texts Relating to the Old Testament* by James B. Pritchard by permission of Princeton University Press. Copyright, 1950, 1955, by Princeton University Press. Second Edition, 1955.

James B. Pritchard, *Ancient Near Eastern Texts*, 2nd ed. (Princeton, New Jersey: Princeton University Press, 1955), p. 370 ff.

Thou appearest beautifully on the horizon of heaven,
Thou living Aton, the beginning of life!
When thou art risen on the eastern horizon,
Thou hast filled every land with thy beauty.
Thou art gracious, great, glistening, and high over every land;
Thy rays encompass the lands to the limit of all that thou hast made:
As thou are Re, thou reachest to the end of them;
Thou subduest them for thy beloved son.
Though thou art far away, thy rays are on earth;
Though thou art in their faces, no one knows thy going.

When thou settest in the western horizon,
The land is in darkness, in the manner of death.
They sleep in a room, with heads wrapped up,
Nor sees one eye the other.
All their gods which are under their heads might be stolen,
But they would not perceive it.
Every lion is come forth from his den;
All creeping things, they sting.
Darkness is a shroud, and the earth is in stillness.
For he who made them rests in his horizon.

At daybreak, when thou arisest on the horizon,
When thou shinest as the Aton by day,
Thou drivest away the darkness and givest thy rays.
The Two Lands are in festivity every day,
Awake and standing upon their feet,
For thou hast raised them up.
Washing their bodies, taking their clothing,
Their arms are raised in praise at thy appearance.
All the world, they do their work.

All beasts are content with their pasturage;
Trees and plants are flourishing.
The birds which fly from their nests,
Their wings are stretched out in praise to thy *ka*.
All beasts spring upon their feet.
Whatever flies and alights,
They live when thou hast risen for them.
The ships are sailing north and south as well,
For every way is open at thy appearance.
The fish in the river dart before thy face;
Thy rays are in the midst of the great green sea. . . .

How manifold it is, what thou hast made!
They are hidden from the face of man.
O sole god, like whom there is no other!
Thou didst create the world according to thy desire,
Whilst thou wert alone.
All men, cattle, and wild beasts,
Whatever is on earth, going upon its feet,
And what is on high, flying with its wings. . . .

12 / THE CRUMBLING EMPIRE

The following excerpts are taken from a papyrus written in the eleventh century B.C. *They form part of a narrative concerning Wen-Amon, dignitary of Amon's temple at Karnak, who was sent to Byblos in Phoenicia to fetch wood for the god's ceremonial barge named User-et-Amon. Wen-Amon was detained for more than three months by a local dynast, Ne-su-Ba-neb-Ded, and his wife, Ta-net-Amon, in the Nile Delta, then went by ship to Dor on the northern coast of Palestine where he was delayed by the local prince, and finally via Tyre to Byblos. He brought with him a sculptured image of the god whom he was serving, Amon-of-the-Road, in the hope that he would make his voyage succeed. He managed to accomplish his mission after long negotiations with the prince of Byblos, Zakar-Baal, but had great difficulty escaping the enemies of Egypt who were attempting to capture his ship on the high seas. A storm forced him to land on Cyprus and from there he probably returned to Egypt to tell his tale. His adventures illustrate both the imperial claims of Egypt and the weakness of her position in the Fertile Crescent around 1100* B.C.[13]

And I found him [Zakar-Baal of Byblos] sitting in his upper room, with his back turned to a window, so that the waves of the great Syrian sea broke against the back of his head. So I said unto him: "May Amon

[13] Reprinted from *Ancient Near Eastern Texts Relating to the Old Testament* by James B. Pritchard by permission of Princeton University Press. Copyright, 1950, 1955, by Princeton University Press. Second Edition, 1955.

James B. Pritchard, *Ancient Near Eastern Texts*, 2nd ed. (Princeton, New Jersey: Princeton University Press, 1955), p. 26 ff.

favor you." But he said to me: "How long, up to today, since you came from the place where Amon is?" So I said to him: "Five months and one day up to now." And he said to me: "Well, you're truthful! Where is the letter of Amon which should be in your hand? Where is the dispatch of the High Priest of Amon which should be in your hand?" And I told him: "I gave them to Ne-su-Ba-neb-Ded and Ta-net-Amon." And he was very, very angry, and he said to me: "Now see —neither letters nor dispatches are in your hand! Where is the cedar ship which Ne-su-Ba-neb-Ded gave to you? Where is its Syrian crew? Didn't he turn you over to this foreign ship captain to have him kill you and throw you into the sea? Then with whom would they have looked for the god? And you too—with whom would they have looked for you too?" So he spoke to me.

BUT I SAID TO HIM: "Wasn't it an Egyptian ship? Now it is Egyptian crews which sail under Ne-su-Ba-neb-Ded! He has no Syrian crews." And he said to me: "Aren't there twenty ships here in my harbor which are in commercial relations with Ne-su-Ba-neb-Ded? As to this Sidon, the other place which you have passed, aren't there fifty more ships there which are in commercial relations with Werket-El, and which are drawn up to his house?" And I was silent in this great time.

And he answered and said to me: "On what business have you come?" So I told him: "I have come after the woodwork for the great and august barque of Amon-Re, King of the Gods. Your father did it, your grandfather did it, and you will do it too!" So I spoke to him. But he said to me: "To be sure, they did it! And if you give me something for doing it, I will do it! Why, when my people carried out this commission, Pharaoh—life, prosperity, health!—sent six ships loaded with Egyptian goods, and they unloaded them into their storehouses! You —what is it that you're bringing me—me also?" And he had the journal rolls of his fathers brought, and he had them read out in my presence, and they found a thousand *deben* of silver and all kinds of things in his scrolls.

So he said to me: "If the ruler of Egypt were the lord of mine, and I were his servant also, he would not have to send silver and gold, saying: 'Carry out the commission of Amon!' There would be no carrying of a royal-gift, such as they used to do for my father. As for me—me also—I am not your servant! I am not the servant of him who sent you either! If I cry out to the Lebanon, the heavens open up, and the logs are here lying on the shore of the sea! Give me the sails which you have brought to carry your ships which would hold the logs for Egypt! Give me the ropes which you have brought to lash the cedar, logs which I am to cut down to make you . . . which I shall make for you as the sails of your boats, and the spars will be too heavy and will break, and you will die in the middle of the sea! See, Amon gives voice in the sky, and he puts Seth near him. Now Amon has founded all lands. He has founded them, but he founded first the land of Egypt, from which you come; for skill came out of it, to reach the place where I am, and learning came out of it, to reach the place where I am. What are these silly trips which they have had you make?"

And I said to him: "That's not true! What I am on are no 'silly trips' at all! There is no ship upon the River which does not belong to Amon! The sea is his, and the Lebanon is his, of which you say: 'It is mine!' It forms the nursery for User-et-Amon, the lord of every ship! Why, he spoke—Amon-Re, King of the Gods—and said to Heri-Hor, my master: 'Send me forth!' So he had me come, carrying this great god. But see, you have made this great god spend these twenty-nine days moored in your harbor, although you did not know it. Isn't he here? Isn't he the same as he was? You are stationed here to carry on the commerce of the Lebanon with Amon, its lord. As for your saying that the former kings sent silver and gold—suppose that they had life and health; then they would not have had such things sent! But they had such things sent to your fathers in place of life and health! Now as for Amon-Re, King of the Gods—he is the lord of this life and health, and he was the lord of your fathers. They spent their lifetimes making offering to Amon. And you also—you are the servant of Amon! If you say to Amon: 'Yes, I will do it!' and you carry out his commission, you will live, you will be prosperous, you will be healthy, and you will be good to your entire land and your people! But don't wish for yourself anything belonging to Amon-Re, King of the Gods. Why, a lion wants his own property! Have your secretary brought to me, so that I may send him to Ne-su-Ba-neb-Ded and Ta-net-Amon, the officers whom Amon put in the north of his land, and they will have all kinds of things sent. I shall send him to them to say: 'Let it be brought until I shall go back again to the south, and I shall then have every bit of the debt still due to you brought to you.'" So I spoke to him.

So he entrusted my letter to his messenger, and he loaded in the keel, the bow-post, the stern-post, along with four other hewn timbers —seven in all—and he had them taken to Egypt. And in the first month of the second season his messenger who had gone to Egypt came back to me in Syria. And Ne-su-Ba-neb-Ded and Ta-net-Amon sent: 4 jars and 1 *kak-men* of gold; 5 jars of silver, 10 pieces of clothing in royal linen; 10 *kherd* of good Upper Egyptian linen; 500 rolls of finished papyrus; 500 cowhides; 500 ropes; 20 sacks of lentils; and 30 baskets of fish. And she sent to me personally: 5 pieces of clothing in good Upper Egyptian linen; 1 sack of lentils; and 5 baskets of fish.

And the Prince was glad, and he detailed three hundred men and three hundred cattle, and he put supervisors at their head, to have them cut down the timber. So they cut them down, and they spent the second season lying there.

In the third month of the third season they dragged them to the shore of the sea, and the Prince came out and stood by them. And he sent to me, saying: "Come!" Now when I presented myself near him, the shadow of his lotus-blossom fell upon me. And Pen-Amon, a butler who belonged to him, cut me off, saying: "The shadow of Pharaoh—life, prosperity, health!—your lord, has fallen on you!" But he was angry at him, saying: "Let him alone!"

So I presented myself near him, and he answered and said to me: "See, the commission which my fathers carried out formerly, I have carried it out also, even though you have not done for me what your fathers would have done for me, and you too should have done! See, the last of your woodwork has arrived and is lying here. Do as I wish, and come to load it in—for aren't they going to give it to you? . . .

THE HEBREWS

13 / THE MOSAIC COVENANT

During the second millennium B.C. *various Oriental texts mention the Apiru, a group of nomadic peoples wandering around the fringes of the settled areas of the Fertile Crescent (the area from Mesopotamia, through Syria and Palestine, to Egypt). The Hebrews of the Old Testament may be these nomads. In later centuries, after the Hebrews settled in the land of Canaan, it was clearly established in their tradition that the nomadic groups from which they were descended had merged into a united people by a covenant with their god, Jehovah. In the thirteenth century* B.C. *the Hebrews, under the leadership of Moses, made a covenant with Jehovah in which they promised to worship him and he to protect them. As a result of this covenant Jehovah was said to have given his people a law code, the Ten Commandments; in reality this code is of much later date and was compiled after 500* B.C. *The idea of a covenant between men and their god remained basic to the Judaeo-Christian tradition. The account of the cov-*

enant, as well as the Ten Commandments, are preserved in the book of Exodus *(Chs. 19–20) in the Old Testament.*[14]

In the third month after the children of Israel were gone forth out of the land of Egypt, the same day came they into the wilderness of Sinai. And when they were departed from Rephidim and were come to the wilderness of Sinai, they encamped in the wilderness; and there Israel encamped before the mount. And Moses went up unto God, and Jehovah called unto him out of the mountain saying, Thus shalt thou say to the house of Jacob and tell the children of Israel: Ye have seen what I did unto the Egyptians and how I bare you on eagles' wings and brought you unto myself. Now therefore, if ye will obey my voice indeed and keep my covenant, then ye shall be mine own possession from among all peoples: for all the earth is mine: and ye shall be unto me a kingdom of priests and a holy nation. These are the words which thou shalt speak unto the children of Israel. . . .

And God spake all these words saying, I am Jehovah thy God, who brought thee out of the land of Egypt, out of the house of bondage.

Thou shalt have no other gods before me.

Thou shalt not make unto thee a graven image nor any likeness of any thing that is in heaven above or that is in the earth beneath or that is in the water under the earth: thou shalt not bow down thyself unto them, nor serve them; for I, Jehovah thy God, am a jealous God visiting the iniquity of the fathers upon the children, upon the third and upon the fourth generation of them that hate me, and showing lovingkindness unto thousands of them that love me and keep my commandments.

Thou shalt not take the name of Jehovah thy God in vain; for Jehovah will not hold him guiltless that taketh his name in vain.

Remember the sabbath day to keep it holy. Six days shalt thou labor and do all thy work; but the seventh day is a sabbath unto Jehovah thy God: in it thou shalt not do any work, thou nor thy son nor thy daughter, thy man-servant nor thy maid-servant nor thy cattle nor thy stranger that is within thy gates: for in six days Jehovah made heaven and earth, the sea and all that in them is and rested the seventh day: where Jehovah blessed the sabbath day and hallowed it.

Honor thy father and thy mother that thy days may be long in the land which Jehovah thy God giveth thee.

Thou shalt not kill.

Thou shalt not commit adultery.

Thou shalt not steal.

[14] *The Holy Bible,* newly edited by the American Revision Committee (New York: Thomas Nelson and Sons, 1901), p. 74 ff.

Thou shalt not bear false witness against thy neighbor.

Thou shalt not covet thy neighbor's house, thou shalt not covet thy neighbor's wife nor his man-servant nor his maid-servant nor his ox nor his ass nor anything that is thy neighbor's.

14 / KING DAVID

After their conquest of Canaan the Hebrews consolidated their hold on the land and organized themselves as a settled people. Their wars against the Canaanites, and especially against the Philistines, necessitated the establishment of kingship. Under their second and third kings, David (1000–961 B.C.*) and Solomon (961–922* B.C.*), the Hebrew people became powerful.*

Underlying the two books of Samuel in the Old Testament is a biographical history of King David written by one of his contemporaries—a great piece of historical writing. The historian admires David's achievements, such as the capture of Jerusalem (A), but does not hide his crimes, such as his shameful intrigue against a loyal soldier, Uriah the Hittite, who was away on military duty with the Israelite army under the command of the King's general Joab when the King seduced his wife, Bath-sheba (B). After his crime David was sharply rebuked by Nathan, one of the earliest prophets of Jehova mentioned in the Bible, for having robbed a poor man—a rebuke that foreshadows the principle of social justice preached by later prophets (No. 15).[15]

A. THE CAPTURE OF JERUSALEM

Then came all the tribes of Israel to David unto Hebron and spake saying, Behold, we are thy bone and thy flesh. In times past, when Saul was king over us, it was thou that leddest out and broughtest in Israel: and Jehovah said to thee, Thou shalt be shepherd of my people Israel, and thou shalt be prince over Israel. So all the elders of Israel came to the king of Hebron; and king David made a covenant with them in Hebron before Jehovah: and they anointed David king over Israel. David was thirty years old when he began to reign and he reigned forty years. In Hebron he reigned over Judah seven

[15] *The Holy Bible,* newly edited by the American Revision Committee (New York: Thomas Nelson and Sons, 1901), p. 323 ff., 329 ff.

years and six months; and in Jerusalem he reigned thirty and three years over all Israel and Judah.

And the king and his men went to Jerusalem against the Jebusites, the inhabitants of the land, who spake unto David saying, Except thou take away the blind and the lame, thou shalt not come in hither; thinking David cannot come in hither. Nevertheless David took the stronghold of Zion; the same is the city of David. And David said on that day, Whosoever smiteth the Jebusites, let him get up to the watercourse, and smite the lame and the blind that are hated of David's soul. Wherefore they say, There are the blind and the lame; he cannot come into the house. And David dwelt in the stronghold and called it the city of David. And David built round about from Millo and inward. And David waxed greater and greater; for Jehovah the God of Hosts was with him.

B. DAVID AND BATH-SHEBA

And it came to pass at eventide that David arose from off his bed and walked upon the roof of the king's house: and from the room he saw a woman bathing; and the woman was very beautiful to look upon. And David sent and inquired after the woman. And one said, Is not this Bath-sheba, the daughter of Eliam, the wife of Uriah the Hittite? And David sent mesengers and took her; and she came in unto him, and he lay with her; (for she was purified from her uncleanness;) and she returned unto her house. And the woman conceived; and she sent and told David and said, I am with child.

And David sent to Joab saying, Send me Uriah the Hittite. And Joab sent Uriah to David. And when Uriah was come unto him, David asked of him how Joab did, and how the people fared, and how the war prospered. And David said to Uriah, Go down to thy house and wash thy feet. And Uriah departed out of the king's house, and there followed him a mess of food from the king. But Uriah slept at the door of the king's house with all the servants of his lord and went not down to his house. And when they had told David saying, Uriah went not down unto his house, David said unto Uriah, Art thou not come from a journey? wherefore didst thou not go down unto thy house? And Uriah said unto David, The ark and Israel and Judah abide in booths; and my lord Joab and the servants of my lord are encamped in the open field; shall I then go into my house to eat and to drink and to lie with my wife? as thou livest and as thy soul liveth, I will not do this thing. And David said to Uriah, Tarry here to-day also and to-morrow I will let thee depart. So Uriah abode in Jerusalem that day and the morrow. And when David had called him, he did eat and drink before him; and he made him drunk: and at even he went out to lie on his bed with the servants of his lord but went not down to his house.

And it came to pass in the morning that David wrote a letter to Joab and sent it by the hand of Uriah. And he wrote in the letter saying, Set ye Uriah in the forefront of the hottest battle and retire ye from him that he may be smitten and die. And it came to pass when Joab kept watch upon the city that he assigned Uriah unto the place where he knew that valiant men were. And the men of the city went out and fought with Joab: and there fell some of the people, even of the servants of David; and Uriah the Hittite died also. . . .

And when the wife of Uriah heard that Uriah her husband was dead, she made lamentation for her husband. And when the mourning was past, David sent and took her home to his house, and she became his wife and bare him a son. But the thing that David had done displeased Jehovah.

And Jehovah sent Nathan unto David. And he came unto him, and said unto him, There were two men in one city; the one rich, and the other poor. The rich man had exceeding many flocks and herds; but the poor man had nothing save one little ewe lamb which he had bought and nourished up: and it grew up together with him, and with his children; it did eat of his own morsel and drank of his own cup and lay in his bosom and was unto him as a daughter. And there came a traveller unto the rich man, and he spared to take of his own flock and of his own herd to dress for the wayfaring man that was come unto him, but took the poor man's lamb and dressed it for the man that was come to him. And David's anger was greatly kindled against the man; and he said to Nathan, As Jehovah liveth, the man that hath done this is worthy to die; and he shall restore the lamb fourfold because he did this thing and because he had no pity.

And Nathan said to David, Thou art the man. Thus saith Jehovah the God of Israel, I anointed thee king over Israel, and I delivered thee out of the hand of Saul; and I gave thee thy master's house and thy master's wives into thy bosom and gave thee the house of Israel and of Judah; and if that had been too little, I would have added unto thee such and such things. Wherefore hast thou despised the word of Jehovah to do that which is evil in his sight? thou hast smitten Uriah the Hittite with the sword and hast taken his wife to be thy wife and hast slain him with the sword of the children of Ammon. Now therefore, the sword shall never depart from thy house because thou hast despised me and hast taken the wife of Uriah the Hittite to be thy wife.

15 / AMOS

After King Solomon's death (922 B.C.*) the Hebrew kingdom was divided into two parts, Israel in the North and Judah in the South. Israel was more advanced and sophisticated than its southern neighbor, but it was from the more primitive southern kingdom of Judah that many of the prophets came (see in No. 14B, above, the figure of Nathan). The prophets reminded the people of the two kingdoms of their ancestors' covenant with Jehovah (No. 13). In the land of the Canaanites the Hebrews, so the prophets said, had abandoned the worship of Jehovah and worshiped the Canaanite gods. They taught that Jehovah demanded not ritual but social justice. More and more they came to insist upon the universality of Jehovah until they finally arrived at strict monotheism. The prophet Amos lived around 750* B.C. *in Tekoa, a Judaean village south of Bethlehem. He was a shepherd, active as a prophet primarily in the Northern kingdom.*[16]

Thus saith Jehovah: For three transgressions of Israel, yea for four, I will not turn away the punishment thereof; because they have sold the righteous for silver and the needy for a pair of shoes; they that pant after the dust of the earth on the head of the poor and turn aside the way of the meek; and a man and his father go unto the same maiden to profane my holy name; and they lay themselves down beside every altar upon clothes taken in pledge; and in the house of their God they drink the wine of such as have been fined.

Yet destroyed I the Amorite before them, whose height was like the height of the cedars, and he was strong as the oaks; yet I destroyed his fruit above and his roots from beneath. Also I brought you up out of the land of Egypt and led you forty years in the wilderness to possess the land of the Amorite. And I raised up of your sons for prophets and of your young men for Nazirites. Is it not even thus, O ye children of Israel? saith Jehovah. But ye gave the Nazirites wine to drink and commanded the prophets saying, prophesy not. . . .

Hear this word that Jehovah hath spoken against you, O children of Israel, against the whole family which I brought up out of the land of Egypt saying, You only have I known of all the families of the earth: therefore I will visit upon you all your iniquities. Shall two

[16] *The Holy Bible,* newly edited by the American Revision Committee (New York: Thomas Nelson and Sons, 1901), pp. 906–9.

walk together except they have agreed? Will a lion roar in the forest when he hath no prey? will a young lion cry out of his den if he have taken nothing? Can a bird fall in a snare upon the earth where no gin is set for him? shall a snare spring up from the ground and have taken nothing at all? Shall the trumpet be blown in a city and the people not be afraid? shall evil befall a city, and Jehovah hath not done it? Surely the Lord Jehovah will do nothing, except he reveal his secret unto his servants the prophets. The lion hath roared: who will not fear? The Lord Jehovah hath spoken; who can but prophesy? . . .

Hear this word, ye kine of Bashan that are in the mountain of Samaria, that oppress the poor, that crush the needy, that say unto their lords, Bring and let us drink. The Lord Jehovah hath sworn by his holiness that, lo, the days shall come upon you that they shall take you away with hooks and your residue with fish-hooks. And ye shall go out at the breaches, every one straight before her; and ye shall cast yourselves into Harmon, saith Jehovah. . . .

Hear ye this word which I take up for a lamentation over you, O house of Israel. The virgin of Israel is fallen; she shall no more rise; she is cast down upon her land; there is none to raise her up. For thus saith the Lord Jehovah: The city that went forth a thousand shall have a hundred left and that which went forth a hundred shall have ten left, to the house of Israel.

For thus saith Jehovah unto the house of Israel, Seek ye me and ye shall live; but seek not Beth-el nor enter into Gilgal and pass not to Beer-sheba: for Gilgal shall surely go into captivity, and Beth-el shall come to nought. Seek Jehovah and ye shall live; lest he break out like fire in the house of Joseph and it devour and there be none to quench it in Beth-el. . . .

Woe unto you that desire the day of Jehovah! Wherefore would ye have the day of Jehovah? It is darkness and not light. As if a man did flee from a lion, and a bear met him; or went into the house and leaned his hand on the wall, and a serpent bit him. Shall not the day of Jehovah be darkness and not light? even very dark, and no brightness in it?

I hate, I despise your feasts and I will take no delight in your solemn assemblies. Yea, though ye offer me your burnt-offerings and meal-offerings, I will not accept them; neither will I regard the peace-offerings of your fat beasts. Take thou away from me the noise of thy songs; for I will not hear the melody of thy viols. But let justice roll down as waters and righteousness as a mighty stream.

Did ye bring unto me sacrifices and offerings in the wilderness forty years, O house of Israel? Yea, ye have borne the tabernacle of your king and the shrine of your images, the star of your god, which ye made to yourselves. Therefore will I cause you to go into captivity beyond Damascus, saith Jehovah whose name is the God of hosts. . . .

Thus he showed me and behold, the Lord stood beside a wall made by a plumbline, with a plumbline in his hand. And Jehovah said unto me, Amos, what seest thou? and I said, A plumbline. Then said the Lord, Behold I will set a plumbline in the midst of my people Israel; I will not again pass by them any more; and the high places of Isaac shall be desolate, and the sanctuaries of Israel shall be laid waste; and I will rise against the house of Jeroboam with the sword.

Then Amaziah the priest of Beth-el sent to Jeroboam king of Israel saying, Amos hath conspired against thee in the midst of the house of Israel: the land is not able to bear all his words. For thus Amos saith, Jeroboam shall die by the sword, and Israel shall surely be led away captive out of his land. Also Amaziah said unto Amos, O thou seer, go, flee thou away into the land of Judah and there eat bread and prophesy there; but prophesy not again any more at Beth-el; for it is the king's sanctuary and it is a royal house.

Then answered Amos and said to Amaziah, I was no prophet neither was I a prophet's son; but I was a herdsman and a dresser of sycamore-trees; and Jehovah took me from following the flock and Jehovah said unto me, Go, prophesy unto my people Israel. Now therefore hear thou the word of Jehovah: Thou sayest, Prophesy not against Israel and drop not thy word against the house of Isaac; therefore thus saith Jehovah: Thy wife shall be a harlot in the city, and thy sons and thy daughters shall fall by the sword, and thy land shall be divided by line; and thou thyself shall die in a land that is unclean, and Israel shall surely be led away captive out of his land.

16 / A CAMPAIGN OF KING SENNACHERIB OF ASSYRIA: THE JUDAEAN RECORD

Sennacherib's attack upon Judaea (701 B.C.) was recorded not only in the Assyrian annals (No. 3B) but also in the chronicles of Judah.[17]

[17] *The Holy Bible,* newly edited by the American Revision Committee (New York: Thomas Nelson and Sons, 1901), pp. 405–8.

Now in the fourteenth year of king Hezekiah did Sennacherib king of Assyria come up against all the fortified cities of Judah and took them. And Hezekiah, king of Judah, sent to the king of Assyria to Lachish saying, I have offended; return from me: that which you puttest on me will I bear. And the king of Assyria appointed unto Hezekiah king of Judah three hundred talents of silver and thirty talents of gold. And Hezekiah gave him all the silver that was found in the house of Jehovah, and in the treasures of the king's house. At that time did Hezekiah cut off the gold from the doors of the temple of Jehovah and from the pillars which Hezekiah king of Judah had overlaid and gave it to the Assyrians. And the king of Assyria sent Tartan and Rab-saris and Rabshakeh from Lachish to king Hezekiah with a great army unto Jerusalem. And they went up and came to Jerusalem. . . .

[The Assyrian generals then summon King Hezekiah of Judaea and the inhabitants of Jerusalem to surrender and not to trust in relief from Egypt or in the help of Jehovah. Hezekiah in turn receives encouraging oracles from the prophet Isaiah.]

And it came to pass that night that the angel of Jehovah went forth and smote in the camp of the Assyrians a hundred fourscore and five thousand: and when men arose early in the morning, behold, these were all dead bodies. So Sennacherib king of Assyria departed and went and returned and dwelt at Nineveh.

17 / THE CREATION OF THE WORLD AND OF MAN

The prophets' insistence on Jehovah's universality eventually produced the belief that Jehovah was the only god (see introduction to No. 15) and that he had created the world and man. In the fifth century B.C. *a priestly writer described the process of creation, an account that has many similarities to, as well as differences from, the Akkadian epic of creation (No. 4) and must therefore derive from very ancient sources. There follows immediately a second, older, and somewhat different account of the creation of man, in which man is made by divine breath from dust.*[18]

In the beginning God created the heavens and the earth. And the earth was waste and void; and darkness was upon the face of the deep: and the Spirit of God moved upon the face of the waters. And God said, Let there be light: and there was light. And God saw the light that it was good: and God divided the light from the darkness. And God called the light Day, and the darkness he called Night. And there was evening and there was morning, one day.

And God said, Let there be a firmament in the midst of the waters, and let it divide the waters from the waters. And God made the firmament and divided the water which were under the firmament from the waters which were above the firmament; and it was so. And God called the firmament Heaven. And there was evening and there was morning, a second day.

And God said, Let the waters under the heavens be gathered together unto one place and let the dry land appear; and it was so. And God called the dry land Earth; and the gathering together of the waters called he Seas; and God saw that it was good. And God said, Let the earth put forth grass, herbs yielding seed and fruit-trees bearing fruit after their kind wherein is the seed thereof, upon the earth: and it was so. And the earth brought forth grass, herbs yielding seed after their kind; and God saw that it was good. And there was evening and there was morning, a third day.

And God said, Let there be lights in the firmament of heavens to divide the day from the night; and let them be for signs and for seasons and for days and years; and let them be for lights in the firmament of heaven to give light upon the earth; and it was so. And God made the two great lights; the greater light to rule the day and the lesser light to rule the night; he made the stars also. And God set them in the firmament of heaven to give light upon the earth and to rule over the day and over the night and to divide the light from the darkness; and God saw that it was good. And there was evening and there was morning, a fourth day.

And God said, Let the waters swarm with swarms of living creatures and let birds fly above the earth in the open firmament of heaven. And God created the great sea-monsters and every living creature that moveth wherewith the waters swarmed after their kind and every winged bird after its kind; and God saw that it was good. And God blessed them saying, Be fruitful and multiply and fill the waters in

18 *The Holy Bible,* newly edited by the American Revision Committee (New York: Thomas Nelson and Sons, 1901), p. 1 ff.

the seas and let birds multiply on the earth. And there was evening and there was morning, a fifth day.

And God said, Let the earth bring forth living creatures after their kind, cattle, and creeping things and beasts of the earth after their kind; and it was so. And God made the beasts of the earth after their kind and the cattle after their kind and everything that creepeth upon the ground after its kind; and God saw that it was good. And God said, Let us make man in our image, after our likeness and let them have dominion over the fish of the sea and over the birds of the heavens and over the cattle and over all the earth and over every creeping thing that creepeth upon the earth. And God created man in his own image, in the image of God created he him; male and female created he them. And God blessed them: and God said unto them, Be fruitful and multiply and replenish the earth and subdue it; and have dominion over the fish of the sea and over the birds of the heavens and over every living thing that moveth upon the earth. And God said, Behold, I have given you every herb yielding seed which is upon the face of all the earth and every tree in which is the fruit of a tree yielding seed; to you it shall be for food; and to every beast of the earth, and to every bird of the heavens and to every thing that creepeth upon the earth wherein there is life I have given every green herb for food; and it was so. And God saw every thing that he had made, and behold it was very good. And there was evening and there was morning, the sixth day.

And the heavens and the earth were finished and all the host of them. And on the seventh day God finished his work which he had made. And God blessed the seventh day and hallowed it; because that in it he rested from all his work which God had created and had made.

These are the generations of the heavens and of the earth when they were created in the day that Jehovah God made earth and heaven. And no plant of the field was yet in the earth, and no herb of the field had yet sprung up; for Jehovah God had not caused it to rain upon the earth; and there was not a man to till the ground; but there went up a mist from the earth and watered the whole face of the ground. And Jehovah God formed men of the dust of the ground and breathed into his nostrils the breath of life; and man became a living soul.

18 / THE FLOOD

As the biblical account of creation shows striking resemblances to the Akkadian creation epic (No. 4), so the description of the Flood in Genesis (Ch. 7) is clearly related to

Utnapishtim's tale of the Flood in the story of Gilgamesh (No. 5). Like Utnapishtim, Noah was instructed by the deity to build himself an ark, and specifications were given for its construction.[19]

And the flood was forty days upon the earth; and the waters increased and bare up the ark and it was lifted up above the earth. And the waters prevailed and increased greatly upon the earth; and the ark went upon the face of the waters. And the waters prevailed exceedingly upon the earth, and all the high mountains that were under the whole heaven were covered. Fifteen cubits upward did the waters prevail, and the mountains were covered. And all flesh died that moved upon the earth, both birds and cattle and beasts and every creeping thing that creepeth upon the earth and every man; all in whose nostrils was the breath of the spirit of life, of all that was on the dry land, died. And every living thing was destroyed that was upon the face of the ground, both men and cattle and creeping things and birds of the heavens; and they were destroyed from the earth; and Noah only was left and they that were with him in the ark. And the waters prevailed upon the earth a hundred and fifty days.

And God remembered Noah and all the beasts and all the cattle that were with him in the ark; and God made a wind to pass over the earth, and the waters assuaged, the fountains also of the deep and the windows of heaven were stopped, and the rain from heaven was restrained, and the waters returned from off the earth continually; and after the end of a hundred and fifty days the waters decreased. And the ark rested in the seventh month, on the seventeenth day of the month, upon the mountains of Ararat. And the waters decreased continually until the tenth month; in the tenth month, on the first day of the month, were the tops of the mountains seen.

And it came to pass at the end of forty days that Noah opened the window of the ark which he had made; and he sent forth a raven and it went forth to and fro until the waters were dried up from off the earth. And he sent forth a dove from him to see if the waters were abated from off the face of the ground; but the dove found no rest for the sole of her foot and she returned unto him to the ark; for the waters were on the face of the whole earth; and he put forth his hand and took her and brought her in unto him into the ark. And he stayed yet other seven days; and again he sent forth the dove out of the ark; and the dove came in to him at eventide; and, lo, in her mouth

19 *The Holy Bible,* newly edited by the American Revision Committee (New York: Thomas Nelson and Sons, 1901), p. 7.

an olive-leaf plucked off; so Noah knew that the waters were abated from off the earth. And he stayed yet other seven days and sent forth the dove; and she returned not again unto him any more.

19 / A JEWISH VIEW OF HISTORY

The book of Daniel in the Old Testament was probably written between 168 and 165 B.C., *when the Jews were being attacked by the Seleucid king Antiochus IV Epiphanes (175–164* B.C.*). Its hero allegedly lived in the Neo-Babylonian empire around 600* B.C. *The book contains stories about Daniel and Daniel's visions. In the vision printed below, the four beasts represented the Babylonian, Median, Persian, and Seleucid kingdoms. The fourth beast had ten horns, probably a reference to ten Seleucid rulers. The little horn stood for Antiochus Epiphanes. The main point of the prophecy is that in the future the fourth beast, the Seleucid kingdom, will be judged and killed by God ("one that was ancient of days"). In other words, the kingdom of the heathens will be overcome, and the Jewish people will rule. At the end of time a mysterious figure, "one like unto a son of man," will be given universal and everlasting dominion. The vision was interpreted for Daniel; he was told that the mysterious figure refers to the "saints of the Most High," i.e., the Jewish people or a Jewish group called the* Hasidim, *the Pious. A great deal of speculation developed in late ancient and medieval times around the figure called "one like unto a son of man," and it was often understood to refer to a Messianic king.*[20]

In the first year of Belshazzar king of Babylon Daniel had a dream and visions of his head upon his bed; then he wrote the dream and told the sum of the matters. Daniel spake and said, I saw in my vision by night, and, behold, the four winds of heaven brake forth upon the great sea. And four great beasts came up from the sea, diverse one from another. The first was like a lion and had eagle's wings: I beheld

[20] *The Holy Bible,* newly edited by the American Revision Committee (New York: Thomas Nelson and Sons, 1901), p. 885 ff.

till the wings thereof were plucked, and it was lifted up from the earth, and made to stand upon two feet as a man; and a man's heart was given to it. And behold, another beast, a second like to a bear; and it was raised up on one side, and three ribs were in its mouth between its teeth; and they said thus unto it, Arise, devour much flesh. After this I beheld and lo, another, like a leopard, which had upon its back four wings of a bird; the beast had also four heads; and dominion was given to it. After this I saw in the night visions and behold, a fourth beast, terrible and powerful and strong exceedingly; and it had great iron teeth; it devoured and brake in pieces and stamped the residue with its feet; and it was diverse from all the beasts that were before it; and it had ten horns. I considered the horns and behold, there came up among them another horn, a little one, before which three of the first horns were plucked up by the roots; and behold in this horn were eyes like the eyes of a man and a mouth speaking great things.

I beheld till thrones were placed and one that was ancient of days did sit: his raiment was white as snow, and the hair of his head like pure wool; his throne was fiery flames, and the wheels thereof burning fire. A fiery stream issued and came forth from before him; thousands of thousands ministered unto him, and ten thousand times ten thousand stood before him: the judgment was set, and the books were opened. I beheld at that time because of the voice of the great words which the horn spake: I beheld even till the beast was slain, and its body destroyed, and it was given to be burned with fire. And as for the rest of the beasts, their dominion was taken away; yet their lives were prolonged for a season and a time.

I saw in the night-visions and behold, there came with the clouds of heaven one like unto a son of man, and he came even to the ancient of days, and they brought him near before him. And there was given him dominion and glory and a kingdom that all the peoples, nations and languages should serve him; his dominion is an ever-lasting dominion which shall not pass away and his kingdom that which shall not be destroyed.

As for me, Daniel, my spirit was grieved in the midst of my body, and the visions of my head troubled me. I came near unto one of them that stood by and asked him the truth concerning all this. So he told me and made me know the interpretation of the things. These great beasts, which are four, are four kings that shall arise out of the earth. But the saints of the Most High shall receive the kingdom, and possess the kingdom for ever, even for ever and ever.

II / BRONZE AGE AND EARLY IRON AGE IN GREECE

20 / ALAN J. B. WACE: THE COMING OF THE GREEKS

The sources for earliest Greek history are primarily archaeological. Archaeologists distinguish the Bronze Age from the Iron Age and consider the Dorian Invasion (circa *1100* B.C.*) the dividing line between the two epochs. Within the Bronze Age they distinguish three periods: Early, Middle, and Late (or Mycenaean,* circa *1580–1100* B.C.*). Bronze Age culture in mainland Greece is called Helladic; in Crete, Minoan; on the other islands, Cycladic. The historical results of archaeological investigations are summarized by Professor Wace.*[1] *He discusses two principal problems: first, at what time did the ancestors of the Greeks appear in the Mediterranean World, and second, was the Mycenaean civilization of the second half of the second millennium* B.C. *Oriental or Greek?*

The first stage of civilization in Greece is represented by the prehistoric mounds of Thessaly and contemporary sites in Central and Southern Greece. The earliest layers are Neolithic, and though we cannot

[1] Alan J. B. Wace, in Michael Ventris and John Chadwick, *Documents in Mycenaean Greek* (New York: Cambridge University Press, 1956), pp. XIX–XXII, XXVI–XXVIII. Reprinted by permission of Cambridge University Press.

as yet suggest even an approximate date, they probably are not later than the fourth millenium B.C. Their earliest inhabitants had reached a pottery stage of development and (to judge by the presence of Melian obsidian) were able to cross the narrow seas. We know nothing of their origin, which is still a matter of archaeological debate. They were succeeded at the beginning of the Bronze Age by a new people who, to judge from their artefacts, were racially dissimilar. This new people used copper and later bronze and made pottery of a more sophisticated type, but had not yet learnt the potter's wheel. It would appear that this people introduced into Greece many words, mostly place and plant names, ending in *-nthos, -assos, -ttos* and *-ēnē* which are recognized as non-Indo-European: such words are Korinthos, *terebinthos, asaminthos,* Parnassos, Hymettos, Mykēnē. The original home of the Early Helladic people is usually placed in south-western Asia Minor, where similar place-names occur, but there is as yet no proof for this. This folk was akin to the contemporary Bronze Age people of the Cyclades and of Crete, and thus we can recognize that the cultures of the Early Bronze Age in these areas were not only contemporary but closely related. These cultures may not have been actually sisters, but were probably at least first cousins.

The Early Helladic people overran the Mainland, and presumably did not extirpate the Neolithic folk but coalesced with the survivors. In any case, as far as we can tell, they were not Indo-European. . . .

With the beginning of the Middle Bronze Age on the Mainland of Greece in the nineteenth century B.C. a new element appears. In the stratification of excavated sites such as Korakou, Eutresis and Lianokladi it is obvious that there is no transition or evolution from the Early Bronze Age culture to that of the Middle Bronze Age. It is clear that a new factor at this time came into Greece; and since the material signs of its culture, pottery (which was made on the wheel), house plans, tombs, and in general all artefacts, differ markedly from those of the preceding Early Bronze Age, we assume that these differences mean a difference of race. This new racial element presumably in its turn also overrun and amalgamated with the survivors of the Early Helladic inhabitants. From this time onwards there is no similar sign of any cultural break: the Middle Bronze Age develops slowly and naturally into the Late Bronze Age. This can be seen clearly in the pottery from the Late Middle Helladic grave circle at Mycenae recently excavated by Dr. Papademetriou and Professor George Mylonas. Likewise at the end of the Late Bronze Age there can be observed, in spite of the more or less general destruction of the principal sites like Mycenae and Tiryns, a similar gradual change in culture (visible most of all in the pottery) from the end of the Bronze Age into the Early Iron Age. From the Early Iron Age henceforward there is no break in the development of culture in Greece: the Early Iron Age evolves naturally into the Orientalizing and Archaic periods and so into the great Classical Age of Greece. Thus by a process of elimination we deduce that since neither the Neolithic nor the Early Helladic people were Indo-Europeans, that is Greeks, then the Middle Helladic people who introduced into Greece the mysterious pottery called Minyan Ware (the characteristic pottery of the Middle Bronze Age) were probably the first Greeks to enter Hellas. So far no signs of their presence in the north of the Balkan peninsula can be found, and apart from Troy we have no indications of their presence in Asia Minor. The original home of the Greeks still remains a problem awaiting solution.

The Middle Helladic people apparently did not immediately come into contact with Crete and the Minoan culture; they met however in Melos, where at Phylakopi Kamares ware and Minyan ware are found side by side in the same Middle Cycladic strata. Towards the end of the Middle Bronze Age some of the painted Middle Helladic pottery shows signs of Cretan (Kamares) influence, but actual imports from Crete are rare. During the transition from the Middle to the Late Bronze Age the Mainland people became at last fully aware of the Minoan culture, which influenced the Mainland in much the same way as that in which classical Greek culture influenced Etruria. Just as in Crete the latest Middle Minoan products almost abruptly change into the new style of Late Minoan I, so on the Mainland the last style of Middle Helladic gives way rather suddenly to the bloom of Late Helladic I. The oversea connexions of the Mainland in this and the following period are to be seen in the fact that the "Aegean" pottery found in Egypt at this date is Late Helladic and not Late Minoan. Little or no Middle Helladic pottery has been observed in Crete; but Melian vases of Middle Cycladic III date were found in the Knossian temple repositories of Middle Minoan III, and a small vase of Knossian faïence of the same period in Shaft Grave A of the new Middle Helladic grave circle at Mycenae. At all events from Late Minoan I/Late Helladic I onwards the contacts between Crete, Knossos in particular, and the Mainland (as exemplified at Mycenae) were frequent and intimate. The trained eye can, however, nearly always distinguish between Cretan and Mainland vases. The Zakro cups, for instance, are quite different in fabric from their contemporaries on the Mainland. In the succeeding Late Minoan II or Palace Period, actual Mainland vases are found at Knossos and imitations of them are common, for instance the Ephyraean goblets of Knossos. . . .

[Wace then offers further evidence to support his thesis that Knossos differed from the rest of Crete: thus Linear B tablets, "Ephyrean"

pottery, alabaster vases are frequent on the Greek mainland, but are found on Crete only at Knossos. Other features of mainland provenance, such as the large Palace Style jars, beehive tombs, throne rooms, and the green porphyry used for making stone vases were imported to Knossos. On the basis of such considerations Wace arrives at the following conclusions:]

Thus the general belief was spreading among those who had devoted serious study to the problem and knew the actual objects (in short, the excavators and field archaeologists) and who had already deduced that the Mycenaeans must be Greeks, that at this time Knossos must have been at least under strong Mainland influence, perhaps even under the rule of a Mainland prince. It was consequently suggested that the destruction of Knossos at the close of the fifteenth century (at the end of Late Minoan II) was not due to an invasion from overseas or an earthquake, but to a revolt of the native Cretans, the "Minoans," against the intruding Greek dynasty or overlords. The deductions about Mainland influence at Knossos were based on facts, archaeological facts, the value of which far outweighs all theories and hypotheses about Minoan empires and colonies.

The Aegean archaeologists naturally believed that the "Mycenaeans" of the Mainland were Greeks, and that they would have spoken and written Greek. Thus the discovery of the Pylos tablets in 1939 and their obvious similarity in script and probably in language with the Linear B tablets from Knossos posed an entirely new problem, which could only be solved by the decipherment of the script. The "Minoans" naturally held that the Pylos tablets proved the Minoan conquest of the Mainland. One scholar even suggested that the tablets were loot from Knossos! The "Mainlanders" believed that the Pylos tablets ought to be written in Greek, and toyed with the idea that the Knossos tablets might be Greek also, though even they did not then see the wider implications of the result of all this. (Whether the language of the Mainland, probably then Greek, was the same as that of Crete cannot yet be determined.)

In 1952, as explained below, Mr. Ventris announced his decipherment of the Linear B script as Greek, and many things thereupon became clear and the archaeological deductions received linguistic confirmation, a great triumph for both methods. Working independently, the archaeologists and the linguists had come to the same conclusions. It is not often that learned researches support one another so decisively or so neatly.

Thus at one stroke what is practically a revolution has taken place in Greek studies. The prehistoric period of the Middle and Late Bronze Ages on the Mainland (Middle and Late Helladic) must now be recognized as Hellenic; we cannot include Crete, because we cannot yet read the Minoan Linear A script, which represents a different language from the Linear B script, and thus the Minoan culture cannot be called Hellenic. We must in future differentiate between the Linear A Minoan script and the Linear B Mycenaean script; for the latter is far commoner on the Mainland, where it is found from Orchomenos in the north to Pylos in the south, than it is in Crete.

We must in future speak of pre-Classical and Classical Greek art and culture. From the beginning of Schliemann's discoveries at Mycenae the conservatism of classical archaeologists has obstructed progress in the study of Greek civilization as a whole. Because the pre-Classical Mycenaean culture was in many ways naturally unlike the culture of Classical Greece of the sixth, fifth, and fourth centuries B.C., archaeologists refused to believe that it could possibly be Greek. They could hardly have expected that the culture of Mycenae, one thousand years older, and that of Periclean Athens would be the same. The more, however, we study Mycenaean art and culture, the more we find in it elements that anticipate Classical Greek art.

From the first, because Mycenaean art was unlike Classical Greek art, it was dismissed as oriental. Even when it was admitted that the Greeks might have arrived in Greece at the beginning of the Middle Bronze Age, it was stated that Greek art did not develop until one thousand years later, after an interregnum of chaos. One writer for example says: "When the sun of Homer rose out of the darkness of this wild time, it shone over the ruins of Creto-Mycenaean culture; but the new life of pure Hellenism grew up out of its ruins." We are told that the first creation of Greek art was the Geometric style, as though it had suddenly descended from Olympus about 1000 B.C. These "orthodox" archaeologists never reflected for one moment on the growth and evolution of the Geometric style. We know now that it evolved gradually from the pre-Classical culture of the Late Bronze Age, just as that in its turn evolved from the culture of the Middle Bronze Age. Nature does not work *per saltus* but by slow and sometimes painful processes of growth and change and development. In any study of Greek art to concentrate on the Classical period alone is a fatal mistake. The true student of Greek art must begin his studies with the Middle Bronze Age at least; also he must not end his studies with the death of Alexander, as so many do, and refuse even to look at Hellenistic art.

Schliemann in the enthusiasm of his first discoveries was overawed by the "experts" who insisted that his finds could not be Greek but must be Phoenician, Asiatic and so on. When he found frescoes at Mycenae, the "experts" insisted that they could not possibly be prehistoric and deterred him from publishing them. Other "experts" have held that there is a great chasm between pre-Classical and Classical Greece. An Oxford professor wrote as late as 1911: "The chasm dividing prehistoric and historic Greece is growing wider and deeper; and those who were at first disposed to leap over it now recognize such feats are impossible." It is this spirit which has impeded progress in our studies of pre-Classical Greece. Now, with the revelation of pre-Homeric Greek going back to the fifteenth century B.C., we have before us a great opportunity to discard old assumptions and the shibboleths once regarded almost as sacred dogma.

The history of Greece and of Greek culture will have to be rewritten from the outlook of our present knowledge, and as more pre-Classical texts are found and deciphered, so our knowledge will grow. Greek art is one and indivisible, and has a continuous history from the first arrival of the Greeks. A fresh examination of the legends of early Greece must also be undertaken to estimate their archaeological and historical value.

21 / ALAN J. B. WACE: MYCENAE–CAPITAL OF AGAMEMNON

The ruins of Mycenae in the Peloponnesus have given its name to the first Greek civilization—the Mycenaean Age. Excavations on the site were begun by Heinrich Schliemann in 1874 and have been continuing since that time. A reconstruction of the history of this important Bronze Age site on the basis of these excavations is summarized in the following section by Professor Wace.[2] *It should be noted that the summary was written prior to the decipherment of Linear B tablets (No. 22) and consequently before Professor Wace had fully elaborated his "mainland theory," i.e., his thesis that during the Mycenaean Age Knossos was under mainland influence, in contrast to Sir Arthur Evans' position that Knossos was the primary center (No. 20).*

[2] Reprinted from *Mycenae. An Archaeological History and Guide* by A. J. B. Wace by permission of Princeton University Press, copyright, 1949, by Princeton University, pp. 21–3. The excerpt will be most rewarding if read in conjunction with photographs of Mycenae, such as those published in Professor Wace's book.

The citadel was first occupied by man about 3000–2800 B.C., at the beginning of the Early Bronze Age. Remains of this period have been found on the summit and in the neighborhood of the Lion Gate and on another isolated hill, Kalkani, to the west, which has a good spring at its foot and therefore was also inhabited early. With the next period, the Middle Bronze Age about 2200–1600 B.C., when it is believed the first Greeks entered Greece, the prosperity of Mycenae began. As the power of Mycenae grew, so gradually from the middle of this period onward she came in contact with the civilization of Crete, was much attracted by it, and began to imitate Cretan manners, customs, culture, and art. A fortification wall was built round the summit of the citadel and within it was probably the residence of the prince or ruler. There were houses on the western slope and also on some of the neighboring hills. At the western foot of the hard limestone rock which forms the upper part of the citadel lay the cemetery. Part of this, including the Grave Circle, is now within the Cyclopean walls and part lies outside just to the west of the Lion Gate.

Throughout the period Mycenae seems to have grown in wealth and power and at its close two of its princes were laid in a shaft grave dug in the middle of the cemetery. This is the oldest of the six famous royal shaft graves found by Schliemann and Stamatakes and is known to archaeologists as the sixth shaft grave.

During the three phases of the Late Bronze Age the power and wealth of Mycenae increased still more. During the first phase, 1600–1500 B.C., other princes and princesses of the royal family were laid with all their treasures in five other shaft graves dug beside the one just mentioned. They probably belonged to one dynasty which we might call the Shaft Grave Dynasty. It seems to have ruled approximately a century and was contemporary with the kings of the early eighteenth dynasty in Egypt, with which country Mycenae already had commercial relations.

Not long before the end of this phase and during the second, 1500–1400 B.C., the princes of Mycenae were buried in the great tholos tombs, six of which antedate 1400 B.C. This change in the burial customs of the princes perhaps indicates a change of dynasty, and we might say that the Shaft Grave Dynasty was succeeded by the Tholos Tomb Dynasty. It was under these princes that Cretan fashions attained their greatest popularity, and the florid and exuberant Cretan style is much in evidence. In these two phases the ordinary civilian population did not live in the citadel, which was reserved for the royal family, the court, the officers of government and their families and attendants, but in separate settlements on the neighboring hills, such as Kalkani and the ridge above the Treasury of Atreus. In the sides of these hills they dug out burial places in the form of chamber tombs, the contents of which vividly illustrate the life of the Mycenaeans. A residence for the prince and his family existed from this time at least on the summit of the citadel, but no details about it are now recoverable.

The zenith of Mycenae's greatness was reached in the third and last phase of the Late Bronze Age, about 1400–1150 B.C. At the beginning of this phase the power of Crete was overthrown and Mycenae and the states of the Mainland were free to develop unhindered. The princes who now ruled Mycenae were not only powerful but must also have been rich. The source of their wealth is unknown but it has been suggested with considerable probability that in the mountains of Argolis behind Mycenae were copper mines which then, in the Bronze Age, would have been a most valuable source of revenue. Soon after the middle of the fourteenth century the citadel was enlarged and refortified by the construction of the Cyclopean walls with the Lion and Postern Gates. On the summit a new palace arose. This included a spacious court with a hall of state (*megaron*) and other official and domestic apartments, such as a throne room, a bathroom, and a shrine. The walls were covered with gay frescoes among which military scenes are prominent. Within the Lion Gate the shaft graves of the earlier dynasty were enclosed by the Grave Circle and became a sacred area. The greatest of the tholos tombs, the so-called Treasury of Atreus, is so similar in construction to the Lion Gate that it is conceivable that it was the tomb of the prince who built the palace and refortified and enlarged the citadel. Within the fortress there was, besides the palace, accommodation for the prince's family and officers with their attendants and presumably, too, for soldiers and slaves and some of the essential craftsmen. These all lived in houses adapted to their means and needs, built on terraces within the walls, which enclosed two wells and storehouses. There was a good system of drainage. The streets, however, were narrow lanes except for the main road which leads to the palace from the Lion Gate up to the great ramp and zigzag embankment, and justifies the Homeric epithet of Mycenae, "city of wide streets." The civilian population lived as before in settlements on the neighboring hills with springs close at hand, and their tombs were rock-cut chambers hewn out in the hillsides. Outside the Lion Gate was a cluster of buildings, perhaps inns for travelers or booths of traders and craftsmen to supply the inhabitants of the citadel with the food and goods they needed. Mycenae was the administrative center of a considerable dominion. High roads built through the Argive hills with culverts and bridges show that the rulers of this state organized both for peace and for war. The houses and the tombs and the objects found in them show that the standard of life was high for the period and that the Mycenaeans were an artistic and cultured race. Their architecture and what we can conjecture of their administration proves their intelligence, and the simple refinement of their decoration is refreshing after the exuberance of the Cretan style, fashionable in the first two phases of this age. The influence of Mycenae, commercial and political, extended over the Greek Mainland and adjacent islands and spread abroad to Sicily, Macedonia, Thrace, Troas, Asia Minor, Cilicia, Cyprus, Syria, Palestine, and Egypt. Homer's picture of the authority of Agamemnon is not exaggerated.

During the last phase the development of Mycenae did not stand still. In the thirteenth century B.C. the citadel was enlarged to the northeast and an underground cistern was constructed outside the walls with secret access from within, so that the garrison could have a constant supply of water. The palace, which seems to have suffered from a fire, was reconstructed and redecorated and a grand staircase was built as an approach to the court and state apartments. The so-called Tomb of Clytemnestra is that of a successor to the prince buried in the Treasury of Atreus. To this date also belongs a large house, the House of Columns, practically a small palace, on the east side of the citadel.

Throughout this period 1400–1100 B.C. all the evidence indicates that Mycenae was a strong and flourishing state, the seat of a powerful dynasty with a wide dominion. It corresponds admirably with our idea of the stronghold which was the capital of Agamemnon, king of men, *primus inter pares* of the Greek princes before Troy and holder of the supreme sovereignty granted by Zeus. After the Trojan War came the collapse at the beginning of the Early Iron Age. Toward the end of the twelfth century Mycenae was destroyed, but how its fall came about we do not know. All the buildings within the citadel which have been excavated were destroyed by fire and, if we may judge by the lack of precious things in them, they were apparently looted first.

This was the political convulsion which the Greeks called the Return of the Heraclidae or the Dorian Invasion. What were the circumstances which really led to it we cannot tell.

22 / EVIDENCE OF THE LINEAR B TABLETS

Prior to 1952 Mycenaean Civilization was known from archaeological excavations and, to a certain extent, from Homer's epics. From 1886 on, inscribed objects from Crete began to be recovered, and in 1939 similar objects in large numbers came to light during American excavations at Pylos in the Peloponnesus. Attempts to decipher the scripts, which began immediately after the discovery of the first finds, were rewarded when in 1952 Michael Ventris succeeded in deciphering one of the scripts ("Linear B"). The tablets proved to contain administrative records and inventories written in an old form of the Greek language. The decipherment, now accepted by most scholars, inaugurated a new field of study. While detailed conclusions must, in view of the youth of the field, be tentative, two important general results are beyond doubt. First, the bearers of Mycenaean Civilization were Greeks. Second, in the Mycenaean Age political organization was characterized by a vast and specialized bureaucracy interested in and capable of maintaining elaborate written records on all conceivable forms of human activity. The last conclusion in particular was one for which scholars had been entirely unprepared on the basis of Homer's evidence. The two examples given here may serve to illustrate the nature of the Linear B texts.

One tablet from Pylos (A) is concerned with different quantities of wheat seed connected with land owned by various officials. The nature of the connection is uncertain. The tablets may record actual transactions referring to wheat seed. The alternative is that there existed a standard density of sowing and that the quantities of wheat simply indicate the acreage owned by each official. The chief interest of the tablet lies in the references to high officials at Pylos. The largest amount of seed is assigned to the king (wanax). *Next to him stands the military leader* (lawagetes). *The three fief-holders together are allotted as much seed as the king alone. Finally the land of the religious association receives a very small allotment. A great number of other officials are named by other tablets—for example, feudal lords called* pasiren *(related to Homer's term for "king,"* basileus*) and councils* (kerosija, *kindred to the classical* gerousia).

The other tablet from Pylos translated in (B) contains what is probably a religious calendar for ten days of a certain month. It records offerings of cups and bowls made at the shrines of certain named gods and goddesses. The human beings (men and women) mentioned carry the cups and bowls. The greatest interest of the tablet lies in the names of deities. Some of them are well known from later Greece: Zeus, Poseidon, Hera, Hermes (other tablets add Apollo, Athena, Artemis, perhaps Dionysus and Hephaistos). Other gods or goddesses are less well attested in later times (Iphimedeia, Diwja, the Dove-goddess, the Mistress). It may be significant that at Pylos Poseidon leads the list of deities (see Homer, Odyssey, *II, 44).*[3]

A. OFFICIALS AT PYLOS

1. The preserve of the king, seed at so much: 3600 liters wheat
2. The preserve of the military leader, seed at so much: 1200 liters wheat
3. (The lands) of the fief-holders, so much seed: 3600 liters wheat; and (there are) so many fief-holders: three
4. The unencumbered (land) of the cult association, seed at so much: 720 liters wheat

B. GODS AND CULTS AT PYLOS

Obverse

(1st) Pylos: perform a certain action at the (shrine) of Poseidon and . . . the town, and bring the gifts and bring those to carry them.

One gold cup, two women. . . .

(2nd) Pylos: perform a certain action at the (shrines) of the Dove-goddess and of Iphemedeia and of Diwja, and bring the gifts and bring those to carry them.

To the Dove-goddess: one gold bowl, one woman.

To Iphemedeia: one gold bowl.

To Diwja: one gold bowl, one woman.

To Hermes . . . : one gold cup, one man.

(3rd) Pylos: perform a certain action at the (shrine) of Zeus, and bring the gifts and bring those to carry them.

To Zeus: one gold bowl, one man.

To Hera: one gold bowl, one woman.

To Drimios the priest of Zeus: one gold bowl, [one man?].

(4) blank.

(5) Pylos: blank.

[3] Michael Ventris and John Chadwick, *Documents in Mycenaean Greek* (New York: Cambridge University Press, 1956), pp. 266, 287. Reprinted by permission of Cambridge University Press.

23 / STERLING DOW: THE MYCENAEAN HEGEMONY

In the Middle Bronze Age the Greek occupants of Mycenae came in contact with the civilization of Minoan Crete and began to be affected by Cretan customs and art. Mycenaean power reached its zenith in the Late Bronze Age, about 1450–1150 B.C., *when Mycenae was the leading state on the Greek mainland and controlled many islands in the Aegean Sea.*[4]

Mykenai in Greece. Apart from the usual farms, pastures, and groves, the resources of Mykenai are altogether unknown to us: how was procured the gold of the Shaft Graves and the wherewithal to build a fleet. Mykenai itself was well situated, but so were many other towns. With silver, marble, and clay, Classical Athens had at least modest non-agricultural resources for Empire; but for Mykenai no special local sources of wealth whatever can be specified.

It was the start which was difficult. In time, perhaps early in the 300–400 years of Greek occupation before Grave Circle A, territory was surely added. The minimum which ought to be imagined is shown best by Pylos in the Linear B tablets: however their detail is to be interpreted, unquestionably they show extensive territorial control. Something like this, as much or more, should be imagined for Mykenai.

A second stage, whenever attained, would be the close alliance, based on marriage perhaps rather than on conquest, with Lakedaimon, thus giving control all the way south to the Lakonian Gulf, also the Taygetan promontory, and in Messenia as far as, and including, Pedasos-Methone.

Earlier perhaps than this Mainland expansion was a third phase, the conquest of Crete. In any case the problem of resources, difficult (for us) in the Sixteenth Century—so that the obtaining of the gold etc. for the 19 burials in Grave Circle A remains a problem—in the later

[4] Reprinted from "The Greeks in the Bronze Age," *Rapports* II of XIe Congrès des Sciences Historiques, Comité International des Sciences Historiques, Göteborg, Stockholm, Uppsala, 1960. Copyright by Almqvist & Wiksell, 1960.

Sterling Dow, "The Greeks in the Bronze Age," *Rapports* II of XIe Congrès des Sciences Historiques, Comité International des Sciences Historiques, Göteborg, Stockholm, Uppsala, 1960, pp. 19–26.

Fifteenth and in the Fourteenth Century is no problem at all. Revenues sufficed for the walls, the palace, the tholoi; for all the furnishings, of which just enough remains to give a hint, of the palace; and of the tholoi, where virtually nothing remains.

The Form of the Hegemony. If we try to formulate some notion of the organization of the Aegean under Mykenai, we find a number of indications as guides:

1. In the Ancient tradition as a whole, Mykenai is not given a thalassocracy. Thucydides makes Minos, but not Agamemnon, anticipate the features of the Athenian Empire. Agamemnon has naval power and islands, but their character would seem to be that of an extension of the kingdom.

2. The Catalogue of Ships, however doubtful its division of the Argolid into two, may well echo historical truth in not making the *relation* (not, of course, the absolute figures) of Agamemnon's naval power to the rest of Greece resemble that of Athens later. Agamemnon has available 160 ships, of which he loans the Arkadioi 60: the implicit suggestion that he could man only 100 is in the direction of realism. The next largest power, Pylos, has 90; then come Tiryns and Crete each with 80.

3. The Linear B tablets from Knossos, as we have seen, reveal there a chief of state (*Wanax*) with a high official at his side, just as in an independent kingdom. Mykenai may well have controlled the place and received much of the income, but in form Knossos was apparently independent.

4. In the *Iliad,* Agamemnon does not by any means occupy the position of Emperor in relation to the other Kings. He is a *primus inter pares,* though with the emphasis on the *primus.* The weaker he appears personally, the more he must be conceded to owe to his acknowledged headship of Greece; close reading will show, I think, that this position is really conceded very fully by the poet, however much his plot forced him to make Agamemnon appear weak personally.

5. These considerations, varied in source and doubtless in value, accord best with the Hittite evidence as most recently interpreted. This interpretation leads not for the first time, but more imperatively than before, to the identification of Rhodes as the great Greek power with which the Hittites dealt. Hittite documents of the Fourteenth and Thirteenth centuries refer some 20 times to Akhkhijawā, more easily transliterated Ahhijawa, which was evidently their (inaccurate) rendition of 'Αχαιϝία, that is, Achaea. If Ahhijawa cannot be Mykenai itself—the evidence is awkward both ways—then what we have is an independent state of considerable power in the eastern Aegean. Here again Mykenai appears as having no empire, or rather, Greek power is fragmented.

If the foregoing does not mislead, we can contrast the Minoan

Thalassocracy with the Mykenaian Hegemony. Like Classical Corinth, perhaps, Mykenai was content with the profits of trade, and sought no empire. Colonies were sent out, but for the revenue of trade if for any; not for other power, and not for the extortion of tribute. As against the many Minoas, spread abroad, there is only the one Mykenai. . . .

Troy. If this view of Bronze Age fortifications is acceptable, the expedition against Troy can be explained in simple terms. The old notion that Troy obnoxiously controlled the Dardanelles, and thus Black Sea commerce, by levying toll on shipping, or on goods trans-shipped, is happily defunct. There was no such commerce, and the destruction of Troy VIIa did not open it up. Another explanation of the war is needed.

Like all such forts, Troy VIIa held royal treasure. It was not the rich place that Troy VI had been, but the prospective plunder was worth the effort. Epic poetry later altered the purpose to a romantic one, and glamorized the whole expedition, just as epic poetry would be expected to do.

A few facts appear to survive criticism. There *was* a Greek expedition against Troy VIIa; Mykenai under Agamemnon commanded it; numerous allies took part. The fort was packed with people, and proved hard to capture. The Greeks succeeded, after which they pillaged, burned, and departed. Epic exaggerated all the details, especially the size of the Greek force, and the time it took. Gross inaccuracies about the site crept in: they would not worry epic poets. So much seems clear. The real problems are in another sphere, viz. chronology.

[In a section entitled "The Relative Order of Events," the author then establishes his view that the Greek expedition against Troy must have taken place circa *1240* B.C., *before the Mediterranean world was attacked by invaders* (circa *1223* B.C.) *and before the commerce of Mykenai was reduced to a trickle in the second half of the thirteenth century.]*

The Destruction of the Palace Bureaucracies. Certain phenomena, when seen in relation, give an insight into the "mind" of Bronze Age Greece. (1) With their interest in astonishingly petty details, the tablets show a bookkeeping-shopkeeping mentality. (2) The economy in some sense is planned. The object of the plan, or at least *one* object, is to fill the palace magazines with agricultural produce (Knossos) and the shelves with thousands of vases (Pylos), the sale of which would increase the royal treasures (Mykenai, Grave Circle A). (3) In other royal economies, i.e. in states where the king's income is very large (taxes, tribute, booty), and his expenses (army/bodyguard, court, royal burials) are less, treasure can accumulate to enormous totals (cf. the Achaemenids and the Ptolemies). (4) The safety of the treasure naturally becomes a grave concern: hence walls are built if a menace exists. (5) The treasures cannot be kept secret, but become known, however inaccurately; hence wars such as the expedition against Troy, since people who are obsessed with their own treasures naturally want to add to them the treasures of others.

(6) Within each such state, and considering them from the point of view of the subjects, it seems clear that the authority of the monarch and his bureaucracy over a great many subjects was tremendous. People appear to have lived within an elaborate framework of *system*, features of which were specialization under central control, with writing used to communicate and preserve orders and records. To some extent intricate and complex, the different functions—commerce and agriculture and manufacture—depended on each other. If treasure and the safe-guarding of it were dominant concerns in the king's mind, subservience and care in fulfilling his duties in the system dominated the subject. The subject knew no other way of life.

All of this was highly "civilized" and one may conjecture that it was fragile. Destroy the palace, and the whole community was wrecked. This happened. Pylos, the last palace to be built, was perhaps the first to go, ca. 1200 B.C., the rest very soon, in the next decades, at latest not after 1150. The Dorian destroyers were savage enough to have ended less fragile organizations than the palace bureaucracies. As it was, the disruption of commerce brought down the whole of society. This fragility explains why, even without Dorians on the Akropolis, Attika also went under. The economy was geared to certain exports and imports; they ended, and the invaders were soon ravaging the Attic countryside. The Akropolis they could not take, but destruction was complete without that.

Linear B can teach us two large facts, still not wholly assimilated, about the destruction. One is about illiteracy. Hitherto it has been fairly clear that illiteracy was due to the failure of interest on the part of older people in teaching the younger to read and write; and in an equally complete failure of interest on the part of the younger to want to learn. Now we can understand much better the failure of interest. It was caused by the utter collapse of a system which had engrossed the lives of those who wrote and who read. When the system collapsed overnight, the incentive to literacy was not all that went with it, but but people's very lives. There were no more careers for the palace bureaucrats, the craftsmen, the officers, even for the more highly trained slaves. Probably most of them had to go dig in the fields. There was a reversion to primitive economy.

The other large historical fact taught by Linear B is the abruptness of the governmental change. The Classical Greeks were inherently, persistently conservative, in that the greatest changes were regularly accompanied by retention of something old. As in Rome and in other states also, the King might be largely or almost completely supplanted; but there was still at Athens, throughout its history down to Constantine or beyond, an officer entitled *Basileus,* not to mention, for centuries at least, four *Phylobasileis.* But when the destruction of the Twelfth Century took place, the chief of state, the *Wanax,* was evidently completely abolished. He was part of the bureaucracy, the supreme part, so integral that his title did not survive, even in some conservative nominal manner, any more than did the bureaucracy. The epic tradition too lost any accurate and conscious memory of the office.

The effect of the Dorian invasions was not just the destruction of property. It was profoundly a mental event. The state was almost literally decapitated. The whole organization and the whole mentality at the top—that of the palace bureaucracy—went. Small local officials, numerous in each state, whose title had been *Basileus* and was significantly kept, replaced the one *Wanax.* The state was broken up into smaller local units. Attika, for instance, had to be united all over again.

The Dorians and the three centuries *plus* of Dark Age which they initiated were the most fearful and (for civilization at the time) costly disaster in European history. But they were not an unmixed evil. Linear B literacy, had it lasted any length of time, would have been an incubus upon the Greek mind. That has been clear for some time. Can we not add to it a similar statement about the palace bureaucracies? They had created Mykenai, Tiryns, Pylos, much else; but their work was done, they had no future, at least none easily imagined. Even in cities where there may have been opportunities, as in Athens, no one tried to recreate palace bureaucracies. They too would have become an incubus, a faulty syllabary of thought where a flexible alphabet was needed. Even though fine things were rubbed out by the Dorians, too many and unnecessarily, on the whole it was well for Europe that the slate was wiped clean. Hesiod knew enough to deplore the Iron Age, yet without it there would have been no Hesiod, and all that came down to his greater compeer Homer would never have had the qualities which oral testing produces.

24 / THE TAWAGALAWAS LETTER

Most scholars are agreed that the Mycenaean Greeks are referred to in the Hittite archives. The Hittites had dominated Asia Minor since 2000 B.C. *from their capital at Boghazkoi. Their empire reached its height from 1400–1200, when it vied with Egypt for the control of Syria. Hittite texts frequently refer to a king and kingdom of Ahhijawā and a city of Millawanda, probably the Hittite equivalents of the Achaeans (Greeks) and Miletus. The most interesting text is the following letter. It was written by one of the greatest of Hittite kings, either Mursilis II (1339–1306* B.C.*) or his son Muwatallis (1306–1282* B.C.*), to an unnamed king of Ahhijawā. The Hittite ruler complains of two residents of Millawanda, a city belonging to the king of Ahhijawā. One of them, Tawagalawas, after having offered to become a vassal of the Hittite king, waged war against him. The other, Pijamaradus, a Hittite subject, had stolen seven thousand of the king's prisoners, had found asylum at Millawanda, and there had enjoyed the protection of Atpās, representative of the king of Ahhijawā. The exact location of Ahhijawā is uncertain, but a good case has been made for its being the island of Rhodes, off the Southern shore of Asia Minor (alternatives: Mycenae, Crete, Cyprus). The document reveals the Hittites, a land power, dealing in the late fourteenth or early thirteenth century* B.C. *on equal terms with Ahhijawā, a naval power, able to attack the shores of Asia Minor and controlling a small area (Millawanda/Miletus) in Asia Minor.*[5]

I have to complain of the insolent and treacherous conduct of one Tawagalawas. We come into contact in the land of Luqqā [Lycia]; and he offered to become a vassal of the Hittite Empire. I agreed, and sent an officer of most exalted rank to conduct him to my presence: he had the audacity to complain that the officer's rank was not exalted enough; he insulted my ambassador in public, and demanded that he be declared vassal-king there and then without the formality of interview. Very well: I order him, if he desires to become a vassal of mine, to make sure that no troops of his are to be found in Ijalanda when I arrive there. And what do I find when I arrive at Ijalanda?—The troops of Tawagalawas, fighting on the side of my enemies. I defeat them, take many prisoners, devastate the district,—scrupulously leaving the fortress of Atrija intact out of respect for my treaty with you. Now comes a Hittite subject, Pijamaradus by name, steals my 7,000 prisoners, and makes off to your city Millawanda. I command him to return to me: he disobeys. I write to you: you send a surly message un-

[5] Denys L. Page, *History and the Homeric Iliad* (Berkeley and Los Angeles: University of California Press, 1959), p. 11 ff. Reprinted by permission of University of California Press.

accompanied by gift or greeting, to say that you have ordered your representative in Millawanda, a certain Atpās, to deliver Pijamaradus up. Nothing happens, so I go to fetch him. I enter your city Millawanda, for I have something to say to Pijamaradus, and it would be well that your subjects there should hear me say it. But my visit is not a success. I ask for Tawagalawas: he is not at home. I should like to see Pijamaradus: he has gone to sea. You refer me to your representative Atpās: I find that both he and his brother are married to daughters of Pijamaradus; they are not likely either to give me satisfaction or to give you an unbiassed account of these transactions, though they have had the pleasure of listening to the speech which I had prepared for their father-in-law, and they have promised under oath to make a true report to you. Meantime I receive from you a most insolent message, adopting a tone tolerated only between equals, forbidding me to remove Pijamaradus from Millawanda. Now I have a proposal to make: give me Pijamaradus, and I promise that he shall come to no harm. I will send a high dignitary of the Hittite court, a kinsman by marriage of my own queen, as a hostage for him. If I can make a satisfactory settlement with Pijamaradus, well and good; if not, he shall return to your territory unharmed, and you shall keep my royal hostage until then. Are you aware, and is it with your blessing, that Pijamaradus is going round saying that he intends to leave his wife and family, and incidentally my 7,000 prisoners, under your protection while he makes continual inroads on my dominions? Kindly tell him either to settle down peacefully in your country, or to return to my country. Do not let him use Ahhijawā as a base for operations against me. You and I are friends. There has been no quarrel between us since we came to terms in the matter of Wilusa: the trouble there was all my fault, and I promise it shall not happen again. As for my military occupation of your city Millawanda, please regard it as a friendly visit. I am sorry that in the past you have had occasion to accuse me of being aggressive and of sending impolite messages: I was young then, and carried away in the heat of action. I may add that I also have had harsh words from you; and I suggest that the fault may lie not with ourselves but with our messengers; let us bring them to trial, cut off their heads, mutilate their bodies, and live henceforth in perfect friendship.

III / THE EARLY GREEK CITY-STATE AND THE CONFLICT WITH PERSIA

25 / THE EVIDENCE OF HOMER

According to Herodotus, Homer lived no earlier than four hundred years before his own time, i.e., in the ninth century B.C. *The events described in the* Iliad *and the* Odyssey, *however—the Greek war against Troy and the return of the heroes from Troy—took place in the thirteenth (twelfth?) century. The principal historical problem posed by Homer's poems is this: do they reflect the civilization of the Mycenaean Age or of Homer's own period? Most scholars agree that they present a mixture of Mycenaean and post-Mycenaean elements. This mixture is the product of the poet's imagination, and its constituent parts cannot have coexisted in any given historical era. No single date can therefore be assigned to the civilization described in the* Iliad *and the* Odyssey; *each feature and element must be dated separately.*

In the following excerpt (A) from Iliad *II, the Argive host is ruled by the typical organs of the city-state of post-Dorian Greece: King, Council of Nobles, Assembly of People. Nestor suggests that the warriors be marshalled according to the post-Dorian kinship groups (tribes and clans) to which they belong by birth. Yet the possibility cannot be excluded that a similar organization had existed in the Mycenaean Age. Furthermore, it would appear more likely that the overlordship exercised by Agamemnon, King of Mycenae in Argos, over the other Greek groups belongs to the Mycenaean Age rather than to a later period. Odysseus' attitude toward the commoner Thersites is indicative of the aristocratic outlook of epic poetry.*

After Patroclus' death Achilles decides to re-enter the battle before Troy. His divine mother Thetis persuades the god Hephaistos to forge new armor for her son. The shield made by Hephaistos is a work of art which provides a description of a peaceful city and a besieged city. In the former city the principal activities are a religious ceremony and a trial for homicide. The second city is wealthy, and its wealth consists primarily of cattle. Homer's description of Achilles' shield (B) gives a vivid description of archaic life in peace and war.[1]

A. KING, COUNCIL, AND ASSEMBLY

Now the goddess Dawn drew close to tall Olympos
with her message of light to Zeus and the other immortals.
But Agamemnon commanded his clear-voiced heralds to summon
by proclamation to assembly the flowing-haired Achaians,
and the heralds made their cry and the men were assembled swiftly.
First he held a council session of the high-hearted princes
beside the ship of Nestor, the king of the race of Pylos.
Summoning these he compacted before them his close counsel:
'Hear me, friends: in my sleep a Dream divine came to me
through the immortal night, and in appearance and stature
and figure it most closely resembled splendid Nestor.
It came and stood above my head and spoke a word to me:
"Son of wise Atreus breaker of horses, are you sleeping?
He should not sleep night long who is a man burdened with counsels
and responsibility for a people and cares so numerous.
Now listen quickly to what I say, since I am a messenger
from Zeus, who far away cares much for you and is pitiful.
Zeus bids you arm the flowing-haired Achaians for battle

[1] Reprinted from *The Iliad of Homer*, by Richmond Lattimore, trans., by permission of The University of Chicago Press. Copyright, 1951, by The University of Chicago, pp. 77–85, 388–91.

in all haste; since now you might take the wide-wayed city
of the Trojans. For no longer are the gods who live on Olympos
arguing the matter, since Hera has forced them all over
by her supplication, and evils are in store for the Trojans
by Zeus' will. Keep this within your heart." So speaking
the Dream went away on wings, and sweet sleep released me.
Come then, let us see if we can arm the sons of the Achaians.
Yet first, since it is the right way, I will make trial of them
by words, and tell them even to flee in their benched vessels.
Do you take stations here and there, to check them with orders.'
  He spoke thus, and sat down again, and among them rose up
Nestor, he who ruled as a king in sandy Pylos.
He in kind intention toward all stood forth and addressed them:
'Friends who are leaders of the Argives and keep their counsel,
had it been any other Achaian who told of this dream
we should have called it a lie and we might rather have turned from it.
Now he who claims to be the best of the Achaians has seen it.
Come then, let us see if we can arm the sons of the Achaians.'
  So he spoke and led the way departing from the council,
and the rest rose to their feet, the sceptred kings, obeying
the shepherd of the people, and the army thronged behind them.
Like the swarms of clustering bees that issue forever
in fresh bursts from the hollow in the stone, and hang like
bunched grapes as they hover beneath the flowers in springtime
fluttering in swarms together this way and that way,
so the many nations of men from the ships and the shelters
along the front of the deep sea beach marched in order
by companies to the assembly, and walked blazing among them,
Zeus' messenger, to hasten them along. Thus they were assembled
and the place of their assembly was shaken, and the earth groaned
as the people took their positions and there was tumult. Nine heralds
shouting set about putting them in order, to make them cease their
clamour and listen to the kings beloved of Zeus. The people
took their seats in sober fashion and were marshalled in their places
and gave over their clamouring. Powerful Agamemnon
stood up holding the sceptre Hephaistos had wrought him carefully.
Hephaistos gave it to Zeus the king, the son of Kronos,
and Zeus in turn gave it to the courier Argeiphontes,
and lord Hermes gave it to Pelops, driver of horses,
and Pelops again gave it to Atreus, the shepherd of the people.
Atreus dying left it to Thyestes of the rich flocks,
and Thyestes left it in turn to Agamemnon to carry
and to be lord of many islands and over all Argos.
Leaning upon this sceptre he spoke and addressed the Argives:

'Fighting men and friends, o Danaans, henchmen of Ares:
Zeus son of Kronos has caught me fast in bitter futility.
He is hard; who before this time promised me and consented
that I might sack strong-walled Ilion and sail homeward.
Now he has devised a vile deception, and bids me go back
to Argos in dishonour having lost many of my people.
Such is the way it will be pleasing to Zeus, who is too strong,
who before now has broken the crests of many cities
and will break them again, since his power is beyond all others.
And this shall be a thing of shame for the men hereafter
to be told, that so strong, so great a host of Achaians
carried on and fought in vain a war that was useless
against men fewer than they, with no accomplishment shown for it;
since if both sides were to be willing, Achaians and Trojans,
to cut faithful oaths of truce, and both to be numbered,
and the Trojans were to be counted by those with homes in the city,
while we were to be allotted in tens, we Achaians,
and each one of our tens chose a man of Troy to pour wine for it,
still there would be many tens left without a wine steward.
By so much I claim we sons of the Achaians outnumber
the Trojans—those who live in the city; but there are companions
from other cities in their numbers, wielders of the spear, to help them,
who drive me hard back again and will not allow me,
despite my will, to sack the well-founded stronghold of Ilion.
And now nine years of mighty Zeus have gone by, and the timbers
of our ships have rotted away and the cables are broken
and far away our own wives and our young children
are sitting within our halls and wait for us, while still our work here
stays forever unfinished as it is, for whose sake we came hither.
Come then, do as I say, let us all be won over; let us
run away with our ships to the beloved land of our fathers
since no longer now shall we capture Troy of the wide ways.'

[The Assembly breaks up, and the Achaean warriors get the ships ready for the homeward journey. The goddesses Hera and Athena intervene and persuade Odysseus to put an end to the flight of the Achaeans. Odysseus is successful.]

So he went through the army marshalling it, until once more
they swept back into the assembly place from the ships and the shelters
clamorously, as when from the thunderous sea the surf-beat
crashes upon the great beach, and the whole sea is in tumult.
Now the rest had sat down, and were orderly in their places,
but one man, Thersites of the endless speech, still scolded,

who knew within his head many words, but disorderly;
vain, and without decency, to quarrel with the princes
with any word he thought might be amusing to the Argives.
This was the ugliest man who came beneath Ilion. He was
bandy-legged and went lame of one foot, with shoulders
stooped and drawn together over his chest, and above this
his skull went up to a point with the wool grown sparsely upon it.
Beyond all others Achilleus hated him, and Odysseus.
These two he was forever abusing, but now at brilliant
Agamemnon he clashed the shrill noise of his abuse. The Achaians
were furiously angry with him, their minds resentful.
But he, crying the words aloud, scolded Agamemnon:
'Son of Atreus, what thing further do you want, or find fault with
now? Your shelters are filled with bronze, there are plenty of the choicest
women for you within your shelter, whom we Achaians
give to you first of all whenever we capture some stronghold.
Or is it still more gold you will be wanting, that some son
of the Trojans, breakers of horses, brings as ransom out of Ilion,
one that I, or some other Achaian, capture and bring in?
Is it some young woman to lie with in love and keep her
all to yourself apart from the others? It is not right for
you, their leader, to lead in sorrow the sons of the Achaians.
My good fools, poor abuses, you women, not men, of Achaia,
let us go back home in our ships, and leave this man here
by himself in Troy to mull his prizes of honour
that he may find out whether or not we others are helping him.
And now he has dishonoured Achilleus, a man much better
than he is. He has taken his prize by force and keeps her.
But there is no gall in Achilleus' heart, and he is forgiving.
Otherwise, son of Atreus, this were your last outrage.'
  So he spoke, Thersites, abusing Agamemnon
the shepherd of the people. But brilliant Odysseus swiftly
came beside him scowling and laid a harsh word upon him:
'Fluent orator though you be, Thersites, your words are
ill-considered. Stop, nor stand up alone against princes.
Out of all those who came beneath Ilion with Atreides
I assert there is no worse man than you are. Therefore
you shall not lift up your mouth to argue with princes,
cast reproaches into their teeth, nor sustain the homegoing.
We do not even know clearly how these things will be accomplished,
whether we sons of the Achaians shall win home well or badly;
yet you sit here throwing abuse at Agamemnon,
Atreus' son, the shepherd of the people, because the Danaan
fighters give him much. You argue nothing but scandal.

And this also will I tell you, and it will be a thing accomplished.
If once more I find you playing the fool, as you are now,
nevermore let the head of Odysseus sit on his shoulders,
let me nevermore be called Telemachos' father,
if I do not take you and strip away your personal clothing,
your mantle and your tunic that cover over your nakedness,
and send you thus bare and howling back to the fast ships,
whipping you out of the assembly place with the strokes of indignity.'
  So he spoke and dashed the sceptre against his back and
shoulders, and he doubled over, and a round tear dropped from him,
and a bloody welt stood up between his shoulders under
the golden sceptre's stroke, and he sat down again, frightened,
in pain, and looking helplessly about wiped off the tear-drops.
Sorry though the men were they laughed over him happily,
and thus they would speak to each other, each looking at the man next
him: 'Come now: Odysseus has done excellent things by thousands,
bringing forward good counsels and ordering armed encounters;
but now this is far the best thing he has ever accomplished
among the Argives, to keep this thrower of words, this braggart
out of assembly. Never again will his proud heart stir him
up, to wrangle with the princes in words of revilement.'
  So the multitude spoke, but Odysseus, sacker of cities,
stood up holding the staff, and beside him grey-eyed Athene
in the likeness of a herald enjoined the people to silence,
that at once the foremost and the utmost sons of the Achaians
might listen to him speaking and deliberate his counsel.
He in kind intention toward all stood forth and addressed them:
'Son of Atreus: now, my lord, the Achaians are trying
to make you into a thing of reproach in the sight of all mortal
men, and not fulfilling the promise they undertook once
as they set forth to come here from horse-pasturing Argos,
to go home only after you had sacked strong-walled Ilion.
For as if they were young children or widowed women
they cry out and complain to each other about going homeward.
In truth, it is a hard thing, to be grieved with desire for going.
Any man who stays away one month from his own wife
with his intricate ship is impatient, one whom the storm winds
of winter and the sea rising keep back. And for us now
this is the ninth of the circling years that we wait here. Therefore
I cannot find fault with the Achaians for their impatience
beside the curved ships; yet always it is disgraceful
to wait long and at the end to go home empty-handed.
No, but be patient, friends, and stay yet a little longer
until we know whether Kalchas' prophecy is true or is not true.

For I remember this thing well in my heart, and you all are
witnesses, whom the spirits of death have not carried away from us;
yesterday and before, at Aulis, when the ships of the Achaians
were gathered bringing disaster to the Trojans and Priam,
and we beside a spring and upon the sacred altars
were accomplishing complete hecatombs to the immortals
under a fair plane tree whence ran the shining of water.
There appeared a great sign; a snake, his back blood-mottled,
a thing of horror, cast into the light by the very Olympian,
wound its way from under the altar and made toward the plane tree.
Thereupon were innocent children, the young of the sparrow,
cowering underneath the leaves at the uttermost branch tip,
eight of them, and the mother was the ninth, who bore these children.
The snake ate them all after their pitiful screaming,
and the mother crying aloud for her young ones, fluttered about him,
and as she shrilled he caught her by the wing and coiled around her.
After he had eaten the sparrow herself with her children
the god who had shown the snake forth made him a monument,
striking him stone, the son of devious-devising Kronos,
and we standing about marvelled at the thing that had been done.
So as the terror and the god's monsters came into the hecatomb
Kalchas straightaway spoke before us interpreting the gods' will:
"Why are you turned voiceless, you flowing-haired Achaians?
Zeus of the counsels has shown us this great portent: a thing late,
late to be accomplished, whose glory shall perish never.
As this snake has eaten the sparrow herself with her children,
eight of them, and the mother was the ninth, who bore them,
so for years as many as this shall we fight in this place
and in the tenth year we shall take the city of the wide ways."
So he spoke to us then; now all this is being accomplished.
Come then, you strong-greaved Achaians, let every man stay
here, until we have taken the great citadel of Priam.'
So he spoke, and the Argives shouted aloud, and about them
the ships echoed terribly to the roaring Achaians
as they cried out applause to the word of godlike Odysseus.

B. THE SHIELD OF ACHILLES: THE CITY-STATE IN PEACE AND WAR

First of all he forged a shield that was huge and heavy,
elaborating it about, and threw around it a shining
triple rim that glittered, and the shield strap was cast of silver.
There were five folds composing the shield itself, and upon it
he elaborated many things in his skill and craftsmanship.

He made the earth upon it, and the sky, and the sea's water,
and the tireless sun, and the moon waxing into her fullness,
and on it all the constellations that festoon the heavens,
the Pleiades and the Hyades and the strength of Orion
and the Bear, whom men give also the name of the Wagon,
who turns about in a fixed place and looks at Orion
and she alone is never plunged in the wash of the Ocean.
On it he wrought in all their beauty two cities of mortal
men. And there were marriages in one, and festivals.
They were leading the brides along the city from their maiden chambers
under the flaring of torches, and the loud bride song was arising.
The young men followed the circles of the dance, and among them
the flutes and lyres kept up their clamour as in the meantime
the women standing each at the door of her court admired them.
The people were assembled in the market place, where a quarrel
had arisen, and two men were disputing over the blood price
for a man who had been killed. One man promised full restitution
in a public statement, but the other refused and would accept nothing.
Both then made for an arbitrator, to have a decision;
and people were speaking up on either side, to help both men.
But the herald kept the people in hand, as meanwhile the elders
were in session on benches of polished stone in the sacred circle
and held in their hands the staves of the heralds who lift their voices.
The two men rushed before these, and took turns speaking their cases,
and between them lay on the ground two talents of gold, to be given
to that judge who in this case spoke the straightest opinion.
But around the other city were lying two forces of armed men
shining in their war gear. For one side counsel was divided
whether to storm and sack, or share between both sides the property
and all the possessions the lovely citadel held hard within it.
But the city's people were not giving way, and armed for an ambush.
Their beloved wives and their little children stood on the rampart
to hold it, and with them the men with age upon them, but meanwhile
the others went out. And Ares led them, and Pallas Athene.
These were gold, both, and golden raiment upon them, and they were
beautiful and huge in their armour, being divinities,
and conspicuous from afar, but the people around them were smaller.
These, when they were come to the place that was set for their ambush,
in a river, where there was a watering place for all animals,
there they sat down in place shrouding themselves in the bright bronze.
But apart from these were sitting two men to watch for the rest of them
and waiting until they could see the sheep and the shambling cattle,
who appeared presently, and two herdsmen went along with them
playing happily on pipes, and took no thought of the treachery.

Those others saw them, and made a rush, and quickly thereafter
cut off on both sides the herds of cattle and the beautiful
flocks of shining sheep, and killed the shepherds upon them.
But the other army, as soon as they heard the uproar arising
from the cattle, as they sat in their councils, suddenly mounted
behind their light-foot horses, and went after, and soon overtook them.
These stood their ground and fought a battle by the banks of the river,
and they were making casts at each other with their spears bronze-headed; and Hate was there with Confusion among them, and Death
the destructive; she was holding a live man with a new wound, and
another one unhurt, and dragged a dead man by the feet through
the carnage. The clothing upon her shoulders showed strong red with
men's blood. All closed together like living men and fought with
each other and dragged away from each other the corpses of those
who had fallen.

26 / THE AGE OF COLONIZATION

From the eighth to the sixth century B.C. *several Greek cities on the mainland, on the Aegean islands, and in Asia Minor solved domestic political, social, and economic problems by sending some of their sons to colonize new cities. Information happens to be particularly plentiful for the founding of the city of Cyrene in North Africa by settlers from the Aegean island of Thera* (circa 630 B.C.).

The following text (A) was recorded on a stone found at Cyrene in North Africa and first published in 1928. The authenticity of the text has been questioned, but according to recent scholarship it is held to reproduce the original agreement made at Thera in the seventh century B.C., *with the possible exception of some words inserted by a later editor. If this is so, this unique text provides a vivid illustration of the atmosphere of crisis usually preceding the dispatch of a colony. The young men of the island are drafted for this dangerous and uncertain expedition overseas. Their property and citizenship rights at Thera are safeguarded for five years against the possibility of failure. Penalties of death and confiscation are meted out to shirkers and relatives who grant them asylum. All these provisions give evidence of the growing authority of the city-state, Thera, over the inhabitants. The primitive ceremony of the waxen images placed the agreement made at Thera under religious sanction.*[2]

The next excerpt (B) is taken from the History *of Herodotus of Halicarnassus (born* circa *484* B.C.*). In the chapters selected below he collected the various accounts current in the fifth century at Thera and Cyrene concerning the foundation of the latter city. The theme of the entire* History *is the Persian War and its antecedents, but excursuses and flashbacks of all kinds abound (the story of Cyrene is an example). To write this great work, the "father of history" traveled widely: to Cyrene and Egypt, Babylonia, Scythia, Athens and Southern Italy, but not to Palestine and the western Mediterranean. He spent considerable time at Athens and participated in the Athenian colony at Thurii (443* B.C.*). The* History *ends with the Athenian siege of Sestos in 478* B.C.[3]

A. OATH OF THE FOUNDERS

Oath (Agreement?) of the Founders

It was resolved by the Assembly [at Thera]. Since Apollo spontaneously ordered Battus and the Theraeans to colonize Cyrene, the Theraeans are determined to send to Libya Battus as leader and king; and the Theraeans shall sail as his companions. They shall sail on equal terms from each household, one son from each. Men in the prime of youth are to be enlisted from all the districts. Of the other Theraeans any free man may sail if he wishes. If the colonists occupy the settlement, men from the same households who later land in Libya shall share in citizenship, shall be eligible for office, and shall be allotted unoccupied land. But if they fail to occupy the settlement and if the people of Thera are unable to help them and if for five years they are beset by privation, then they may without fear leave the land [and return] to Thera, [receive back] their property and be citizens. He who refuses to sail when the city sends him shall be liable to the death penalty and his property shall be confiscated. Any father who gives refuge or asylum (?) to his son or any brother who [does the same] for his brother shall suffer the same penalty as the person refusing to sail.

On these terms they swore oaths (made an agreement?), both those who stayed behind and those who sailed to found the colony. And they

[2] Translation by the editor from text edited by A. J. Graham, *Journal of Hellenic Studies*, **80** (1960), 94 ff.

[3] George Rawlinson, *The History of Herodotus* (New York: D. Appleton and Co., 1860), Vol. III, pp. 103–4; 106–8.

invoked curses on those who violated the terms and did not abide by them, whether living in Libya or staying behind. They fashioned waxen images and all together, men, women, boys and girls, watched (?) [them] burn while pronouncing curses, [saying that] any person who did not abide by this oath (agreement) but violated it should waste away and melt like the images, he and his son and his property; but that those who abided by this oath (agreement), whether they sailed to Libya or stayed behind, should find much happiness, they and their sons.

B. LATER ACCOUNTS ON MOTHER CITY AND COLONY

Grinus (they say), the son of Aesanius, a descendant of Theras, and king of the island of Thera, went to Delphi to offer a hecatomb on behalf of his native city. He was accompanied by a large number of the citizens, and among the rest by Battus, the son of Polymnestus, who belonged to the Minyan family of the Euphemidae. On Grinus consulting the oracle about sundry matters, the Pythoness gave him for answer, "that he should found a city in Libya." Grinus replied to this: "I, O king, am too far advanced in years, and too inactive, for such a work. Bid one of these youngsters undertake it." As he spoke, he pointed towards Battus; and thus the matter rested for some time. When the embassy returned to Thera, small account was taken of the oracle by the Theraeans, as they were quite ignorant where Libya was, and were not so venturesome as to send out a colony in the dark.

Seven years passed from the utterance of the oracle, and not a drop of rain fell in Thera: all the trees in the island, except one, were killed with the drought. The Theraeans upon this sent to Delphi, and were reminded reproachfully, that they had never colonised Libya. . . . A few persons then sailed from Thera to reconnoitre. Guided by Corobius to the island of Platea, they left him there with provisions for a certain number of months, and returned home with all speed to give their countrymen an account of the island. . . .

The Theraeans who had left Corobius at Platea, when they reached Thera, told their countrymen that they had colonised an island on the coast of Libya. They of Thera, upon this, resolved that men should be sent to join the colony from each of their seven districts, and that the brothers in every family should draw lots to determine who were to go. Battus was chosen to be king and leader of the colony. So these men departed for Platea on board of two penteconters. . . .

With these he [Battus] proceeded to Libya, but within a little time, not knowing what else to do, the men returned and arrived off Thera. The Theraeans, when they saw the vessels approaching, received them with showers of missiles, would not allow them to come near the shore, and ordered the men to sail back from whence they came. Thus compelled to return, they settled on an island near the Libyan coast, which (as I have already said) was called Platea. In size it is reported to have been about equal to the city of Cyrene, as it now stands.

In this place they continued two years, but at the end of that time, as their ill luck still followed them, they left the island to the care of one of their number, and went in a body to Delphi, where they made complaint at the shrine, to the effect that, notwithstanding they had colonised Libya, they prospered as poorly as before. Hereon the Pythoness made them the following answer:—

> "Knowest thou better than I, fair Libya abounding in fleeces?
> Better the stranger than he who has trod it? Oh! clever Theraeans!"

Battus and his friends, when they heard this, sailed back to Platea: it was plain the god would not hold them acquitted of the colony till they were absolutely in Libya. So, taking with them the man whom they had left upon the island, they made a settlement on the mainland directly opposite Platea, fixing themselves at a place called Aziris, which is closed in on both sides by the most beautiful hills, and on one side is washed by a river.

Here they remained six years, at the end of which time the Libyans induced them to move, promising that they would lead them to a better situation. So the Greeks left Aziris, and were conducted by the Libyans towards the west, their journey being so arranged, by the calculations of their guides, that they passed in the night the most beautiful district of the whole country, which is the region called Irasa. The Libyans brought them to a spring, which goes by the name of Apollo's fountain, and told them—"Here, Grecians, is the proper place for you to settle; for here the sky leaks."

27 / LYRIC POETRY: SOLON OF ATHENS ON GOOD GOVERNMENT

Greek lyric poetry originated in Asia Minor in the seventh century B.C. *and was heavily influenced by the Homeric epics, yet it differed profoundly from them, for its twin subjects were the poet as an individual and various groups to which he belonged, notably the city-state. As in other respects, Athens was late in making its contribution to the new genre, but in due time it produced masterpieces. Solon was born in Athens around 640* B.C. *and was elected archon with the extraordinary powers of a "reconciler" for 594/3. In the elegy printed below he sees his native Athens endangered by the covetousness and unrighteousness of her citizens. Discord, factionalism, and civil war are rampant, the poor are sold into slavery. He foresees that* Dikē, *the personification of Right, will exact punishment from the entire community. At the end of the poem Solon proclaims to his fellow Athenians the advice of his inner self: ill government* (dysnomiē) *must be replaced by good government* (eunomiē), *the greatest blessing for mortal men.*[4]

Our city, however, will never perish—so it is decreed by Zeus and willed by the blessed immortal gods. For this daughter of a mighty sire, a great-hearted guardian indeed, Pallas Athena, protects her with her hands. But her citizens, corrupted by wealth, as well as the unjust minds of the people's leaders are determined to ruin the great city by their foolish acts—they are destined to suffer much pain because of their great pride. For they cannot restrain their insolence, nor prepare peacefully the present festive banquet. . . . They yield to unrighteous deeds and prosper. . . . They steal and rob, each in different ways, not sparing either sacred or public possessions, and do not heed the holy foundations of Justice. Silently she bears witness to happenings both present and past and in time she arrives, unfailingly, to exact the penalty. Inevitably this sore affects the entire city, quickly it brings evil serfdom, or awakens internal discord and slumbering war that destroys the lovable prime of many men. For in gatherings dear to the unrighteous the beloved city is soon brought low by her enemies. Such are the evils rampant among the people, and many among the Poor set foot in a foreign land, sold into slavery and bound with shameful fetters. . . . Thus the common evil enters every home and the outer doors will no longer be able to keep it out. Over the fence it leaps and unfailingly finds every man even if he flees and hides in the innermost recess of his room. Here are the warnings that my mind bids me proclaim to the Athenians: bad government brings many evils upon a city, but good government makes all its parts orderly and perfect. Often it shackles the unrighteous, it makes smooth the rough elements, it puts an end to insolence, it restrains pride, it withers the blossoms of ruin in their growth, it makes straight crooked judgments, it

[4] Translated by the editor from Demosthenes, *On the False Embassy*, § 255.

smoothes arrogant deeds, it puts an end to deeds of sedition, an end to the wrath of troublesome strife. Through it all parts of the world of men are made perfect and prudent.

28 / WERNER JAEGER: THE RISE OF GREEK PHILOSOPHY

Philosophy, one of the greatest achievements of the human mind, first arose in colonial Greece, in Ionia, in the sixth century B.C. *Much profound thought had preceded philosophical thought in the Orient and in Greece (see Nos. 4, 5, 10). Yet philosophical thought possessed powers and qualities quite unlike the mythical thought of previous religious thinkers and poets.*

Werner Jaeger, for many years a professor at Harvard, was an outstanding authority on Greek thought and his survey of the ideals of Greek culture is one of the great works of twentieth-century scholarship. Excerpt A is Jaeger's view of the origin and nature of Greek philosophy.

The "natural philosophers" of Ionia were concerned with Nature (physis) *and tried to discover in Nature a unifying principle* (arche). *Individual philosophers defined this unifying principle in different ways. One of the earliest writers was Anaximander* (circa *560* B.C.), *who defined this principle as the Non-Limited* (apeiron): *"It is necessary that things should pass into that from which they are born. For things must pay one another the penalty and compensation for their injustice according to the ordinance of time." Excerpt B is Werner Jaeger's interpretation of Anaximander's famous fragment.*[5]

A. ORIGIN AND NATURE OF PHILOSOPHICAL THOUGHT

The natural philosophers of the sixth century started by inquiring into the origin of the universe, its physis. Physis gave its name to the

[5] From *Paideia: The Ideals of Greek Culture*, by Werner Jaeger, translated by Gilbert Highet. Copyright 1939, 1943, 1944, by Oxford University Press, Inc., and Basil Blackwell. Reprinted by permission. Vol. I, pp. 155–6, 159–61.

whole intellectual movement and to the type of thinking which it created; and that is not unjustified, if we only remember the original significance of the Greek word, and do not introduce the modern idea of physics. For the problem of the origin of things—which we should call a metaphysical problem—was in fact always their chief interest; and their physical theories and discoveries were subordinate to it. It is true that a rational science of nature was created by the same movement, but it was at first embedded in metaphysical speculation, and only gradually became an independent branch of research. In the Greek conception of physics two subjects are confused: the inquiry into the origin of the universe (which compels reason to move beyond phenomena observed by the senses), and the comprehension of everything which proceeds from that origin and now exists (*ta onta*), by empirical investigation (*historiē*). It was natural that the inquisitive nature of the Ionians, the great explorers and observers, should make them push their investigations to the point where the ultimate problems arise; and equally natural that, once they had asked what the universe was and how it came into existence, they should find themselves impelled to extend their knowledge of facts and to explain individual phenomena. Since Egypt and the Near Eastern countries were neighbours of Ionia, it is highly probable (and the probability is supported by sound tradition) that these older civilizations, through constant intellectual intercourse with the Ionians, influenced them not only to adopt their technical discoveries and skills in surveying, navigation, and astronomy, but also to penetrate the deeper problems to which the Egyptian and Oriental myths of creation and divinity gave answers far different from those of the Greeks.

But it was an innovation in the very principles of thought when the Ionians, assimilating and elaborating the empirical knowledge of celestial and natural phenomena which they got from the Orient, used that knowledge independently to help them discover the origin and nature of the universe; and when they subjected the myths dealing with the real and visible world, the myths of creation, to theoretical and causal inquiry. That is the true origin of scientific thought. That is the historical achievement of the Greeks. No doubt they took some time to free themselves from the domination of the myth; but their liberation was a rational and scientific process, as is shown by the fact that it was one continuous movement, carried on by the independent but connected investigations of a number of philosophers. The birthplace of Ionian natural philosophy is held to be Miletus, the metropolis of Ionian civilization: for the lives of the first three cosmologists Thales, Anaximander, and Anaxagoras, cover the period down to the destruction of Miletus by the Persians at the beginning of the fifth century B.C. The violent interruption of three generations of high intellectual achievement by the brutal invasion of external historical fate is not more obvious than the continuity of the work done by these great philosophers, and their peculiar intellectual type—which has rather anachronistically been called the "Milesian school." Yet they asked their questions and pursued their investigations in one definite direction; and they established the methods and the concepts which were to be used by subsequent Greek natural philosophers down to Democritus and Aristotle.

B. ANAXIMANDER OF MILETUS ON THE ORIGIN OF NATURAL OBJECTS

It should be obvious that Anaximander is speaking of the pleonexia or aggrandisement of things against one another. Existence in itself is not a sin—that is a non-Greek idea. The words are a personification of the strife between things, which is compared to a lawsuit among men. We must picture an Ionian city-state. There is the market-place where suits are heard and decisions are given; and the judge sitting on the bench to ordain the compensation to be paid. The judge is Time. We know him from Solon's political poems: his power is inevitable. When one of the contestants has taken too much from the other, the judge deprives him of his excess and gives it to the other to make up the deficiency. Solon's idea was this: Dikē [Justice] does not depend on human, earthly justice; nor does she act by sudden temporary strokes of divine punishment, as the old religion of Hesiod's time held; her power is immanent, manifested in the process by which all inequalities compensate themselves in time; and that inevitable process is the "punishment of Zeus," or "divine requital." Anaximander goes much further. He holds that this eternal process of compensation is at work not only in human life but in the whole world. The immanent compensatory process in human life induces him to believe that nature too with its forces and oppositions is subject to an immanent rule of law like mankind, and that it is this rule of law which regulates coming-to-be and passing-away throughout creation.

To a modern eye this appears to be the dawn of the majestic idea that all nature is subject to universal laws. But Anaximander was not thinking of the monotonous causal series which modern scientists construct. He was formulating a moral, not a physical law of nature. There is a deeply religious meaning in his conception that natural phenomena are governed by a moral standard. It is not a compendious description of events, but justification of the nature of the universe: he shows creation to be a cosmos "writ large"—namely a community of things under law. Its meaning and its purpose is the continuous and inescapable process of coming-to-be and passing-away—the process which is hardest for simple men, with their passion for life, to bear and understand. We do not know whether Anaximander himself used the word *cosmos* in this connexion: it is used by his successor Anaximenes, if the fragment in which it occurs is correctly attributed to him. But actually Anaximander's idea of the eternal power of Dikē ruling natural phenomena implies the idea of a cosmos, although not exactly in the later sense of the word. Therefore we are justified in describing his conception of the universe as the spiritual discovery of the cosmos. The discovery could not be made anywhere but in the depths of the human soul. It has nothing to do with telescopes, observatories, or any kind of empirical research. It was produced by intuitive thought, the same kind of thought which created the idea (also ascribed to Anaximander) of the infinite number of universes. No doubt the philosophical idea of a cosmos entails a break with current religious beliefs. But it also entails the magnificent new realization that Being is divine, despite the horror of impermanence and annihilation which (as the poets show) saddened and perplexed all that generation.

29 / THE CREATION OF ATHENIAN DEMOCRACY AND NAVAL POWER

Athens received a democratic constitution in the age of Solon. Soon after his reforms, however, regionalism and rivalry of noble clans tore the state asunder. The result was the tyranny of Peisistratus and his sons. After the expulsion of Hippias (510 B.C.*) Cleisthenes the Alcmaeonid introduced constitutional reforms which made Athenian democracy a reality. He dissolved the four existing tribes in which membership was based on kinship and established in their stead ten new tribes. The ten Cleisthenian tribes had only the name in common with the earlier tribes. To each of the new tribes villages* (demes) *from different regions of Attica (suburbs of Athens; coast; inland district) were assigned, and in each tribe men from these different regions were obliged to cooperate in the political life of the Athenian city-state. Thus both the regionalism and the power of the aristocratic clans were* *overcome. The new tribes became the basis for the political institutions of the state, especially the Council of Five Hundred created by Cleisthenes. The danger of a new tyranny was eliminated by the establishment of ostracism, and the foundations of Athenian naval power were laid from the proceeds of a lucky strike in the silver mines of Attica. The following excerpt derives from Aristotle's* Constitution of Athens, *a work preserved on papyrus and first discovered in 1880.*[6]

And when this time he [Cleisthenes] had become Chief of the multitude, in the fourth year after the deposition of the tyrants, in the archonship of Isagoras [508 B.C.], he first divided the whole body into ten tribes instead of the existing four, wishing to mix them up, in order that more might take part in the government; from which arose the saying, "Don't draw distinctions between tribes," addressed to those who want to inquire into people's clans. Next he made the Council to consist of five hundred members instead of four hundred, fifty from each Tribe, whereas under the old system there had been a hundred. This was the reason why he did not arrange them in twelve tribes, in order that he might not have to use the existing division of the Thirds (for the four Tribes contained twelve thirds), with the result that the multitude would not have been mixed up. He also portioned out the land among the demes into thirty parts, ten belonging to the suburbs, ten to the coast, and ten to the inland district; and he gave these parts the name of Thirds by lot, three to each, in order that each Tribe might have a share in all the districts. And he made all the inhabitants in each of the demes fellow-demesmen of one another, in order that they might not call attention to the newly enfranchised citizens by addressing people by their fathers' names, but designate people officially by their demes; owing to which Athenians in private life also use the names of their demes as surnames. And he also appointed Demarchs, having the same duties as the former Ship-commissioners, for he put the demes in the place of the Ship-commissions. He named some of the demes from their localities, but others from their founders, for the demes were no longer all corresponding to the places. The clans and brotherhoods and priesthoods belonging to the various demes he allowed to remain on the ancestral plan. As eponymous deities of the Tribes he instituted ten tutelary heroes selected by an oracle of the Pythian priestess from a previously chosen list of a hundred.

[6] Reprinted by permission of the publishers from the Loeb Classical Library, H. Rackham, *Aristotle, The Athenian Constitution* (Cambridge, Mass.: Harvard University Press; London: William Heinemann Ltd., 1935), pp. 63–71.

These reforms made the constitution much more democratic than that of Solon; for it had come about that the tyranny had obliterated the laws of Solon by disuse, and Cleisthenes aiming at the multitude had instituted other new ones, including the enactment of the law about ostracism. First of all, in the fifth year after these enactments [504 B.C.], in the archonship of Hermocreon, they instituted the oath of induction for the Council of Five Hundred that is still in use. Next they began to elect Generals by tribes, one from each tribe, while the whole army was under the command of the War-lord. Eleven years afterwards came their victory in the battle of Marathon [490 B.C.]; and in the archonship of Phaenippus [488 B.C.], two years after the victory, the people being now in high courage, they put in force for the first time the law about ostracism, which had been enacted owing to the suspicion felt against the men in the positions of power because Peisistratus when leader of the people and general set himself up as tyrant. The first person banished by ostracism was one of his relatives, Hipparchus son of Charmus of the deme of Collytus, the desire to banish whom had been Cleisthenes' principal motive in making the law. For the Athenians permitted all friends of the tyrants that had not taken part with them in their offences during the disorders to dwell in the city,—in this the customary mildness of the people was displayed; and Hipparchus was the leader and chief of these persons. But directly afterwards, in the next year, in the archonship of Telesinus [487 B.C.], they elected the Nine Archons by lot, tribe by tribe, from a preliminary list of five hundred chosen by the demesmen: this was the date of the first election on these lines, after the tyranny, the previous Archons having all been elected by vote. And Megacles son of Hippocrates of the deme Alopekē was ostracized. For three years they went on ostracizing the friends of the tyrants, at whom the legislation had been aimed, but afterwards in the fourth year it was also used to remove any other person who seemed to be too great; the first person unconnected with the tyranny to be ostracized was Xanthippus son of Ariphron. Two years later, in the archonship of Nicomedes [483 B.C.], in consequence of the discovery of the mines at Maronea, the working of which had given the state a profit of a hundred talents, the advice was given by some persons that the money should be distributed among the people; but Themistocles prevented this, not saying what use he would make of the money, but recommending that it should be lent to the hundred richest Athenians, each receiving a talent, so that if they should spend it in a satisfactory manner, the state would have the advantage, but if they did not, the state should call in the money from the borrowers. On these terms the money was put at his disposal, and he used it to get a fleet of a hundred triremes built, each of the hundred borrowers having one ship built, and with these they fought the naval battle at Salamis [480 B.C.] against the barbarians. And it was during this period that Aristeides son of Lysimachus was ostracized. Three years later in the archonship of Hypsechides they allowed all the persons ostracized to return, because of the expedition of Xerxes [480 B.C.] and they fixed a boundary thenceforward for persons ostracized, prohibiting them from living within a line drawn from Geraestus to Scyllaeum under penalty of absolute loss of citizenship.

30 / THE PERSIAN WARS

At the beginning of the fifth century B.C. *the Greek cities in Asia Minor rebelled against the Persian Empire, which had controlled them since the second half of the sixth century. Athens and Eretria gave modest aid to the rebels. Consequently, after the rebellion was suppressed (494* B.C.*), the Persian King Darius felt that his hold over his Western satrapies (Ionia and Lydia) would not be secure until the Greek islands and mainland were incorporated in his dominions. Thus began the Persian attacks on Greece. The fighting in mainland Greece lasted until 479* B.C.*, but in the Aegean at large and on the coast of Asia Minor it continued down to the Peace of Callias (449–8* B.C.*).*

The most important narrative source on the Persian War is the History *of Herodotus (on whom see introduction to No. 26). Herodotus described the failure of the first expedition sent out by King Darius against mainland Greece under Mardonius in 492 and the defeat of a second expedition at the hands of the Athenians at Marathon (490). Darius' son, King Xerxes, inherited from his father the project of a punitive expedition against mainland Greece.*

During his travels Herodotus spent much time in Athens in the Periclean Age. Excerpt A, like other sections of his History, *clearly shows the influence of the Athenian climate of opinion. It is also interesting as a statement on the function of naval power.*[7] *Excerpt B is taken from Aeschylus' (see No. 34) play* The Persians, *produced in 472* B.C. *The poet was present at the battle of Salamis and incorporated his memories of this event into a Messenger's*

[7] George Rawlinson, *The History of Herodotus,* Vol. IV (New York: D. Appleton and Co., 1860), pp. 96–7.

report delivered at the Persian court in the presence of the Queen Mother Atossa shortly after the Greek victory.[8] *Excerpt C is Herodotus' account of the same battle.*[9]

A. ATHENIANS THE SAVIOURS OF GREECE

To return, however, to my main subject,—the expedition of the Persian king, though it was in name directed against Athens, threatened really the whole of Greece. And of this the Greeks were aware some time before, but they did not all view the matter in the same light. Some of them had given the Persian earth and water and were bold on this account, deeming themselves thereby secured against suffering hurt from the barbarian army; while others, who had refused compliance, were thrown into extreme alarm. For whereas they considered all the ships in Greece too few to engage the enemy, it was plain that the greater number of states would take no part in the war, but warmly favoured the Medes.

And here I feel constrained to deliver an opinion, which most men, I know, will mislike, but which, as it seems to me to be true, I am determined not to withhold. Had the Athenians from fear of the approaching danger quitted their country or had they without quitting it submitted to the power of Xerxes, there would certainly have been no attempt to resist the Persians by sea; in which case, the course of events by land would have been the following. Though the Peloponnesians might have carried ever so many breastworks across the Isthmus, yet their allies would have fallen off from the Lacedaemonians, not by voluntary desertion, but because town after town must have been taken by the fleet of the barbarians; and so the Lacedaemonians would at last have stood alone and standing alone would have displayed prodigies of valour and died nobly. Either they would have done thus or else, before it came to that extremity, seeing one Greek state after another embrace the cause of the Medes, they would have come to terms with King Xerxes;—and thus, either way Greece would have been brought under Persia. For I cannot understand of what possible use the walls across the Isthmus could have been, if the King had had the mastery of the sea. If then a man should now say that the Athenians were the saviours of Greece, he would not exceed the truth. For they truly held the scales and whichever side they espoused must

[8] Reprinted by permission of the publishers and the Loeb Classical Library, H. W. Smyth, translator, *Aeschylus,* Volume I (Cambridge, Mass.: Harvard University Press, 1938), pp. 141–53.

[9] George Rawlinson, *The History of Herodotus,* Vol. IV (New York: D. Appleton and Co., 1860), pp. 284 ff.

have carried the day. They too it was who, when they had determined to maintain the freedom of Greece, roused up that portion of the Greek nation which had not gone over to the Medes and so, next to the gods, they repulsed the invader. Even the terrible oracles which reached them from Delphi and struck fear into their hearts failed to persuade them to fly from Greece. They had the courage to remain faithful to their land and await the coming of the foe.

B. SALAMIS: THE PLAYWRIGHT'S ACCOUNT

MESSENGER

My Queen, some destructive power or evil spirit, that appeared I know not whence, caused the beginning of our utter rout. A Hellene, from the Athenian host, came to thy son Xerxes and told this tale: that, when the gloom of sable night should set in, the Hellenes would not hold their station, but, springing upon the rowing benches of their ships, would seek, some here, some there, to preserve their lives by stealthy flight. But Xerxes, on hearing this, not comprehending the wile of the Hellene nor yet that the gods grudged him success, straightway gave charge to all his captains to this effect—that, when the sun had ceased to illumine the earth with his beams, and darkness had covered the precincts of the sky, they should bring up in serried order the main body of the fleet, disposed in triple line, to bar the exits and the sounding straits, and station other ships in a circle around the island of Ajax; with the warning that, should the Hellenes escape an evil doom, finding by stealth some means of flight for their fleet, it had been decreed that every captain should lose his head. So he commanded in full confidence of heart, since he knew not the issue purposed of the gods. Our crews then, with no lack of order but with an obedient spirit, prepared their evening meal, while each sailor looped his oar about its thole-pin so that it fitted well. But when the light of the sun had faded and night drew on, each master of an oar and each man versed in arms went on board. The long galleys cheered each other, line by line; and they held their course as each captain had been ordered, and all the livelong night the commanders of the fleet kept their whole force cruising to and fro across the strait. Night began to wane, yet the fleet of the Hellenes in no wise endeavoured to put forth by stealth. When, however, radiant Day with her white coursers shone over all the land, first of all from the Hellenes rang out loud a cheer like unto a song of triumph, and, at the same instant, clear from the island crags Echo returned an answering cry. Terror fell on all the barbarians, balked of their purpose; for not as in flight did in that hour the Hellenes chant their solemn paean, but as men rushing to the onset with the courage of gallant hearts. The trumpet with its blast fired all their line; and instantly, at the word of command, with the even stroke of foaming oars they smote the briny deep. Swiftly they all hove clear into view. Their right wing, well marshalled, led on foremost in orderly advance, next their whole armament bore out against us, and at the same time a mighty shout greeted our ears: "On, ye sons of Hellas! Free your native land, free your children, your wives, the fanes of your fathers' gods, and the tombs of your ancestors. Now you battle for your all." And now from our side arose responsive the mingled clamour of Persian speech; the time brooked no delay, but instantly ship dashed against ship its bronze-sheathed beak. It was a ship of Hellas that began the charge and sheared off entire the curved stern of a Phoenician barque. Each captain drove his ship straight against some other ship. At first, indeed, the stream of the Persian armament held its own; but when the mass of our ships had been crowded in the narrows, and none could render another aid, and each crashed its bronze-faced beak against each of its own line, they shivered their whole array of oars; while the Hellenic galleys, not heedless of their chance, hemmed them in and battered them on every side. The hulls of our vessels rolled over and the sea was hidden from our sight, strewn as it was with wrecks and slaughtered men. The shores and reefs were crowded with our dead, and every ship that formed a part of the barbarian fleet plied its oars in disorderly flight. But, as if our men were tunnies or some haul of fish, the foe kept striking and hacking them with broken oars and fragments of wrecked ships; and groans and shrieks together filled the open sea until the face of sable night hid the scene. But the multitude of our disasters I could not narrate in full at thy request even were I to make a ten days' story of my tale. Be well assured of this—there never perished in a single day so great a multitude of men.

ATOSSA

Alas! In sooth a mighty sea of troubles has burst upon the Persians and the entire barbarian race.

MESSENGER

Be well assured of this, the disaster is not as yet half told. So dire an affliction of calamity fell upon them as to outweigh these ills, aye twice over.

ATOSSA

But what fortune could have befallen yet more malign than this? Speak! What is this other disaster thou sayest came upon our host, sinking the scale to greater weight of ill?

MESSENGER

What Persians were in their life's prime, bravest in spirit, preeminent for noble birth, and ever among the foremost in loyalty unto the King himself—these have fallen ignobly by a most inglorious doom.

ATOSSA

Ah, wretched that I am, my friends, by reason of this cruel pass! By what manner of death sayest thou they perished?

MESSENGER

There is an island fronting Salamis, small, a dangerous anchorage for ships; and upon its sea-washed shore dance-loving Pan is wont to tread. Thither Xerxes dispatched these, his choicest troops, in order that when the Hellenic foe, wrecked from out his ships, should seek escape in safety to the island, they might slaughter his force, an easy prey, and rescue their comrades from the narrows of the sea. Grievously did he misjudge the issue. For when some god had given the glory to the Hellenes in the battle on the sea, that self-same day, fencing their bodies in armour of goodly bronze, they bounded from their ships and encircled the whole island round about, so that our men were at a loss which way to turn. Oft-time they were struck by stones slung from their hands, and arrows sped from the bowstring kept ever falling upon them and working them destruction. At last the Hellenes, charging with one shout, smote them and hacked to pieces the limbs of the poor wretches, until they had utterly destroyed the life of all. Xerxes groaned aloud when he beheld the depth of the disaster; for he occupied a seat commanding a clear view of all the armament—a lofty eminence hard by the open sea. Rending his robes and uttering a loud wail, he forthwith gave orders to his force on land and dismissed them in disorderly flight. Such, besides the one already told, is the disaster thou must bewail.

ATOSSA

O hateful divinity, how hast thou foiled the purpose of the Persians! Cruel was the vengeance brought upon himself that my son designed for illustrious Athens, and the barbarians whom aforetime Marathon destroyed were not enough. For them my son thought to exact retribution, and has drawn upon himself so great a multitude of woes. But the ships that escaped destruction—tell me of them. Where didst thou leave them? Know'st thou to make clear report?

MESSENGER

The commanders of the ships that still remained fled with a rush in disorder before the wind. As for the survivors of the army, they perished in Boeotian land, some distressed by thirst beside a refreshing spring, while some of us, exhausted and panting, won our way to the land of the Phocians, to Doris and the Melian gulf, where the Spercheus waters the plain with kindly stream. Thence the soil of the Achaean land and the cities of the Thessalians received us, sore in want of food. There it was that full many perished of thirst and hunger —for we were oppressed by both. And we came to the Magnesian land and to the country of the Macedonians, to the ford of the Axius and Bolbe's reedy fens, and to Mount Pangaeus, in Edonian land. But on that night the god roused winter before its time and froze the stream of sacred Strymon from shore to shore; and many a man who ere that had held the gods in no esteem, implored them then in supplication as he worshipped earth and heaven. But when our host had made an end of its fervent invocation of the gods, it ventured to pass across the ice-bound stream. And whosoever of us started on his way before the beams of the sun-god were dispersed abroad, found himself in safety; for the bright orb of the sun with its burning rays heated the mid-passage and pierced it with its flames. One upon another our men sank in, and fortunate indeed was he whose breath of life was sundered soonest. All who survived and won to safety, when they had made their way through Thrace, as they best could, with grievous hardships, escaped and reached—and few they were indeed—the land of hearth and home; so that the city of the Persians well may make lament in regret for the best beloved youth of the land. My tale is true. Yet much remains untold of the ills launched by Heaven upon the Persians.

C. SALAMIS: THE HISTORIAN'S ACCOUNT

Meanwhile, the Grecian fleet, which had left Artemisium, proceeded to Salamis, at the request of the Athenians, and there cast anchor. The Athenians had begged them to take up this position, in order that they might convey their women and children out of Attica and further might deliberate upon the course which it now behoved them to follow. Disappointed in the hopes which they had previously entertained, they were about to hold a council concerning the present posture of their affairs. For they had looked to see the Peloponnesians drawn up in full force to resist the enemy in Boeotia but found nothing of what they had expected; nay, they learnt that the Greeks of those parts, only concerning themselves about their own safety, were building a wall across the Isthmus and intended to guard the Peloponnese and let the rest of Greece take its chance. These tidings caused them to make the request whereof I spoke that the combined fleet should anchor at Salamis.

So while the rest of the fleet lay to off this island, the Athenians cast anchor along their own coast. Immediately upon their arrival proclamation was made that every Athenian should save his children and household as he best could; whereupon some sent their families to Egina, some to Salamis, but the greater number to Troezen. This removal was made with all possible haste, partly from a desire to obey the advice of the oracle, but still more for another reason. The Athenians say that they have in their acropolis a huge serpent which lives in the temple and is the guardian of the whole place. Nor do they only say this, but, as if the serpent really dwelt there, every month they lay out its food which consists of a honey-cake. Up to this time the honey-cake had always been consumed; but now it remained untouched. So the priestess told the people what had happened; whereupon they left Athens the more readily since they believed that the goddess had already abandoned the citadel. As soon as all was removed, the Athenians sailed back to their station.

And now, the remainder of the Grecian sea-force, hearing that the fleet which had been at Artemisium, was come to Salamis, joined it at that island from Troezen—orders having been issued previously that the ships should muster at Pogon, the port of the Troezenians. The vessels collected were many more in number than those which had fought at Artemisium and were furnished by more cities. The admiral was the same who had commanded before, to wit Eurybiades, the son of Eurycleides, who was a Spartan, but not of the family of the kings: the city, however, which sent by far the greatest number of ships and the best sailors was Athens.

[There follows the muster of the Hellenic allies participating in the battle of Salamis. The total was 378 triremes, of which 180 were furnished by Athens.]

Orders were now given to stand out to sea; and the ships proceeded towards Salamis and took up the stations to which they were directed, without let or hindrance from the enemy. The day, however, was too far spent for them to begin the battle since night already approached: so they prepared to engage upon the morrow. The Greeks, meanwhile, were in great distress and alarm, more especially those of the Peloponnese; who were troubled that they had been kept at Salamis to fight on behalf of the Athenian territory; and feared that if they should suffer defeat, they would be pent up and besieged in an island while their own country was left unprotected.

The same night the land army of the barbarians began its march towards the Peloponnese where, however, all that was possible had been done to prevent the enemy from forcing an entry by land. As soon as ever news reached the Peloponnese of the death of Leonidas and his companions at Thermopylae, the inhabitants flocked together from the various cities and encamped at the Isthmus under the command of Cleombrotus, son of Anaxandridas and brother of Leonidas. Here their first care was to block up the Scironian way; after which it was determined in council to build a wall across the Isthmus. As the number assembled amounted to many tens of thousands, and there was not one who did not give himself to the work, it was soon finished. Stones, bricks, timber, baskets filled full of sand, were used in the building; and not a moment was lost by those who gave their aid, for they laboured without ceasing either by night or day. . . .

So the Greeks at the Isthmus toiled unceasingly as though in the greatest peril; since they never imagined that any great success would be gained by the fleet. The Greeks at Salamis, on the other hand, when they heard what the rest were about, felt greatly alarmed; but their fear was not so much for themselves as for the Peloponnese. At first they conversed together in low tones, each man with his fellow, secretly, and marvelled at the folly shown by Eurybiades; but presently the smothered feeling broke out and another assembly was held; whereat the old subjects provoked much talk from the speakers, one side maintaining that it was best to sail to the Peloponnese and risk battle for that instead of abiding at Salamis and fighting for a land already taken by the enemy; while the other, which consisted of the Athenians, Eginetans and Megarians was urgent to remain and have the battle fought where they were.

Then Themistocles, when he saw that the Peloponnesians would carry the vote against him, went out secretly from the council and instructing a certain man what he should say sent him on board a merchant ship to the fleet of the Medes. The man's name was Sicinnus; he was one of Themistocles' household slaves and acted as tutor to his sons; in after times, when the Thespians were admitting persons to citizenship, Themistocles made him a Thespian and a rich man to boot. The ship brought Sicinnus to the Persian fleet, and there he delivered his message to the leaders in these words:—

"The Athenian commander has sent me to you privily, without the knowledge of the other Greeks. He is a well-wisher to the king's cause, and would rather success should attend on you than on his countrymen; wherefore he bids me tell you, that fear has seized the Greeks and they are meditating a hasty flight. Now then it is open to you to achieve the best work that ever ye wrought, if only ye will hinder their escaping. They no longer agree among themselves, so that they will not now make any resistance—nay, 'tis likely ye may see a fight already begun between such as favour and such as oppose your cause." The messenger, when he had thus expressed himself, departed and was seen no more.

Then the captains, believing all that the messenger had said, proceeded to land a large body of Persian troops on the islet of Psyttaleia, which lies between Salamis and the mainland; after which, about the hour of midnight, they advanced their western wing towards Salamis so as to inclose the Greeks. At the same time the force stationed about Ceos and Cynosura moved forward and filled the whole strait as far as Munychia with their ships. This advance was made to prevent the Greeks from escaping by flight and to block them up in Salamis where it was thought that vengeance might be taken upon them for the battles fought near Artemisium. The Persian troops were landed on the islet of Psyttaleia because, as soon as the battle began, the men and wrecks were likely to be drifted thither, as the isle lay in the very path of the coming fight,—and they would thus be able to save their own men and destroy those of the enemy. All these movements were made in silence that the Greeks might have no knowledge of them; and they occupied the whole night so that the men had no time to get their sleep. . . .

Meanwhile, among the captains at Salamis, the strife of words grew fierce. As yet they did not know that they were encompassed, but imagined that the barbarians remained in the same places where they had seen them the day before.

In the midst of their contention, Aristides, the son of Lysimachus, who had crossed from Egina, arrived in Salamis. He was an Athenian and had been ostracised by the commonalty; yet I believe from what I have heard concerning his character that there was not in all Athens a man so worthy or so just as he. He now came to the council and standing outside called for Themistocles. Now Themistocles was not his friend, but his most determined enemy. However, under the pressure of the great dangers impending, Aristides forgot their feud and called Themistocles out of the council, since he wished to confer with him. He had heard before his arrival of the impatience of the Peloponnesians to withdraw the fleet to the Isthmus. As soon therefore as Themistocles came forth, Aristides addressed him in these words:—

"Our rivalry at all times and especially at the present season ought to be a struggle which of us shall most advantage our country. Let me then say to thee that so far as regards the departure of the Peloponnesians from this place much talk and little will be found precisely alike. I have seen with my own eyes that which I now report; that, however much the Corinthians or Eurybiades himself may wish it, they cannot now retreat; for we are enclosed on every side by the enemy. Go in to them, and make this known."

"Thy advice is excellent," answered the other, "and thy tidings are also good. That which I earnestly desired to happen, thine eyes have beheld accomplished. Know that what the Medes have now done was at my instance; for it was necessary, as our men would not fight here at their own free will, to make them fight whether they would or no. But come now, as thou hast brought the good news, go in and tell it. For if I speak to them, they will think it a feigned tale and will not believe that the barbarians have inclosed us around. Therefore do thou go to them and inform them how matters stand. If they believe thee, 'twill be for the best; but if otherwise, it will not harm. For it is impossible that they should now flee away if we are indeed shut in on all sides, as thou sayest."

Then Aristides entered the assembly and spoke to the captains: he had come, he told them, from Egina, and had but barely escaped the blockading vessels—the Greek fleet was entirely inclosed by the ships of Xerxes—and he advised them to get themselves in readiness to resist the foe. Having said so much, he withdrew. And now another contest arose, for the greater part of the captains would not believe the tidings.

But while they still doubted, a Tenian trireme, commanded by Panaetius the son of Sosimenes, deserted from the Persians and joined the Greeks bringing full intelligence. For this reason the Tenians were inscribed upon the tripod at Delphi among those who overthrew the barbarians. With this ship, which deserted to their side at Salamis, and the Lemnian vessel which came over before at Artemisium, the Greek fleet was brought to the full number of 380 ships; otherwise it fell short by two of that amount.

The Greeks now, not doubting what the Tenians told them, made ready for the coming fight. At the dawn of day, all the men-at-arms were assembled together, and speeches were made to them, of which the best was that of Themistocles; who throughout contrasted what was noble with what was base and bade them, in all that came within the range of man's nature and constitution, always to make choice of the nobler part. Having thus wound up his discourse, he told them to go at once on board their ships, which they accordingly did; and about this time the trireme, that had been sent to Egina for the Aeacidae, returned; whereupon the Greeks put to sea with all their fleet.

The fleet had scarce left the land when they were attacked by the barbarians. At once most of the Greeks began to back water and were about touching the shore, when Ameinias of Pallene, one of the Athenian captains, darted forth in front of the line and charged a ship of the enemy. The two vessels became entangled and could not separate whereupon the rest of the fleet came up to help Ameinias and engaged with the Persians. Such is the account which the Athenians give of the way in which the battle began; but the Eginetans maintain that the vessel which had been to Egina for the Aeacidae was the one that brought on the fight. It also reported that a phantom in the form of a woman appeared to the Greeks and in a voice that was heard from end to end of the fleet cheered them on to the fight; first, however, rebuking them and saying—"Strange men, how long are ye going to back water?"

Against the Athenians who held the western extremity of the line towards Eleusis were placed the Phoenicians; against the Lacedaemonians whose station was eastward towards the Piraeus, the Ionians.

Of these last a few only followed the advice of Themistocles to fight backwardly; the greater number did far otherwise. I could mention here the names of many trierarchs who took vessels from the Greeks, but I shall pass over all excepting Theomestor the son of Androdamas and Phylacus the son of Histiaeus, both Samians. I show this preference to them, inasmuch as for this service Theomestor was made tyrant of Samos by the Persians while Phylacus was enrolled among the king's benefactors and presented with a large estate in land. In the Persian tongue the kin's benefactors are called *Orosangs*.

Far the greater number of the Persian ships engaged in this battle were disabled—either by the Athenians or by the Eginetans. For as the Greeks fought in order and kept their line while the barbarians were in confusion and had no plan in anything that they did, the issue of the battle could scarce be other than it was. Yet the Persians fought far more bravely here than at Euboea and indeed surpassed themselves; each did his utmost through fear of Xerxes, for each thought that the king's eye was upon himself. . . .

The Greeks who gained the greatest glory of all in the sea fight of Salamis were the Eginetans and after them the Athenians. The individuals of most distinction were Polycritus the Eginetan and two Athenians, Eumenes of Anagyrus and Ameinias of Pallene; the latter of whom had pressed Artemisia [queen of Halicarnassus] so hard. And assuredly if he had known that the vessel carried Artemisia on board, he would never have given over the chase till he had either succeeded in taking her or else been taken himself. For the Athenian captains had received special orders touching the queen, and moreover a reward of ten thousand drachmas had been proclaimed for any one who should make her prisoner; since there was great indignation felt that a woman should appear in arms against Athens. However, as I said before, she escaped; and so did some others whose ships survived the engagement; and these were all now essembled at the port of Phalerum. . . .

In the midst of the confusion Aristides, the son of Lysimachus, the Athenian of whom I lately spoke as a man of the greatest excellence, performed the following service. He took a number of the Athenian heavy-armed troops who had previously been stationed along the shore of Salamis and landing with them on the islet of Psyttaleia, slew all the Persians by whom it was occupied.

As soon as the sea-fight was ended, the Greeks drew together to Salamis all the wrecks that were to be found in that quarter and prepared themselves for another engagement, supposing that the king would renew the fight with the vessels which still remained to him. Many of the wrecks had been carried away by a westerly wind to the cost of Attica, where they were thrown upon the strip of shore called Colias. Thus not only were the prophecies of Bacis and Musaeus concerning this battle fulfilled completely, but likewise, by the place to which the wrecks were drifted, the prediction of Lysistratus, an Athenian soothsayer, uttered many years before these events and quite forgotten at the time by all the Greeks, was fully accomplished. The words were:

> "Then shall the sight of the oars fill Colian dames with amazement."

Now this must have happened as soon as the king was departed. Xerxes, when he saw the extent of his loss, began to be afraid lest the Greeks might be counselled by the Ionians or without their advice might determine to sail straight to the Hellespont and break down the bridges there; in which case he would be blocked up in Europe and run great risk of perishing. He therefore made up his mind to fly; but as he wished to hide his purpose alike from the Greeks and from his own people, he set to work to carry a mound across the channel to Salamis, and at the same time began fastening a number of Phoenician merchant ships together to serve at once for a bridge and a wall. He likewise made many warlike preparations as if he were about to engage the Greeks once more at sea. Now, when these things were seen, all grew fully persuaded that the king was bent on remaining and intended to push the war in good earnest. Mardonius, however, was in no respect deceived; for long acquaintance enabled him to read all the king's thoughts. Meanwhile Xerxes though engaged in this way sent off a messenger to carry intelligence of his misfortune to Persia.

IV / "FIFTY YEARS PERIOD" AND THE PERICLEAN AGE

31 / LEADING PERSONALITIES AND POLITICAL PROGRAMS

As the story of the Persian Wars soon became embroidered with legend, so did the biographies of the great men who had led the Greeks to victory. This was particularly true of Themistocles (A), the creator of Athenian naval power and the chief architect of the naval victory of Salamis. He was admired by Herodotus (No. 30C). Thucydides, normally sparing in his praise of individuals, goes out of his way to record his judgment of Themistocles.[1]

After the ostracism of Themistocles (circa 470 B.C.*) Cimon, son of Miltiades, became Athens' leading statesman. He favored a vigorous pursuit of the war against Persia and harmonious cooperation with Sparta. The biographer Plutarch of Chaerona* (circa *46–120* A.D.*), in his* Parallel Lives of *Greek and Roman statesmen and generals, collected much of the biographical information current in later centuries. It should be borne in mind, however, that he wrote his biographies in an out-of-the-way province of the Roman Empire at a time when it had become difficult even for a*

[1] Richard Crawley, *The History of the Peloponnesian War by Thucydides* (London: Longman's, Green and Co., 1874), p. 88 ff.

Greek to understand the political life of the free city-state. The historical value of Plutarch's biographies therefore varies with the reliability of the sources at his disposal. Plutarch's biography of Cimon (B) is especially valuable because parts of it are based on the personal reminiscences of one of Cimon's contemporaries, the poet Ion of Chios.[2]

Plutarch thought that Pericles began his political career as a demagogue and changed into a statesman concerned for the Athenian state after the ostracism (in 443 or 442 B.C.*) of his rival Thucydides, the son of Melesias (to be distinguished from the historian Thucydides, the son of Olorus). Plutarch's view represents an attempt to harmonize the disagreement of his sources. Of these sources some, such as Thucydides in his* History, *praised Pericles' statemanship, while others, such as Plato, condemned Pericles' democratic policies. Plutarch's biography, in the section on Pericles' building program (C), makes clear the political issues existing between Pericles and Thucydides the son of Melesias. The latter, as spokesman for Athenian oligarchs, objected to the use of the funds of the Delian League for the beautification of Athens. Pericles, on the other hand, the leader of the democratic party, claimed that the money contributed by the members of the Delian League belonged to Athens and could be used by her at her discretion, provided only that Athens carried on the common defense against Persia. The Periclean building program thus emerges as a means of providing employment for the population of Athens. Most of the buildings mentioned by Plutarch are standing, in more or less ruined form, and bear out the biographer's favorable judgment.*[3]

A. THEMISTOCLES

Thucydides: Portrait of a Self-Made Man

For Themistocles was a man who exhibited the most indubitable signs of genius; indeed, in this particular he has a claim on our admiration quite extraordinary and unparalleled. By his own native capacity, alike unformed and unsupplemented by study, he was at

[2] A. H. Clough, *Plutarch's Lives,* Vol. III (Boston: Little, Brown and Company, 1905), pp. 209–10, 220–22.

[3] A. H. Clough, *Plutarch's Lives,* Vol. I (Boston: Little, Brown and Company, 1905), pp. 326–7, 329–30, 334–40, 369.

once the best judge in those sudden crises which admit of little or of no deliberation, and the best prophet of the future, even to its most distant possibilities. An able theoretical expositor of all that came within the sphere of his practice, he was not without the power of passing an adequate judgment in matters in which he had no experience. He could also excellently divine the good and evil which lay hid in the unseen future. In fine, whether we consider the extent of his natural powers, or the slightness of his application, this extraordinary man must be allowed to have surpassed all others in the faculty of intuitively meeting an emergency. Disease was the real cause of his death; though there is a story of his having ended his life by poison, on finding himself unable to fulfil his promises to the king. However this may be, there is a monument to him in the market-place of Asiatic Magnesia. He was governor of the district, the king [of Persia] having given him Magnesia, which brought in fifty talents a year, for bread, Lampsacus, which was considered to be the richest wine country, for wine, and Myos for other provisions. His bones, it is said, were conveyed home by his relatives in accordance with his wishes, and interred in Attic ground. This was done without the knowledge of the Athenians; as it is against the law to bury in Attica an outlaw for treason.

B. CIMON

Ion relates that when he [Cimon] was a young man, and recently come from Chios to Athens, he chanced to sup with Cimon, at Laomedon's house. After supper, when they had, according to custom, poured out wine to the honor of the gods, Cimon was desired by the company to give them a song, which he did with sufficient success, and received the commendations of the company, who remarked on his superiority to Themistocles, who, on a like occasion, had declared he had never learnt to sing, nor to play, and only knew how to make a city rich and powerful. After talking of things incident to such entertainments, they entered upon the particulars of the several actions for which Cimon had been famous. And when they were mentioning the most signal, he told them they had omitted one, upon which he valued himself most for address and good contrivance. He gave this account of it. When the allies had taken a great number of the barbarians prisoners in Sestos and Byzantium, they gave him the preference to divide the booty; he accordingly put the prisoners in one lot, and the spoils of their rich attire and jewels in the other. This the allies complained of as an unequal division; but he gave them their choice to take which lot they would, for that the Athenians should be content with that which they refused. Herophytus of Samos advised them to take the ornaments for their share, and leave the slaves to the Athenians; and Cimon went away, and was much laughed at for his ridiculous division. For the allies carried away the golden bracelets, and armlets, and collars, and purple robes, and the Athenians had only the naked bodies of the captives, which they could make no advantage of, being unused to labor. But a little while after, the friends and kinsmen of the prisoners coming from Lydia and Phrygia, redeemed every one his relations at a high ransom; so that by this means Cimon got so much treasure that he maintained his whole fleet of galleys with the money for four months; and yet there was some left to lay up in the treasury at Athens. . . .

In the fourth year of the reign of Archidamus, the son of Zeuxidamus, king of Sparta, there happened in the country of Lacedaemon, the greatest earthquake that was known in the memory of man; the earth opened into chasms, and the mountain Taygetus was so shaken, that some of the rocky points of it fell down, and except five houses, all the town of Sparta was shattered to pieces. They say, that a little before any motion was perceived, as the young men and the boys just grown up were exercising themselves together in the middle of the portico, a hare, of a sudden, started out just by them, which the young men, though all naked and daubed with oil, ran after for sport. No sooner were they gone from the place than the gymnasium fell down upon the boys who had stayed behind, and killed them all. Their tomb is to this day called Sismatias. Archidamus, by the present danger made apprehensive of what might follow, and seeing the citizens intent upon removing the most valuable of their goods out of their houses, commanded an alarm to be sounded, as if an enemy were coming upon them, in order that they should collect about him in a body, with arms. It was this alone that saved Sparta at that time, for the Helots were got together from the country about, with design to surprise the Spartans, and overpower those whom the earthquake had spared. But finding them armed and well prepared, they retired into the towns and openly made war with them, gaining over a number of the Laconians of the country districts; while at the same time the Messenians, also, made an attack upon the Spartans, who therefore dispatched Periclidas to Athens to solicit succors, of whom Aristophanes says in mockery that he came and

> In a red jacket, at the altars seated,
> With a white face, for men and arms entreated.

This Ephialtes opposed, protesting that they ought not to raise up or assist a city that was a rival to Athens; but that being down, it were best to keep her so, and let the pride and arrogance of Sparta be trodden under. But Cimon, as Critias says, preferring the safety of Lacedaemon to the aggrandizement of his own country, so persuaded the people, that he soon marched out with a large army to their relief. Ion records, also, the most successful expression which he used to move the Athenians. "They ought not to suffer Greece to be lamed, nor their own city to be deprived of her yoke-fellow."

In his return from aiding the Lacedaemonians, he passed with his army through the territory of Corinth; whereupon Lachartus reproached him for bringing his army into the country, without first asking leave of the people. For he that knocks at another man's door ought not to enter the house till the master gives him leave. "But you, Corinthians, O Lachartus," said Cimon, "did not knock at the gates of the Cleonaeans and Megarians, but broke them down, and entered by force, thinking that all places should be open to the stronger." And having thus rallied the Corinthians, he passed on with his army. Some time after this, the Lacedaemonians sent a second time to desire succors of the Athenians against the Messenians and Helots, who had seized upon Ithome. But when they came, fearing their boldness and gallantry, of all that came to their assistance, they sent them only back, alleging they were designing innovations. The Athenians returned home, enraged at this usage, and vented their anger upon all those who were favorers of the Lacedaemonians; and seizing some slight occasion, they banished Cimon for ten years, which is the time prescribed to those that are banished by the ostracism.

C. PLUTARCH: PERICLES, THE DEMOCRATIC STATESMAN

Pericles, while yet but a young man, stood in considerable apprehension of the people, as he was thought in face and figure to be very like the tyrant Peisistratus, and those of great age remarked upon the sweetness of his voice, and his volubility and rapidity in speaking, and were struck with amazement at the resemblance. Reflecting, too, that he had a considerable estate, and was descended of a noble family, and had friends of great influence, he was fearful all this might bring him to be banished as a dangerous person; and for this reason meddled not at all with state affairs, but in military service showed himself of a brave and intrepid nature. But when Aristides was now dead, and Themistocles driven out, Cimon was for the most part kept abroad by the expeditions he made in parts out of Greece; Pericles, seeing things in this posture, now advanced and took his side, not with the rich and few, but with the many and poor, contrary to his natural bent, which was far from democratical; but, most likely, fearing he might fall under suspicion of aiming at arbitrary power, and seeing

Cimon on the side of the aristocracy, and much beloved by the better and more distinguished people, he joined the party of the people, with a view at once both to secure himself and procure means against Cimon.

He immediately entered, also, on quite a new course of life and management of his time. For he was never seen to walk in any street but that which led to the marketplace and the council-hall, and he avoided invitations of friends to supper, and all friendly visiting and intercourse whatever; in all the time he had to do with the public, which was not a little, he was never known to have gone to any of his friends to a supper, except that once when his near kinsman Euryptolemus married, he remained present till the ceremony of the drink-offering, and then immediately rose from table and went his way. For these friendly meetings are very quick to defeat any assumed superiority, and in intimate familiarity an exterior of gravity is hard to maintain. Real excellence, indeed, is most recognized when most openly looked into; and in really good men, nothing which meets the eyes of external observers so truly deserves their admiration, as their daily common life does that of their nearer friends. Pericles, however, to avoid any feeling of commonness, or any satiety on the part of the people, presented himself at intervals only, not speaking to every business, nor at all times coming into the assembly, but, as Critolaus says, reserving himself, like the Salaminian galley, for great occasions, while matters of lesser importance were despatched by friends or other speakers under his direction. . . .

Since Thucydides describes the rule of Pericles as an aristocratical government, that went by the name of a democracy, but was, indeed, the supremacy of a single great man [see No. 42], while many others say, on the contrary, that by him the common people were first encouraged and led on to such evils as appropriations of subject territory; allowances for attending theatres, payments for performing public duties, and by these bad habits were, under the influence of his public measures, changed from a sober, thrifty people, that maintained themselves by their own labors, to lovers of expense, intemperance, and license, let us examine the cause of this change by the actual matters of fact.

At the first, as has been said, when he set himself against Cimon's great authority, he did caress the people. Finding himself come short of his competitor in wealth and money, by which advantages the other was enabled to take care of the poor, inviting every day some one or other of the citizens that was in want to supper, and bestowing clothes on the aged people, and breaking down the hedges and enclosures of his grounds, that all that would might freely gather what fruit they pleased, Pericles, thus outdone in popular arts, by the advice of one Damonides of Oea, as Aristotle states, turned to the distribution of the public moneys; and in a short time having bought the people over, what with moneys allowed for shows and for service on juries, and what with other forms of pay and largess, he made use of them against the Council of Areopagus, of which he himself was no member, as having never been appointed by lot either chief archon, or lawgiver, or king, or captain. For from of old these offices were conferred on persons by lot, and they who had acquitted themselves duly in the discharge of them were advanced to the court of Areopagus. And so Pericles, having secured his power and interest with the populace, directed the exertions of his party against this council with such success, that most of these causes and matters which had been used to be tried there, were, by the agency of Ephialtes, removed from its cognizance; Cimon, also, was banished by ostracism as a favorer of the Lacedaemonians and a hater of the people, though in wealth and noble birth he was among the first, and had won several most glorious victories over the barbarians, and had filled the city with money and spoils of war; as is recorded in the history of his life. So vast an authority had Pericles obtained among the people. . . .

That which gave most pleasure and ornament to the city of Athens, and the greatest admiration and even astonishment to all strangers, and that which now is Greece's only evidence that the power she boasts of and her ancient wealth are no romance or idle story, was his construction of the public and sacred buildings. Yet this was that of all his actions in the government which his enemies most looked upon and cavilled at in the popular assemblies, crying out how that the commonwealth of Athens had lost its reputation and was ill-spoken of abroad for removing the common treasure of the Greeks from the isle of Delos into their own custody; and how that their fairest excuse for so doing, namely, that they took it away for fear the barbarians should seize it, and on purpose to secure it in a safe place, this Pericles had made unavailable, and how that "Greece cannot but resent it as an insufferable affront, and consider herself to be tyrannized over openly, when she sees the treasure, which was contributed by her upon a necessity for the war, wantonly lavished out by us upon our city, to gild her all over, and to adorn and set her forth, as it were some vain woman, hung round with precious stones and figures and temples, which cost a world of money."

Pericles, on the other hand, informed the people, that they were in no way obliged to give any account of those moneys to their allies, so long as they maintained their defence, and kept off the barbarians from attacking them; while in the mean time they did not so much as supply one horse or man or ship, but only found money for the service; "which money," said he, "is not theirs that give it, but theirs that receive it, if so be they perform the conditions upon which they receive it." And that it was good reason, that, now the city was sufficiently provided and stored with all things necessary for the war, they should convert the overplus of its wealth to such undertakings, as would hereafter, when completed, give them eternal honor, and, for the present, while in process, freely supply all the inhabitants with plenty. With their variety of workmanship and of occasions for service, which summon all arts and trades and require all hands to be employed about them, they do actually put the whole city, in a manner, into state-pay; while at the same time she is both beautified and maintained by herself. For as those who are of age and strength for war are provided for and maintained in the armaments abroad by their pay out of the public stock, so, it being his desire and design that the undisciplined mechanic multitude that stayed at home should not go without their share of public salaries, and yet should not have them given them for sitting still and doing nothing, to that end he thought fit to bring in among them, with the approbation of the people, these vast projects of buildings and designs of works, that would be of some continuance before they were finished, and would give employment to numerous arts, so that the part of the people that stayed at home might, no less than those that were at sea or in garrisons or on expeditions, have a fair and just occasion of receiving the benefit and having their share of the public moneys.

The materials were stone, brass, ivory, gold, ebony, cypress-wood; and the arts or trades that wrought and fashioned them were smiths and carpenters, moulders, founders and braziers, stone-cutters, dyers, goldsmiths, ivory-workers, painters, embroiderers, turners; those again that conveyed them to the town for use, merchants and mariners and ship-masters by sea, and by land, cartwrights, cattle-breeders, waggoners, rope-makers, flax-workers, shoe-makers, and leather-dressers, road-makers, miners. And every trade in the same nature, as a captain in an army his particular company of soldiers under him, had its own hired company of journeymen and laborers belonging to it banded together as in array, to be as it were the instrument and body for the performance of the services. Thus, to say all in a word, the occasions and services of these public works distributed plenty through every age and condition.

As then grew the works up, no less stately in size than exquisite in form, the workmen striving to outvie the material and the design with the beauty of their workmanship, yet the most wonderful thing of all was the rapidity of their execution. Undertakings, any one of which singly might have required, they thought, for their completion, several successions and ages of men, were every one of them accomplished in the height and prime of one man's political service. Although they say, too, that Zeuxis once, having heard Agatharchus the painter boast of despatching his work with speed and ease, replied, "I take a long time." For ease and speed in doing a thing do not give the work lasting solidity or exactness of beauty; the expenditure of time allowed to a man's pains beforehand for the production of a thing is repaid by way of interest with a vital force for its preservation when once produced. For which reason Pericles's works are especially admired, as having been made quickly, to last long. For every particular piece of his work was immediately, even at that time, for its beauty and elegance, antique; and yet in its vigor and freshness looks to this day as if it were just executed. There is a sort of bloom of newness upon those works of his, preserving them from the touch of time, as if they had some perennial spirit and undying vitality mingled in the composition of them.

Phidias had the oversight of all the works, and was surveyor-general, though upon the various portions of other great masters and workmen were employed. For Callicrates and Ictinus built the Parthenon; the chapel at Eleusis, where the mysteries were celebrated, was begun by Coroebus, who erected the pillars that stand upon the floor or pavement, and joined them to the architraves; and after his death Metagnes of Xypete added the frieze and the upper line of columns; Xenocles of Cholargus roofed or arched the lantern on the top of the temple of Castor and Pollux; and the long wall, which Socrates says he himself heard Pericles propose to the people, was undertaken by Callicrates. This work Cratinus ridicules, as long in finishing,—

> Tis long since Pericles, if words would do it,
> Talk'd up the wall; yet adds not one mite to it.

The Odeum, or music-room, which in its interior was full of seats and ranges of pillars, and outside had its roof made to slope and descend from one single point at the top, was constructed, we are told, in imitation of the king of Persia's pavilion; this likewise by Pericles's order; which Cratinus again, in his comedy called the Thracian Women, made an occasion of raillery,—

> So, we see here,
> Jupiter Long-pate Pericles appear.
> Since ostracism time, he's laid aside his head,
> And wears the new Odeum in its stead.

Pericles, also, eager for distinction, then first obtained the decree for a contest in musical skill to be held yearly at the Panathenaea, and he himself, being chosen judge, arranged the order and method in which the competitors should sing and play on the flute and on the harp. And both at that time, and at other times also, they sat in this music-room to see and hear all such trials of skill.

The propylaea, or entrances to the Acropolis, were finished in five years' time, Mnesicles being the principal architect. A strange accident happened in the course of building, which showed that the goddess was not averse to the work, but was aiding and cooperating to bring it to perfection. One of the artificers, the quickest and the handiest workman among them all, with a slip of his foot fell down from a great height, and lay in a miserable condition, the physicians having no hopes of his recovery. When Pericles was in distress about this, Athena appeared to him at night in a dream, and ordered a course of treatment, which he applied, and in a short time and with great ease cured the man. And upon this occasion it was that he set up a brass statue of Athena, surnamed Health, in the citadel near the altar, which they say was there before. But it was Phidias who wrought the goddess's image in gold, and he has his name inscribed on the pedestal as the workman of it; and indeed the whole work in a manner was under his charge, and he had, as we have said already, the oversight over all the artists and workmen, through Pericles's friendship for him; and this, indeed, made him much envied, and his patron shamefully slandered with stories, as if Phidias were in the habit of receiving, for Pericles's use, freeborn women that came to see the works. The comic writers of the town, when they had got hold of this story, made much of it, and bespattered him with all the ribaldry they could invent, charging him falsely with the wife of Menippus, one who was his friend and served as lieutenant under him in the wars; and with the birds kept by Pyrilampes, an acquaintance of Pericles, who, they pretended, used to give presents of peacocks to Pericles's female friends. And how can one wonder at any number of strange assertions from men whose whole lives were devoted to mockery, and who were ready at any time to sacrifice the reputation of their superiors to vulgar envy and spite, as to some evil genius, when even Stesimbrotus the Thasian has dared to lay to the charge of Pericles a monstrous and fabulous piece of criminality with his son's wife? So very difficult a matter is it to trace and find out the truth of any thing by history, when, on the one hand, those who afterwards write it find long periods of time intercepting their view and, on the other hand, the contemporary records of any actions and lives, partly through envy and ill-will, partly through favor and flattery, pervert and distort truth.

When the orators, who sided with Thucydides [son of Melesias] and his party, were at one time crying out, as their custom was, against Pericles, as one who squandered away the public money, and made havoc of the state revenues, he rose in the open assembly and put the question to the people, whether they thought that he had laid out much; and they saying, "Too much, a great deal," "Then," said he, "since it is so, let the cost not go to your account, but to mine; and let the inscription upon the buildings stand in my name." When they heard him says thus, whether it were out of a surprise to see the greatness of his spirit, or out of emulation of the glory of the works, they cried aloud, bidding him to spend on, and lay out what he thought fit from the public purse, and to spare no cost, till all were finished.

At length, coming to a final contest with Thucydides, which of the two should ostracize the other out of the country, and having gone through this peril, he threw his antagonist out, and broke up the confederacy that had been organized against him. So that now all schism and division being at an end, and the city brought to evenness and unity, he got all Athens and all affairs that pertained to the Athenians into his own hands, their tributes, their armies, and their galleys, the islands, the sea, and their wide-extended power, partly over other Greeks and partly over barbarians, and all that empire, which they possessed, founded and fortified upon subject nations and royal friendships and alliances. . . .

When he was now near his end, the best of the citizens and those of his friends who were left alive, sitting about him, were speaking of the greatness of his merit, and his power, and reckoning up his famous actions and the number of his victories; for there were no less than nine trophies, which, as their chief commander and conqueror of their enemies, he had set up, for the honor of this city. They talked thus together among themselves, as though he were unable to understand or mind what they said, but had now lost his consciousness. He had listened, however, all the while, and attended to all, and speaking out among them, said, that he wondered they should commend and take notice of things which were as much owing to fortune as to any thing else, and had happened to many other commanders, and, at the same time, should not speak or make mention of that which was the most excellent and greatest thing of all. "For," said he, "no Athenian, through my means, ever wore mourning."

32 / ATHENS AND EMPIRE: THE ERYTHRAE DECREE

The Delian League had been founded in 478–477 B.C. *as a confederacy of equals under Athenian leadership and had been designed to carry on the war against Persia. As time went on Athenian leadership became tyrannical. Athens forced members to remain in the League and began to interfere in the domestic affairs of member states.*

The following text was inscribed on a marble slab found on the Acropolis at Athens, now unfortunately lost. It contains a decree passed by the Athenian assembly (ekklesia) *about 455* B.C. *The purpose of the decree is to ensure that the Ionian city of Erythrae, a member state of the Delian League on the Asiatic mainland opposite Chios, would always be ruled by a council friendly to Athens. The overseers and commandant of the permanent Athenian garrison at Erythrae are Athenian officials.*[4]

1. (A few letters only are left of the prescript.)
2. The Erythraeans shall bring to the Greater Panathenaea offerings worth not less than three minas. The ten Commissioners of the Sacrifices shall distribute the meat among those of the Erythraeans who are present, a drachma's worth to each. If the sacrificial animals are acceptable, but are not worth three minas as above stated, the Cattle-Buyers shall purchase oxen for sacrifice and the account shall be charged to the *demos* of the Erythraeans; and anyone so desiring may feast upon the meat.
3. There shall be a council of the Erythraeans, filled by lot, and consisting of one hundred and twenty men. A man so appointed shall undergo scrutiny before the council and it shall not be lawful for anyone under thirty years of age to be a councillor. Those who are disqualified shall be liable to prosecution and shall not be councillors within four years. The council shall be drawn by lot and established at present by the overseers and the commandant of the garrison, in future by the council (in office) and the commandant.
4. Each of those who are to be councillors at Erythrae shall, before entering office, swear by Zeus and Apollo and Demeter, imprecating destruction upon himself and upon his children if he commits perjury; and he shall swear the oath upon the burning sacrifices. The councillors in office shall compel the performance of these things; and if they fail to do so, they may be fined 1000 drachmae or whatever the sum the Erythraean people may decree for them to pay. The councillors shall swear in the following terms:
5. I will be councillor as well and truly as I am able for the people of the Erythraeans and of the Athenians and of the Allies. And I will not revolt against the commonwealth of the Athenians, or against the Allies

[4] From G. W. Botsford and E. G. Sihler, *Hellenic Civilization* (New York: Columbia University Press, 1915), pp. 260–62. Reprinted by permission of Columbia University Press.

of the Athenians, either of my own accord or at the will of another. Neither will I desert them, either of my own accord or at the will of another. Neither will I receive back, either of my own accord or at the will of another, any one of those who fled to the Medes, except with the sanction of the Athenians and of the (Erythraean) people. Neither will I drive away any who are remaining, except with the sanction of the Athenians and of the people.

6. If any Erythraean shall kill another Erythraean, let him be put to death. If anyone shall be condemned to perpetual banishment, let him be banished [at the same time?] from the (territory of the) Athenian alliance, and let his property be confiscated by the Erythraeans. If anyone is convicted of attempting to betray the city of the Erythraeans to the tyrants, let him be put to death [with impunity], both himself (?) and his children unless [the rest of the inscription is fragmentary.]

33 / A CRITIQUE OF DEMOCRATIC PRINCIPLES AND THEIR APPLICATION

This work, entitled "The Constitution of Athens," is transmitted among the works of Xenophon (circa 430–354 B.C.). It is earlier than Xenophon, however, and is variously dated by scholars between 435 and 415 B.C. The pamphlet represents the view of an Athenian oligarch (for this reason the author as well as the work are often referred to as the "Old Oligarch"). The author disapproves violently of the principles of Athenian democracy because in his opinion they favor the baser element among the population and discriminate against the better people. Contrary to general Greek opinion, however, the Old Oligarch maintains that, given its premises (to which he personally objects), Athenian democracy goes about its preservation in a wise way. He understands clearly the connection of Athenian democracy with naval power: it is the common people of Athens that row her men-of-war. He recognizes the egalitarianism and freedom of Athenian public life. The Old Oligarch is proud of Athenian naval and economic power and does not object to Athenian interference in the internal affairs of member states of the empire (see No. 32). He refers to the operation of Athenian democracy with its tension between oligarchs and democrats; to the division among citizens, resident aliens, and slaves; to Athenian religious cults and theatrical performances; and to the passion of Athenians for lawsuits. The principal value of this political pamphlet lies in the light it sheds on Athenian democracy and imperialism.[5]

Now, as concerning the Polity of the Athenians, and the type or manner of constitution which they have chosen, I praise it not, in so far as the very choice involves the welfare of the baser folk as opposed to that of the better class. I repeat, I withhold my praise so far; but, given the fact that this is the type agreed upon, I propose to show that they set about its preservation in the right way; and that those other transactions in connection with it, which are looked upon as blunders by the rest of the Hellenic world, are the reverse.

In the first place, I maintain, it is only just that the poorer classes and the People of Athens should be better off than the men of birth and wealth, seeing that it is the people who man the fleet, and put round the city her girdle of power. The steersman, the boatswain, the lieutenant, the look-out-man at the prow, the shipwright—these are the people who engird the city with power, far more than her heavy infantry and men of birth and quality. This being the case, it seems only just that offices of state should be thrown open to every one both in the ballot and the show of hands, and that the right of speech should belong to any one who likes, without restriction. For, observe, there are many of these offices which, according as they are in good or in bad hands, are a source of safety or of danger to the People, and in these the People prudently abstains from sharing; as, for instance, it does not think it incumbent on itself to share in the functions of the general or of the commander of cavalry. The sovereign People recognises the fact that in forgoing the personal exercise of these offices, and leaving them to the control of the more powerful citizens, it secures the balance of advantage to itself. It is only those departments of government which bring emolument and assist the private estate that the People cares to keep in its own hands.

In the next place, in regard to what some people are puzzled to explain—the fact that everywhere greater consideration is shown to the base, to poor people and to common folk, than to persons of good quality,—for far from being a matter of surprise, this, as can be shown,

[5] H. G. Dakyns, *The Works of Xenophon,* Vol. II (London and New York: Macmillan and Co., 1892), pp. 275–92.

is the keystone of the preservation of the democracy. It is these poor people, this common folk, this riff-raff, whose prosperity, combined with the growth of their numbers, enhances the democracy. Whereas, a shifting of fortune to the advantage of the wealthy and the better classes implies the establishment on the part of the commonalty of a strong power in opposition to itself. In fact, all the world over, the cream of society is in opposition to democracy. Naturally, since the smallest amount of intemperance and injustice, together with the highest scrupulousness in the pursuit of excellence, is to be found in the ranks of the better class, while within the ranks of the People will be found the greatest amount of ignorance, disorderliness, rascality,—poverty acting as a stronger incentive to base conduct, not to speak of lack of education and ignorance, traceable to the lack of means which afflicts the average mankind. . . .

The objection may be raised that it was a mistake to allow the universal right of speech and a seat in council. These should have been reserved for the cleverest, the flower of the community. But here, again, it will be found that they are acting with wise deliberation in granting to even the baser sort the right of speech, for supposing only the better people might speak, or sit in council, blessings would fall to the lot of those like themselves, but to the commonalty the reverse of blessings. Whereas now, any one who likes, any base fellow, may get up and discover something to the advantage of himself and his equals. It may be retorted: "And what sort of advantage either for himself or for the People can such a fellow be expected to hit upon?" The answer to which is, that in their judgment the ignorance and the baseness of this fellow, together with his goodwill, are worth a great deal more to them than your superior person's virtue and wisdom, coupled with animosity. What it comes to therefore, is that a state founded upon such institutions will not be the best state; but, given a democracy, these are the right means to secure its preservation. The People, it must be borne in mind, does not demand that the city should be well governed and itself a slave. It desires to be free and to be master. As to bad legislation it does not concern itself about that. In fact, what you believe to be bad legislation is the very source of the People's strength and freedom. But if you seek for good legislation, in the first place you will see the cleverest members of the community laying down the laws for the rest. And in the next place, the better class will curb and chastise the lower orders; the better class will deliberate in behalf of the state, and not suffer crack-brained fellows to sit in Council, or to speak or vote in the Assembly. No doubt; but under the weight of such blessings the People will in a very short time be reduced to slavery.

Another point is the extraordinary amount of license granted to slaves and resident aliens at Athens, where a blow is illegal, and a slave will not step aside to let you pass him in the street. I will explain the reason of this peculiar custom. Supposing it were legal for a slave to be beaten by a citizen, it would frequently happen that an Athenian might be mistaken for a slave or an alien and receive a beating; since the Athenian People is not better clothed than the slave or alien, nor in personal appearance is there any superiority. Or if the fact itself that slaves in Athens are allowed to indulge in luxury, and indeed in some cases to live magnificently, be found astonishing, this too, it can be shown, is done of set purpose. Where you have a naval power dependent upon wealth we must perforce be slaves to our slaves, in order that we may get in our slave-rents, and let the real slave go free. Where you have wealthy slaves it ceases to be advantageous that my slave should stand in awe of you. In Lacedaemon my slave stands in awe of you. But if your slave is in awe of me, there will be a risk in his own person. It is for this reason then that we have established an equality between our slaves and freemen; and again between our resident aliens and full citizens, because the city stands in need of her resident aliens to meet the requirements of such a multiplicity of arts and for the purposes of her navy. That is, I repeat, the justification of the equality conferred upon our resident aliens.

Citizens devoting their time to gymnastics and to the cultivation of music are not to be found in Athens; the sovereign People has disestablished them, not from any disbelief in the beauty and honour of such training, but recognising the fact that these are things the cultivation of which is beyond its power. On the same principle, in the case of the choregia, the gymnasiarchy, and the trierarchy, the fact is recognised that it is the rich man who trains the chorus, and the People for whom the chorus is trained; it is the rich man who is trierarch or gymnasiarch, and the People that profits by their labours. In fact, what the People looks upon as its right is to pocket the money. To sing and run and dance and man the vessels is well enough, but only in order that the People may be the gainer, while the rich are made poorer. And so in the courts of justice, justice is not more an object of concern to the jurymen than what touches personal advantage.

To speak next of the allies, and in reference to the point that emissaries from Athens come out, and, according to common opinion, calumniate and vent their hatred upon the better sort of people, this is done on the principle that the ruler cannot help being hated by those whom he rules; but that if wealth and respectability are to wield power in the subject cities, the empire of the Athenian People has but a short lease of existence. This explains why the better people are punished with infamy, robbed of their money, driven from their homes, and put to death, while the baser sort are promoted to honour.

On the other hand, the better Athenians throw their aegis over the better class in the allied cities. And why? Because they recognize that it is to the interest of their own class at all times to protect the best element in the cities. It may be urged that if it comes to strength and power the real strength of Athens lies in the capacity of her allies to contribute their money quota. But to the democratic mind it appears a higher advantage still for the individual Athenian to get hold of the wealth of her allies, leaving them only enough to live upon and to cultivate their estates, but powerless to harbour treacherous designs. . . .

As to heavy infantry, an arm the deficiency of which at Athens is well recognized, this is how the matter stands. They recognise the fact that, in reference to the hostile power, they are themselves inferior, and must be, even if their heavy infantry were more numerous. But relatively to the allies, who bring in the tribute, their strength even on land is enormous. And they are persuaded that their heavy infantry is sufficient for all purposes, provided they retain this superiority. Apart from all else, to a certain extent fortune must be held responsible for the actual condition. The subjects of a power which is dominant by land have it open to them to form contingents from several small states and to muster in force for battle. But with the subjects of a naval power it is different. As far as they are groups of islanders it is impossible for their states to meet together for united action, for the sea lies between them, and the dominant power is master of the sea. And even if it were possible for them to assemble in some single island unobserved, they would only do so to perish by famine. And as to the states subject to Athens which are not islanders, but situated on the continent, the larger are held in check by need and the small ones absolutely by fear, since there is no state in existence which does not depend upon imports and exports, and these she will forfeit if she does not lend a willing ear to those who are masters by sea. In the next place, a power dominant by sea can do certain things which a land power is debarred from doing; as, for instance, ravage the territory of a superior, since it is always possible to coast along to some point, where either there is no hostile force to deal with or merely a small body; and in case of an advance in force on the part of the enemy they can take to their ships and sail away. Such a performance is attended with less difficulty than that experienced by the relieving force on land. Again, it is open to a power so dominating by sea to leave its own territory and sail off on as long a voyage as you please. Whereas the land power cannot place more than a few days' journey between itself and its own territory, for marches are slow affairs; and it is not possible for an army on the march to have food supplies to last for any great length of time. Such an army must either march through friendly territory or it must force a way by victory in battle. The voyager meanwhile has it in his power to disembark at any point where he finds himself in superior force, or, at the worst, to coast by until he reaches either a friendly district or an enemy too weak to resist. Again, those diseases to which the fruits of the earth are liable as visitations from heaven fall severely on a land power, but are scarcely felt by the naval power, for such sicknesses do not visit the whole earth everywhere at once. So that the ruler of the sea can get in supplies from a thriving district. And if one may descend to more trifling particulars, it is to this same lordship of the sea that the Athenians owe the discovery, in the first place, of many of the luxuries of life through intercourse with other countries. So that the choice things of Sicily and Italy, of Cyprus and Egypt and Lydia, of Pontus or Peloponnese, or wheresoever else it be, are all swept, as it were, into one centre, and all owing, as I say, to their maritime empire. And again, in process of listening to every form of speech they have selected this from one place and that from another—for themselves. So much so that while the rest of the Hellenes employ each pretty much their own peculiar mode of speech, habit of life, and style of dress, the Athenians have adopted a composite type, to which all sections of Hellas, and the foreigner alike, have contributed.

As regards sacrifices and temples and festivals and sacred enclosures, the People sees that it is not possible for every poor citizen to do sacrifice and hold festival, or to set up temples and to inhabit a large and beautiful city. But it has hit upon a means of meeting the difficulty. They sacrifice—that is, the whole state sacrifices—at the public cost a large number of victims; but it is the People that keeps holiday and distributes the victims by lot amongst its members. Rich men have in some cases private gymnasia and baths with dressing-rooms, but the People takes care to have built at the public cost a number of palaestras, dressing-rooms and bathing establishments for its own special use, and the mob gets the benefit of the majority of these, rather than the select few or the well-to-do.

As to wealth, the Athenians are exceptionally placed with regard to Hellenic and foreign communities alike, in their ability to hold it. For, given that some state or other is rich in timber for shipbuilding, where is it to find a market for the product except by persuading the ruler of the sea? Or, suppose the wealth of some state or other to consist of iron, or may be bronze, or of linen yarn, where will it find a market except by permission of the supreme maritime power? Yet these are the very things, you see, which I need for my ships. Timber I must have from one, and from another iron, from a third bronze, from a fourth linen yarn, from a fifth wax, etc. Besides which they will not suffer their antagonists in those parts to carry these products elsewhither, or they will cease to use the sea. Accordingly I, without one stroke of labour, extract from the land and possess all these good things, thanks to my supremacy on the sea; whilst not a single other state possesses the two of them. Not timber, for instance, and yarn together, the same city. But where yarn is abundant, the soil will be light and devoid of timber. And in the same way bronze and iron will not be products of the same city. And so for the rest, never two, or at best three, in one state, but one thing here and another thing there. Moreover, above and beyond what has been said, the coastline of every mainland presents either some jutting promontory, or adjacent island, or narrow strait of some sort, so that those who are masters of the sea can come to moorings at one of these points and wreak vengeance on the inhabitants of the mainland.

There is just one thing which the Athenians lack. Supposing they were the inhabitants of an island, and were still, as now, rulers of the sea, they would have had in their power to work whatever mischief they liked, and to suffer no evil in return (as long as they kept command of the sea), neither the ravaging of their territory nor the expectation of any enemy's approach. Whereas at present the farming portion of the community and the wealthy landowners are ready to cringe before the enemy overmuch, whilst the People, knowing full well that, come what may, not one stock or stone of their property will suffer, nothing will be cut down, nothing burnt, lives in freedom from alarm, without fawning at the enemy's approach. Besides this, there is another fear from which they would have been exempt in an island home—the apprehension of the city being at any time betrayed by their oligarchs and the gates thrown open, and an enemy bursting suddenly in. How could incidents like these have taken place if an island had been their home? Again, had they inhabited an island there would have been no stirring of sedition against the people; whereas at present, in the event of faction, those who set it on foot base their hopes of success on the introduction of an enemy by land. But people inhabiting an island would be free from all anxiety on that score. Since, however, they did not chance to inhabit an island from the first, what they now do is this—they deposit their property in the islands, trusting to their command of the sea, and they suffer the soil of Attica to be ravaged without a sigh. To expend pity on that, they know, would be to deprive themselves of other blessings still more precious. . . .

In the same spirit it is not allowed to caricature on the comic stage or otherwise libel the People, because they do not care to hear themselves ill spoken of. But if any one has a desire to satirise his neighbour he has full leave to do so. And this because they are well aware that, as a general rule, the person caricatured does not belong to the people, or the masses. He is more likely to be some wealthy or well-born person, or man of means and influence. In fact, but few poor people and of the popular stamp incur the comic lash, or if they do they have brought it on themselves by excessive love of meddling or some covetous self-seeking at the expense of the People, so that no particular annoyance is felt at seeing such folk satirised.

What, then, I venture to assert is, that the People of Athens has no difficulty in recognising which of its citizens are of the better sort and which the opposite. And so recognising those who are serviceable and advantageous to itself, even though they be base, the People loves them; but the good folk they are disposed the rather to hate. This virtue of theirs, the People holds, is not engrained in their nature for any good to itself, but rather for its injury. In direct opposition to this, there are some persons who, being born of the People, are yet by natural instinct not commoners. For my part I pardon the People its own democracy, as indeed, it is pardonable in any one to do good to himself. But the man who, not being himself one of the People, prefers to live in a state democratically governed rather than in an oligarchical state may be said to smooth his own path towards iniquity. He knows that a bad man has a better chance of slipping through the fingers of justice in a democratic than in an oligarchical state.

I repeat that my position concerning the policy of the Athenians is this: the type of polity is not to my taste, but given that a democratic form of government has been agreed upon, they do seem to me to go the right way to preserve the democracy by the adoption of the particular type which I have set forth.

But there are other objections brought, as I am aware, against the Athenians, by certain people, and to this effect. It not seldom happens, they tell us, that a man is unable to transact a piece of business with the Council or the People, even if he sit waiting a whole year. Now this does happen at Athens, and for no other reason save that, owing to the immense mass of affairs, they are unable to work off all the business on hand and dismiss the applicants. And how in the world should they be able, considering in the first place, that they, the Athenians, have more festivals to celebrate than any other state throughout the length and breadth of Hellas? [During these festivals, of course, the transaction of any sort of affairs is still more out of the question.] In the next place, only consider the number of cases they have to decide—what with private suits and public causes and scrutinies of accounts, etc., more than the whole of the rest of mankind put together; while the Council has multifarious points to advise upon concerning peace and war, concerning ways and means, concerning the framing and passing of laws, and concerning the thousand and one matters affecting the state perpetually occurring, and endless questions touching the allies; besides the receipt of the tribute, the superintendence of dockyards and temples, etc. Can, I ask again, any one find it at all surprising that, with all these affairs on their hands, they are unequal to doing business with all the world? . . .

There is another point in which it is sometimes felt that the Athenians are ill advised, in their adoption, namely, of the less respectable party, in a state divided by faction. But if so, they do it advisedly. If they chose the more respectable, they would be adopting those whose views and interests differ from their own, for there is no state in which the best element is friendly to the people. It is the worst element which in every state favours the democracy—on the principle that like favours like. It is simple enough then. The Athenians choose what is most akin to themselves. Also on every occasion on which they have attempted to side with the better classes, it has not fared well with them, but within a short interval the democratic party has been enslaved, as for instance in Boeotia; or, as when they chose the aristocrats of the Milesians, and within a short time these revolted and cut the people to pieces; or, as when they chose the Lacedaemonians as against the Messenians, and within a short time the Lacedaemonians subjugated the Messenians and went to war against Athens.

I seem to overhear a retort, "No one, of course, is deprived of his civil rights at Athens unjustly." My answer is, that there are some who are unjustly deprived of their civil rights, though the cases are certainly rare. But it will take more than a few to attack the democracy at Athens, since you may take it as an established fact, it is not the man who has lost his civil rights justly that takes the matter to heart, but the victims, if any, of injustice. But how in the world can any one imagine that many are in a state of civil disability at Athens, where the People and the holders of office are one and the same? It is from iniquitous exercise of office, from iniquity exhibited either in speech or action, and the like circumstances that citizens are punished with deprivation of civil rights in Athens. Due reflection on these matters will serve to dispel the notion that there is any danger at Athens from persons visited with disfranchisement.

34 / GREEK TRAGEDY

The origin of tragedy, one of Greece's greatest contributions to Western Civilization, is shrouded in uncertainty. There are reasons to believe that it was an import into Attica from Dorian lands and that it developed from performances which were entirely lyric and musical. It may have been Thespis who, in 534

B.C. *at Athens, added an actor and speeches to choral productions. In Attica in the fifth century tragedies were performed under the auspices of the city-state at the Great Dionysia, a spring festival dedicated to the god Dionysus. Each year three poets competed, each entering three tragedies and a satyr play. From these circumstances it follows that the Attic tragedy was normally a religious ceremony which dealt with religious problems. The subject of tragedy was usually an episode from Greek myth illustrating the relation of man to the higher powers. In this volume space allows (but see No. 30B) only a few excerpts from the earliest Athenian dramatist, Aeschylus (525/4?–456* B.C.*). They are taken from the trilogy, the* Oresteia, *composed of three tragedies: the* Agamemnon, *the* Libation Bearers, *and the* Eumenides. *The trilogy was first performed in 458, i.e., early in the Periclean Age, when Athens was waging war on two fronts—against Persia and against Sparta. The noble Council of the Areopagus had then recently been stripped of most of its political powers (462–1), and Athens had concluded an alliance with Sparta's enemy, Argos (461). In the trilogy, Agamemnon, who in the epic poems had been depicted as king of Mycenae, is represented as king of Argos.*

The action of the first play of the trilogy, the Agamemnon, *begins shortly prior to Agamemnon's triumphant return from conquered Troy to his native Argos. A chorus of Argive elders, in the first ode of the play (A), tells in ominous fashion of the sailing of the great armada ten years earlier. At that time, due to the wrath of the goddess Artemis, the fleet had been prevented from sailing for Aulis because there was no wind. The seer Calchas had advised Agamemnon that Artemis demanded the sacrifice of his daughter Iphigeneia. Torn between his love for his daughter and his position as leader of the armada, Agamemnon finally had carried out Artemis' request.*

Messages reach Argos that the Greek host has captured Troy and that Agamemnon is soon to return. In the choral ode that follows (B) the Chorus comments on the fate of Troy. In Aeschylus' opinion Troy has been punished for the crime of Paris (son of King Priam) who had seduced Helen, the wife of his host Menelaos. The poet objects solemnly to the opinion, widely held, that prosperity leads to destruction. Against this common opinion he upholds his belief in a just government of the world.

In the Agamemnon, *the king is murdered by his wife Clytemnestra. One of the reasons for Clytemnestra's action is that Aga-*

memnon had slaughtered their daughter Iphigeneia. In the second play, the Libation Bearers, *their son Orestes, under orders from Zeus and Apollo, takes revenge for his father's murder by killing his mother. In the last play of the trilogy, the* Eumenides, *Orestes is pursued by the Chorus of Furies, ancient deities charged with the function of avenging murder within a family. Orestes takes refuge on the Acropolis of Athens at the foot of the cult statue of Athena; Athena appoints a tribunal of Athenian citizens to judge the contest between the Furies and Orestes, the prototype of the historic Council of the Areopagus (which retained its jurisdiction in cases of homicide even after the reforms of 462–1). The court is evenly divided, and Athena as chairman casts the decisive ballot in favor of Orestes (C). Her argument is that, as she herself had no mother, she is on the side of her father Zeus (who had approved of Orestes' deed) and of Agamemnon as the male partner in marriage. The trial of Orestes reveals the preponderance of the male element in Athenian society; but note that Athena warns her Athenians not to ban fear and just terrors, that is, reverence and restraint, altogether from the city. The trilogy closes with the reconciliation of the Furies, who are transformed into the* Eumenides *("The Kindly Ones") and become protectresses of Athens.*[6]

A. A KING'S DILEMMA

Zeus, whatever he may be, if this name
pleases him in invocation,
thus I call upon him.
I have pondered everything
yet I cannot find a way,
only Zeus, to cast this dead weight of ignorance
finally from out my brain.

He who in time long ago was great,
throbbing with gigantic strength,
shall be as if he never were, unspoken.
He who followed him has found
his master, and is gone.
Cry aloud without fear the victory of Zeus,

[6] Reprinted from *The Complete Greek Tragedies,* ed. by David Grene and Richmond Lattimore, by permission of The University of Chicago Press. Copyright, 1953, by the University of Chicago. *Aeschylus, Oresteia,* translated by Richmond Lattimore, pp. 39–42, 57–8, 159–63.

you will not have failed the truth:
Zeus, who guided men to think,
who has laid it down that wisdom
comes alone through suffering.
Still there drips in sleep against the heart
grief of memory; against
our pleasure we are temperate.
From the gods who sit in grandeur
grace comes somehow violent.

On that day the elder king
of the Achaean ships, no more
strict against the prophet's word,
turned with the crosswinds of fortune,
when no ship sailed, no pail was full,
and the Achaean people sulked
fast against the shore at Aulis
facing Chalcis, where the tides ebb and surge:

and winds blew from the Strymon, bearing
sick idleness, ships tied fast, and hunger,
distraction of the mind, carelessness
for hull and cable;
with time's length bent to double measure
by delay crumbled the flower and pride
of Argos. Then against the bitter wind
the seer's voice clashed out
another medicine
more hateful yet, and spoke of Artemis, so that the kings
dashed their staves to the ground and could not hold their tears.

The elder lord spoke aloud before them:
"My fate is angry if I disobey these,
but angry if I slaughter
this child, the beauty of my house,
with maiden blood shed staining
these father's hands beside the altar.
What of these things goes now without disaster?
How shall I fail my ships
and lose my faith of battle?
For them to urge such sacrifice of innocent blood
angrily, for their wrath is great—it is right. May all be well yet."

But when necessity's yoke was put upon him
he changed, and from the heart the breath came bitter

and sacrilegious, utterly infidel,
to warp a will now to be stopped at nothing.
The sickening in men's minds, tough,
reckless in fresh cruelty brings daring. He endured then
to sacrifice his daughter
to stay the strength of war waged for a woman,
first offering for the ships' sake.
Her supplications and her cries of father
were nothing, nor the child's lamentation
to kings passioned for battle.
The father prayed, called to his men to lift her
with strength of hand swept in her robes aloft
and prone above the altar, as you might lift
a goat for sacrifice, with guards
against the lips' sweet edge, to check
the curse cried on the house of Atreus
by force of bit and speech drowned in strength.

Pouring then to the ground her saffron mantle
she struck the sacrificers with
the eyes' arrows of pity,
lovely as in a painted scene, and striving
to speak—as many times
at the kind festive table of her father
she had sung, and in the clear voice of a stainless maiden
with love had graced the song
of worship when the third cup was poured.

What happened next I saw not, neither speak it.
The crafts of Calchas fail not of outcome.
Justice so moves that those only learn
who suffer; and the future
you shall know when it has come; before then, forget it.
It is grief too soon given.
All will come clear in the next dawn's sunlight.
Let good fortune follow these things as
she who is here desires,
our Apian land's singlehearted protectress.

B. EVIL: THE PUNISHMENT FOR PRIDE

And that which first came to the city of Ilium,
call it a dream of calm

and the wind dying,
the loveliness and luxury of much gold,
the melting shafts of the eyes' glances,
the blossom that breaks the heart with longing.
But she turned in mid-step of her course to make
bitter the consummation,
whirling on Priam's people
to blight with her touch and nearness.
Zeus hospitable sent her,
a vengeance to make brides weep.

It has been made long since and grown old among men,
this saying: human wealth
grown to fulness of stature
breeds again nor dies without issue.
From high good fortune in the blood
blossoms the quenchless agony.
Far from others I hold my own
mind; only the act of evil
breeds others to follow,
young sins in its own likeness.
Houses clear in their right are given
children in all loveliness.

But Pride aging is made
in men's dark actions
ripe with the young pride
late or soon when the dawn of destiny
comes and birth is given
to the spirit none may fight nor beat down,
sinful Daring; and in those halls
the black visaged Disasters stamped
in the likeness of their fathers.

And Righteousness is a shining in
the smoke of mean houses.
Her blessing is on the just man.
From high walls starred with gold by reeking hands
she turns back
with eyes that glance away to the simple in heart,
spurning the strength of gold
stamped false with flattery.
And all things she steers to fulfillment.

C. ATHENS AS AGENT OF MORALITY

ATHENE

If it please you, men of Attica, hear my decree
now, on this first case of bloodletting I have judged.
For Aegeus' population, this forevermore
shall be the ground where justices deliberate.
Here is the Hill of Ares, here the Amazons
encamped and built their shelters when they came in arms
for spite of Theseus, here they piled their rival towers
to rise, new city, and dare his city long ago,
and slew their beasts for Ares. So this rock is named
from then the Hill of Ares. Here the reverence
of citizens, their fear and kindred do-no-wrong
shall hold by day and in the blessing of night alike
all while the people do not muddy their own laws
with foul infusions. But if bright water you stain
with mud, you nevermore will find it fit to drink.
No anarchy, no rule of a single master. Thus
I advise my citizens to govern and to grace,
and not to cast fear utterly from your city. What
man who fears nothing at all is ever righteous? Such
be your just terrors, and you may deserve and have
salvation for your citadel, your land's defence,
such as is nowhere else found among men, neither
among the Scythians, nor the land that Pelops held.
I establish this tribunal. It shall be untouched
by money-making, grave but quick to wrath, watchful to
protect those who sleep, a sentry on the land.
These words I have unreeled are for my citizens,
advice into the future. All must stand upright
now, take each man his ballot in his hand, think on
his oath, and make his judgment. For my word is said.

CHORUS

I give you counsel by no means to disregard
this company. We can be a weight to crush your land.

APOLLO

I speak too. I command you to fear, and not
make void the yield of oracles from Zeus and me.

CHORUS

You honor bloody actions where you have no right.
The oracles you give shall be no longer clean.

APOLLO

My father's purposes are twisted then. For he
was appealed to by Ixion, the first murderer.

CHORUS

Talk! But for my part, if I do not win the case,
I shall come back to this land and it will feel my weight.

APOLLO

Neither among the elder nor the younger gods
have you consideration. I shall win this suit.

CHORUS

Such was your action in the house of Pheres. Then
you beguiled the Fates to let mortals go free from death.

APOLLO

Is it not right to do well by the man who shows
your worship, and above all when he stands in need?

CHORUS

You won the ancient goddesses over with wine
and so destroyed the orders of an elder time.

APOLLO

You shall not win the issue of this suit, but shall
be made to void your poison to no enemy's hurt.

CHORUS

Since you, a young god, would ride down my elder age,
I must stay here and listen to how the trial goes,
being yet uncertain to loose my anger on the state.

ATHENE

It is my task to render final judgment here.
This is a ballot for Orestes I shall cast.
There is no mother anywhere who gave me birth,
and, but for marriage, I am always for the male
with all my heart, and strongly on my father's side.
So, in a case where the wife has killed her husband, lord
of the house, her death shall not mean most to me. And if
the other votes are even, then Orestes wins.
You of the jurymen who have this duty assigned,
shake out the ballots from the vessels, with all speed.

ORESTES

Phoebus Apollo, what will the decision be?

CHORUS

Darkness of night, our mother, are you here to watch?

ORESTES

This is the end for me. The noose, or else the light.

CHORUS

Here our destruction, or our high duties confirmed.

APOLLO
Shake out the votes accurately, Athenian friends.
Be careful as you pick them up. Make no mistake.
In the lapse of judgment great disaster comes. The cast
of a single ballot has restored a house entire.
ATHENE
The man before us has escaped the charge of blood.
The ballots are in equal number for each side.
ORESTES
Pallas Athene, you have kept my house alive.
When I had lost the land of my fathers you gave me
a place to live. Among the Hellenes they shall say:
"A man of Argos lives again in the estates
of his father, all by grace of Pallas Athene, and
Apollo, and with them the all-ordaining god
the Saviour"—who remembers my father's death, who looked
upon my mother's advocates, and rescues me.
I shall go home now, but before I go I swear
to this your country and to this your multitude
of people into all the bigness of time to be,
that never man who holds the helm of my state shall come
against your country in the ordered strength of spears,
but though I lie then in my grave, I still shall wreak
helpless bad luck and misadventure upon all
who stride across the oath that I have sworn: their ways
disconsolate make, their crossings full of evil
augury, so they shall be sorry that they moved.
But while they keep the upright way, and hold in high
regard the city of Pallas, and align their spears
to fight beside her, I shall be their gracious spirit.
And so farewell, you and your city's populace.
May you outwrestle and overthrow all those who come
against you, to your safety and your spears' success.

35 / THE SOPHISTS

The term "sophists" refers to men who were wise or skilled. The Sophists were professional teachers wandering like many of the physicians (Introduction to No. 37) from city to city. As Homer, Hesiod, and the lyric poets had been the educators of Greece in earlier centuries, so the Sophists became the great edu-

cational force in the late fifth century. In an age where political leadership came into the hands of individuals who had not, as in the aristocratic city-state, absorbed the principles of citizenship and statecraft in their ancestral home, there was a need for teachers of political behavior. This need was satisfied by the teaching of the Sophists. In the cities visited by the Sophists young men of ambition flocked to their classes. One of the principal subjects taught by the Sophists was oratory, the art of persuading one's fellow citizen in the assembly or in the law courts to adopt a particular course of action.

The Praise of Helen *was written, tongue in cheek, by Gorgias from Leontini in Sicily (circa 483–376), probably during the earlier stages of the Peloponnesian War (Gorgias visited Athens in 427* B.C.*). It represents a* tour de force, *for in Greece Helen of Troy was generally considered the archetype of wickedness (see No. 34B). Most remarkable in the* Praise of Helen, *and characteristic for the Sophist movement, is the high opinion expressed therein of the power of speech. Characteristic also of sophistic thought is the argumentation from probability and from human nature. After reading this work, one can imagine how the Sophists acquired the reputation of making the weaker argument appear the better. There was frequently a skeptical or even cynical element in the Sophists' teaching, and some members of the profession tended to question and undermine the accepted standards of morality.*[7]

1. The glory (*cosmos*) of a city is courage; of a body, beauty; of a soul, wisdom; of action, virtue; of speech, truth. It is right in all circumstances to praise what is praiseworthy and blame what is blameworthy.
2. It belongs to the same man both to speak the truth and to refute falsehood. Helen is universally condemned and regarded as the symbol of disasters; I wish to subject her story to critical examination, and so rescue her from ignorant calumny.
3. She was of the highest parentage; her reputed father Tyndareus was the most powerful of men; her real father, Zeus, was king of all.
4. From these origins she obtained her divine beauty, by the display of which she inspired love in countless men, and caused the assemblage of a great number of ambitious suitors, some endowed with

[7] Kathleen Freeman, *Ancilla to the Pre-Socratic Philosophers* (Oxford: Basil Blackwell, 1952), pp. 131–3. Reprinted by permission of the publisher.

wealth, others with ancestral fame, others with personal prowess, others with accumulated wisdom.

5. I shall not relate the story of who won Helen or how; to tell an audience what it knows wins belief but gives no pleasure. I shall pass over this period and come to the beginning of my defence, setting out the probable reasons for her journey to Troy.

6. She acted as she did either through Fate and the will of the gods and the decrees of Necessity, or because she was seized by force, or won over by persuasion (or captivated by love). If the first, it is her accuser who deserves blame; for no human foresight can hinder the will of God; the stronger cannot be hindered by the weaker, and God is stronger than man in every way. Therefore if the cause was Fate, Helen cannot be blamed.

7. If she was carried off by force, clearly her abductor wronged her and she was unfortunate. He, a barbarian, committed an act of barbarism, and should receive blame, disgrace and punishment; she, being robbed of her country and friends, deserves pity rather than obloquy.

8. If it was speech that persuaded her and deceived her soul, her defence remains easy. Speech is a great power, which achieves the most divine works by means of the smallest and least visible form; for it can even put a stop to fear, remove grief, create joy, and increase pity. This I shall now prove.

9. All poetry can be called speech in metre. Its hearers shudder with terror, shed tears of pity, and yearn with sad longing; the soul, affected by the words, feels as its own an emotion aroused by the good and ill fortunes of other people's actions and lives.

10. The inspired incantations of words can induce pleasure and avert grief; for the power of the incantations, uniting with the feeling in the soul, soothes and persuades and transports by means of its wizardry. Two types of wizardry and magic have been invented, which are errors in the soul and deceptions in the mind.

11. Their persuasions by means of fictions are innumerable; for if everyone had recollection of the past, knowledge of the present, and foreknowledge of the future, the power of speech would not be so great. But as it is, when men can neither remember the past nor observe the present nor prophesy the future, deception is easy; so that most men offer opinion as advice to the soul. But opinion, being unreliable, involves those who accept it in equally uncertain fortunes.

12. (Text corrupt) Thus, persuasion by speech is equivalent to abduction by force, as she was compelled to agree to what was said, and consent to what was done. It was therefore the persuader, not Helen, who did wrong and should be blamed.

13. That Persuasion, when added to speech, can also make any impression it wishes on the soul, can be shown, firstly, from the arguments

of the meteorologists, who by removing one opinion and implanting another, cause what is incredible and invisible to appear before the eyes of the mind; secondly, from legal contests, in which a speech can sway and persuade a crowd, by the skill of its composition, not by the truth of its statements; thirdly, from the philosophical debates, in which quickness of thought is shown easily altering opinion.

14. The power of speech over the constitution of the soul can be compared with the effect of drugs on the bodily state; just as drugs by driving out different humours from the body can put an end either to the disease or to life, so with speech: different words can induce grief, pleasure or fear; or again, by means of a harmful kind of persuasion, words can drug and bewitch the soul.

15. If Helen was persuaded by love, defence is equally easy. What we see has its own nature, not chosen by us; and the soul is impressed through sight. . . .

19. If therefore Helen's eye, delighted with Paris's form, engendered the passion of love in her soul, this is not remarkable; for if a god is at work with divine power, how can the weaker person resist? And if the disease is human, due to the soul's ignorance, it must not be condemned as a crime but pitied as a misfortune, for it came about through the snares of Fate, not the choice of the will; by the compulsion of love, not by the plottings of art.

20. Therefore, whichever of the four reasons caused Helen's action, she is innocent.

21. I have expunged by my discourse this woman's ill fame, and have fulfilled the object set forth at the outset. I have tried to destroy the unjust blame and the ignorant opinion, and have chosen to write this speech as an Encomium on Helen and an amusement for myself.

36 / WERNER JAEGER: SOCRATES

Socrates of Athens (469–399 B.C.*) left no written works, yet he had a profound effect on all subsequent thought, especially philosophic thought. The works of his pupils, notably Xenophon and Plato, provide much information on his appearance, habits, and even on his thinking. Xenophon represents Socrates as a patriotic and rather prosaic Athenian citizen without much independence of thought. Plato, on the other hand, immortalized*

Socrates in all his dialogues as a great moral teacher who was an inspired and inspiring human being, constantly questioning current prejudice, given to prodigious flights of imagination, endowed with a gift for both good-natured humor and biting sarcasm. The German philosopher Schleiermacher once formulated the Socratic Problem as follows: "What can *Socrates have been, in addition to all Xenophon says he was, without contradicting the characteristic qualities and rules of life that Xenophon definitely declares to have been Socratic—and what* must *he have been, to give Plato the impulse and the justification to portray him as he does in the dialogues?" In 399* B.C. *Socrates was tried as a result of the accusation that he did not believe in the Athenian gods and that he introduced new gods and corrupted the youth. At the end of the trial he was sentenced to death and later executed. Several years after Socrates' death Plato composed the* Apology of Socrates, *which was based on the actual speech given by Socrates during his trial. In the* Apology *Socrates said the following:*

I shall never give up philosophizing and urging you and making my point clear to everyone I meet, saying what I always say: "My good sir, you are an Athenian, a citizen of the city which is greatest and most noted for its wisdom and power; are you not then ashamed to be worrying about your money and how to increase it, and about your reputation, and about your honour, instead of worrying about the knowledge of good and truth and how to improve your soul?" And if anyone contradicts me and says that he does worry about his soul, I shall not let him off at once and go away, but question him and examine him and refute him; and if I think that he does not possess virtue, but simply says he does, I shall reproach him for underestimating what is most valuable, and prizing what is unimportant. I shall do this to everyone I meet, young and old, stranger and citizen—but particularly to you citizens of Athens, because you are nearer to me in blood. For this, you must realize, is God's command to me; and I think that no greater good has ever happened to you than this my service to God. For all that I do is go round and persuade young and old among you not to give so much of your attention to your bodies and your money as to the perfection of your souls.

On the basis of this passage Werner Jaeger, an outstanding authority on the history of Greek philosophy, attempted to answer the Socratic Problem.[8]

[8] From *Paideia: The Ideals of Greek Culture,* by Werner Jaeger, translated by Gilbert Highet. Copyright 1939, 1943, 1944 by Oxford University Press, Inc., and Basil Blackwell. Reprinted by permission. Vol. II, p. 38 ff.

Socrates says that he "philosophizes." Obviously, he does not mean by this that he engages in abstract thought, but that he exhorts and teaches. One of the methods he uses is Socratic examination and refutation of all sham knowledge and artificial excellence (*areté*). That examination is only one part of the whole process as he describes it, although it usually seems to be the most original aspect of it. But before we investigate the character of this dialectical "examination of men"—which is generally considered the essence of Socratic philosophy, because it contains more of the theoretic element than the rest—we must look a little more closely at Socrates' introductory speech of admonition. When he compares the existence of the business man, always panting to make money, with his own higher ideal, his comparison turns on the care or attention which men give to the goods they prize most highly. Instead of care for money-making, Socrates advises care for one's soul (*psychēs therapeia*). This idea appears at the beginning of his speech, and recurs at the end. But there is nothing to prove that the soul is more important than the body or external goods. That is assumed to be obvious, although in practice men do not behave as if it were. For us, there is nothing remarkable in that, at least in theory; in fact, it seems rather a commonplace. But was it so obvious for the Greeks of that age as it is for us, who are the heirs of two thousand years of Christian tradition? Socrates makes the same point in his discussion with the young man in *Protagoras*. There too he begins by saying that his young friend's soul is in danger. The theme of the soul's danger in this connexion is typical of Socrates, and always leads to his summons to take care of the soul. He speaks like a doctor—only his patient is not the physical man but the spiritual being. There is an extraordinarily large number of passages in the writings of his pupils where the care of the soul is described by Socrates as the highest interest of man. Here we can penetrate to the very heart of his view of his own duty and mission: he felt that it was educational, and that the work of education was the service of God. It can be properly described as a religious duty, because it is the duty of "caring for the soul." For, in Socrates' view, the soul is the divine in man. Socrates defines the care of the soul more closely as the care of the knowledge of values and of truth, *phronēsis* and *alētheia*. The soul is no less sharply distinguished from the body than it is from external goods. This implies a Socratic hierarchy of values, and with it a new, clearly graduated theory of goods, which places spiritual goods highest, physical goods below them, and external goods like property and power in the lowest place.

37 / MEDICAL WRITERS

The following excerpts are taken from works attributed to the greatest medical author of the ancient world, Hippocrates, who lived on the island of Cos in the second part of the fifth century B.C. *However, it is doubtful whether the attribution is correct. In fact, the different treatises contained in the "Hippocratic Corpus" differ significantly in their attitudes toward medical and philosophical problems. However this may be, the methods described in the medical treatises had enormous influence on Greek historiography (Thucydides) and philosophy (Plato). Excerpt A stresses the influence of geographic environment (winds, water, etc.) on man's health and character. Note that the physicians referred to in this excerpt traveled from city to city, particularly in times of "epidemics." Excerpt B is remarkable as evidence of the dissociation of Greek medicine from magic and of the identification of the brain as the seat of consciousness. Note that "sacred disease" was the accepted term for epilepsy.*[9]

A. GEOGRAPHIC AND POLITICAL ENVIRONMENTS AFFECT HEALTH

Whoever wishes to pursue properly the science of medicine must proceed thus. First, he ought to consider what effects each season of the year can produce; for the seasons are not at all alike, but differ widely both in themselves and at their changes. The next point is the hot winds and the cold, especially those that are universal, but also those that are peculiar to each particular region. He must also consider the properties of the waters; for as these differ in taste and in weight, so the property of each is far different from that of any other. Therefore, on arrival at a town with which he is unfamiliar, a physician should examine its position with respect to the winds and to the risings of the sun. For a northern, a southern, an eastern, and a western aspect has each its own individual property. He must consider with the greatest care both these things and how the natives are off for water, whether they use marshy, soft waters, or such as are hard and come from rocky

[9] Reprinted by permission of the publishers from the Loeb Classical Library, translated by W. H. S. Jones, *Hippocrates* (Cambridge, Mass.: Harvard University Press; London: William Heinemann Ltd., 1939): *Airs, Waters and Places,* Vol. I, pp. 71–3, 105–9, 115–17; *The Sacred Disease,* Vol. II, pp. 139–45, 151–3, 175, 179–83.

heights, or brackish and harsh. The soil, too, whether bare and dry or wooded and watered, hollow and hot or high and cold. The mode of life also of the inhabitants that is pleasing to them, whether they are heavy drinkers, taking lunch, and inactive, or athletic, industrious, eating much and drinking little.

Using this evidence he must examine the several problems that arise. For if a physician know these things well, by preference all of them, but at any rate most, he will not, on arrival at a town with which he is unfamiliar, be ignorant of the local diseases, or of the nature of those that commonly prevail; so that he will not be at a loss in the treatment of diseases, or make blunders, as is likely to be the case if he have not this knowledge before he consider his several problems. As time and the year passes he will be able to tell what epidemic diseases will attack the city either in summer or in winter, as well as those peculiar to the individual which are likely to occur through change in mode of life. For knowing the changes of the seasons, and the risings and settings of the stars, with the circumstances of each of these phenomena, he will know beforehand the nature of the year that is coming. Through these considerations and by learning the times beforehand, he will have full knowledge of each particular case, will succeed best in securing health, and will achieve the greatest triumphs in the practice of his art. If it be thought that all this belongs to meteorology, he will find out, on second thoughts, that the contribution of astronomy to medicine is not a very small one but a very great one indeed. For with the seasons men's diseases, like their digestive organs, suffer change. . . .

So much for the changes of the seasons. Now I intend to compare Asia and Europe, and to show how they differ in every respect, and how the nations of the one differ entirely in physique from those of the other. It would take too long to describe them all, so I will set forth my views about the most important and the greatest differences. I hold that Asia differs very widely from Europe in the nature of all its inhabitants and of all its vegetation. For everything in Asia grows to far greater beauty and size; the one region is less wild than the other, the character of the inhabitants is milder and more gentle. The cause of this is the temperate climate, because it lies towards the east midway between the risings of the sun, and farther away than is Europe from the cold. Growth and freedom from wildness are most fostered when nothing is forcibly predominant, but equality in every respect prevails. Asia, however, is not everywhere uniform; the region, however, situated midway between the heat and the cold is very fruitful, very wooded and very mild; it has splendid water, whether from rain or from springs. While it is not burnt up with the heat nor dried up by drought and want of water, it is not oppressed with cold, nor yet damp and wet with excessive rains and snow. Here the harvests are likely to be plentiful, both those from seed and those which the earth bestows of her own accord, the fruit of which men use, turning wild to cultivated and transplanting them to a suitable soil. The cattle too reared there are likely to flourish, and especially to bring forth the sturdiest young and rear them to be very fine creatures. The men will be well nourished, of very fine physique and very tall, differing from one another but little either in physique or stature. This region, both in character and in the mildness of its seasons, might fairly be said to bear a close resemblance to spring. Courage, endurance, industry and high spirit could not arise in such conditions either among the natives or among immigrants, but pleasure must be supreme . . . wherefore in the beasts they are of many shapes. . . .

With regard to the lack of spirit and of courage among the inhabitants, the chief reason why Asiatics are less warlike and more gentle in character than Europeans is the uniformity of the seasons, which show no violent changes either towards heat or towards cold, but are equable. For there occur no mental shocks nor violent physical change, which are more likely to steel the temper and impart to it a fierce passion than is a monotonous sameness. For it is changes of all things that rouse the temper of man and prevent its stagnation. For these reasons, I think, Asiatics are feeble. . . .

B. EPILEPSY A DISEASE OF THE BRAIN

I am about to discuss the disease called "sacred." It is not, in my opinion, any more divine or more sacred than other diseases, but has a natural cause, and its supposed divine origin is due to men's inexperience, and to their wonder at its peculiar character. Now while men continue to believe in its divine origin because they are at a loss to understand it, they really disprove its divinity by the facile method of healing which they adopt, consisting as it does of purifications and incantations. But if it is to be considered divine just because it is wonderful, there will be not one sacred disease but many, for I will show that other diseases are no less wonderful and portentous, and yet nobody considers them sacred. For instance, quotidian fevers, tertians and quartans seem to me to be no less sacred and godsent than this disease, but nobody wonders at them. Then again one can see men who are mad and delirious from no obvious cause, and committing many strange acts; while in their sleep, to my knowledge, many groan and shriek, others choke, others dart up and rush out of doors, being delirious until they wake, when they become as healthy and rational as they were before, though pale and weak; and this happens not once but many times. Many other instances, of various kinds, could be given, but time does not permit us to speak of each separately. . . .

Accordingly I hold that those who attempt in this manner [magic] to cure these diseases cannot consider them either sacred or divine; for when they are removed by such purifications and by such treatment as this, there is nothing to prevent the production of attacks in men by devices that are similar. If so, something human is to blame, and not godhead. He who by purifications and magic can take away such an affection can also by similar means bring it on, so that by this argument the action of godhead is disproved. By these sayings and devices they claim superior knowledge, and deceive men by prescribing for them purifications and cleansing, most of their talk turning on the interventions of gods and spirits. Yet in my opinion their discussions show, not piety, as they think, but impiety rather, implying that the gods do not exist, and what they call piety and the divine is, as I shall prove, impious and unholy. . . .

But this disease is in my opinion no more divine than any other; it has the same nature as other diseases, and the cause that gives rise to individual diseases. It is also curable, no less than other illnesses, unless by long lapse of time it be so ingrained as to be more powerful than the remedies that are applied. Its origin, like that of other diseases, lies in heredity. For if a phlegmatic parent has a phlegmatic child, a bilious parent a bilious child, a consumptive parent a consumptive child, and a splenetic parent a splenetic child, there is nothing to prevent some of the children suffering from this disease when one or the other of the parents suffered from it; for the seed comes from every part of the body, healthy seed from the healthy parts, diseased seed from the diseased parts. Another strong proof that this disease is no more divine than any other is that it affects the naturally phlegmatic, but does not attack the bilious. Yet, if it were more divine than others, this disease ought to have attacked all equally, without making any difference between bilious and phlegmatic.

The fact is that the cause of this affection, as of the more serious diseases generally, is the brain. . . .

Men ought to know that from the brain, and from the brain only, arise our pleasures, joys, and laughter and jests, as well as our sorrows, pains, griefs and tears. Through it, in particular, we think, see, hear, and distinguish the ugly from the beautiful, the bad from the good, the pleasant from the unpleasant, in some cases using custom as a test, in others perceiving them from their utility. It is the same thing which makes us mad or delirious, inspires us with dread and fear, whether by night or by day, brings sleeplessness, inopportune mistakes, aimless anxieties, absent-mindedness, and acts that are contrary to habit. These things that we suffer all come from the brain, when it is not healthy, but becomes abnormally hot, cold, moist, or dry, or suffers any other unnatural affection to which it was not accustomed. Madness comes from its moistness. When the brain is abnormally moist, of necessity it moves, and when it moves neither sight nor hearing are still, but we see or hear now one thing and now another, and the tongue speaks in accordance with the things seen and heard on any occasion. But all the time the brain is still a man is intelligent. . . .

In these ways I hold that the brain is the most powerful organ of the human body, for when it is healthy it is an interpreter to us of the phenomena caused by the air, as it is the air that gives it intelligence. Eyes, ears, tongue, hands and feet act in accordance with the discernment of the brain; in fact the whole body participates in intelligence in proportion to its participation in air. To consciousness the brain is the messenger. For when a man draws breath into himself, the air first reaches the body, though it leaves in the brain its quintessence, and all that it has of intelligence and sense. If it reached the body first and the brain afterwards, it would leave discernment in the flesh and the veins, and reach the brain hot, and not pure but mixed with the humour from flesh and blood, so as to have lost its perfect nature. . . .

V / THUCYDIDES AND THE GREAT PELOPONNESIAN WAR

The readings in this part are taken from Thucydides' History. *They are printed here in the order in which they appear in the text (see also No. 31A). Thucydides was an Athenian* (circa *460–400* B.C.) *who took part in the war during the early stages. In 424* B.C. *he was elected to the office of* strategos, *or "general," and was exiled in the same year because he had failed to protect Amphipolis from the Peloponnesians under Brasidas. He returned to Athens at the end of the Peloponnesian War. His work covers the war to the Athenian naval victory of Cynossema (411* B.C.*). There are traces of incompleteness in several parts of the work.*[1]

38 / THE IMPORTANCE OF THE TOPIC

Thucydides, an Athenian, wrote the history of the war between the Peloponnesians and the Athenians, beginning at the moment that it broke out and believing that it would be a great war and more worthy of relation than any that had preceded it. This belief was not without its grounds. The preparations of both the combatants were in every department in the last state of perfection; and he could see the rest of the Hellenic race taking sides in the quarrel; those who delayed doing so at once having it in contemplation. Indeed this was the greatest movement yet known in history, not only of the Hellenes, but of a

[1] Richard Crawley, *The History of the Peloponnesian War by Thucydides* (London: Longman's, Green and Co., 1874), p. 1. Thucydides refers to himself by his name.

large part of the barbarian world—I had almost said, of mankind. For though the events of remote antiquity, and even those that more immediately precede the war, could not from lapse of time be clearly ascertained, yet the evidences which an inquiry carried as far back as was practicable leads me to trust all point to the conclusion that there was nothing on a great scale, either in war or in other matters.

39 / HISTORICAL METHOD AND CAUSES OF WAR

In the first sentences Thucydides emphasizes the greatness of his subject (see No. 38). In the following excerpt he explains his method. He distinguishes narration from speeches. He claims that his narrative materials rest on conscientious research into facts and details and that he rejects both poetic legend and historical romance, the latter surely an implied criticism of Herodotus. The speeches, on the other hand, represent a characteristic device used by Thucydides in which a balance is held between what the speaker actually said and what Thucydides believes he should have said. They often contain, therefore, the historian's judgment on men and events. At the end of the section Thucydides discusses the causes of the Peloponnesian War, in which he distinguishes the "real cause" from the "grounds of complaint" (affairs of Epidamnus and Potidaea).[2]

The conclusions I have drawn from the proofs quoted may, I believe, safely be relied on. Assuredly they will not be disturbed either by the lays of a poet displaying the exaggeration of his craft, or by the compositions of the chroniclers that are attractive at truth's expense; the subjects they treat of being out of the reach of evidence, and time having robbed most of them of historical value by enthroning them in the region of legend. Turning from these, we can rest satisfied with having proceeded upon the clearest data and having arrived at conclusions as exact as can be expected in matters of such antiquity. To come to this war; despite the known disposition of the actors in a

[2] *Ibid.*, pp. 13–15.

struggle to overrate its importance, and when it is over to return to their admiration of earlier events, yet an examination of the facts will show that it was much greater than its predecessors.

With reference to the speeches in this history, some were delivered before the war began, others while it was going on; some I heard myself, others I got from various quarters; it was in all cases difficult to carry them word for word in one's memory, so my habit has been to make the speakers say what was in my opinion demanded of them by the various occasions, of course adhering as closely as possible to the general sense of what they really said. And with reference to the narrative of events, far from permitting myself to derive it from the first source that came to hand, I did not even trust my own impressions, but it rests partly on what I saw myself, partly on what others saw for me, the accuracy of their report being always tried by the most severe and detailed tests possible. My conclusions have cost me some labour from the want of coincidence between accounts of the same occurrences by different eye-witnesses, arising sometimes from deficient memory, sometimes from deficient impartiality. The absence of romance in my history will, I fear, detract somewhat from its interest; but if it be judged useful by those inquirers who desire an exact knowledge of the past as an aid to the interpretation of the future, which in the course of human things must resemble if it does not reflect it, I shall be content. In fine, I have written my work to be a possession for all time and not merely as the exploit of a passing hour.

The Median war, the greatest achievement of past times, yet found a speedy decision in two actions by sea and two by land. The Peloponnesian war was prolonged to an immense length, and long as it was it was short without parallel for the misfortunes that it brought upon Hellas. Never had so many cities been taken and laid desolate, here by the barbarians, here by the parties contending (the old inhabitants being sometimes removed to make room for others); never was there so much banishing and blood-shedding, now on the field of battle, now in the strife of action. Old stories of occurrences handed down by tradition, but scantily confirmed by experience, suddenly ceased to be incredible; there were earthquakes of unparalleled extent and violence; eclipses of the sun occurred with a frequency unrecorded in previous history; there were great droughts in sundry places and consequent famines, and that most calamitous and awfully fatal visitation, the plague. All this came upon them with the late war, which was begun by the Athenians and Peloponnesians by the dissolution of the thirty years' truce made after the conquest of Euboea. To the question why they broke the treaty, I answer by placing first an account of their grounds of complaint and points of difference, that no one may ever have to ask the immediate cause which plunged the Hellenes into a war of such magnitude. The real cause I consider to be the one which was formally most kept out of sight. The growth of the power of Athens, and the terror which this inspired, made war a necessity to Lacedaemon.

40 / SPARTAN AND ATHENIAN NATIONAL CHARACTERS

In carrying out his program (see No. 39), Thucydides describes Athens' interference in the war between Corinth and her colony of Corcyra and the Athenian siege of Corinth's colony of Potidaea. Corinth now presses for a declaration of war by the Peloponnesian League against Athens. In 432 B.C. the league is summoned to meet at Sparta to discuss Corinthian accusations that Athens had violated the Thirty Years' Truce (445 B.C.). At this meeting Corinthian envoys deliver a speech in which they urge the league, especially Sparta, to go to war against Athens. In the course of their speech the Corinthians compare Spartans (Lacedaemonians) and Athenians in a dramatic way.[3]

"You, Lacedaemonians, of all the Hellenes are alone inactive, and defend yourselves not by doing anything but by looking as if you would do something; you alone wait till the power of an enemy is becoming twice its original size, instead of crushing it in its infancy. And yet the world used to say that you were to be depended upon; but in your case, we fear, it said more than the truth. The Mede, we ourselves know, had time to come from the ends of the earth to Peloponnese, without any force of yours worthy of the name advancing to meet him. But this was a distant enemy. Well, Athens at all events is a near neighbour, and yet Athens you utterly disregard; against Athens you prefer to act on the defensive instead of on the offensive,

[3] Richard Crawley, *The History of the Peloponnesian War by Thucydides* (London: Longman's, Green and Co., 1874), pp. 43–5.

and to make it an affair of chances by deferring the struggle till she has grown far stronger than at first. And yet you know that on the whole the rock on which the barbarian was wrecked was himself, and that if our present enemy Athens has not again and again annihilated us, we owe it more to her blunders than to your protection. Indeed, expectations from you have before now been the ruin of some, whose faith induced them to omit preparation.

"We hope that none of you will consider these words of remonstrance to be rather words of hostility; men remonstrate with friends who are in error, accusations they reserve for enemies who have wronged them. Besides, we consider that a rebuke which might be fitly administered by others may be fitly administered by us, particularly when we contemplate the great contrast between the two national characters; a contrast of which, as far as we can see, you have little perception, having never yet considered what sort of antagonists you will encounter in the Athenians, how widely, how absolutely different from yourselves. The Athenians are addicted to innovation, and their designs are characterized by equal swiftness of conception and execution; you have a genius for keeping what you have got, accompanied by a total want of invention, and a habit of never executing even what is necessary. Again, they are adventurous beyond their power, and daring beyond their judgment, they are sanguine in danger; your wont is to attempt less than is justified by your power, to mistrust even what is sanctioned by your judgment, and to fancy that you will never survive a danger. Further, there is promptitude on their side against procrastination on yours; they are never at home, you are never from it: for they hope by their absence to extend their acquisitions, you fear by your advance to endanger what you have left behind. They follow up a success as far as possible and recoil from reverse as little as possible. Again their bodies they use in their country's cause as if they belonged to any one but themselves, their intellect they jealously husband to be employed in her service. A scheme unexecuted is with them a positive loss, a successful enterprise a comparative failure. The deficiency created by the miscarriage of an undertaking is soon filled up by fresh hopes; for they alone are enabled to call a thing hoped for a thing got, by the speed with which they act upon their resolutions. Thus they toil on in troubles and dangers all the days of their life, with little opportunity for enjoying, being ever engaged in getting: and because in their estimation a holiday is only to do what the occasion demands, and tranquility undisturbed is no less of a misfortune than restless occupation. So that to say that they were born never themselves to rest nor to let others do so, would for a short account be a true account of their character."

41 / ATHENS: IDEALS AND DISASTER

Thucydides describes the first Peloponnesian invasion of Attica and reports its material and psychological effects upon the inhabitants. He also writes of the first Athenian enterprises by land and by sea during 431. There follow two of the most famous passages in Thucydides' work: The Funeral Oration delivered by Pericles during the winter of 431–30 at the public funeral of the Athenian victims of the first year of warfare, and the account of the plague which ravaged Attica from 430 B.C. *onward. The Funeral Oration gives an idealized description of the Athenian city-state. It should be borne in mind that most of Pericles' general pronouncements refer to specific Athenian institutions or events of Athenian history and that the speech will prove most interesting if these allusions are understood (best commentary throughout Alfred Zimmern's classic* Greek Commonwealth, *especially in Chapter VIII). With brutal abruptness Thucydides follows Pericles' statement of Athenian ideals with the account of the plague. This passage reveals the effect of Greek medicine on Thucydides' historical thought, and is remarkable, among other things, for its emphasis on the psychological and moral effects of the disease.*[4]

"I shall begin with our ancestors: it is both just and proper that they should have the honour of the first mention on an occasion like the present. They dwelt in the country without break in the succession from generation to generation, and handed it down free to the present time by their valour. And if they deserve praise, much more do our immediate fathers, who added to their inheritance the empire which we now possess, and spared no pains to be able to leave their acquisitions to us of the present generation. Lastly, there are few parts of our dominions that have not been augmented by those of us here, who are still for the most part in the vigour of life; while the mother country has been furnished by us with everything that can enable her to depend on her own resources whether for war or for peace. That part of our history which tells of the military achievements which gave us our several possessions, or of the ready valour with which we or our

[4] Richard Crawley, *The History of the Peloponnesian War by Thucydides* (London: Longman's, Green and Co., 1874), pp. 121–34.

fathers stemmed the tide of Hellenic or foreign aggression, is a theme too familiar to my hearers for me to dilate on, and I shall therefore pass it. But what was the road by which we reached our position, what the form of government under which our greatness grew, what the national habits out of which it sprang; these are questions which I may try to solve before I proceed to my panegyric upon these men; since I think this to be a subject upon which on the present occasion a speaker may properly dwell, and to which the whole assemblage, whether citizens or foreigners, may listen with advantage.

"Our constitution does not copy the laws of neighbouring states; but we are rather a pattern to others than imitators ourselves. Its administration favours the many instead of the few; this is why it is called a democracy. If we look to the laws, they afford equal justice to all in their private differences; if to social standing, advancement in public life falls to reputation for capacity, class considerations not being allowed to interfere with merit; while as to poverty, if a man is able to serve the state, he is not hindered by the obscurity of his condition. The freedom which we enjoy in our government extends also to our ordinary life. There, far from exercising a jealous surveillance over each other, we do not feel called upon to be angry with our neighbour for doing what he likes or even to indulge in those injurious looks which cannot fail to be offensive, although they inflict no positive penalty. But all this ease in our private relations does not make us lawless as citizens. Against this fear is our chief safeguard, teaching us to obey the magistrates and the laws, particularly such as regard the protection of the injured whether they are actually on the statute book or belong to that code which, although unwritten, yet cannot be broken without acknowledged disgrace.

"Further, we provide plenty of means for the mind to refresh itself from business. At stated periods of the year we celebrate games and sacrifices; besides which the elegance of our private establishments forms a daily source of pleasure and helps to banish the spleen; while the magnitude of our city draws the produce of the world into our harbour, so that to the Athenian the fruits of other countries are as familiar a luxury as those of his own.

"If we turn to our military policy, there also we differ from our antagonists. We throw open our city to the world, and never by alien acts exclude foreigners from any opportunity of learning or observing, although the eyes of an enemy may occasionally profit by our liberality; trusting less in system and policy than to the native spirit of our citizens; while in education where our rivals from their very cradles by a painful discipline seek after manliness, at Athens we live exactly as we please, and yet are just as ready to encounter every legitimate danger. In proof of this it may be noticed that the

Lacedaemonians never invade our country with a contingent, but with the whole of their confederates; while we Athenians advance unsupported into the territory of a neighbor, and fighting upon a foreign soil usually vanquish with ease men who are defending their homes. While our united force was never yet encountered by any enemy, through our being at once occupied with our marine and being by land continually dispatched upon a hundred different services; so that, wherever they engage with some such fraction of our strength, a success against a detachment is magnified into a victory over the nation, and a defeat into a reverse suffered at the hands of our entire people. And yet if with habits not of labour but of ease, and courage not of art but of nature, we are still willing to encounter danger, we have the double advantage of escaping the experience of hardships in anticipation and of facing them in the hour of need as fearlessly as those who are never free from them.

"Nor are these the only points in which our city is worthy of admiration. Cultivating refinement without extravagance and knowledge without effeminacy, we employ our wealth more for use than for show, and place the real disgrace of poverty not in owning to the fact but in declining the struggle against it. Our public men have, besides politics, their private affairs to attend to, and our ordinary citizens, though occupied with the pursuits of industry, are still fair judges of public matters; for, unlike any other nation, regarding him who takes no part in these duties not as unambitious but as useless, we Athenians are able to judge at all events if we cannot originate, and instead of looking on discussion as a stumbling-block in the way of action, we think it an indispensable preliminary to any wise action at all. Again, in our enterprises we present the singular spectacle of daring and deliberation, each carried to its highest point, and both united in the same persons; although usually decision is the fruit of ignorance, hesitation of reflexion. But the palm of courage will surely be adjudged most justly to those who best know the difference between hardship and pleasure and yet are never tempted to shrink from danger. In generosity we are equally singular, acquiring our friends by conferring, not by receiving favours. Yet, of course, the doer of the favour is the firmer friend of the two, in order by continued kindness to keep the recipient in his debt; while the debtor feels less keenly from the very consciousness that the return he makes will be a payment, not a free gift. And it is only the Athenians who, fearless of consequences, confer their benefits not from calculations of expediency, but in the confidence of liberality.

"In short, I say that as a city we are the school of Hellas; while I doubt if the world can produce a man, who where he has only himself to depend upon, is equal to so many emergencies, and graced by so happy a versatility as the Athenian. And that this is no mere boast thrown out for the occasion, but plain matter of fact, the power of the state acquired by these habits proves. For Athens alone of her contemporaries is found when tested to be greater than her reputation, and alone gives no occasion to her assailants to blush at the antagonist by whom they have been worsted, or to her subjects to question her title by merit to rule. Rather, the admiration of the present and succeeding ages will be ours, because we have shown our power not by more representatives but by mighty proofs; and because far from needing a Homer for our panegyrist, or other of his craft whose verses might charm for the moment only for the impression which they gave to melt at the touch of fact, we have forced every sea and land to be the highway of our daring, and everywhere, whether for evil or for good, have left imperishable monuments behind us. Such is the Athens for which these men, in the assertion of their determination not to part with her, nobly fought and died; and well may every one of their survivors be ready to suffer in her cause.

"Indeed if I have dwelt at some length upon the character of our country, it has been to show that our stake in the struggle is not the same as theirs who have no such blessings to lose, and also that the panegyric of the men over whom I am now speaking might be by definite proofs established. That panegyric is now in a great measure complete; for the Athens that I have celebrated is only what the heroism of these and their like have made her, men whose fame, unlike that of most Hellenes, will be found to be only commensurate with their deserts. And if a test of worth be wanted, it is to be found in their closing scene, and this not only in the cases in which it set the final seal upon their merit, but also in those in which it gave the first intimation of their having any. For there is justice in the claim that steadfastness in his country's battles should be as a cloak to cover a man's other imperfections; since the good action has blotted out the bad, and his merit as a citizen more than outweighed his demerits as an individual. But none of these allowed either wealth with its prospect of future enjoyment to unnerve his spirit, or poverty with its hope of a day of freedom and riches to tempt him to shrink from danger. No, holding that vengeance upon their enemies was more to be desired than any personal blessings and reckoning this to be the most glorious of hazards, they joyfully determined to accept the risk, and making sure of their vengeance to leave their wishes to take care of themselves; and committing to hope the uncertainty of final success, to trust to action in the business before them. Thus choosing to die resisting, rather than to live submitting, they fled only from dishonour, but met danger face to face, and after one brief moment, while at the summit of their fortune, were taken away not from their fear, but from their glory.

"So died these men as became Athenians. You, their survivors, must determine to have as unaltering a resolution in the field, though you may pray that it may have a happier issue. And not contented with a mere hearsay notion of the advantages which are involved in the defence of your country, though these would furnish a valuable text to a speaker even before an audience so alive to them as the present, you must yourselves realise the power of Athens, and feed your eyes upon her from day to day, till love of her fills your hearts; and then when all her greatness shall break upon you, you must reflect that it was by courage, sense of duty and a keen feeling of honour in action that men were enabled to acquire all this, and that no personal failure in an enterprise could make them consent to deprive their country of their valour, but they laid it at her feet as the most glorious contribution that they could offer. For this offering of their lives made in common by them all they each of them individually received that renown which never grows old, and for a sepulchre, not so much that in which their bones have been deposited, but that noblest of shrines wherein their glory is laid up to be eternally remembered upon every occasion on which deed or story shall fall for its commemoration. For heroes have the whole earth for their tomb; and in lands far from their own, where the column with its epitaph declares it, there is enshrined in every breast a record unwritten with no tablet to preserve it, except that of the heart. These take as your model, and judging happiness to be the fruit of freedom and freedom of valour, never decline the dangers of war. For it is not the miserable that would most justly be unsparing of their lives; these have nothing to hope for: it is rather they to whom continued life may bring reverses as yet unknown, and to whom a fall, if it came, would be most tremendous in its consequences. And surely, to a man of spirits, the degradation of his being a coward must be immeasurably more grievous than the unfelt death which strikes him in the midst of his strength and patriotism. . . ."

Such was the funeral that took place during this winter, with which the first year of the war came to an end. In the first days of summer [430 B.C.] the Lacedaemonians and their allies, with two-thirds of their forces as before, invaded Attica, under the command of Archidamus, son of Zeuxidamus, king of Lacedaemon, and sat down and laid waste to the country. Not many days after their arrival in Attica the plague first began to show itself among the Athenians. It was said that it had visited many places previously about Lemnos and elsewhere; but a pestilence of such extent and mortality was nowhere remembered.

Neither were the physicians at first of any service, ignorant as they were of the proper way to treat it, but they died themselves the most thickly, as they visited the sick most often; nor did any human art succeed any better. Supplications in the temples, divinations and so forth were found equally futile till the overwhelming nature of the disaster at last put a stop to them altogether.

It first began, it is said, in the parts of Ethiopia above Egypt, and thence descended into Egypt and Libya and into most of the king's country. Suddenly falling upon Athens, it first attacked the population in Piraeus,—which was the occasion of their saying that the Peloponnesians had poisoned the reservoirs, there being as yet no wells there—and afterwards appeared in the upper city, when the deaths became much more frequent. All speculation as to its origin and its causes, if causes can be found adequate to produce so great a disturbance, I leave to other writers, whether lay or professional; for myself, I shall simply set down its nature, and explain the symptoms by which perhaps it may be recognised by the student, if it should ever break out again. This I can the better do as I had the disease myself and watched its operation in the case of others.

That year then is admitted to have been otherwise unprecedentedly free from sickness; and such few cases as occurred, all determined in this. As a rule, however, there was no ostensible cause; but people in good health were all of a sudden attacked by violent heats in the head and redness and inflammation in the eyes, the inward parts such as the throat or tongue becoming bloody and emitting an unnatural and fetid breath. These symptoms were followed by sneezing and hoarseness, after which the pain soon reached the chest and produced a hard cough. When it fixed in the stomach, it upset it; and discharges of bile of every kind named by physicians ensued, accompanied by very great depression. In most cases also an ineffectual retching followed, producing violent spasms, which in some cases ceased soon after, in others much later. Externally the body was not very hot to the touch, nor pale in its appearance, but reddish, livid and breaking out into small pustules and ulcers. But internally it burned so that the patient could not bear to have on him clothing or linen even of the very lightest description; or indeed to be otherwise than stark naked. What they would have liked best would have been to throw themselves into cold water; as indeed was done by some of the neglected sick, who plunged into the rain-tanks in their agonies of unquenchable thirst; though it made no difference whether they drank little or much. Besides this, the miserable feeling of not being able to rest or sleep never ceased to torment them. The body meanwhile did not waste away so long as the distemper was at its height, but held out to a marvel against its ravages; so that when they succumbed, as in most cases, on the seventh or eighth day to the internal inflammation, they had still some strength in them. But if they passed this stage, and the disease descended further into the bowels, inducing a violent ulceration there accompanied by severe diarrhoea, this brought on a weakness which was generally fatal. For the disorder first settled in the head, ran its course from thence through the whole of the body, and even where it did not prove mortal, it still left its mark on the extremities; for it settled in the privy parts, the fingers and the toes, and many escaped with the loss of these, some too with that of their eyes. Others again were seized with an entire loss of memory on their first recovery and did not know either themselves or their friends.

But while the nature of the distemper was such as to baffle all description and its attacks almost too grievous for human nature to endure, it was still in the following circumstance that its difference from all ordinary disorders was most clearly shown. All the birds and beasts that prey upon human bodies, either abstained from touching them (though there were many lying unburied), or died after tasting them. In proof of this, it was noticed that birds of this kind actually disappeared; they were not about the bodies or indeed to be seen at all. But of course the effects which I have mentioned could best be studied in a domestic animal like the dog.

Such then, if we pass over the varieties of particular cases, which were many and peculiar, were the general features of the distemper. Meanwhile the town enjoyed an immunity from all the ordinary disorders; or if any case occurred, it ended in this. Some died in neglect, others in the midst of every attention. No remedy was found that could be used as a specific; for what did good in one case, did harm in another. Strong and weak constitutions proved equally incapable of resistance, all alike being swept away, although dieted with the utmost precaution. By far the most terrible feature in the malady was the dejection which ensued when any one felt himself sickening, for the despair into which they instantly fell took away their power of resistance and left them a much easier prey to the disorder; besides which, there was the awful spectacle of men dying like sheep, through having caught the infection in nursing each other. This caused the greatest mortality. On the one hand, if they were afraid to visit each other, they perished from neglect; indeed many houses were emptied of their inmates for want of a nurse: on the other, if they ventured to do so, death was the consequence. This was especially the case with such as made any pretensions to goodness: honour made them unsparing of themselves in their attendance in their friends' houses, where even the members of the family were at last worn out by the moans of the dying and succumbed to the force of the disaster. Yet it was with those who had recovered from the disease that the sick and the dying found most compassion. These knew what it was from experience and had now no fear for themselves; for the same man was never attacked twice—never at least fatally. And such persons not only received the congratulations of others, but themselves also, in the elation of the moment, half entertained the vain hope that they were for the future safe from any disease whatsoever.

An aggravation of the existing calamity was the influx from the country into the city, and this was especially felt by the new arrivals. As there were no houses to receive them, they had to be lodged at the hot season of the year in stifling cabins where the mortality raged without restraint. Bodies lay one upon another in the agonies of thirst, and half-dead creatures reeled about the streets and gathered round all the fountains in their longing for water. The sacred places also in which they had quartered themselves were full of corpses of persons that had died there just as they were; for as the disaster passed all bound, men, not knowing what was to become of them, became utterly careless of everything, whether sacred or profane. All the burial rites before in use were entirely upset, and they buried the bodies as best they could. Many from want of the proper appliances, through so many of their friends having died already, had recourse to the most shameless sepultures: sometimes getting the start of those who had raised a pile, they threw their own dead body upon the stranger's pyre and ignited it; sometimes they tossed the corpse which they were carrying on the top of another that was burning and so went off.

Nor was this the only form of lawless extravagance which owed its origin to the plague. Men now coolly ventured on what they had formerly done in a corner, and not just as they pleased, seeing the rapid transitions produced by persons in prosperity suddenly dying and those who before had nothing succeeding to their property. So they resolved to spend quickly and enjoy themselves, regarding their lives and riches as alike things of a day. Perseverance in what men called honour was popular with none, it was so uncertain whether they would be spared to attain the object; but present enjoyment and all that contributed to it was laid down as both honourable and useful. Fear of gods or law of man there was none to restrain them. As for the first, they judged it to be just the same whether they worshipped them or not, as they saw all alike perishing; and for the last, no one expected to live to be brought to trial for his offences, but felt that a far severer sentence had been already passed upon them and hung ever over their heads, and before this fell it was only reasonable to enjoy life a little.

Such was the nature of the calamity, and heavily did it weigh on the Athenians; death raging within the city and devastation without. Among other things which they remembered in their distress was, very naturally, the following verse which the old men said had long ago been uttered:

A Dorian war shall come and with it death.

At any rate a dispute arose as to whether dearth and not death had not been the word in the verse; but at the present juncture, it was of course decided in favour of the latter. I fancy, however, that if another Dorian war should ever afterwards come upon us, and a dearth should happen to accompany it, the verse will probably be read accordingly. The oracle also which had been given to the Lacedaemonians was now remembered by those who knew of it. When the God was asked whether they should go to war, he answered that if they put their might into it, victory would be theirs, and that he would himself be with them. With this oracle events were supposed to tally. For the plague broke out as soon as the Peloponnesians invaded Attica, and never entering Peloponnese (not at least to an extent worth noticing), committed its worst ravages at Athens, and next to Athens at the most populous of the other towns. Such was the history of the plague.

42 / PERICLES AND HIS SUCCESSORS

Pericles died in the fall of 429, a victim of the plague. Thucydides, who admired Pericles above all others, includes in his work an evaluation of this great statesman in which he compares Pericles to his successors. The passage is interesting also for Thucydides' view of the later stages of the Peloponnesian War.[5] *See also No. 31C.*

As long as he [Pericles] was at the head of the state during the peace, he pursued a moderate and conservative policy; and in his time its greatness was at its height. When the war broke out, here also he seems to have rightly gauged the power of his country. He outlived its commencement two years and six months, and the correctness of his previsions respecting it became better known by his death. He told them to wait quietly, to pay attention to their marine, to attempt no new conquests, and to expose the city to no hazards during the war, and doing this, promised them a favourable result. What they did was the

[5] Richard Crawley, *The History of the Peloponnesian War by Thucydides* (London: Longman's, Green and Co., 1874), p. 141 ff.

very contrary, allowing private ambitions and private interests, in matters apparently quite foreign to the war, to lead them into projects unjust both to themselves and to their allies—projects whose success would only conduce to the honour and advantage of private persons and whose failure entailed certain disaster on the country in the war. The causes of this are not far to seek. Pericles indeed, by his rank, ability, and known integrity, was enabled to exercise an independent control over the multitude—in short, to lead them instead of being led by them; for as he never sought power by improper means, he was never compelled to flatter them, but, on the contrary, enjoyed so high an estimation that he could afford to anger them by contradiction. Whenever he saw them unseasonably and insolently elated, he would with a word reduce them to alarm; on the other hand, if they fell victims to a panic, he could at once restore them to confidence. In short, what was nominally a democracy became in his hands government by the first citizen. With his successors it was different. More on a level with one another and each grasping at supremacy, they ended by committing even the conduct of state affairs to the whims of the multitude. This, as might have been expected in a great and sovereign state, produced a host of blunders and amongst them the Sicilian expedition; though this failed not so much through a miscalculation of the power of those against whom it was sent as through a fault in the senders in not taking the best measures after its departure, but choosing rather to occupy themselves with private cabals for the leadership of the commons by which they not only paralysed operations in the field, but also first introduced civil discord at home. Yet after losing most of their fleet besides other forces in Sicily, and with faction already dominant in the city, they could still for three years make head against their original adversaries, joined not only by the Sicilians, but also by their own allies nearly all in revolt and at last by the king's son, Cyrus, who furnished the funds for the Peloponnesian navy. Nor did they finally succumb till they fell the victims of their own intestine disorders. So superfluously abundant were the resources from which the genius of Pericles foresaw an easy triumph in the war over the unaided forces of the Peloponnesians.

43 / WAR AND REVOLUTION

Thucydides continues his account of the "Archidamian War" after the death of Pericles. In 427 B.C. *a civil war occurred on the island of Corcyra between oligarchs (the Few) and demo-*

crats (the Many). In the course of the revolution Athens intervened on the side of the democrats, the Peloponnesians on that of the oligarchs. Atrocities were committed by both parties, including incendiarism, murder, and enforced suicide. Thucydides avails himself of this first instance of a domestic revolution during the Peloponnesian War to provide an analysis of the events.[6]

So bloody was the march of the revolution, and the impression which it made was the greater as it was one of the first to occur. Later on, one may say, the whole Hellenic world was convulsed; struggles being everywhere made by the popular chiefs to bring in the Athenians and by the oligarchs to introduce the Lacedaemonians. In peace there would have been neither the pretext nor the wish to make such an invitation; but in war, with an alliance always at the command of either faction for the hurt of their adversaries and their own corresponding advantage, opportunities for bringing in the foreigner were never wanting to the revolutionary parties. The sufferings which revolution entailed upon the cities were many and terrible, such as have occurred and always will occur as long as the nature of mankind remains the same; though in a severer or milder form and varying in their symptoms according to the variety of the particular cases. In peace and prosperity states and individuals have better sentiments because they do not find themselves suddenly confronted with imperious necessities; but war takes away the easy supply of daily wants and so proves a rough master that brings most men's characters to a level with their fortunes. Revolution thus ran its course from city to city, and the places which it arrived at last, from having heard what had been done before, carried to a still greater excess the refinement of their inventions, as manifested in the cunning of their enterprises and the atrocity of their reprisals. Words had to change their ordinary meaning and to take that which was now given them. Reckless audacity became courage staunch to its associates; prudent hesitation, specious cowardice; moderation was held to be a cloak for unmanliness; ability to see all sides of a question, inaptness to act on any. Frantic violence became the attribute of manliness; safe plotting, a justifiable means of self-defence. The advocate of extreme measures was always trustworthy; his opponent a man to be suspected. To succeed in a plot was to have a shrewd head, to divine a plot a still shrewder; but to try to provide against having to do either was to break up your party and to be afraid of your adversaries. In fine, to

[6] Richard Crawley, *The History of the Peloponnesian War by Thucydides* (London: Longman's, Green and Co., 1874), pp. 224–7.

forestall an intending criminal, or to suggest the idea of a crime where it was wanting, was equally commended, until even blood became a weaker tie than party, from the superior readiness of those united by the latter to dare everything without reserve; such associations not having in view the blessings derivable from established institutions but being formed by ambition for their overthrow; while the confidence of their members in each other rested less on any religious sanction than upon complicity in crime. The fair proposals of an adversary were met with jealous precautions by the stronger of the two and not with a generous confidence. Revenge also was held of more account than self-preservation. Oaths of reconciliation, being only proffered on either side to meet an immediate difficulty, only held good so long as no other weapon was at hand; but when opportunity offered, he who first ventured to seize it and to take his enemy off his guard thought this perfidious vengeance sweeter than an open one since, considerations of safety apart, success by treachery won him the palm of knowingness. Indeed, rogues are oftener called clever than simpletons honest, and men are as ashamed of being the one as they are proud of being the other. The cause of all these evils was the lust for power felt by greed and ambition, and out of this came violence of parties once engaged in contention. The leaders in the cities, each provided with the fairest professions, on the one side with the cry of political equality of the people, on the other of an ordered aristocracy, sought prizes for themselves in those public interests which they pretend to cherish, and, recoiling from no means in their struggles for ascendancy, dared and went through with the direct excesses; which were met in their turn with reprisals still more terrible, which, instead of stopping at what justice or the good of the state demanded, were only limited by the party caprice of the moment; unjust legal condemnations or the authority of the strong arm being with equal readiness involved to glut the animosities of the hour. Thus religion was in honour with neither party; but the use of fair names to arrive at guilty ends was in high reputation. Meanwhile, the moderate part of the citizens perished between the two, either for not joining in the quarrel, or because envy would not suffer them to escape.

Thus every form of iniquity took root in the Hellenic countries by reason of the troubles. The ancient simplicity into which honour so largely entered was laughed down and disappeared; and society became divided into camps in which no man trusted his fellow. To put an end to this, there was neither promise to be depended upon nor oath that could command respect; but all parties dwelling rather in their calculation upon the hopelessness of a permanent state of things were more intent upon self-defence than capable of confidence. In this contest the blunter wits were most successful. Apprehensive of their own deficiencies and of the cleverness of their antagonists, they feared to be worsted in debate and to be surprised by the combinations of their more versatile opponents and so at once boldly had recourse to action; while their adversaries arrogantly thinking that they should know in time and that it was unnecessary to secure by action what policy afforded often fell victims to their want of precaution.

Meanwhile Corcyra gave the first example of most of the crimes alluded to; of the reprisals exacted by the governed who had never experienced equitable treatment or indeed aught but insolence from their rulers—when their hour came; of the iniquitous resolves of those who desired to get rid of their accustomed poverty and ardently coveted their neighbours' goods; and lastly, of the savage and pitiless excesses into which men who had begun the struggle not in a class but in a party spirit were hurried by their ungovernable passions. In the confusion into which life was now thrown in the cities, human nature, always rebelling against the law and now its master, gladly showed itself ungoverned in passion, above respect for justice and the enemy of all superiority; since revenge would not have been set above religion and gain above justice, had it not been for the fatal power of envy. Indeed men too often take upon themselves in the prosecution of their revenge to set the example of doing away with those general laws to which all alike can look for salvation in adversity, instead of allowing them to subsist against the day of danger when their aid may be required.

44 / ATHENIAN DESPOTISM AND AMORALISM

Athenian despotism and amoralism is clearly revealed in a dialogue between Athenian envoys and the magistrates of the small Aegean island of Melos (416 B.C.). Melos, a colony of Sparta, had repeatedly refused to join the Athenian alliance and was now attacked by an Athenian expeditionary force. The Athenian attack was entirely unprovoked. The Athenian arguments are heavily influenced by the thought of the Sophists (No. 35). In the end the island was betrayed to the Athenians after a long and difficult siege. Athens executed all adult males and sold the Melian women and children into slavery. Xenophon reports that when news of the Sicilian disaster first reached Athens in 413 B.C., the Athenians feared that Sparta would punish them as they had punished Sparta's colony, Melos.[7]

The Athenians also made an expedition against the isle of Melos with thirty ships of their own, six Chian and two Lesbian vessels, sixteen hundred heavy infantry, three hundred archers and twenty mounted archers from Athens, and about fifteen hundred heavy infantry from the allies and the islanders. The Melians are a colony of Lacedaemon that would not submit to the Athenians like the other islanders and at first remained neutral and took no part in the struggle, but afterwards, upon the Athenians using violence and plundering their territory, assumed an attitude of open hostility. Cleomedes, son of Lycomedes, and Tisias, son of Tisimachus, the generals, encamping in their territory with the above armament, before doing any harm to their land, sent envoys to negotiate. These the Melians did not bring before the people, but bade them state the object of their mission to the magistrates and the few; upon which the Athenian envoys spoke as follows:—

ATHENIANS.—Since the negotiations are not to go on before the people, in order that we may not be able to speak straight on without interruption, and deceive the ears of the multitude by seductive arguments which would pass without refutation (for we know that this is the meaning of our being brought before the few), what if you who sit there were to pursue a method more cautious still! Make no set speech yourselves, but take us up at whatever you do not like and settle that before going any farther. And first tell us if this proposition of ours suits you.

The Melian commissioners answered:

MELIANS.—To the fairness of quietly instructing each other as you propose there is nothing to object; but your military preparations are too far advanced to agree with what you say, as we see you are come to be judges in your own cause and that all we can reasonably expect from this negotiation is war, if we prove to have right on our side and refuse to submit, and in the contrary case, slavery.

ATHENIANS.—If you have met to reason about presentiments of the future or for anything else than to consult for the safety of your state upon the facts that you see before you, we will give over; otherwise we will go on.

MELIANS.—It is natural and excusable for men in our position to turn more ways than one both in thought and utterance. However, the

[7] Richard Crawley, *The History of the Peloponnesian War by Thucydides* (London: Longman's, Green and Co., 1874), pp. 396–401.

question in this conference is, as you say, the safety of our country; and the discussion, if you please, can proceed in the way which you propose.

ATHENIANS.—For ourselves, we shall not trouble you with specious pretences—either of how we have a right to our empire because we overthrew the Mede or are now attacking you because of wrong that you have done us—and make a long speech which would not be believed; and in return we hope that you, instead of thinking to influence us by saying that you did not join the Lacedaemonians, although their colonists, or that you have done us no wrong, will aim at what is feasible holding in view the real sentiments of us both; since you know as well as we do that right, as the world goes, is only in question between equals in power while the strong do what they can and the weak suffer what they must.

MELIANS.—For our parts then we think it expedient—we speak as we are obliged, since you enjoin us to let right alone and talk only of interest—that you should not destroy the privilege so useful to all of being allowed in danger to invoke what is fair and right and even to profit by arguments not strictly valid if they can be got to pass current. And you are as much interested in this as any, as your fall would be a signal for the heaviest vengeance and an example for the world to meditate upon.

ATHENIANS.—The end of our empire, if end it should, does not frighten us; a rival empire like Lacedaemon, even if Lacedaemon was our real antagonist, is not so terrible to the vanquished as subjects who by themselves attack and overpower their rulers. This, however, is a risk that we are content to take. We will now proceed to show you that we are come here in the interest of our empire and that we shall say what we are now going to say for the preservation of your country; as we would fain exercise that empire over you without trouble and see you preserved for the good of us both.

MELIANS.—And how, pray, could it turn out as good for us to serve as for you to rule?

ATHENIANS.—Because you would have the advantage of submitting before suffering the worst, and we should gain by not destroying you.

MELIANS.—So that you would not consent to our being neutral, friends instead of enemies, but allies of neither side.

ATHENIANS.—No; for your hostility cannot so much hurt us as your friendship will be an argument to our subjects of our weakness and your enmity of our power.

MELIANS.—Is that your subjects' idea of equity, to put those who have nothing to do with you in the same category with peoples that are most of them your own colonists, and some conquered rebels?

ATHENIANS.—As far as right goes they think one has as much of it as the other and that if any maintain their independence it is because they are strong and that if we do not molest them it is because we are afraid; so that besides extending our empire we should gain in security by your subjection; the fact that you are islanders and weaker than others rendering it all the more important that you should not succeed in baffling the masters of the sea.

MELIANS.—But do you consider that there is no security in the policy which we indicate? For here again if you debar us from talking about justice and invite us to obey your interest, we also must explain ours and try to persuade you if the two happen to coincide. How can you avoid making enemies of all existing neutrals who shall look at our case and conclude from it that one day or another you will attack them? And what is this but to make greater the enemies that you have already, and to force others to become so who would otherwise have never thought of it?

ATHENIANS.—Why, the fact is that continentals generally give us but little alarm; the liberty which they enjoy will long prevent their taking precautions against us; it is rather islanders like yourselves, outside our empire, and subjects smarting under the yoke, who would be the most likely to take a rash step and lead themselves and us into obvious danger.

MELIANS.—Well then, if you risk so much to retain your empire, and your subjects to get rid of it, it were surely great baseness and cowardice in us who are still free not to try everything that can be tried before submitting to your yoke.

ATHENIANS.—Not if you are well advised, the contest not being an equal one with honour as the prize and shame as the penalty, but a question of self-preservation and of not resisting those who are far stronger than you are.

MELIANS.—But we know that the fortune of war is sometimes more impartial than the disproportion of numbers might lead one to suppose; and for us to submit is to give ourselves over to despair, while action still leaves us hope of maintaining ourselves.

ATHENIANS.—Hope, danger's comforter, may be indulged in by those who have enough and to spare, if not without loss, at all events without ruin; but its nature is to be extravagant, and those who go so far as to put their all upon the venture see it in its true colours only when they are ruined; but so long as the discovery would enable them to guard against it, it is never found wanting. Let not this be the case with you who are weak and hang on a single turn of the scale; nor be like the vulgar who, abandoning such security as human means may still afford, when visible hopes fail them in extremity, turn to invisible, to prophecies and oracles and other such inventions that delude men with hopes to their destruction.

MELIANS.—You may be sure that we are as well aware as you of the difficulty of contending against your power and fortune unless the terms be equal. But we trust with the help of the gods that our fortunes may be as good as yours since we are just men fighting against unjust, and that what we want in power will be made up by the alliance of the Lacedaemonians who are bound, if only for very shame, to come to the aid of their kindred. Our confidence, therefore, after all is not so utterly irrational.

ATHENIANS.—When you speak of the favour of the gods, we may as fairly hope for that as yourselves; neither our pretensions nor our conduct being in any way contrary to what men believe of the gods, or practise among themselves. Of the gods we believe, and of men we know, that by a necessary law of their nature they rule wherever they can. And it is not as if we were the first to make this law, or to act upon it when made: we found it existing before us; and shall leave it to exist for ever after us; all we do is to make use of it, knowing that you and everybody else, having the same power as we have, would do the same as we do. Thus, as far as the gods are concerned, we have no fear and no reason to fear that we shall have the worse. But when we come to your notion about the Lacedaemonians which leads you to believe that shame will make them help you, here we bless your simplicity but do not envy your folly. The Lacedaemonians, when themselves or their country's laws are in question, are the worthiest men alive; of their conduct towards others much might be said, but no clearer idea of it could be given than by shortly saying that of all the men we know they most indubitably consider what is agreeable honourable and what is expedient just. Such a way of thinking does not promise much for the safety which you now unreasonably count upon. . . .

45 / THE GREAT BLUNDER

In Thucydides' History *the Melian outrage is followed immediately by the account of the Sicilian Expedition (415–413 B.C.). Called upon by the city of Egeste (or Segesta) in Sicily to help them in a local war against their neighbors at Selinuntum, the Athenians elected Alcibiades, Nicias, and Lamachus to command the Sicilian Expedition. Nicias was elected against his will, and in a meeting of the Assembly he advised against the expedition. Alcibiades and others spoke eloquently in favor of it, however, and swayed the Assembly. Nicias made one last attempt to dissuade the Athenians by stressing the difficulties of this venture, but it was in vain. Thucydides' narrative breathes the spirit of buoyancy and boldness, but also of greed and foolhardiness, which inspired Athens on this fateful occasion.*[8]

The Athenians at once voted that the generals should have full powers in the matter of the numbers of the army and of the expedition generally to do as they judged best for the interests of Athens. After this the preparations began; messages being sent to the allies and the rolls drawn up at home. And as the city had just recovered from the plague and the long war, and a number of young men had grown up and capital had accumulated by reason of the truce, everything was the more easily provided. . . .

After this the departure for Sicily took place, it being now about midsummer. Most of the allies, with the corn transports and the smaller craft and the rest of the expedition, had already received orders to muster at Corcyra, to cross the Ionian sea from thence in a body to the Iapygian promontory. But the Athenians themselves and such of their allies as happened to be with them went down to Piraeus upon a day appointed at daybreak and began to man the ships for putting out to sea. With them also went down the whole population, one may say, of the city, both citizens and foreigners; the inhabitants of the country each escorting those that belonged to them, their friends, their relatives or their sons, with hope and lamentation upon their way, as they thought of the conquests which they hoped to make or of the friends whom they might never see again, considering the long voyage which they were going to make from their country. Indeed, at this moment, when they were now upon the point of parting from one another, the danger came more home to them than when they voted for the expedition; although the strength of the armament and the profuse provision which they remarked in every department was a sight that could not but comfort them. As for the foreigners and the rest of the crowd, they simply went to see a sight worth looking at and passing all belief.

Indeed this armament that first sailed out was by far the most costly and splendid Hellenic force that had ever been sent out by a single city up to that time. In mere number of ships and heavy infantry that against Epidaurus under Pericles and the same when going against Potidaea under Hagnon was not inferior; containing as it did four thousand Athenian heavy infantry, three hundred horse and one hun-

[8] Richard Crawley, *The History of the Peloponnesian War by Thucydides* (London: Longman's, Green & Co., 1874), pp. 423–8.

dred galleys accompanied by fifty Lesbian and Chian vessels and many allies besides. But these were sent upon a short voyage and with a scanty equipment. The present expedition was formed in contemplation of a long term of service by land and sea alike and was furnished with ships and troops so as to be ready for either as required. The fleet had been elaborately equipped at great cost to the captains and the state; the treasury giving a drachma a day to each seaman and providing empty ships, sixty men of war and forty transports, which the captains manned with the best crews obtainable, giving a bounty in addition to the pay from the treasury to the thranitae and crews generally, besides spending lavishly upon figure-heads and equipments and one and all making the utmost exertions to enable their own ships to excel in beauty and fast sailing. Meanwhile the land forces had been picked from the best muster-rolls and vied with each other in paying great attention to their arms and personal accoutrements. From this resulted not only a rivalry among themselves in their different departments, but an idea among the rest of the Hellenes that it was more a display of power and resources than an armament against an enemy. For if any one had counted up the public expenditure of the state and the private outlay of individuals, that is to say, the sums which the state had already spent upon the expedition and was sending out in the hands of the generals and those which individuals had expended upon their personal outfit or as captains of galleys had laid out and were still to lay out upon their vessels; and if he had added to this the journey money which each was likely to have provided himself with, independently of the pay from the treasury, for a voyage of such length and what the soldiers or traders took with them for the purpose of exchange—it would have been found that many talents in all were being taken out of the city. Indeed the expedition was not less famous from wonder at its boldness and by the splendour of its appearance than for its overwhelming strength as compared with the peoples against whom it was directed and for the fact that this was the longest passage from home hitherto attempted and the most ambitious in its objects, considering the resources of those who undertook it.

The ships now being manned and everything put on board with which they meant to sail, the trumpet commanded silence and the prayers customary before puting out to sea were offered, not in each ship by itself, but by all together to the voice of a herald; and bowls of wine were mixed through all the armament, and libations made by the soldiers and their officers in gold and silver goblets. In their prayers joined also the crowds on shore, the citizens and all others that wished them well. The hymn sung and the libations finished, they put out to sea, and first sailing out in column then raced each other as far as Aegina, and so hastened to reach Corcyra, where the rest of the allied forces were also assembling.

46 / "TOTAL DESTRUCTION"

After the defeat in the Great Harbor of Syracuse, the Athenians decided to withdraw their army by means of an overland march.[9]

After this, Nicias and Demosthenes now thinking that enough had been done in the way of preparation, the removal of the army took place upon the second day after the sea fight. It was a lamentable scene, not merely from the single circumstance that they were retreating after having lost all their ships, their great hopes gone and themselves and the state in peril; but also in leaving the camp there were things most grievous for every eye and heart to contemplate. The dead lay unburied, and each man as he recognized a friend among them shuddered with grief and horror; while the living whom they were leaving behind, wounded or sick, were to the living far more shocking than the dead and more to be pitied than those who had perished. These fell to entreating and bewailing until their friends knew not what to do, begging them to take them and loudly calling to each individual comrade or relative whom they could see, hanging upon the necks of their tent-fellows in the act of departure and following as far as they could, and when their bodily strength failed them, not being left behind without much crying and calling upon heaven. So that the whole army being filled with tears and distracted after this fashion found it not easy to go, even from an enemy's land, where they had already suffered evils too great for tears and in the unknown future before them feared to suffer still. Dejection and self-condemnation were also rife among them. Indeed they could only be compared to a starved-out town, and that no small one, escaping; the whole multitude upon the march being not less than forty thousand men, all of whom carried anything they could which might be of use, and the heavy infantry and troopers, contrary to their wont, their own victuals, in some cases for want of servants, in others through not

[9] Richard Crawley, *The History of the Peloponnesian War by Thucydides* (London: Longman's, Green and Co., 1874), pp. 533–5, 540 ff., 543.

trusting them; as they had long been deserting and now did so in greater numbers than ever. Yet even thus they did not carry enough, as there was no longer food in the camp. Moreover their disgrace generally and the universality of their sufferings, however to a certain extent alleviated by being borne in company, were still felt at the moment a heavy burden, especially when they contrasted the splendour and glory of their setting out with the humiliation in which it had ended. For this was by far the greatest reverse that ever befell an Hellenic army. They had come to enslave others, and were departing in fear of being enslaved themselves: they had sailed out with prayer and paeans, and now started to go back with omens directly contrary; travelling by land instead of by sea, and trusting not in their fleet but in their heavy infantry. Nevertheless the greatness of the danger still impending made all this appear tolerable. . . .

[The retreating Athenian army under Nicias and Demosthenes suffered constant harassment from the Syracusans, who tried to block their slow and wearisome advance. The Syracusans managed to divide the Athenian army and to force Demosthenes and his contingent to surrender. Nicias and his troops were eliminated on the following day at the River Assinarus (413 B.C.*).]*

As soon as it was day Nicias put his army in motion, pressed as before by the Syracusans and their allies, pelted from every side by their missiles and struck down by their javelins. The Athenians pushed on for the Assinarus, impelled by the attacks made upon them from every side by a numerous cavalry and the swarm of other arms, fancying that they should breathe more freely if once across the river and driven on also by their exhaustion and craving for water. Once there they rushed in and all order was at an end, each man wanting to cross first, and the attacks of the enemy making it difficult to cross at all, since they were forced to huddle together, and so fell against and trod down one another, some dying immediately upon the javelins, others getting entangled together and stumbling over the articles of baggage, without being able to rise again. Meanwhile the opposite bank which was steep was lined by the Syracusans, who showered missiles down upon the Athenians, most of them drinking greedily and heaped together in disorder in the hollow bed of the river. The Peloponnesians also came down and butchered them, especially those in the water, which was thus immediately spoiled, but which they went on drinking just the same, mud and all, bloody as it was, most even fighting to have it. . . .

[Nicias now surrenders to the Spartan general Gylippus. Athenian and allied casualties on the River Assinarus were "not exceeded by

any in this Sicilian war," and the survivors of the expeditionary force were made prisoners and eventually sold into slavery. Nicias and Demosthenes were executed. Of Nicias' death Thucydides remarks that "of all the Hellenes in my time, [Nicias] least deserved such a fate, seeing that the whole course of his life had been regulated with strict attention to virtue." Thucydides concludes his account of the Sicilian Expedition as follows:]

This was the greatest Hellenic achievement of any in this war, or, in my opinion, in Hellenic history; at once most glorious to the victors, and most calamitous to the conquered. They were beaten at all points and altogether; all that they suffered was great; they were destroyed, as the saying is, with a total destruction—their fleet, their army—there was nothing that was not destroyed, and few out of many returned home.

VI / THE GREEK WORLD IN THE FOURTH AND THIRD CENTURIES B.C.

The Great Peloponnesian War was followed by much warfare among the city-states in the competition for leadership in Greece. Victorious Sparta, who abused her power, soon became more hated than Athens had been during her period of hegemony. Moreover, under King Agesilaus, Sparta had become involved in war against Persia both in Asia Minor and on the mainland. As a result of her wars against Persia and the main cities of Greece, Sparta's military situation deteriorated markedly during the first decade of the fourth century. Consequently, from 392 on she tried to obtain peace terms from Persia. These negotiations culminated in the "King's Peace" (387–386 B.C.*), which was finally accepted by all of Greece. It was, however, considered a humiliation inasmuch as the King of Persia was able to dictate his terms to the Greek world.*

47 / THE KING'S PEACE (387-386 B.C.)

Xenophon of Athens (430–354 B.C.*) had been a pupil of Socrates and had seen years of military service against Persia, partially under Spartan leadership. In his* Hellenic History *he* *continued Thucydides' narrative down to 362* B.C. *In this work he described both Spartan negotiations with Persia and the peace itself. The principal Spartan negotiator was Antalcidas, who was supported by Tiribazus, Persian satrap of Ionia. Antalcidas not only managed to obtain from King Artaxerxes peace terms that were favorable to Sparta, but also overcame the resistance of the principal cities, Athens and Thebes, to these terms.*[1]

Antalcidas had now returned from the Persian court with Tiribazus. The negotiations had been successful. He had secured the alliance of the Persian king and his military cooperation in case the Athenians and their allies refused to abide by the peace which the king dictated. . . .

The Athenians could not but watch with alarm the growth of the enemy's fleet, and began to fear a repetition of their former discomfiture. To be trampled under foot by the hostile power seemed indeed no remote possibility, now that the Lacedaemonians had procured an ally in the person of the Persian monarch, and they were in little less than a state of siege themselves, pestered as they were by privateers from Aegina. On all these grounds the Athenians became passionately desirous of peace. The Lacedaemonians were equally out of humour with the war for various reasons—what with their garrison duties, one mora [a division of the Spartan army] at Lechaeum and another at Orchomenus, and the necessity of keeping watch and ward on the states, if loyal not to lose them, if disaffected to prevent their revolt; not to mention that reciprocity of annoyance of which Corinth was the centre. So again the Argives had a strong appetite for peace; they knew that the ban had been called out against them, and, it was plain, that no fictitious alteration of the calendar would any longer stand them in good stead. Hence, when Tiribazus issued a summons calling on all who were willing to listen to the terms of peace sent down by the king to present themselves, the invitation was promptly accepted. At the opening of the conclave Tiribazus pointed to the king's seal attached to the document, and proceeded to read the contents, which ran as follows:

"The king, Artaxerxes, deems it just that the cities in Asia, with the islands of Clazomenae and Cyprus, should belong to himself; the rest of the Hellenic cities he thinks it just to leave independent, both small and great, with the exception of Lemnos, Imbros, and Scyros, which three are to belong to Athens as of yore. Should any of the

[1] H. G. Dakyns, *The Works of Xenophon,* Vol. II (London and New York: Macmillan and Co., 1892), pp. 96–100.

parties concerned not accept this peace, I, Artaxerxes, will war against him or them with those who share my views. This will I do by land and by sea, with ships and with money."

After listening to the above declaration the ambassadors from the several states proceeded to report the same to their respective governments. One and all of these took the oaths to ratify and confirm the terms unreservedly, with the exception of the Thebans, who claimed to take the oaths in behalf of all Boeotians. This claim Agesilaus repudiated.

48 / ISOCRATES: SPOKESMAN OF RECONCILIATION AMONG GREEKS AND OF WARFARE AGAINST PERSIA

One of Athens' most famous orators in the fourth century was Isocrates (436–338 B.C.), who had been a pupil of the Sophist Gorgias (No. 35) and at another time of Socrates. From the former he had adopted the principle that the orator should concern himself with public issues; from the latter he had inherited his concern for morality. Some years before Plato founded the Academy, a school of philosophy (No. 51), Isocrates founded a school for orators (392 B.C.). He numbered among his pupils men of great importance: the Athenian general Timotheus, the historians Ephorus and Theopompus, the philosopher Speusippus. Isocrates' "orations" were in fact never delivered, but were published as political pamphlets. In a sense the program of Isocrates triumphed in the formation of the Corinthian League (No. 50) and in Alexander's campaigns (No. 53).

With the publication of the Panegyricus *(A) in 380 B.C. Isocrates followed in the footsteps of his teacher Gorgias, who in 408 B.C. had addressed the Greeks at the Olympic festival. The* Panegyricus *was written against the background of the King's Peace*

(No. 47), which Isocrates felt to be a humiliation of Greece. The program developed in the "speech" is a reaction against that shameful peace.

A generation after the Panegyricus, *Isocrates, then ninety years old, wrote his* Address to Philip *(B). Much had happened during the intervening period. Athens had rebuilt her empire, but, contrary to Isocrates' hopes as expressed in the* Panegyricus, *she had not been able to unify Greece. Thebes had repeatedly defeated Sparta and had made her own bid for leadership in Greece, but this episode lasted a few years only. In 359* B.C. *Philip II had ascended the throne of the Macedonians, a Greek people less advanced than the people of the great city-states of the fourth century. By war and internal reforms Philip had quickly strengthened his backward country and won a number of military successes against Athens and other Greek cities. In 346* B.C. *he had agreed to a peace while Isocrates was writing his* Address to Philip, *in which his political program was expressed as still centering around a pan-Hellenic offensive against Persia. Philip was to bring about a reconciliation among the principal Greek cities, which were Argos, Sparta, Thebes, and Athens, and then to lead united Greece in a great war against Persia. But while in the earlier work Athens was to be the leader in this great enterprise, Isocrates now entrusted this task to the King of Macedon. In the course of the speech Isocrates referred to the tyrant Jason of Pherae (in Thessaly, + 370* B.C.*), who had contemplated a Greek attack upon Persia.*[2]

A. THE PANEGYRICUS

As to our public interests, the speakers who no sooner come before us than they inform us that we must compose our enmities against each other and turn against the barbarians, rehearsing the misfortunes which have come upon us from our mutual warfare and the advantages which will result from a campaign against our natural enemy—these men do speak the truth, but they do not start at the point from which they could best bring these things to pass. For the Hellenes are subject, some to us, others to the Lacedaemonians, the polities by

[2] Reprinted by permission of the publishers from the Loeb Classical Library, trans. by George Norlin, *Isocrates* (Cambridge, Mass.: Harvard University Press; London: William Heinemann Ltd.; New York: G. P. Putnam's Sons, 1928), Vol. I, pp. 127–31, 231–7, 319–21, 323–7.

which they govern their states having thus divided most of them. If any man, therefore, thinks that before he brings the leading states into friendly relations, the rest will unite in doing any good thing, he is all too simple and out of touch with the actual conditions. No, the man who does not aim merely to make an oratorical display, but desires to accomplish something as well, must seek out such arguments as will persuade these two states to share and share alike with each other, to divide the supremacy between them, and to wrest from the barbarians the advantages which at the present time they desire to seize for themselves at the expense of the Hellenes.

Now our own city could easily be induced to adopt this policy, but at present the Lacedaemonians are still hard to persuade; for they have inherited the false doctrine that leadership is theirs by ancestral right. If, however, one should prove to them that this honour belongs to us rather than to them, perhaps they might give up splitting hairs about this question and pursue their true interests.

So, then, the other speakers also should have made this their starting-point and should not have given advice on matters about which we agree before instructing us on the points about which we disagree. I, at all events, am justified by a twofold motive in devoting most of my attention to these points: first and foremost, in order that some good may come of it, and that we may put an end to our mutual rivalries and unite in a war against the barbarian; and, secondly, if this is impossible, in order that I may show who they are that stand in the way of the happiness of the Hellenes, and that all may be made to see that even as in times past Athens justly held the sovereignty of the sea, so now she not unjustly lays claim to the hegemony. . . .

[Isocrates then discusses in detail Athenian achievements. He proceeds to contrast Athenian imperialism such as it had existed in the fifth century with that of Sparta in the fourth. He concludes that Athenian imperialism was far more enlightened and more beneficial to the allies than that of Sparta and gives reasons why a war against Persia is advisable, timely, and likely to succeed.]

It is not possible for us to cement an enduring peace unless we join together in a war against the barbarians, nor for the Hellenes to attain concord until we wrest our material advantages from one and the same source and wage our wars against one and the same enemy. When these conditions have been realized, and when we have been freed from the poverty which afflicts our lives—a thing that breaks up friendships, perverts the affections of kindred into enmity, and plunges the whole world into war and strife—then surely we shall enjoy a spirit of concord, and the good will which we shall feel towards each other will be genuine. For all these reasons, we must make it our paramount duty to transfer the war with all speed from our boundaries to the continent, since the only benefit which we can reap from the wars which we have waged against each other is by resolving that the experience which we have gained from them shall be employed against the barbarians.

But is it not well, you may perhaps ask, on account of the Treaty, to curb ourselves and not be over-hasty or make the expedition too soon, seeing that the states which have gained their freedom through the Treaty feel grateful toward the King, because they believe that it was through him that they gained their independence, while those states which have been delivered over to the barbarians complain very bitterly of the Lacedaemonians and only less bitterly of the other Hellenes who entered into the peace, because in their view, they were forced by them into slavery? But, I reply, is it not our duty to annul this agreement, which has given birth to such a sentiment—the sentiment that the barbarian cares tenderly for Hellas, and stands guard over her peace, while among ourselves are to be found those who outrage and evilly entreat her? The crowning absurdity of all, however, is the fact that among the articles which are written in the agreement it is only the worst which we guard and observe. For those which guarantee the independence of the islands and of the cities in Europe have long since been broken and are dead letters on the pillars, while those which bring shame upon us and by which many of our allies have been given over to the enemy—these remain intact, and we all regard them as binding upon us, though we ought to have expunged them and not allowed them to stand a single day, looking upon them as commands, and not as compacts; for who does not know that a compact is something which is fair and impartial to both parties, while a command is something which puts one side at a disadvantage unjustly? On this ground we may justly complain of our envoys who negotiated this peace, because, although dispatched by the Hellenes, they made the Treaty in the interest of the barbarians. For they ought, no matter whether they took the view that each of the states concerned should retain its original territory, or that each should extend its sovereignty over all that it had acquired by conquest, or that we should each retain control over what we held when peace was declared—they ought, I say, to have adopted definitely some one of these views, applying the principle impartially to all, and on this basis to have drafted the articles of the Treaty. But instead of that, they assigned no honour whatsoever to our city or to Lacedaemon, while they set up the barbarian as lord of all Asia; as if we had gone to war for his sake, or as if the rule of the Persians had been long established, and we were only just now founding our cities—whereas in fact it is they who have only recently attained this place of honour, while Athens and Lacedaemon have been throughout their entire history a power among the Hellenes.

I think, however, that I shall show still more clearly both the dishonour which we have suffered, and the advantage which the King has gained by putting the matter in this way: All the world which lies beneath the firmament being divided into two parts, the one called Asia, the other Europe, he has taken half of it by the Treaty, as if he were apportioning the earth with Zeus, and not making compacts with men. Yes, and he has compelled us to engrave this Treaty on pillars of stone and place it in our public temples—a trophy far more glorious for him than those which are set up on fields of battle; for the latter are for minor deeds and a single success, but this treaty stands as a memorial of the entire war and of the humiliation of the whole of Hellas.

These things may well rouse our indignation and make us look to the means by which we shall take vengeance for the past and set the future right. For verily it is shameful for us, who in our private life think the barbarians are fit only to be used as household slaves, to permit by our public policy so many of our allies to be enslaved by them; and it is disgraceful for us, when our fathers who engaged in the Trojan expedition because of the rape of one woman, all shared so deeply in the indignation of the wronged that they did not stop waging war until they had laid in ruins the city of him who had dared to commit the crime,—it is disgraceful for us, I say, now that all Hellas is being continually outraged, to take not a single step to wreak a common vengeance, although we have it in our power to accomplish deeds as lofty as our dreams. For this war is the only war which is better than peace; it will be more like a sacred mission than a military expedition; and it will profit equally both those who crave the quiet life and those who are eager for war; for it will enable the former to reap the fruits of their own possessions in security and the latter to win great wealth from the possession of our foes.

B. THE ADDRESS TO PHILIP

[Jason of Pherae] without having achieved anything comparable to what you have done won the highest renown, not from what he did, but from what he said; for he kept talking as if he intended to cross over to the continent and make war upon the King. Now since Jason by use of words alone advanced himself so far, what opinion must we expect the world will have of you if you actually do this thing; above all, if you undertake to conquer the whole empire of the King, or, at any rate, to wrest from it a vast extent of territory and sever from it—to use a current phrase—"Asia from Cilicia to Sinope"; and if, furthermore, you undertake to establish cities in this region, and to settle in permanent abodes those who now, for lack of the daily necessities of life, are wandering from place to place and committing outrages upon whomsoever they encounter? If we do not stop these men from banding together, by providing sufficient livelihood for them, they will grow before we know it into so great a multitude as to be a terror no less to the Hellenes than to the barbarians. But we pay no heed to them; nay, we shut our eyes to the fact that a terrible menace which threatens us all alike is waxing day by day. It is therefore the duty of a man who is high-minded, who is a lover of Hellas, who has a broader vision than the rest of the world, to employ these bands in a war against the barbarians, to strip from that empire all the territory which I defined a moment ago, to deliver these homeless wanderers from the ills by which they are afflicted and which they inflict upon others, to collect them into cities, and with these cities to fix the boundary of Hellas, making of them buffer states to shield us all. For by doing this, you will not only make them prosperous, but you will put us all on a footing of security. If, however, you do not succeed in these objects, this much you will at any rate easily accomplish,—the liberation of the cities which are on the coast of Asia. . . .

Therefore, since the others are so lacking in spirit, I think it is opportune for you to head the war against the King; and, while it is only natural for the other descendants of Heracles, and for men who are under the bonds of their polities and laws, to cleave fondly to that state in which they happen to dwell, it is your privilege, as one who has been blessed with untrammelled freedom, to consider all Hellas your fatherland, as did the founder of your race, and to be as ready to brave perils for her sake as for the things about which you are personally most concerned.

Perhaps there are those—men capable of nothing else but criticism—who will venture to rebuke me because I have chosen to challenge you to the task of leading the expedition against the barbarians and of taking Hellas under your care, while I have passed over my own city. Well, if I were trying to present this matter to any others before having broached it to my own country, which has thrice freed Hellas—twice from the barbarians and once from the Lacedaemonian yoke—I should confess my error. In truth, however, it will be found that I turned to Athens first of all and endeavoured to win her over to this cause with all the earnestness of which my nature is capable, but when I perceived that she cared less for what I said than for the ravings of the platform orators, I gave her up, although I did not abandon my efforts. Wherefore I might justly be praised on every hand, because throughout my whole life I have constantly employed such powers as

I possess in warring on the barbarians, in condemning those who opposed my plan, and in striving to arouse to action whoever I think will best be able to benefit the Hellenes in any way or rob the barbarians of their present prosperity. Consequently, I am now addressing myself to you, although I am not unaware that when I am proposing this course many will look at it askance, but that when you are actually carrying it out all will rejoice in it; for no one has had any part in what I have proposed, but when the benefits from it shall have been realized in fact, everyone without fail will have to look to have his portion.

Consider also what a disgrace it is to sit idly by and see Asia flourishing more than Europe and the barbarians enjoying a greater prosperity than the Hellenes; and, what is more, to see those who derive their power from Cyrus, who as a child was cast out by his mother on the public highway, addressed by the title of "The Great King," while the descendants of Heracles, who because of his virtue was exalted by his father to the rank of a god, are addressed by meaner titles than they. We must not allow this state of affairs to go on; no, we must change and reverse it entirely.

49 / DEMOSTHENES: SPOKESMAN OF DEFENSE AGAINST PHILIP OF MACEDON

Demosthenes (384–322 B.C.) was younger than Isocrates and advocated a different political program. He delivered his first speech on a public issue in 354, five years after Philip II had become King of Macedon. From 351 on, his political career was devoted to the purpose of alerting the people of Athens to the Macedonian danger. His hour of triumph came when, in 338, Athens concluded an alliance with her old enemy, Thebes, but the hour was too late. In the same year Philip II defeated the allies in the disastrous battle of Chaeronea. Demosthenes, who survived this defeat by many years, carried on intrigues against Macedon and finally committed suicide in 322 B.C.

In 352 B.C. Philip intervened in Thessaly, plundered the coast of Attica, and raided the Athenian possessions in the Aegean

Sea. The First Philippic *(A) was delivered by Demosthenes in 351.*

The Third Philippic *(B) was delivered by Demosthenes in 341* B.C. *By this time Philip's power had grown alarmingly. In 348 he had taken Olynthus on the Chalcidice, in spite of Athenian aid. This was followed by his annexation of portions of Thrace. In spite of the Peace of Philocrates concluded with Athens in 346* B.C., *Philip then intervened in a Sacred War (concerned with control over the pan-Hellenic sanctuary at Delphi) and as a consequence was elected a member of the Amphictyonic Council administering Delphi. By 345 he controlled Thessaly and was causing trouble in the Peloponnesus. In 342 Macedonian forces were installed in Euboea and then proceeded to annex all of Thrace and to threaten Byzantium. These successes were due not only to Philip's military "innovations" (especially his improved siege warfare), but also to his reliance on bribery on a grand scale, which provided him with collaborators in all the cities of Greece.*[3]

A. THE FIRST PHILIPPIC

If any among you, Athenians, deem Philip hard to be conquered, looking at the magnitude of his existing power, and the loss by us of all our strongholds, they reason rightly, but should reflect, that once we held Pydna and Potidaea and Methone and all the region round about as our own, and many of the nations now leagued with him were independent and free, and preferred our friendship to his. Had Philip then taken it into his head, that it was difficult to contend with Athens, when she had so many fortresses to infest his country, and he was destitute of allies, nothing that he has accomplished would he have undertaken, and never would he have acquired so large a dominion. But he saw well, Athenians, that all these places are the open prizes of war, that the possessions of the absent naturally belong to the present, those of the remiss to them that will venture and toil. Acting on such principle, he has won everything and keeps it, either by way of conquest, or by friendly attachment and alliance; for all men will side with and respect those, whom they see prepared and willing to make proper exertion. If you, Athenians, will adopt this principle now, though you did not before, and every man, where he can and ought to give his service to the state, be ready to give it without excuse, the wealthy to contribute, the able-bodied to enlist; in a

[3] Charles R. Kennedy, *The Olynthiac and Other Public Orations of Demosthenes* (London: George Bell and Sons, 1903), pp. 62–7, 117–8, 124, 126–7.

word, plainly, if you will become your own masters, and cease each expecting to do nothing himself, while his neighbour does everything for him, you shall then with heaven's permission recover your own, and get back what has been frittered away, and chastise Philip. Do not imagine, that his empire is everlastingly secured to him as a god. There are those who hate and fear and envy him, Athenians, even among those that seem most friendly; and all feelings that are in other men belong, we may assume, to his confederates. But now they are cowed, having no refuge through your tardiness and indolence, which I say you must abandon forthwith. For you see, Athenians, the case, to what pitch of arrogance the man has advanced, who leaves you not even the choice of action or inaction, but threatens and uses (they say) outrageous language, and, unable to rest in possession of his conquests, continually widens their circle, and whilst we dally and delay, throws his net all around us. When then, Athenians, when will ye act as becomes you? In what event? In that of necessity, I suppose. And how should we regard the events happening now? Methinks, to freemen the strongest necessity is the disgrace of their condition. Or tell me, do ye like walking about and asking one another:—is there any news? Why, could there be greater news than a man of Macedonia subduing Athenians, and directing the affairs of Greece? Is Philip dead? No, but he is sick. And what matters it to you? Should anything befall this man, you will soon create another Philip, if you attend to business thus. For even he has been exalted not so much by his own strength, as by our negligence. And again; should anything happen to him; should fortune, which still takes better care of us than we of ourselves, be good enough to accomplish this; observe that, being on the spot, you would step in while things were in confusion, and manage them as you pleased; but as you now are, though occasion offered Amphipolis, you would not be in a position to accept it, with neither forces nor counsels at hand.

However, as to the importance of a general zeal in the discharge of duty, believing you are convinced and satisfied, I say no more.

As to the kind of force which I think may extricate you from your difficulties, the amount, the supplies of money, the best and speediest method (in my judgment) of providing all the necessaries, I shall endeavor to inform you forthwith, making only one request, men of Athens. When you have heard all, determine; prejudge not before. And let none think I delay our operations, because I recommend an entirely new force. Not those that cry, quickly! today! speak most to the purpose; (for what has already happened we shall not be able to prevent by our present armament); but he that shows what and how great and whence procured must be the force capable of enduring till either we have advisedly terminated the war, or overcome our enemies; for so shall we escape annoyance in future. This I think I am able to show, without offence to any other man who has a plan to offer. My promise indeed is large; it shall be tested by the performance; and you shall be my judges.

First, then, Athenians, I say we must provide fifty warships, and hold ourselves prepared, in case of emergency, to embark and sail. I require also an equipment of transports for half the cavalry and sufficient boats. This we must have ready against his sudden marches from his own country to Thermopylae, the Chersonese, Olynthus, and anywhere he likes. For he should entertain the belief, that possibly you may rouse from this over-carelessness, and start off, as you did to Euboea, and formerly (they say) to Haliartus, and very lately to Thermopylae. And although you should not pursue just the course I would advise, it is no slight matter, that Philip, knowing you to be in readiness—know it he will for certain; there are too many among our own people who report everything to him—may either keep quiet from apprehension, or, not heeding your arrangements, be taken off his guard, there being nothing to prevent your sailing, if he give you a chance, to attack the territories. Such an armament, I say, ought instantly to be agreed upon and provided. But besides, men of Athens, you should keep in hand some force, that will incessantly make war and annoy him: none of your ten or twenty thousand mercenaries, not your forces on paper, but one that shall belong to the state, and, whether you appoint one or more generals, or this or that man or any other, shall obey and follow him. Subsistence too I require for it. What the force shall be, how large, from what source maintained, how rendered efficient, I will show you, stating every particular. Mercenaries I recommend—and beware of doing what has often been injurious—thinking all measures below the occasion, adopting the strongest in your decrees, you fail to accomplish the least—rather, I say, perform and procure a little, add to it afterwards, if it prove insufficient. I advise then two thousand soldiers in all, five hundred to be Athenians, of whatever age you think right, serving a limited time, not long, but such time as you think right, so as to relieve one another: the rest should be mercenaries. And with them two hundred horse, fifty at least Athenians, like the foot, on the same terms of service; and transports for them. Well; what besides? Ten swift galleys: for, as Philip has a navy, we must have swift galleys also, to convoy our power. How shall subsistence for these troops be provided? I will state and explain; but first let me tell you, why I consider a force of this amount sufficient, and why I wish the men to be citizens.

Of that amount, Athenians, because it is impossible for us now to raise an army capable of meeting him in the field: we must plunder and adopt such kind of warfare at first: our force, therefore, must not be over-large (for there is not pay or subsistence) nor altogether mean. Citizens I wish to attend and go on board, because I hear that formerly the state maintained mercenary troops at Corinth, commanded by Polystratus and Iphicrates and Chabrias and some others, and that you served with them yourselves; and I am told, that these mercenaries fighting by your side and you by theirs defeated the Lacedaemonians. But ever since your hirelings have served by themselves, they have been vanquishing your friends and allies, while your enemies have become unduly great. Just glancing at the war of our state, they go off to Artabazus, or anywhere rather, and the general follows, naturally; for it is impossible to command without giving pay. What therefore ask I? To remove the excuses both of general and soldiers, by supplying pay, and attaching native soldiers, as inspectors of the general's conduct. The way we manage things now is a mockery. For if you were asked: Are you at peace, Athenians? No, indeed, you would say; we are at war with Philip. Did you not choose from yourselves ten captains and generals, and also captains and two generals of horse? How are they employed? Except one man, whom you commission on service abroad, the rest conduct your processions with the sacrificers. Like puppet-makers, you elect your infantry and cavalry officers for the market-place, not for war. Consider, Athenians; should there not be native captains, a native general of horse, your own commanders, that the force might really be the state's? Or should your general of horse sail to Lemnos, while Menelaus commands the cavalry fighting for your possessions? I speak not as objecting to the man, but he ought to be elected by you, whoever the person be. . . .

B. THE THIRD PHILIPPIC

I will first then examine and determine this point, whether it be in our power to deliberate peace or war. If the country may be at peace, if it depends on us, (to begin with this) I say we ought to maintain peace, and I call upon the affirmant to move a resolution, to take some measure, and not to palter with us. But if another, having arms in his hand and a large force around him, amuses you with the name of peace, while he carries on the operations of war, what is left but to defend yourselves? You may profess to be at peace, if you like, as he does; I quarrel not with that. But if any man supposes this to be a peace, which will enable Philip to master all else and attack you last, he is a madman, or he talks of a peace observed towards him by you, not towards you by him. This it is that Philip purchases by all his expenditure, the privilege of assailing you without being assailed in turn.

If we really wait until he avows that he is at war with us, we are the simplest of mortals: for he would not declare that, though he marched even against Attica and Piraeus, at least if we may judge from his conduct to others. For example, to the Olynthians he declared, when he was forty furlongs from their city, that there was no alternative, but either they must quit Olynthus or he Macedonia; though before that time, whenever he was accused of such an intent, he took it ill and sent ambassadors to justify himself. Again, he marched towards the Phocians as if they were allies, and there were Phocian envoys who accompanied his march, and many among you contended that his advance would not benefit the Thebans. And he came into Thessaly of late as a friend and ally, yet he has taken possession of Pherae: and lastly he told these wretched people of Oreus, that he had sent his soldiers out of good-will to visit them, as he heard they were in trouble and dissension, and it was the part of allies and true friends to lend assistance on such occasions. People who would never have harmed him, though they might have adopted measures of defence, he chose to deceive rather than warn them of his attack; and think ye he would declare war against you before he began it and that while you are willing to be deceived? Impossible. He would be the silliest of mankind, if, whilst you the injured parties make no complaint against him, but are accusing your own countrymen, he should terminate your intestine strife and jealousies, warn you to turn against him, and remove the pretexts of his hirelings for asserting, to amuse you, that he makes no war upon Athens. O heavens! would any rational being judge by words rather than by actions, who is at peace with him and who at war? Surely none. . . .

[Demosthenes then discusses Philip's treacherous attacks on several Greek cities.]

But what has caused the mischief? There must be some cause, some good reason, why the Greeks were so eager for liberty then, and now are eager for servitude. There was something, men of Athens, something in the hearts of the multitude then, which there is not now, which overcame the wealth of Persia and maintained the freedom of Greece, and quailed not under any battle by land or sea; the loss whereof has ruined all, and thrown the affairs of Greece into confusion. What was this? Nothing subtle or clever: simply that whoever took money from the aspirants for power or the corruptors of Greece were universally detested: it was dreadful to be convicted of bribery; the severest punishment was inflicted on the guilty, and there was no intercession or pardon. The favourable moments for enterprise, which fortune frequently offers to the careless against the vigilant, to them that will do nothing against those that discharge all their duty, could not be bought from orators or generals; no more could mutual concord, nor distrust of tyrants and barbarians, nor anything of the kind. But now all such principles have been sold as in open market, and those imported in exchange, by which Greece is ruined and diseased. What are they? Envy where a man gets a bribe; laughter if he confesses it; mercy to the convicted; hatred of those that denounce the crime: all the usual attendants upon corruption. For as to ships and men and revenues and abundance of other materials, all that may be reckoned as constituting national strength—assuredly the Greeks of our day are more fully and perfectly supplied with such advantages than Greeks of the olden time. But they are all rendered useless, unavailable, unprofitable, by the agency of these traffickers. . . .

There is a foolish saying of persons who wish to make us easy, that Philip is not yet as powerful as the Lacedaemonians were formerly, who ruled everywhere by land and sea, and had the king for their ally, and nothing withstood them; yet Athens resisted even that nation, and was not destroyed. I myself believe, that, while everything has received great improvement, and the present bears no resemblance to the past, nothing has been so changed and improved as the practice of war. For anciently, as I am informed, the Lacedaemonians and all Grecian people would for four or five months, during the season only, invade and ravage the land of their enemies with heavy-armed and national troops, and return home again: and their ideas were so old-fashioned, or rather national, they never purchased an advantage from any; theirs was a legitimate and open warfare. But now you doubtless perceive, that the majority of disasters have been effected by treason; nothing is done in fair field or combat. You hear of Philip marching where he pleases, not because he commands troops of the line, but because he has attached to him a host of skirmishers, cavalry, archers, mercenaries, and the like. When with these he falls upon a people in civil dissension, and none (for mistrust) will march out to defend the country, he applies engines and besieges them. I need not mention, that he makes no difference between winter and summer, that he has no stated season of repose. You, knowing these things, reflecting on them, must not let the war approach your territories, nor get your necks broken, relying on the simplicity of the old war with the Lacedaemonians, but take the longest time beforehand for defensive measures and preparations, see that he stirs not from home, avoid any decisive engagement. For a war, if we choose, men of Athens, to pursue a right course, we have many natural advantages; such as the position of his kingdom, which we may extensively plunder and ravage, and a thousand more, but for a battle he is better trained than we are. . . .

50 / KING PHILIP'S COMMON PEACE

After his victory at Chaeronea over Athens and Thebes (338 B.C.) Philip II concluded a peace treaty with the Greek states at a congress of Corinth. The terms of the treaty are reflected in an Athenian inscription containing the oath to be sworn by representatives of the city-states participating in the "common peace" and a (mutilated) list of these states. According to the peace terms, states participating were forbidden to wage war upon each other and to change their constitutions. Philip wished by the pacification of Greece to obtain Greek manpower for his war against Persia. He was to be the military leader of the participating states, and they were to be represented in accordance with their military contributions on a Common Council. There is controversy among scholars as to whether the inscription records merely the peace treaty or whether it also refers to an alliance, the "Corinthian League." There is no mention in the inscription of the fact that Philip assured the maintenance of peace in Greece by establishing Macedonian garrisons at Thebes, Ambracia, Chalcis, and Corinth. Sparta refused to accept the peace terms. The principle that the number of votes held by each city in the Common Council was proportionate to its military contribution distinguished the Corinthian League from the earlier Athenian alliances, in which each state had had one vote.[4]

OATH

I swear by Zeus, Earth, Sun, Poseidon, Athena, Ares and all the gods and goddesses: I will abide by the peace and will not invalidate the treaty made with Philip the Macedonian, and I will not bear arms for the purpose of injury against any of those that abide by the oaths, either by land or by sea. I will not seize for the purpose of war a city or fort (or place) or harbor belonging to any of those that share in the peace, by any art or device whatever. I will not overthrow the kingship of Philip and his descendants or the governments existing

[4] G. W. Botsford and E. G. Sihler, *Hellenic Civilization* (New York: Columbia University Press, 1915), p. 420 ff., revised after M. N. Tod, *A Selection of Greek Historical Inscriptions,* Vol. II (Oxford: Clarendon Press, 1948), No. 177, pp. 224–5). Reprinted by permission of Columbia University Press.

in the respective states at the time when they swore the oaths regarding the peace. I will do nothing contrary to this treaty either in person or by allowing another, in so far as I can prevent; and if any one shall commit any violation of the agreement, I will give aid to those who need it at the time, according as they may demand. I will wage war upon him who violates the common peace, according to the decision of the Common Council and the orders of the Leader. And I will not desert. . . .

[There follows a badly mutilated list of Greek states participating in the "common peace." Each name is followed by a numeral indicating the number of votes held in the Common Council by each member of the Corinthian League. This number varies from one to ten and is proportionate to the strength of military and naval contingents on which Philip is entitled to call.]

51 / PLATO'S THEORY OF FORMS

The fourth century B.C. *is the age of Plato of Athens (429–347). The principal formative influence on Plato's philosophy was Socrates (No. 36), and Plato in turn had a decisive impact on all later philosophy. After Socrates' execution (399* B.C.*) Plato left Athens in despair. About 385 he returned and began to teach at Athens near the grove of the hero Academus. His school, the Academy, attracted some of the foremost mathematicians and scientists of the age. One of Plato's purposes in founding the Academy was to train the political leaders of Athens. Plato also demonstrated his concern for practical politics by three visits to Syracuse, where he tried unsuccessfully to establish a regime compatible with his political philosophy. In his dialogues Plato is generally concerned with virtue or with particular virtues (courage, justice, temperance, etc.). For Plato human virtue is a kind of knowledge, and the discussion therefore normally centers on a characterization of knowledge and its objects. True knowledge, as distinguished from mere opinion, must be the same at all times—must exist independent of the particular circumstances of the knowing individual. Consequently the true and real objects of knowledge are forms or ideas, called* eidē *by Plato, as* *opposed to particular objects in the natural world. Such forms, according to Platonic "idealism," exist independent of human minds. Natural objects are named courageous, just, beautiful, etc., after such ideal qualities because they are their copies or participate in them. Plato exposits his Theory of Forms in many of his dialogues and with ever new imagery. The following excerpt is taken from the* Symposium.

The Symposium *focuses on love. Several speeches praise the power of Love, but the climactic speech is assigned, as usual, to Socrates. Yet Socrates does not offer as his own his remarks concerning Love. He claims that as a young man he had heard its praise sung by an inspired prophetess, Diotima of Mantineia, who saw the nature of Love as the love of wisdom* (philosophia). *Love of wisdom, according to Diotima, was the love for the Platonic forms.*[5]

"Into these love-matters even you, Socrates, might haply be initiated; but I doubt if you could approach the rites and revelations to which these, for the properly instructed, are merely the avenue. However I will speak of them," she said, "and will not stint my best endeavours; only you on your part must try your best to follow. He who would proceed rightly in this business must not merely begin from his youth to encounter beautiful bodies. In the first place, indeed, if his conductor guides him aright, he must be in love with one particular body, and engender beautiful converse therein; but next he must remark how the beauty attached to this or that body is cognate to that which is attached to any other, and that if he means to ensue beauty in form, it is gross folly not to regard as one and the same the beauty belonging to all; and so, having grasped this truth, he must make himself a lover of all beautiful bodies, and slacken the stress of his feeling for one by contemning it and counting it a trifle. But his next advance will be to set a higher value on the beauty of souls than on that of the body, so that however little the grace that may bloom in any likely soul it shall suffice him for loving and caring, and for bringing forth and soliciting such converse as will tend to the betterment of the young; and that finally he may be constrained to contemplate the beautiful as appearing in our observances and our laws, and to

[5] Reprinted by permission of the publishers from the Loeb Classical Library translated by W. R. M. Lamb, *Plato,* Volume V, *Lysis, Symposium, Gorgias* (Cambridge, Mass.: Harvard University Press; London: William Heinemann Ltd., 1939), pp. 201–9.

behold it all bound together in kinship and so estimate the body's beauty as a slight affair. From observances he should be led on to the branches of knowledge, that there also he may behold a province of beauty, and by looking thus on beauty in the mass may escape from the mean, meticulous slavery of a single instance, where he must centre all his care, like a lackey, upon the beauty of a particular child or man or single observance; and turning rather towards the main ocean of the beautiful may by contemplation of this bring forth in all their splendour many fair fruits of discourse and meditation in a plenteous crop of philosophy; until with the strength and increase there acquired he desires a certain single knowledge connected with a beauty which has yet to be told. And here, I pray you," said she, "give me the very best of your attention.

"When a man has been thus far tutored in the lore of love, passing from view to view of beautiful things, in the right and regular ascent, suddenly he will have revealed to him, as he draws to the close of his dealings in love, a wondrous vision, beautiful in its nature; and this, Socrates, is the final object of all those previous toils. First of all, it is ever-existent and neither comes to be nor perishes, neither waxes nor wanes; next, it is not beautiful in part and in part ugly, nor is it such at such a time and other at another, nor in one respect beautiful and in another ugly, nor so affected by position as to seem beautiful to some and ugly to others. Nor again will our initiate find the beautiful presented to him in the guise of a face or of hands or any other portion of the body, nor as a particular description or piece of knowledge, nor as existing somewhere in another substance, such as an animal or the earth or sky or any other thing; but existing ever in singularity of form independent by itself, while all the multitude of beautiful things partake of it in such wise that, though all of them are coming to be and perishing, it grows neither greater nor less, and is affected by no thing. So when a man by the right method of boy-loving ascends from these particulars and begins to descry that beauty, he is almost able to lay hold of the final secret. Such is the right approach or induction to love-matters. Beginning from obvious beauties he must for the sake of that highest beauty be ever climbing aloft, as on the rungs of a ladder, from one to two, and from two to all beautiful bodies; from personal beauty he proceeds to beautiful observances, from observance to beautiful learning, and from learning at last to that particular study which is concerned with the beautiful itself and that alone; so that in the end he comes to know the very essence of beauty. In that state of life above all others, my dear Socrates," said the Mantinean woman, "a man finds it truly worth while to live, as he contemplates essential beauty. This, when once beheld, will outshine your gold and your vesture, your beautiful boys and striplings, whose aspect now so astounds you and makes you and many another, at the sight and constant society of your darlings, ready to do without either food or drink if that were any way possible, and only gaze upon them and have their company. But tell me, what would happen if one of you had the fortune to look upon essential beauty entire, pure and unalloyed; not infected with the flesh and colour of humanity, and ever so much more of mortal trash? What if he could behold the divine beauty itself, in its unique form? Do you call it a pitiful life for a man to lead—looking that way, observing that vision by the proper means, and having it ever with him? Do but consider," she said, "that there only will it befall him, as he sees the beautiful through that which makes it visible, to breed not illusions but true examples of virtue, since his contact is not with illusion but with truth. So when he has begotten a true virtue and has reared it up he is destined to win the friendship of Heaven; he, above all men, is immortal."

52 / ARISTOTLE'S CRITICISM OF THE PLATONIC THEORY OF FORMS

Aristotle (384–322 B.C.), a native of Stagirus in Chalcidice, joined Plato's Academy in 348–347 B.C. Though an ardent admirer of Plato throughout his life, Aristotle at an early stage began to think independently and to criticize the theories of his master. The following excerpt is taken from Aristotle's Nicomachean Ethics. *Here Aristotle is concerned with Plato's notion of forms or ideas and especially with the highest form of all, which played a large role in Plato's thought—the Form of the Good. Like Plato he believes in the forms. Unlike Plato, however, he is of the opinion that a form does not exist apart from natural objects, but represents an element of likeness or analogy in the objects named after a particular form.*[6]

[6] F. H. Peters, *The Nicomachean Ethics of Aristotle,* 15th ed. (London: Kegan Paul, Trench, Trubner and Co., Ltd., n.d.), pp. 8–12.

Dismissing these views, then, we have now to consider the "universal good," and to state the difficulties which it presents; though such an inquiry is not a pleasant task in view of our friendship for the authors of the doctrine of ideas [Plato]. But we venture to think that this is the right course, and that in the interests of truth we ought to sacrifice even what is nearest to us, especially as we call ourselves philosophers. Both are dear to us, but it is a sacred duty to give the preference to truth. . . .

It is evident that there will thus be two classes of goods: one good in themselves, the other good as means to the former. Let us separate then from the things that are merely useful those that are good in themselves, and inquire if they are called good by reference to one common idea or type.

Now what kind of things would one call "good in themselves"? Surely those things that we pursue even apart from their consequences, such as wisdom and sight and certain pleasures and certain honours; for although we sometimes pursue these things as means, no one could refuse to rank them among the things that are good in themselves.

If these be excluded, nothing is good in itself except the idea; and then the type or form will be meaningless.

If however, these are ranked among the things that are good in themselves, then it must be shown that the goodness of all of them can be defined in the same terms, as white has the same meaning when applied to snow and to white lead.

But, in fact, we have to give a separate and different account of the goodness of honour and wisdom and pleasure.

Good, then, is not a term that is applied to all these things alike in the same sense or with reference to one common idea or form.

But how then do these things come to be called good? for they do not appear to have received the same name merely by chance. Perhaps it is because they all proceed from one source, or all conduce to one end; or perhaps it is rather in virtue of some analogy, just as we call the reason the eye of the soul because it bears the same relation to the soul that the eye does to the body, and so on.

But we may dismiss these questions at present; for to discuss them in detail belongs more properly to another branch of philosophy.

And for the same reason we may dismiss the further consideration of the idea; for even granting that this term "good," which is applied to all these different things, has one and the same meaning throughout, or that there is an absolute good apart from these particulars, it is evident that this good will not be anything that man can realize or attain: but it is a good of this kind that we are now seeking.

It might, perhaps, be thought that it would nevertheless be well to make ourselves acquainted with this universal good, with a view to the goods that are attainable and realizable. With this for a pattern, it may be said, we shall more readily discern our own good, and discerning achieve it.

There certainly is some plausibility in this argument, but it seems to be at variance with the existing sciences; for though they are all aiming at some good and striving to make up their deficiencies, they neglect to inquire about this universal good. And yet it is scarce likely that the professors of the several arts and sciences should not know, nor even look for, what would help them so much.

And indeed I am at a loss to know how the weaver or the carpenter would be furthered in his art by a knowledge of his absolute good, or how a man would be rendered more able to heal the sick or to command an army by contemplation of the pure form or idea. For it seems to me that the physician does not even seek for health in this abstract way, but seeks for the health of man, or rather of some particular man, for it is individuals that he has to heal.

53 / ALEXANDER THE GREAT

At the age of twenty, in 366 B.C., Alexander of Macedon succeeded his father, Philip II. The most reliable surviving history of his expedition into Asia was written in the second century A.D. by Arrian of Nicomedia. While this author lived half a millennium after the events which he recorded, he had at his disposal Ptolemy's history of Alexander, and Ptolemy in turn had access to the official journal of Alexander's reign.

In 336 the Corinthian League (No. 50) elected Alexander its leader in his father's place for the projected campaign against Persia. In 334 Alexander crossed the Hellespont. He defeated Persian armies at the river Granicus, at Issus and at Gaugamela. Alexander conquered the Persian Empire and advanced eastward as far as the river Hyphasis, the modern Beas, a tributary of the Indus. He intended to march further east, to the Ganges and beyond, but the army mutinied and he was forced to abandon these plans. He returned to Mesopotamia after incredible hardships and arrived at Susa in 324 B.C. At the time of his death (323 B.C.) he was preparing a new expedition to circumnavigate Arabia.

After Alexander's return he faced dissension among his Macedonian troops following his decision to send his disabled veterans back to the homeland. This was misinterpreted by the Macedonian soldiers to mean that Alexander wished to rely henceforth on Persians rather than Macedonians. Alexander's speech delivered on this occasion, is interesting because he reviews the remarkable rise of Macedon from an underdeveloped country to an imperial power. The prayer recited by Alexander at the banquet of reconciliation reveals his ultimate objective: harmony and community of rule between Macedonians and Persians.[7]

When he [Alexander] arrived at Opis, he collected the Macedonians and announced that he intended to discharge from the army those who were useless for military service either from age or from being maimed in the limbs; and he said he would send them back to their own abodes. He also promised to give those who went back as much as would make them special objects of envy to those at home and arouse in the other Macedonians the wish to share similar dangers and labours. Alexander said this, no doubt, for the purpose of pleasing the Macedonians; but on the contrary they were, not without reason, offended by the speech which he delivered, thinking that now they were despised by him and deemed to be quite useless for military service. Indeed, throughout the whole of this expedition they had been offended at many other things; for his adoption of the Persian dress, thereby exhibiting his contempt for their opinion, caused them grief, as did also his accoutring the foreign soldiers called Epigoni in the Macedonian style, and the mixing of the alien horsemen among the ranks of the Companions. Therefore they could not remain silent and control themselves, but urged him to dismiss all of them from his army; and they advised him to prosecute the war in company with his father, deriding Ammon by this remark. When Alexander heard this (for at that time he was more hasty in temper than heretofore, and no longer, as of old, indulgent to the Macedonians from having a retinue of foreign attendants), leaping down from the platform with his officers around him, he ordered the most conspicuous of the men who had tried to stir up the multitude to sedition to be arrested. He himself pointed out with his hand to the shield-bearing guards those whom they were to arrest, to the number of thirteen; and he ordered these to be led away to execution. When the rest, stricken with terror, became silent, he mounted the platform and spoke as follows:—

[7] E. J. Chinnock, *The Anabasis of Alexander, etc.* (London: Hodder and Stoughton, 1884), pp. 381–90.

"The speech which I am about to deliver will not be for the purpose of checking your start homeward, for, so far as I am concerned, you may depart wherever you wish; but because I wish you to know what kind of men you were originally and how you have been transformed since you came into our service. In the first place, as is reasonable, I shall begin my speech from my father Philip. For he found you vagabonds and destitute of means, most of you clad in hides, feeding a few sheep up the mountain sides, for the protection of which you had to fight with small success against Illyrians, Triballians, and the border Thracians. Instead of the hides he gave you cloaks to wear, and from the mountains he led you down into the plains, and made you capable of fighting the neighbouring barbarians, so that you were no longer compelled to preserve yourselves by trusting rather to the inaccessible strongholds than to your own valour. He made you colonists of cities, which he adorned with useful laws and customs; and from being slaves and subjects, he made you rulers over those very barbarians by whom you yourselves, as well as your property, were previously liable to be plundered and ravaged. He also added the greater part of Thrace to Macedonia, and by seizing the most conveniently situated places on the sea-coast, he spread abundance over the land from commerce, and made the working of the mines a secure employment. He made you rulers over the Thessalians, of whom you had formerly been in mortal fear; and by humbling the nation of the Phòcians, he rendered the avenue into Greece broad and easy for you, instead of being narrow and difficult. The Athenians and Thebans, who were always lying in wait to attack Macedonia, he humbled to such a degree—I also then rendering him my personal aid in the campaign—that instead of paying tribute to the former and being vassals to the latter, those States in their turn procure security to themselves by our assistance. He penetrated into the Peloponnese, and after regulating its affairs, was publicly declared commander-in-chief of all the rest of Greece in the expedition against the Persian, adding this glory not more to himself than to the commonwealth of the Macedonians. These were the advantages which accrued to you from my father Philip; great indeed if looked at by themselves, but small if compared with those you have obtained from me. For though I inherited from my father only a few gold and silver goblets, and there were not even sixty talents in the treasury, and though I found myself charged with a debt of 500 talents owing by Philip, and I was obliged myself to borrow 800 talents in addition to these, I started from the country which could not decently support you, and forthwith laid open to you the passage of the Hellespont, though at that time the Persians held the sovereignty of the sea. Having overpowered the viceroys of Darius with my cavalry, I added to your empire the whole of Ionia, the whole of Aeolis, both Phrygias and Lydia, and I took Miletus by siege. All the other places I gained by voluntary surrender, and I granted you the privilege of appropriating the wealth found in them. The riches of Egypt and Cyrene, which I acquired without fighting a battle, have come to you. Coele-Syria, Palestine, and Mesopotamia are your property. Babylon, Bactra and Susa are yours. The wealth of the Lydians, the treasures of the Persians, and the riches of the Indians are yours; and so is the External Sea. You are viceroys, you are generals, you are captains. What then have I reserved to myself after all these labours, except this purple robe and this diadem? I have appropriated nothing myself, nor can any one point out my treasures, except these possessions of yours or the things which I am guarding on your behalf. Individually, however, I have no motive to guard them, since I feed on the same fare as you do, and I take only the same amount of sleep. Nay, I do not think that my fare is as good as that of those among you who live luxuriously; and I know that I often sit up at night to watch for you, that you may be able to sleep.

"But some one may say, that while you endured toil and fatigue, I have acquired these things as your leader without myself sharing the toil and fatigue. But who is there of you who knows that he has endured greater toil for me than I have for him? Come now! whoever of you has wounds, let him strip and show them, and I will show mine in turn; for there is no part of my body, in front at any rate, remaining free from wounds; nor is there any kind of weapon used either for close combat or for hurling at the enemy, the traces of which I do not bear on my person. For I have been wounded with the sword in close fight, I have been shot with arrows, and I have been struck with missiles projected from engines of war; and though oftentimes I have been hit with stones and bolts of wood for the sake of your lives, your glory, and your wealth, I am still leading you as conquerors over all the land and sea, all rivers, mountains and plains. I have celebrated your wedding with my own, and the children of many of you will be akin to my children. Moreover I have liquidated the debts of all those who had incurred them, without inquiring too closely for what purpose they were contracted, though you receive such high pay, and carry off so much booty whenever there is booty to be got after a siege. Most of you have golden crowns, the eternal memorials of your valor and of the honor you receive from me. Whoever has been killed, has met with a glorious end and has been honoured with a splendid burial. Brazen statues of most of the slain have been erected at home, and their parents are held in honour, being released from all public service and from taxation. But no one of you has ever been killed in flight under my leadership. And now I was intending to send back those of you who are unfit for service, objects of envy to those at home; but since you all wish to depart, depart all of you! Go back and report at home that your king Alexander, the conqueror of the Persians, Medes, Bactrians, and Sacians; the man who has subjugated the Uxians, Arachotians, and Drangians; who has also acquired the rule of the Parthians, Chorasmians, and Hyrcanians, as far as the Caspian Sea; who has marched over the Caucasus, through the Caspian Gates; who has crossed the rivers Oxus and Tanais, and the Indus besides, which has never been crossed by any one else except Dionysus; who has also crossed the Hydaspes, Acesines, and Hydraotes, and who would have crossed the Hyphasis, if you had not shrunk back with alarm; who has penetrated into the Great Sea by both the mouths of the Indus; who has marched through the desert of Gadrosia, where no one ever marched before with an army; who on his route acquired possession of Carmania and the land of the Oritians, in addition to his other conquests, his fleet having in the meantime already sailed round the coast of the sea which extends from India to Persia—report that when you returned to Susa you deserted him and went away, handing him over to the protection of conquered foreigners. Perhaps this report of yours will be both glorious to you in the eyes of men and devout forsooth in the eyes of the gods. Depart!"

Having thus spoken, he leaped down quickly from the platform, and entered the palace, where he paid no attention to the decoration of his person, nor was any of his Companions admitted to see him. Not even on the morrow was any one of them admitted to an audience; but on the third day he summoned the select Persians within, and among them he distributed the commands of the brigades, and made the rule that only those whom he had proclaimed his kinsmen, should have the honour of saluting him with a kiss. But the Macedonians who heard the speech were thoroughly astonished at the moment, and remained there in silence near the platform; nor when he retired did any of them accompany the king, except his personal Companions and the confidential body-guards. Though they remained, most of them had nothing to do or say; and yet they were unwilling to retire. But when the news was reported to them about the Persians and Medes, that the military commands were being given to Persians, that the foreign soldiers were being selected and divided into companies, that a Persian footguard, Persian foot Companions, a Persian regiment of men with silver shields, as well as the cavalry Companions, and another royal regiment of cavalry distinct from these, were being called Macedonian names, they were no longer able to restrain themselves; but running in a body to the palace, they cast their weapons there in front of the gates as a sign of supplication to the king. Standing in front of the gates, they shouted, beseeching to be allowed to enter, and saying that they were willing to surrender the men who had been the instigators of the disturbance on that occasion, and those who had begun the clamour. They also declared they would not retire from the gates either day or night, unless Alexander would take some pity upon them. When he was informed of this, he came out without delay; and seeing them lying on the ground in humble guise, and hearing most of them lamenting with loud voice, tears began to flow also from his own eyes. He made an effort to say something to them, but they continued their importunate entreaties. At length one of them, Callines by name, a man conspicuous both for his age and because he was captain of the Companion cavalry, spoke as follows:—"O king, what grieves the Macedonians is, that thou hast already made some of the Persians kinsmen to thyself, and that Persians are called Alexander's kinsmen, and have the honour of saluting thee with a kiss; whereas none of the Macedonians have as yet enjoyed this honour." Then Alexander, interrupting him, said:—"But all of you without exception I consider my kinsmen, and so from this time I shall call you." When he had said this, Callines advanced and saluted him with a kiss, and so did all those who wished to salute him. Then they took up their weapons and returned to the camp, shouting and singing a song of thanksgiving to Apollo. After this Alexander offered sacrifice to the gods to whom it was his custom to sacrifice, and gave a public banquet, over which he himself presided, with the Macedonians sitting around him; and next to them the Persians; after whom came the men of other nations, honoured for their personal rank or for some meritorious action. The king and his guests drew wine from the same bowl and poured out the same libations, both the Grecian prophets and the Magians commencing the ceremony. He prayed for other blessings, and especially that harmony and community of rule might exist between the Macedonians and Persians. The common account is, that those who took part in this banquet were 9,000 in number, that all of them poured out one libation, and after it sang a song of thanksgiving to Apollo.

54 / THE PTOLEMAIC MONOPOLY ON OIL

In the Hellenistic Age the wealth of the Ptolemaic dynasty rested on the prosperity of Egypt. All land belonged to the king, and large sectors of the economy were administered as royal monopolies: oil, papyrus, mines, quarries, saltworks, natron pits, textiles, banking. Oil, the perfect monopoly, was made by serfs in royal factories from sesame, croton (castor-oil plant), and cnecus and colocynth (gourd seeds). Production, processing (including the workers), distribution (including the retailers), and imports were closely supervised by a large bureaucracy headed by the dioecetes (minister of finance). The administration of the oil monopoly is known from an elaborate papyrus dating from 259 B.C. *which contains administrative regulations concerning this product.*

Papyrus, the normal writing material of the ancient world, was made from the stem of a plant growing in the Nile. While in most parts of the ancient world papyrus texts were lost, in Egypt they were often preserved due to the dry climate.[8]

Year 27, Loius 10. Corrected in the office of Apollonius the dioecetes.

[The persons authorized shall buy the produce from the cultivators at the following rates:] for each artaba of sesame containing thirty choenices, prepared for grinding, 8 drachmae, for each artaba of croton containing thirty choenices, prepared for grinding, 4 drachmae, for each artaba of cnecus, prepared for grinding, 1 drachma 2 obols, for each artaba of colocynth 4 obols, of linseed 3 obols. . . .

They [buyers] shall sell the oil in the country at the rate of 48 drachmae in copper for a metretes of sesame oil or cnecus oil containing 12 choes, and at the rate of 30 drachmae for a metretes of castor oil, colocynth oil, or lamp oil. . . .

In Alexandria and the whole of Libya they shall sell it at the rate of 48 drachmae for a metretes of sesame oil and 48 drachmae for a metretes of castor oil. . . . And they shall provide an amount sufficient for the demands of purchasers, selling it throughout the country in all the cities and towns by . . . measures which have been tested by the oeconomus and the controller.

They shall exhibit the land sown to the director of the contract with the oeconomus and the controller, and if after measuring it they find that the right number of arurae has not been sown, the nomarch and the toparch and the oeconomus and the controller shall, each who is responsible, forfeit to the Crown 2 talents, and to the holders of the contract for each artaba of sesame which they ought to have received 2 drachmae, and for each artaba of croton 1 drachma, together with

[8] Reprinted by permission of the publishers from the Loeb Classical Library, translated by C. C. Edgar and A. S. Hunt, *Select Papyri,* Volume II (Cambridge, Mass.: Harvard University Press; London: William Heinemann Ltd., 1934), pp. 11–31.

the profit which would have been made on the sesame oil and the castor oil. The dioecetes shall exact the payment from them. . . .

They shall not allow the oil-makers appointed in each nome to migrate to another nome. Any oilmaker who goes elsewhere shall be subject to arrest by the director of the contract and the oeconomus and the controller. . . .

The contractors and the checking clerk appointed by the oeconomus and controller shall have authority over all the oil-makers in the nome and over the factories and the plant, and shall seal up the implements during the time when there is no work.

They shall compel the oil-makers to work every day and shall stay beside them, and they shall each day make into oil not less than 1 artaba of sesame at each mortar, and 4 artabae of croton, and 1 of cnecus, and they shall pay as wages for crushing 4 artabae of sesame . . . drachmae, and for . . . artabae of croton 4 drachmae, and for . . . artabae of cnecus 8 drachmae. . . .

The agent appointed by the oeconomus and the controller shall register the names of the dealers in each city and of the retailers, and together with the managers of the contract arrange with them how much oil and castor oil they are to take and sell from day to day; and in Alexandria they shall arrange with the traders; and they shall make a written agreement with each of them, with those in the country every month, with those in Alexandria . . .

Whatever quantity of oil and castor oil the dealers and retailers in each village agree to dispose of, the oeconomus and the controller shall convey the full quantity of each kind to each village before the beginning of the month, and they shall measure it out to dealers and retailers every five days, and shall receive the price, if possible, on the same day, but if not, before the expiry of the five days, and shall pay it into the royal bank, debiting the contract with the cost of transport. . . .

It shall not be lawful to bring [foreign oil] into the interior for sale, either from Alexandria or Pelusium or any other place. Whoever does so shall be deprived of the oil, and shall in addition pay a fine of 100 drachmae for each metretes, and for more or less in proportion.

If any persons carry with them foreign oil for their personal use, those who bring it from Alexandria shall declare it in Alexandria, and shall pay down 12 drachmae for each metretes and for more or less in proportion, and shall obtain a voucher before they bring it inland.

Those who bring it from Pelusium shall pay the tax in Pelusium and obtain a voucher.

The collectors in Alexandria and Pelusium shall place the tax to the credit of the nome to which the oil is brought.

If any persons bringing such oil for their personal use fail to pay the tax or to carry with them the voucher, they shall be deprived of the oil, and shall forfeit in addition 100 drachmae for each metretes. All merchants who carry foreign or Syrian oil from Pelusium across the country to Alexandria shall be exempt from the tax, but shall carry a voucher from the collector stationed at Pelusium and the oeconomus, as is prescribed in the law; likewise for oil which is brought from . . . to Alexandria they shall also carry a voucher from the . . . but if they transport it without (?) a voucher, they shall be deprived of oil.

The contractors shall also appoint agents at Alexandria and Pelusium to check the oil which is dispatched from Syria to Pelusium and Alexandria, and these shall keep the store-houses under seal and check the oil as it is issued.

55 / HELLENISTIC ALEXANDRIA

The poet Theocritus was born in Syracuse and spent part of his life in Alexandria under Ptolemy II Philadelphus (308–246 B.C.*). He wrote a number of "idyls" or small poems. The following poem (Idyl XV) was probably composed in 272* B.C. *It describes the gossiping of two bourgeois ladies in Alexandria, the vastness and overcrowding of the city and the luxury of the royal palace. Remarkable, too, is the melting-pot atmosphere which it portrays: a Sicilian poet here describes a day in the lives of two Syracusan women speaking their native Doric dialect in Alexander's city ruled by a Macedonian dynasty and the celebration of a festival in honor of the Syrian god Adonis, at which a woman of Argive descent sings a hymn to the god.*[9]

GORGO

Is Praxinoë at home?

PRAXINOË

Dear Gorgo, how long it is since you have been here! She *is* at home. The wonder is that you have got here at last! Eunoë, see that she has a chair. Throw a cushion on it too.

GORGO

It does most charmingly as it is.

[9] A. Lang, *Theocritus, Bion and Moschus* (London: Macmillan and Co., Ltd., 1909), pp. 76–84.

PRAXINOË

Do sit down.

GORGO

Oh, what a thing spirit is! I have scarcely got to you alive, Praxinoë! What a huge crowd, what hosts of four-in-hands! Everywhere cavalry boots, everywhere men in uniform! And the road is endless: yes, you really live *too* far away!

PRAXINOË

It is all the fault of that madman of mine. Here he came to the ends of the earth and took—a hole, not a house, and all that we might not be neighbours. The jealous wretch, always the same, ever for spite!

GORGO

Don't talk of your husband, Dinon, like that, my dear girl, before the little boy,—look how he is staring at you! Never mind, Zopyrion, sweet child, she is not speaking about papa.

PRAXINOË

Our Lady! the child takes notice.

GORGO

Nice papa!

PRAXINOË

That papa of his the other day—we call every day 'the other day'—went to get soap and rouge at the shop, and back he came to me with salt—the great big endless fellow!

GORGO

Mine has the same trick, too, a perfect spendthrift—Diocleides! Yesterday he got what he meant for five fleeces, and paid seven shillings a piece for—what do you suppose?—dogskins, shreds of old leather wallets, mere trash—trouble on trouble. But come, take your cloak and shawl. Let us be off to the palace of rich Ptolemy, the King, to see the Adonis; I hear the Queen has provided something splendid!

PRAXINOË

Fine folks do everything finely.

GORGO

What a tale you will have to tell about the things you have seen, to any one who has not seen them! It seems nearly time to go.

PRAXINOË

Idlers have always holiday. Eunoë, bring the water and put it down in the middle of the room, lazy creature that you are. Cats like always to sleep soft! Come, bustle, bring the water; quicker. I want water first, and how she carries it! give it me all the same; don't pour out so much, you extravagant thing. Stupid girl! Why are you wetting my dress? There, stop, I have washed my hands, as heaven would have it. Where is the key of the big chest? Bring it here.

GORGO

Praxinoë, that full body becomes you wonderfully. Tell me how much did the stuff cost you just off the loom?

PRAXINOË

Don't speak of it, Gorgo! More than eight pounds in good silver money,—and the work on it! I nearly slaved my soul out over it!

GORGO

Well, it is *most* successful; all you could wish.

PRAXINOË

Thanks for the pretty speech! Bring my shawl, and set my hat on my head, the fashionable way. No, child, I don't mean to take you. Boo! Bogies! There's a horse that bites! Cry as much as you please, but I cannot have you lamed. Let us be moving. Phyrgia, take the child, and keep him amused, call in the dog, and shut the street door.

[They go into the street.]

Ye gods, what a crowd! How on earth are we ever to get through this coil? They are like ants that no one can measure or number. Many a good deed have you done, Ptolemy; since your father joined the immortals, there's never a malefactor to spoil the passer-by, creeping on him in Egyptian fashion—oh! the tricks those perfect rascals used to play. Birds of a feather, ill jesters, scoundrels all! Dear Gorgo, what will become of us? Here come the King's war-horses! My dear man, don't trample on me. Look, the bay's rearing, see, what temper! Eunoë, you foolhardy girl, will you never keep out of the way? The beast will kill the man that's leading him. What a good thing it is for me that my brat stays safe at home.

GORGO

Courage, Praxinoë. We are safe behind them, now, and they have gone to their station.

PRAXINOË

There! I begin to be myself again. Ever since I was a child I have feared nothing so much as horses and the chilly snake. Come along, the huge mob is overflowing us.

GORGO (TO AN OLD WOMAN)

Are you from the Court, mother?

OLD WOMAN

I am, my child.

PRAXINOË

Is it easy to get there?

OLD WOMAN

The Achaeans got into Troy by trying, my prettiest of ladies. Trying will do everything in the long run.

GORGO

The old wife has spoken her oracles, and off she goes.

PRAXINOË

Women know everything, yes, and how Zeus married Hera!

GORGO

See Praxinoë, what a crowd there is about the doors.

PRAXINOË

Monstrous, Gorgo! Give me your hand, and you, Eunoë, catch hold of Eutychis; never lose hold of her, for fear lest you get lost. Let us all go in together; Eunoë, clutch tight to me. Oh, how tiresome, Gorgo, my muslin veil is torn in two already! For heaven's sake, sir, if you ever wish to be fortunate, take care of my shawl!

STRANGER

I can hardly help myself, but for all that I will be as careful as I can.

PRAXINOË

How close-packed the mob is, they hustle like a herd of swine.

STRANGER

Courage, lady, all is well with us now.

PRAXINOË

Both this year and for ever may all be well with you, my dear sir, for your care of us. A good kind man! We're letting Eunoë get squeezed —come, wretched girl, push your way through. That is the way. We are all on the right side of the door, quoth the bridegroom, when he had shut himself in with his bride.

GORGO

Do come here, Praxinoë. Look first at these embroideries. How light and how lovely! You will call them the garments of the gods.

PRAXINOË

Lady Athene, what spinning women wrought them, what painters designed these drawings, so true they are? How naturally they stand and move, like living creatures, not patterns woven. What a clever thing is man! Ah, and himself—Adonis—how beautiful to behold he lies on his silver couch, with the first down on his cheeks, the thrice-beloved Adonis,—Adonis beloved even among the dead.

A STRANGER

You weariful women, do cease your endless cooing talk! They bore one to death with their eternal broad vowels!

GORGO

Indeed! And where may this person come from? What is it to you if we *are* chatterboxes! Give orders to your own servants, sir. Do you pretend to command ladies of Syracuse? If you must know, we are Corinthians by descent, like Bellerophon himself, and we speak Peloponnesian. Dorian women may lawfully speak Doric, I presume?

PRAXINOË

Lady Persephone, never may we have more than one master. I am not afraid of *your* putting me on short commons.

GORGO

Hush, hush, Praxinoë—the Argive woman's daughter, the great singer, is beginning the *Adonis;* she that won the prize last year for dirge-singing. I am sure she will give us something lovely; see, she is preluding with her airs and graces.

[Follows text of Song of Adonis.]

GORGO

Praxinoë, the woman is cleverer than we fancied! Happy woman to know so much, thrice happy to have so sweet a voice. Well, all the same, it is time to be making for home. Diocleides has not had his dinner, and the man is all vinegar,—don't venture near him when he is kept waiting for dinner. Farewell, beloved Adonis, may you find us glad at your next coming!

VII / EARLY ROME

When the city of Rome was founded, great civilizations in the Near East and in Greece had already risen and fallen. In Greece, in particular, the Dorians had destroyed Mycenaean civilization, and in the first three centuries of the first millennium B.C., *in the areas settled by the remnants of the former population and in those occupied by the conquerors, a new Greek civilization was rising which would culminate one day in the classical Athens of the fifth and fourth centuries.*

Within the complex of ancient civilizations there existed a considerable time lag between developments in the Near East and Greece and in the city of Rome. This time lag remained characteristic for Roman history. In many spheres of activity—political life, economic development and social organization, religious attitudes, and especially intellectual achievement—Rome's evolution was slower than that of contemporary Greece. In some areas, however, the Romans eventually surpassed their Greek masters, especially in the fields of imperial organization and law. Roman organization of the conquests in Italy and later outside of Italy, as well as Roman legislation and jurisprudence, were unmatched anywhere in contemporary Greece.

Another major factor in early Roman history is that a state of practically uninterrupted warfare existed from the time of the city's foundation down to the period of Augustus. Furthermore, except perhaps for the period from the middle of the third to the end of the second centuries B.C., *Rome was divided by serious internal conflicts—first the struggle between patricians and plebeians, later the one between* optimates *and* populares. *Delayed development, foreign warfare, and internal conflicts are the key facts of early Roman history.*

56 / THE FOUNDATION OF ROME

Beginning in the fourth century B.C. *or somewhat earlier, the Romans began to be curious about the origin of their city. Because of Rome's general backwardness, their search for reliable documentary evidence regarding Rome's early history was in vain. There was absolutely no historical literature. In fact, historical literature did not come into being until the late third century* B.C. *Greek literature, however, was flourishing at that time and had connected Italy and Rome with such heroes of Greek mythology as Evander of Arcadia, Odysseus, and Aeneas, son of King Priam of Troy. Roman oral tradition had early invented a founder of the city, named Romulus, who soon became the center of further legendary accretions. In the second century* B.C. *the Romans merged Greek and Roman legends by making Romulus a descendant of Aeneas. The foundation legends are best known in the form given them by Latin writers of the Augustan Age. The following excerpt (A) derives from Livy's* History of Rome *and contains Livy's preface to the entire work as well as part of his account of Rome's foundation. The gigantic work of Titus Livius (59* B.C.–A.D. *17) comprised 142 books, of which only 35 are preserved. It began with the foundation of the city* (ab urbe condita) *and reached down to 9* B.C. *Livy was a great literary artist (his* History *has been called an epic in prose), but he was an uncritical historian. As explained, he was forced by the deficiency of reliable tradition to have recourse to legend for Rome's early history. Yet even for later periods he often availed himself of inferior sources and failed to make full use of what good materials were available. Livy conceived of Roman history in terms of predestination for imperial greatness and attributed success and failure to Rome's moral strength and weakness.*[1]

Literary sources leave no reason to doubt that the first Rome was located near the spot which was later to become the Forum Romanum, *or Rome's marketplace and monumental center. Every inch of ground in that area has been turned over by modern*

[1] George Baker, *The History of Rome by Titus Livius,* Vol. I (New York: Peter A. Mesier, et al., 1823), pp. 1–4, 11–16.

archaeologists, with the result that archaeology can now attempt a reconstruction of the history of the city's foundation and can provide a means of verification for the foundation legends preserved in literature. Excavations in the Roman forum bring to light new materials almost every year. Further reflections yield constantly refined interpretations of the archaeological evidence. The second selection (B) contains a historical synthesis of the archaeological data by Hugh Last. The author distinguishes five stages in the settlement of the Roman area: a settlement on the Palatine Hill, subsequent settlements on the outer hills, a religious union remembered in the festival of the Septimontium, the "City of the Four Regions," and finally, the inclusion of the Aventine Hill. According to him, the transition from the isolated villages to the city of Rome was made with the establishment of the "City of Four Regions" in the seventh century.[2]

A. THE FOUNDATION LEGENDS

Whether in tracing the series of the Roman History from the foundation of the city I shall employ my time to good purpose is a question which I cannot positively determine; nor, were it possible, would I venture to pronounce such determination; for I am aware that the matter is of high antiquity and has been already treated by many others, the latest writers always supposing themselves capable either of throwing some new light on the subject or, by the superiority of their talents for composition, of excelling the more inelegant writers who preceded them. However that may be, I shall at all events derive no small satisfaction from the reflection that my best endeavours have been exerted in transmitting to posterity the achievements of the greatest people in the world; and if, amidst such a multitude of writers, my name should not emerge from obscurity, I shall console myself by attributing it to the eminent merit of those who stand in my way in the pursuit of fame. It may be farther observed that such a subject must require a work of immense extent, as our researches must be carried back through a space of more than seven hundred years; that the state has from very small beginnings gradually increased to such a magnitude that it is now distressed by its own bulk; and that there is every reason to apprehend that the generality of readers will receive

[2] Hugh Last, "The Founding of Rome," in S. A. Cook, F. E. Adcock, M. P. Charlesworth, *The Cambridge Ancient History*, Vol. VII (New York: The Macmillan Company; Cambridge, England: Cambridge University Press, 1928), pp. 354–63. Reprinted by permission of Cambridge University Press.

but little pleasure from the accounts of its first origin or of the times immediately succeeding, but will be impatient to arrive at that period in which the powers of this overgrown state have been long employed in working their own destruction. On the other hand, this much will be derived from my labour, that so long at least as I shall have my thoughts totally occupied in investigating the transactions of such distant ages without being embarrassed by any of those unpleasing considerations in respect of later days which, though they might not have power to warp a writer's mind from the truth, would yet be sufficient to create uneasiness, I shall withdraw myself from the sight of the many evils to which our eyes have been so long accustomed. As to the relations which have been handed down of events prior to the founding of the city or to the circumstances that gave occasion to its being founded and which bear the semblance rather of poetic fictions than of authentic records of history—these I have no intention either to maintain or refute. Antiquity is always indulged with the privilege of rendering the origin of cities more venerable by intermixing divine with human agency; and if any nation may claim the privilege of being allowed to consider its origin as sacred and to attribute it to the operations of the gods, surely the Roman people, who rank so high in military fame, may well expect that while they choose to represent Mars as their own parent and that of their founder, the other nations of the world may acquiesce in this with the same deference with which they acknoweldge their sovereignty. But what degree of attention or credit may be given to these and such-like matters I shall not consider as very material. To the following considerations I wish every one seriously and earnestly to attend; by what kind of men and by what sort of conduct in peace and war the empire has been both acquired and extended; then, as discipline gradually declined, let him follow in his thoughts the structure of ancient morals, at first, as it were, leaning aside, then sinking farther and farther, then beginning to fall precipitate, until he arrives at the present times when our vices have attained to such a height of enormity that we can no longer endure either the burden of them or the sharpness of the necessary remedies. This is the great advantage to be derived from the study of history, indeed the only one which can make it answer any profitable and salutary purpose; for being abundantly furnished with clear and distinct examples of every kind of conduct, we may select for ourselves and for the state to which we belong such as are worthy of imitation; and carefully noting such as being dishonourable in their principles are equally so in their efforts learn to avoid them. Now either partiality to the subject of my intended work misleads me, or there never was any state either greater or of purer morals or richer in good examples than this of Rome; nor was there ever any city into which avarice and luxury made their entrance so late or where poverty and frugality were so highly and so long held in honour, men contracting their desires in proportion to the narrowness of their circumstances. Of late years, indeed, opulence has introduced a greediness for gain, and the boundless variety of dissolute pleasures has created in many a passion for ruining themselves and all around them. But let us, in the first stage at least of this undertaking, avoid gloomy reflections which, when perhaps unavoidable, will not even then be agreeable. If it were customary with us, as it is with poets, we would more willingly begin with good omens and vows and prayers to the gods and goddesses that they would propitiously grant success to our endeavours in the prosecution of so arduous a task. . . .

Romulus and Remus were seized with a desire of building a city in the place where they had been exposed and educated. There were great numbers of Albans and Latins who could be spared for the purpose, and these were joined by a multitude of shepherds; so that all together they formed such a numerous body as gave grounds to hope that Alba and Lavinium would be but small in comparison with the city which they were about to found. These views were interrupted by an evil hereditary in their family, ambition for rule. Hence arose a shameful contest; though they had in the beginning rested their dispute on this amicable footing, that, as they were twins and consequently no title to precedence could be derived from priority of birth, the gods who were guardians of the place should choose by auguries which of the two should give a name to the new city and enjoy the government of it when built. Romulus chose the Palatine, Remus the Aventine mount as their consecrated stands to wait the auguries. We are told that the first omen appeared to Remus, consisting of six vultures; and that after this had been proclaimed, twice that number showed themselves to Romulus; on which each was saluted King by his own followers; the former claiming the kingdom on the ground of the priority of time; the latter on that of the number of the birds. On their meeting an altercation ensued, then blows; and their passions being inflamed by the dispute, the affair proceeded at last to extremity, and murder was the consequence. Remus fell by a blow received in the tumult. There is another account more generally received that Remus, in derision of this brother, leaped over the new wall and that Romulus, enraged thereat, slew him, uttering at the same time this imprecation, "So perish every one that shall hereafter leap over my wall." By these means Romulus came into the sole possession of the government, and the city, when built, was called after the name of its founder. The first buildings which he raised were on the Palatine hill, where he himself had been brought up. To the other deities he performed worship according to the mode of the Albans, but to Hercules according to that of the Greeks as instituted by Evander. . . .

[Livy then tells how the hero Hercules slept near the river Tiber, how the shepherd Cacus stole some of Hercules' cattle and how Cacus was killed by Hercules.]

At that time Evander, a native of Peloponnesus, who had removed hither, governed that part of the country rather through an influence acquired by his merit than any power of sovereignty vested in him. He was highly revered on account of his having introduced the wonderful knowledge of letters, a matter quite new to these men who were ignorant of all the arts; and still more so on account of the supposed divinity of his mother Carmenta, whose prophetic powers had been an object of admiration to those nations before the arrival of the Sibyl in Italy. Evander then being alarmed by the concourse of the shepherds, hastened to the spot where they were assembled in a tumultuous manner about the stranger [Hercules] whom they accused as undeniably guilty of murder; and when he was informed of the fact and of the cause of it, observing the person and mien of the hero, filled with more dignity and majesty than belonged to a human being, he inquired who he was; and being told his name, that of his father and his country, he addressed him in these words; "Hail, Hercules, son of Jove! My mother, the infallible interpreter of the gods, foretold to me that you were destined to increase the number of the celestials and that an altar would be dedicated to you in this place, which a nation, hereafter the most powerful in the world, should distinguish by the name of The Greatest and would offer thereon sacrifices to your honour." Hercules, giving his right hand, replied that "he embraced the omen, and would fulfil the decree of the fates by building and dedicating an altar in the place." There, then, for the first time was performed a sacrifice to Hercules of a chosen heifer taken out of the herd. . . . These were the only foreign rites that Romulus then adopted, showing thereby from the beginning a respect for immortality obtained by merit, a dignity to which his own destiny was conducting him.

After paying due worship to the gods, he summoned the multitude to an assembly; and knowing that they could never be brought to incorporate as one people by any other means than by having their conduct directed by certain rules, he gave them a body of laws; and judging that if he added to the dignity of his own carriage by assuming the ensigns of sovereignty it would help to procure respect to those laws among a rude uninformed people, he adopted a more majestic style of appearance, both with regard to his other appointments and particularly in being attended by twelve lictors. Some think that he was led to fix on this number by that of the birds in the augury which had protended the kingdom to him; I am rather inclined to be of their opinion who suppose that all the officers attendant on magistrates, and among the rest the lictors as well as the number of them, were borrowed from their neighbours, the Etruscans, from whom the curule chair and the gown edged with purple were taken; and that the Etruscans used that number because, their King being elected by the suffrages of twelve states, each state gave him one lictor. Meanwhile the city increased in buildings, which were carried on to an extent proportioned rather to the number of inhabitants they hoped for in future than to what they had at the time. But that its size might not increase beyond its strength, in order to augment his numbers, he had recourse to a practice common among founders of cities who used to feign that the multitude of mean and obscure people thus collected had sprung out of the earth. He opened a sanctuary, in the place where the inclosure now is, on the road down from the Capitol, called the Pass of the Two Groves. Hither fled from the neighbouring states crowds of all sorts without distinction, whether freemen or slaves, led by a fondness for novelty, and this it was that gave solidity to the growing greatness of the city. Having reason now to be pretty well satisfied with his strength, he next made provision that this strength should be regulated by wisdom; and for that purpose he created a hundred senators, either because that number was sufficient or because there were no more than a hundred citizens who could prove their descent from respectable families. They were certainly styled Fathers from their honourable office, and their descendants Patricians.

B. HUGH LAST: THE ARCHAEOLOGICAL FACTS

The summit of the Palatine has an area of roughly twenty-five acres and is divided by a natural depression into an eastern and a western section, of which the former was Palatium proper and the latter bore the name "Cermalus." There is evidence to suggest that at first the communities of these two sites were distinct; but though the name "Cermalus" survived even into imperial times it is clear that the whole population of the hill was very early united. The scarcity of material evidence for primitive occupation must be ascribed in part to the intensity of the use to which the Palatine was put throughout the classical period, at least until the foundation of New Rome; but nevertheless there remains enough to lend archaeological support to the view of the literary authorities. The only authentic burial discovered on the hill itself is an inhumation which cannot be carried back further than the fifth century, but it is not within the limits of the settlement that its cemetery must be sought. Below the slopes of the Velia on its western side there came to light in 1902 a burial-place whose full dimensions cannot be ascertained: but the fragment exposed beside the temple of Antonius and Faustina may be assumed to be typical of the whole. In this *sepulcretum* there is a series of cremations, with which the Volcanal near by has plausibly been connected and which show an undeniable affinity with the cremations of the Alban hills. Though the Alban series has deposits which are definitely earlier than the first at Rome, the cremations of the Forum have begun by the close of the second millenium and extend in all probability into the ninth century B.C. at least, and perhaps beyond.

At a date which the evidence both from Rome and from other parts of Central Italy seems to fix in the neighbourhood of 800 B.C. the *sepulcretum* began to receive the dead of a population distinct from the cremators—of a people whose progress towards Latium can be traced in some detail and the mark of whose presence is inhumation of the body unburnt. From the eighth century these inhumations continue till the sixth, when the cemetery was given up for good. With the draining of the low ground north of the Palatine by the *cloaca maxima,* the history of the Roman Forum begins, and in the history of the business centre of the city the graveyard has no part.

Though demonstrative proof is impossible, there is much plausibility in the view which assigns the cremations of the Forum to the early community of the Palatine. The absence of remains on the hill directs the search for a cemetery outside the limits of the settlement itself, and beyond these limits no site is more obvious than one close by the *col* which served to connect the Palatine with the surrounding country. But the identification does not depend on probability alone. In the necropolis of the Forum the priority of the earlier cremations is proved both by the lower levels at which they are found and by the fact that at the time of the inhumation the cremation-deposits had so far been forgotten that at least one of them was broken into by a later grave. The old inhumations at Rome are probably to be sought on the Esquiline, but from the Esquiline they spread rapidly round the heights to the Forum and the Quirinal. The striking fact about the deposits on the outer hills is that, whereas inhumations are freely found, traces of cremation, and especially of cremations belonging to a time before the burying people arrived, are extremely rare. From this it may be inferred that when, about the end of the ninth century, the inhuming immigrants reached the site of Rome they found the hills of the outer ring only lightly occupied by scattered stragglers of a people whose main settlement was elsewhere, and whose dead lay at the foot of the slopes north of the later Forum. The problem then is to find the home of these cremators. The festival of the Septimontium preserves the memory of a time, early indeed in the history of Rome, but still one at which seven communities had grown up round the site and which consequently is later than the age of the first cremators. Besides the Palatine, the only hills which the necropolis of the Forum might conceivably have served are the Capitoline and Quirinal; but since these two hills, according at least to the most credible of our authorities, were not occupied by any of the seven villages which joined to celebrate the Septimontium, it seems to follow that they cannot claim the first village of all. Thus the Palatine remains, and the consensus of antiquity finds support. . . .

Apart from some cuttings in the rock which have been interpreted as the pole-sockets of primitive *capanne,* nothing has been found in the Palatine earlier than the various cisterns and sundry pieces of wall which may perhaps be dated to the sixth century. The earliest inhabitants probably depended for protection on the natural strength of the hill, assisted by some small defences, probably no more than rough earthworks of the kind still remembered in classical times near the site of one of the Esquiline settlements. On which summit of the Palatine, if both were not occupied, the first village was pitched there is no indication to show, but we may conjecture that before long huts spread over the whole habitable surface of the hill. This brings us to Roma Quadrata.

Roma Quadrata was the name of a shrine on the Palatine containing various objects connected with the foundation of the city; but the term was also used to describe the earliest city recognized by tradition, the city whose limits were those of the Palatine hill. . . .

By a date which falls somewhere within the limits of the eighth century, the outer hills had been freely planted with settlements of the inhuming "Sabines" and the next stage in the history of Rome is marked by the formation of a union, apparently religious in character, to include both the cremators of the Palatine and at least a section of the newcomers. The survival by which the memory of this union was preserved in republican Rome was the festival of the Septimontium; but the evidence for this celebration is so confused that conclusions of historical relevance can only be drawn from it by more or less hazardous conjecture. . . . The wider implications . . . are that the hills of the Septimontium should be found in the Palatine, and certain spurs of the outer heights which lay round about the northern end of the Velia, together with the Velia itself. It is in all ways probable that when Palatine Rome began to grow into something larger the first stage in the expansion was a loose union of the Palatine community, with others round about, and as a record of this stage the festival of the Septimontium may be accepted.

Thus far it is possible to go with tradition; but the further suggestion that the seven communities formed a single city, and that Septimontium was its name, must be rejected. It cannot be doubted that in the late republic, if not before, the word Septimontium was capable of a local signification, but in this sense it properly denoted a district and nothing more. Whatever political or religious ties may have bound the seven villages to one another, the total lack of evidence for any common system of defence indicates the essential difference between the Septimontium and the late Servian City. Individually, of course, the villages may have been fenced, and it is even possible that the stretch of earthwork which survived into historical times had originally belonged to the people of the Subura or the Oppius. But on the nature of the Septimontium in general nothing need be added to the account of Varro—rightly understood—that Septimontium was a name used to denote a certain area at a time in its history before that area was included in the walls of a later city.

The theory which seems to have won credence in classical Rome suggests that the enclosure of the Palatine and other settlements within a single boundary came with the formation of what may be called the City of the Four Regions. For this development the evidence is vague and scanty, but attempts to discredit the Four Regions City as an antiquarian invention have not achieved success. . . . The cogent case for the City of the Four Regions rests on the *pomerium* of republican times. In its original sense *pomerium* seems to have meant the divine boundary of a city, and since it marked the limits of the area specially protected by the city's gods, Varro is wholly plausible in saying that the *pomerium* properly ran outside, and not inside, the defensive walls where such existed. Thus a *pomerium* which encloses a smaller area than that within the Servian wall must be connected with a city earlier in date than this defensive system. It will be seen that the remains of the Servian defences contain evidence for the extent of sixth-century Rome; and since one large region—the Esquiline—is outside the *pomerium* but inside the sixth-century circuit it seems to follow that the *pomerium* must be assigned to something earlier than the so-called Servian City. In addition to the districts of the Septimontium, the *pomerium* of the Republic included Capitoline, Quirinal and Viminal, as well as certain low-lying districts between the hills, of which the Forum is the most important; and such archaeological material as these districts provide suggests that the origin of this city is to be placed in the seventh century.

The choice of a name for this stage of Rome's development is a matter of small importance. "City of the Four Regions" is a modern label, justified to some extent by the fact that, with the possible exception of the Mons Capitolinus and the Roman Forum, the whole area within the *pomerium* which formed the boundary of the seventh-century city, was divided in republican times between the *regiones Suburana, Esquilina, Collina* and *Palatina.* The exception is of some interest. If the ritual of the Argei is early, and not an institution of the third century B.C., as Wissowa has essayed to show, Varro's list of chapels visited by the procession on 16 and 17 March throws valuable light on the city's growth when it suggests that the Capitoline and the low ground beneath it to the east were not included in any one of the Regions. Though a city from which the Capitoline was omitted may be surprising, the explanation of its omission is so obvious as to confirm the suggestion of the evidence. Before the draining of the Forum by the canalization of what later became the Cloaca maxima, the Mons Capitolinus was almost worthless, too small to be an independent stronghold and too isolated to be made part of the Quirinal group. Though no certainty can be attained, it is at least possible that in the earliest city the Capitoline had no place and that its inclusion was due to the later kings with whose building activities it is closely associated. Against such inferences from our knowledge of the four regions no objection can be drawn from the fact that the regions bear the same names as the four urban tribes. Whatever the date of the urban tribes, there is no reason to think that the regions drew their names from the tribes and not *vice versa.* It seems then that in the *pomerium* we have evidence for a city earlier than that of the sixth century, and that in the conjectural limits of the regions there is a hint that this first Rome excluded the Capitoline, which may, like the Esquiline, have been added at the time with which tradition at least connects Servius Tullius.

That the City of the Four Regions was protected by more worldly defences than its *pomerium* there is nothing to show. Evidence for a continuous fortification embracing part of the outer height is wholly lacking until the sixth century brings the wall of Servius. . . .

But it may be said that at present no valid archaeological objection can be brought against the connection of these survivals with the wall ascribed by tradition to the sixth of the kings of Rome. To this stage the addition of the Esquiline, and possibly of the Capitoline, belongs.

Whatever view may be taken of the details related by Livy and

Dionysius about the Icilian rogation of 456, the story probably rests on a basis sound enough to justify the conclusion that in the middle of the fifth century the Aventine was still more or less unoccupied. If this is so, the tale that Ancus Marcius added the Aventine to the city becomes incredible, as indeed it always has been in the light of archaeological evidence for the expansion of Rome; and there is much plausibility in the theory that this hill was first included when the Servian defences were re-organized after the Gallic retreat. The question of the Aventine and its incorporation affects the interpretation of the *cappellaccio* wall because there are traces of this work on the Palatine which could not easily be assigned to a circuit including the Aventine *massif*. Even if proof were forthcoming that the Aventine formed part of the city as early as the sixth century, it would be possible to connect the Palatine remains with the independent defences which that hill may have boasted even after the coming of the Gauls; but if, on the other hand, the Aventine remained outside the defences until the fourth-century reconstruction, then it is possible to say that the whole series of these *cappellaccio* survivals lie on the trace of the fourth-century *enceinte*, except on the slope above the Vallis Murcia where the line was altered, at the time of the restoration, to take in the last of the Roman hills. With the City of the Four Regions this wall can have nothing to do, because the clearest of all the signs it has left are north of the Baths of Diocletian, at a point where the Servian circuit extends as far beyond the *pomerium* as it does anywhere in its course. For the present, and until more light is won, it would be unwise to rule out the possibility that the first wall of Rome which included not only the Palatine but part of the outer heights was built in the sixth century, and that an extension on the Esquiline, as Livy asserts, together possibly with one to include the Capitoline, was really an achievement of the regal period.

Such were the changes of five hundred years. The Palatine settlement, founded not long before the end of the second millenium B.C., had been joined in about 800 by the younger communities of the outer hills. In the eighth century seven of these had begun the common celebration of the Septimontium, and in the seventh these villages, together with those of the Quirinal and Viminal, with or without the Capitoline, had been merged into a single city lying behind a continuous *pomerium*. Next, possibly in the sixth century, a defensive wall was built, which, unless the Capitoline was now for the first time annexed, only deserted the line of the *pomerium* in the northeast, where it was carried forward to enclose a large section of the Esquiline; and finally, in the fourth century, when this was renewed, one more addition was made by the inclusion of the Aventine to the south. Thereafter Rome still grew; but when the fourth-century works had saved the city from the menace of Hannibal, the need for defences slowly disappeared, and Rome became something like the open city which it remained until the Alemannic danger produced the fortifications of Aurelian and Probus.

57 / THE ESTABLISHMENT OF THE ARISTOCRATIC REPUBLIC

The establishment of the republic, traditionally dated at 509 B.C., *was another topic of Roman legend. The significance of the event lay not only in that it marked the overthrow of foreign domination (the Tarquinii were Etruscans), but also the transition from monarchy to an aristocratic regime. The figure of Brutus the Liberator may be an invention altogether. In the following selection Livy describes the consulship and the Senate.*[3]

Henceforward I am to treat of the affairs, civil and military, of a free people, for such the Romans were now become, of annual magistrates and the authority of the laws exalted above that of men. What greatly enhanced the public joy on having attained to this state of freedom was the haughty insolence of the late king; for the former kings governed in such a manner that all of them in succession might deservedly be reckoned as founders of the several parts, at least, of the city which they added to it to accommodate the great numbers of inhabitants whom they themselves introduced. Nor can it be doubted that the same Brutus, who justly merited so great glory for having expelled that haughty king, would have hurt the public interest most materially, had he through an over-hasty zeal for liberty wrested the government from any one of the former princes. For what must have been the consequence if that rabble of shepherds and vagabonds, fugitives from their own countries, having under the sanction of an

[3] George Baker, *The History of Rome by Titus Livius,* Vol. I (New York: Peter A. Mesier, et al., 1823), pp. 100–102.

inviolable asylum obtained liberty or at least impunity, and uncontrolled by dread of kingly power had once been set in commotion by tribunician storms and had in a city where they were strangers engaged in contests with the patricians before the pledges of wives and children, and an affection for the soil itself, which in length of time is acquired from habit, had united their minds in social concord? The state, as yet but a tender shoot, had in that case been torn to pieces by discord; whereas the tranquil moderation of the then government cherished it and by due nourishment brought it forward to such a condition that, its powers being ripened, it was capable of producing the glorious fruit of liberty. The origin of liberty is to be dated from that period, rather on account of the consular government being limited to one year than of any diminution made of the power which had been possessed by the kings. The first consuls enjoyed all their privileges and all their ensigns of authority; in this respect only care was taken not to double the objects of terror by giving the fasces to both the consuls. Brutus, with the consent of his colleague, was first honoured with the fasces, and the zeal which he had shown as the champion of liberty in rescuing it from oppression was not greater than that which he afterwards displayed in the character of its guardian. First of all, while the people were in raptures at their new acquisition of freedom, lest they might afterwards be perverted by the importunities or presents of the princes, he bound them by an oath that they would never suffer any man to assume the authority of king at Rome. Next, in order that the fullness of their body might give the greater weight to the senate, he filled up the number of the senators, which had been diminished by the king's murders, to the amount of three hundred, electing into that body the principal men of equestrian rank; and hence the practice is said to have taken its rise of summoning to the senate those who are fathers and those who are *conscripti;* for they called those who were elected into this new senate *conscripti.* This had a wonderful effect towards producing concord in the state and in attaching the affection of the commons to the patricians.

58 / THE TWELVE TABLES

One of the plebeians' objectives in their conflict with the patricians had been the codification of the law which the patricians administered. Fragments of the law code survived (because it had been memorized and quoted) into much later times. The codification was made in 450–449 B.C. *by two successive committees of ten men, the decemvirs, and represents an authentic and valuable record of Roman life and legal ideas during the first century of the republic.*[4]

TABLE I

Preliminaries to a Trial. Rules for a Trial

If plaintiff summons defendant to court, he shall go. If he does not go, plaintiff shall call witness thereto. Then only shall he take defendant by force.

If defendant shirks or takes to heels, plaintiff shall lay hands on him. . . .

For landowner, landowner shall be protector; but for proletarian person let any one who be willing be protector. . . .

TABLE III

Debt

When debt has been acknowledged, or judgment about matter has been pronounced in court, 30 days must be legitimate time of grace. After that, then arrest of debtor may be made by laying on hands. Bring him into court. If he does not satisfy the judgment, or no one in court offers himself as surety on his behalf, creditor may take defaulter with him. He may bind him either in stocks or in fetters; he may bind him with weight not less than 15 pounds, or with more if he shall so desire. Debtor if he shall wish may live on his own. If he does not live on his own, person [who shall hold him in bonds] shall give him one pound of grits for each day. He may give more if he shall so desire.

(Moreover there was meanwhile the right of compromising, and) unless they made a compromise debtors were held in bond for sixty days. During that time they were brought before the [praetor's] court in the Meeting-Place on three successive market-days, and the amount for which they were judged liable was announced; and on the third market-day they suffered capital punishment or were delivered up for sale abroad, across the Tiber. . . .

On third market-day creditors shall cut pieces. Should they have cut more than their due, it shall be with impunity. . . .

[4] Reprinted by permission of the publishers from the Loeb Classical Library, translated by E. H. Warmington, *Remains of Old Latin,* Volume III (Cambridge, Mass.: Harvard University Press, 1938), pp. 425–505.

TABLE V

Succession. Guardianship

(Our ancestors have seen fit that females, by reason of levity in disposition,) should remain in guardianship even when they have attained their majority. . . . We except the Vestal Virgins. . . .

According as person shall bid regarding his [household] chattels or guardianship of his estate, so shall right be. . . .

If person dies intestate, and has no self-successor, nearest agnate male kinsman shall have possession of deceased's household. . . .

If there is no agnate male kinsman, deceased's clansmen shall have possession of his household. . . .

TABLE VI

Acquisition. Possession

'Usucapio' of movable things requires one year's possession for its completion; but usucapio of an estate and buildings, two years'. . . .

(A woman became subjected to her husband's hand by enjoyment when she had lived as his wedded wife without interruption for one year; for because she had been as it were held by enjoyment in one year's possession, she was transferred to the man's establishment and occupied the status of a daughter; and so there was made in the Law of the Twelve Tables a provision that) any woman who did not wish to be subjected in this manner to the hand of her husband should be absent for three nights in succession every year, and so interrupt the usucapio of each year. . . .

Person shall not dislodge from framework beam fixed in buildings or vineyard. . . .

TABLE VII

Rights Concerning Land

. . . .

Person shall mend roadway. If they keep it not laid with stones, holder of servitude may drive beasts where he shall wish.

Should a tree on a neighbour's farm be bent crooked by the wind and lean over your farm, you may, by the Law of the Twelve Tables, take legal action for removal of that tree. . . .

Moreover a provision of the Law of the Twelve Tables was made that a man might gather up fruit that was falling down on to another man's farm.

TABLE VIII

Torts or Delicts

. . . .

If person has maimed another's limb, let there be retaliation in kind unless he makes agreement for composition with him. . . .

If he has broken or bruised freeman's bone with hand or club, he shall undergo penalty of 300 pieces; if slave's, 150. . . .

If he has done simple harm [to another], penalties shall be 25 pieces. . . .

If a four-footed animal shall be said to have caused pauperies, loss, legal action (for the same is derived from the Law of Twelve Tables. This Law sanctioned) either the surrender of the thing which damaged (that is the animal which committed the damage), or else the offer of assessment for the damage. . . .

For pasturing on, or cutting secretly by night, another's crop acquired by tillage, (a capital punishment was laid down in the Twelve Tables in the case of the) adult malefactor, (and their injunction was) that he be hanged and put to death as a sacrifice to Ceres, (condemned to suffer a penalty heavier than the penalty imposed in the crime of murder; and that) in the case of a person under the age of puberty, at the discretion of the [praetor] either he should be scourged, or for the harm done, composition be made by paying double damages.

(It is ordained that) any person who destroys by burning any building or heap of corn deposited alongside a house shall be bound, scourged, and put to death by burning at the stake provided that he has committed the said misdeed with malice aforethought; but if he shall have committed it by accident, that is, by negligence, it is ordained that he repair the damage, or, if he be too poor to be competent for such punishment, he shall receive a lighter chastisement. . . .

(Trees also received care and attention in ancient law, and provision was made in the Twelve Tables that) any person who had cut down another person's trees with harmful intent should pay 25 *as*-pieces for every tree. . . .

TABLE IX

Public Law

Laws of personal exception must not be proposed; cases in which the penalty affects the "caput" or person of a citizen must not be decided except through the greatest assembly and through those whom the [censors] have placed upon the register of citizens. . . .

(The Law of the Twelve Tables ordains that) he who shall have roused up a public enemy, or handed over a citizen to a public enemy, must suffer capital punishment. . . .

TABLE XI

Supplementary Laws

(When the Board of Ten had put into writing, using the greatest fairness and wisdom, ten tables of laws, they caused to be elected in their stead, for the next year, another Board of Ten, whose good faith and justice have not been praised to a like extent. . . . When they had added two tables of unfair laws, they ordained, by a very inhuman law, that) intermarriage (which is usually permitted even between peoples of separate States) should not take place between our plebeians and our patricians. . . .

59 / THE ORGANIZATION OF THE PLEBS

According to Roman tradition, the commoners (plebeians) of the Early Republic were weighed down by debts and possessed little influence in political life; a revolutionary atmosphere prevailed in Rome. In the course of several centuries of social strife the plebeians were able to win concessions from the patricians, because they were organized and could strike against military service. Livy sets the first secessio *at 492* B.C. *Rome had just triumphed over Volscians, Sabines, and Aequans under the dictatorship of Manlius Valerius.*[5]

The senate were then seized with apprehensions that if the citizens should be discharged from the army, their secret cabals and conspiracies would be renewed; wherefore supposing that, though the levy was made by the dictator, yet as the soldiers had sworn obedience to the consuls they were still bound by that oath, they ordered the legions, under the pretext of hostilities being renewed by the Aequans,

[5] George Baker, *The History of Rome by Titus Livius*, Vol. I (New York: Peter A. Mesier, et al., 1823), pp. 149–51.

to be led out of the city: which step served only to hasten the breaking out of the sedition. It is said that the plebeians at first entertained thoughts of putting the consuls to death in order that they might be thereby discharged from the oath; but being afterwards informed that no religious obligation could be dissolved by an act of wickedness, they, by the advice of a person called Sicinius, retired without waiting for orders from the consuls to the sacred mount beyond the river Anio, about three miles from the city. This account is more generally credited than that given by Piso, who says the secession was made to the Aventine. In this place without any commander, having fortified their camp with a rampart and trench, they remained quiet for several days, taking nothing from any one but necessary subsistence, neither receiving nor giving offence. Great was the consternation in the city; all was fearful suspense and mutual apprehension: the plebeians, who were left behind by their brethren, dreaded the violence of the patricians; the patricians dreaded the plebeians who remained in the city, not knowing whether they ought to wish for their stay or for their departure; but "how long could it be supposed that the multitude which had seceded would remain inactive? And what would be the consequence if in the mean time a foreign war should break out? No glimpse of hope could they see left except in concord between the citizens, which must be re-established in the state on any terms, whether fair or unfair." They determined, therefore, to send as ambassador to the plebeians Menenius Agrippa, a man of eloquence and acceptable to the commons because he had been originally one of their body. He, being admitted into the camp, is said to have related to them the following fable, delivered in antiquated language and an uncouth style:—"At a time when the members of the human body did not, as at present, all unite in one plan, but each member had its own scheme and its own language, the other parts were provoked at seeing that the fruits of all their care, of all their toil and service, were applied to the use of the belly; and that the belly meanwhile remained at its ease and did nothing but enjoy the pleasure provided for it: on this they conspired together that the hand should not bring food to the mouth nor the mouth receive it if offered nor the teeth chew it. While they wished by these angry measures to subdue the belly through hunger, the members themselves and the whole body were, together with it, reduced to the last stage of decay; from thence it appeared that the office of the belly itself was not confined to a slothful indolence; that it not only received nourishment, but supplied it to the others, conveying to every part of the body that blood on which depend our life and vigour by distributing it equally through the veins after having brought it to perfection by digestion of the food." Applying this to the present case, and showing what similitude there was between the dissension of the members and the resentment of the commons against the patricians, he made a considerable impression on the people's minds.

A negotiation was then opened for a reconciliation; and an accommodation was effected on the terms that the plebeians should have magistrates of their own invested with inviolable privileges, who might have power to afford them protection against the consuls; and that it should not be lawful for any of the patricians to hold that office. Accordingly, there were two tribunes of the commons created, Caius Licinius and Lucius Albinius; and these created three colleagues to themselves, among whom was Sicinius, the adviser of the secession: but who the other two were is not agreed: some say that there were only two tribunes created on the sacred mount and that the devoting law was passed there.

60 / ROME OCCUPIED BY GAULS

In 391, not long after the capture of Veii, the Romans suffered a military setback which they never forgot. The Gauls, or Celts, kinsmen of the Italic peoples, occupied Britain, Spain, and France. About 400 B.C. *they migrated into Italy and overcame the Etruscans in northern Italy (henceforth called Cisalpine or Hither Gaul). A call to Rome by the Etruscan city of Clusium for help against a group of Gallic invaders under Brennus precipitated the Gallic attack on Rome. The Romans were defeated in a battle fought on the river Allia.*[6]

Meanwhile, at Rome, when every disposition for the defence of the citadel had been completed as far as was possible in such a conjuncture, the aged crowd withdrew to their houses and there, with a firmness of mind not to be shaken by the approach of death, waited the coming of the enemy; such of them as had held curule offices, choosing to die in that garb which displayed the emblems

[6] George Baker, *The History of Rome by Titus Livius,* Vol. I (New York: Peter A. Mesier, et al., 1823), pp. 478–89.

of their former fortune, of their honours, or of their merit, put on the most splendid robes worn when they draw the chariots of the gods in procession or ride in triumph. Thus habited, they seated themselves in their ivory chairs at the fronts of their houses. Some say that they devoted themselves for the safety of their country and their fellow citizens; and that they sung a hymn upon the occasion, Marcus Fabius, the chief pontiff, dictating the form of words to them. On the side of the Gauls, as the keenness of their rage, excited by the fight, had abated during the night, and as they had neither met any dangerous opposition in the field nor were now taking the city by storm or force, they marched next day without any anger or any heat of passion into the city through the Colline gate, which stood open, and advanced to the Forum, casting round their eyes on the temples of the gods and on the citadel, the only place which had the appearance of making resistance. From thence, leaving a small guard to prevent any attack from the citadel or capitol, they ran about in quest of plunder. Not meeting a human being in the streets, part of them rushed in a body to the houses that stood nearest; part sought the most distant, as expecting to find them untouched and abounding with spoil. Afterwards, being frightened from thence by the very solitude and fearing lest some secret design of the enemy might be put in execution against them while they were thus dispersed, they formed themselves into bodies and returned again to the Forum and places adjoining to it. Finding the houses of the plebeians shut up and the palaces of the nobles standing open, they showed rather greater backwardness to attack these that were open than such as were shut: with such a degree of veneration did they behold men sitting in the porches of those palaces, who, beside their ornaments and apparel more splendid than became mortals, bore the nearest resemblance to gods in the majesty displayed in their looks and the gravity of their countenances. It is said that while they stood gazing as on statues, one of them, Marcus Papirius, provoked the anger of a Gaul by striking him on the head with his ivory sceptre while he was stroking his beard, which at that time was universally worn long; that the slaughter began with him and that the rest were slain in their seats. The nobles being put to death, the remainder of the people met the same fate. The houses were plundered and then set on fire.

However, whether it was that they were not all possessed with a desire of reducing the city to ruins or whether the design had been adopted by the chiefs of the Gauls that some fires should be presented to the view of the besieged for the purpose of terrifying them and to try if they could be compelled to surrender through affection to their own dwellings, or that they had determined that all the houses should not be burned down because whatever remained they could hold as a pledge, by means of which they might work upon the minds of the garrison, the fire did not, during the first day, spread extensively, as is usual in a captured city. The Romans, beholding the enemy from the citadel, who ran up and down through every street, while some new scene of horror arose to their view in every different quarter, were scarcely able to preserve their presence of mind. To whatever side the shouts of the enemy, the cries of women and children, the crackling from the flames, and the crash of falling houses called their attention, thither, deeply shocked at every incident, they turned their eyes, their thought, as if placed by fortune to be spectators of the fall of their country;—left, in short, not for the purpose of protecting anything belonging to them, but merely their own persons, much more deserving of commiseration, indeed, than any before who were ever beleaguered; as by the siege which they had to sustain they were excluded from their native city whilst they saw everything which they held dear in the power of the enemy. Nor was the night which succeeded such a shocking day attended with more tranquility. The morning appeared with an aspect equally dismal; nor did any portion of time relieve them from the sight of a constant succession of new distresses. Loaded and overwhelmed with such a multiplicity of evils, they notwithstanding remitted nought of their firmness; determined, though they should see everything in flames and levelled with the dust, to defend by their bravery the hill which they occupied, small and ill provided as it was, yet being the only refuge of their liberty. And as the same events recurred every day, they became so habituated, as it were, to disasters that, abstracting their thoughts as much as possible from their circumstances, they regarded the arms and the swords in their hands as their only hopes. . . .

[*After a long siege by the Gauls, the Roman garrison on the Capitoline Hill was at the end of its food supply. The besiegers, in turn, were harassed by diseases.*]

The garrison of the capitol was worn down with the fatigue of guards and watches. They had hitherto stood superior to all evils, yet famine was one which nature would not allow to be overcome, so that looking out day after day for some assistance from the dictator and at last not only provisions but hope failing, their arms in the course of relieving the guards at the same time almost weighing down their feeble bodies, they insisted that either a surrender should be made or the enemy bought off on such terms as could be obtained: for the Gauls had given plain intimations that for a small compensation they might be induced to relinquish the siege. The senate then met, and the military tribunes were commissioned to conclude a capitulation. The business was afterwards managed in a conference between Quintus Sulpicius, a military tribune, and Brennus, the chieftain of the Gauls, and a thousand pounds weight of gold was fixed as the ransom of that people, who were afterwards to be rulers of the world. To a transaction so very humiliating in itself insult was added. False weights were brought by the Gauls, and on the tribune objecting to them, the insolent Gaul threw in his sword in addition to the weights and was heard to utter an expression intolerable to Roman ears: "woe to the vanquished."

61 / THE ROMAN POLITICAL SETTLEMENT WITH LATIUM

On many occasions the Romans waged war against their kinsmen in Latium. The last Latin uprising occurred in 340–338 B.C. *and ended in a Roman victory. Rome's treatment of her conquered foes was far from uniform: some communities received full Roman citizenship; others "citizenship without suffrage"; still others lost their land, and Roman garrisons ("colonies") were settled on it. It was this discriminating treatment of the Latins that established Roman hegemony in central Italy and laid the foundations of the Italian Confederacy, at the head of which Rome was to become a world power.*[7]

Before the assembly for electing consuls was called for the ensuing year [334 B.C.], Camillus moved the senate to take into consideration the conduct to be observed towards the states of Latium and proceeded in this manner: "Conscript Fathers, Whatever was to be effected in Latium by means of arms and military operations has now, through the favour of the gods and the valour of your soldiers,

[7] George Baker, *The History of Rome by Titus Livius*, Vol. II (New York: Peter Mesier, et al., 1823), pp. 173–6.

been fully accomplished. The armies of our enemies have been cut to pieces at Pedum and the Astura; all the towns of Latium, and Antium in the Volscian territory, either taken by storm or surrendered, are held by your garrisons. It remains then to be considered, since the frequent rebellions of these people are the cause of so much trouble, by what means we may secure their quiet submission and peaceable behaviour. The attainment of this end the immortal gods have placed within your reach insomuch that they have given you the power of determining whether Latium shall longer exist or not. Ye can therefore ensure to yourselves perpetual peace as far as regards the Latins by the means either of severity or of mercy. Do ye choose to adopt cruel measures against people vanquished and submitting to your authority? Ye may utterly destroy all Latium and make a desert of a country from which, in many and difficult wars, ye have often been supplied with a powerful army of allies. Do ye choose, on the contrary and in conformity to the practice of your ancestors, to augment the Roman state by receiving the vanquished into the number of your citizens? Here is a large addition which ye may acquire by means which will redound most highly to your glory. That government which the subjects feel happy in obeying stands certainly on the firmest of all foundations. But whatever your determination may be, it is necessary that it be speedy; as all those states are at present suspended between hope and fear. It is therefore of importance that ye should be discharged as soon as possible from all solicitude concerning them; and also that, either by punishment or clemency, an immediate impression be made on their minds before they recover from the state of insensibility in which the uncertainty of their fate has thrown them. It was our part to bring the business to such an issue that your deliberations concerning it should be unrestrained in every particular. It is now yours to determine what is most advantageous to yourselves and the commonwealth."

The principal members of the senate highly approved of the consul's statement of the business on the whole: but said that "as the states were differently circumstanced, it would conduce to an easy adjustment of the plan, so as that their resolutions should be conformable to the several merits of each, if he put the question on the case of each state separately." The question was accordingly put and a decree passed with respect to each singly. The Lanuvians were admitted members of the state; the exercise of their public worship was rstored to them with a provision that the grove and temple of Juno Sospita should be in common between the burghers of Lanuvium and the Roman people. On the same terms with these the

Aricians, Nomentans, and Pedans were received into the number of citizens. To the Tusculans the rights of citizens, of which they were already in possession, were continued; and the guilt of the rebellion, instead of being imputed to disaffection in the state, was thrown on a few incendiaries. On the Veliternians, who were Roman citizens of an old standing, in resentment of their having so often arisen in rebellion, severe vengeance was inflicted; their walls were razed and their senate driven into banishment; they were also enjoined to dwell on the farther side of the Tiber with a denunciation that if any of them should be caught on the hither side of that river, the fine to be paid for his discharge should be no less than one thousand *asses* and that the person apprehending him should not release him from confinement until the money should be paid. Into the lands which had belonged to their senators colonists were sent, from the addition of whose numbers Velitrae recovered the appearance of its former populousness. To Antium also a new colony was sent, permission being granted at the same time to the Antians of having themselves enrolled therein if they chose it. The ships of war were taken from them and the people wholly interdicted from meddling with maritime affairs; but the rights of citizens were granted to them. The Tiburtians and Praenestines were amerced in a portion of their lands; not merely on account of their recent crime of rebellion, common to them with the rest of the Latins, but because they had formerly, in disgust at the Roman government, associated in arms with the Gauls, a nation of savages. From the other states they took away the privileges of intermarriage, commerce, and holding assemblies. To the Campanians, in compliment to their horsemen, who had refused to join in rebellion with the Latins, as likewise to the Fundans and Formians because the troops had always found a safe and quiet passage through their territories, the freedom of the state was granted without right of suffrage. The states of Cumae and Suessula, it was decreed, should be placed on the same footing and enjoy the same privileges as Capua. Of the ships of the Antians some were drawn up into the docks at Rome; the rest were burned and, with the prows of these, a pulpit, built in the Forum, was ordered to be decorated, hence called Rostra.

VIII / ROME'S CONQUEST OF THE MEDITERRANEAN

During the last three centuries before the Christian era Rome conquered the Mediterranean world. Her conquests outside Italy of land and peoples with different cultural traditions placed before Rome entirely new administrative tasks. These she found difficult to perform efficiently. Contacts with Greeks in southern Italy, in Sicily, and eventually on the Greek mainland itself immeasurably strengthened the Greek imprint on Roman civilization. Booty acquired by both the state and by individuals in the course of the Punic and Macedonian wars led to social disturbances, revolution, and civil wars. It was left for the princeps, Augustus, to solve these problems—to devise a satisfactory system of provincial administration, to arrive at a viable compromise between Hellenic imports and a revived Roman heritage, and to put an end to civil warfare.

Carthage had been, since at least the mid-fourth century B.C., *a Roman ally. Rome first became involved in warfare against Carthage over the Sicilian city of Messana (modern Messina), just across the straits from southern Italy. At that time the Carthaginians controlled large parts of Sicily, and there was a real danger that they would add this large island to their possessions in North Africa, Sardinia, and Corsica. The Romans had little difficulty in preventing the capture of Messana by the Carthaginians. They then accepted the submission of Carthage's former ally, King Hiero of Syracuse. Once established in Sicily, however, the Romans fell heirs to the old struggle between the Greeks and Carthaginians over the possession of Sicily. In the end Rome managed to eject Carthage from Sicily and to defeat her in several naval engagements. One of the most important aspects of the First Punic War (264–241* B.C.*) was that during that war Rome became a naval power.*

62 / THE SECOND PUNIC WAR (218-201 B.C.)

The peace of 241 B.C. *had been followed in 238 by the entirely unprovoked Roman seizure of the Carthaginian island of Sardinia (238* B.C.*) and by Carthaginian activities in the Iberian Peninsula. In the following excerpt (A) Polybius discusses the causes of the Second Punic War. The historian Polybius of Megalopolis (in Arcadia, circa 200–118?* B.C.*) was an important figure in the public affairs of the Achaean League and was brought to Rome as a hostage at the conclusion of the Third Macedonian War (168* B.C.*). At Rome he became a friend of Scipio Aemilianus, who was to conquer Carthage in the Third Punic War. His work is deliberately factual and sober, "pragmatic," as he calls it. Its theme is the rise of Rome to world domination in the first half of the second century* B.C. *The Roman annalist Quintus Fabius Pictor, cited in the excerpt, was a senator who fought in the war and wrote a history of Rome in the Greek language. The events at the court of the Seleucid ruler Antiochus III, referred to at the end of the selection, occurred in 195* B.C.[1]

At the beginning of the Second Punic War Hannibal invaded Italy and annihilated a consular army at Lake Trasimene in central Italy (217 B.C.*). Quintus Fabius, the* dictator *appointed by the Romans after this disaster, chose delaying tactics rather than risk an open battle. In the end, however, the pressures against Fabius' strategic concepts became too strong, and the Romans ac-*

[1] Evelyn S. Shuckburgh, *The Histories of Polybius*, Vol. I (London: Macmillan, 1889), pp. 171–6.

cepted battle at Cannae in Apulia (216 B.C.*). The result was a Roman disaster of unprecedented magnitude.*

At various points in his account (B), Polybius states solemnly his opinion that Rome's success in conquering the Mediterranean world in the short space of not quite fifty-three years (219–167 B.C.*) was largely due to her constitution and morals. He deals fully with these topics in Book VI, which follows immediately his narrative of Roman and Greek history down to the fateful year of Rome's defeat at Cannae, clearly intending to explain how this Roman catastrophe led to Roman world domination. Polybius states explicitly that his analysis of the Roman constitution applies to the period of Cannae. When Polybius wrote this section (146* B.C.?*) the constitutional harmony described by him was on the point of breaking down, to be succeeded by the struggle of* optimates *and* populares.[2]

A. CAUSATION

Some historians of the Hannibalian war, when they wish to point out to us the causes of this contest between Rome and Carthage, allege first the siege of Saguntum by the Carthaginians, and, secondly, their breach of treaty by crossing the river called by the natives the Iber [Ebro]. But though I should call these the first actions in the war, I cannot admit them to be its causes. One might just as well say that the crossing of Alexander the Great into Asia was the cause of the Persian war, and the descent of Antiochus upon Demetrias the cause of his war with Rome. . . .

Now the Roman annalist Fabius [Pictor] asserts that the cause of the Hannibalian war, besides the injury inflicted upon Saguntum, was the encroaching and ambitious spirit of Hasdrubal. "Having secured great power in Iberia, he returned to Libya with the design of destroying the constitution and reducing Carthage to a despotism. But the leading statesmen, getting timely warning of his intention, banded themselves together and successfully opposed him. Suspecting this, Hasdrubal retired from Libya and thenceforth governed Iberia entirely at his own will without taking any account whatever of the Carthaginian Senate. This policy had had in Hannibal from his earliest youth a zealous supporter and imitator; and when he succeeded to the command in Iberia he continued it; and accordingly,

[2] Evelyn S. Shuckburgh, *The Histories of Polybius,* Vol. I (London: Macmillan, 1889), pp. 468–74, 501–6.

even in the case of this war with Rome, was acting on his own authority and contrary to the wish of the Carthaginians; for none of the men of note in Carthage approved of his attack upon Saguntum." This is the statement of Fabius, who goes on to say, that "after the capture of that city an embassy arrived in Carthage from Rome demanding that Hannibal should be given up on pain of a declaration of war."

Now what answer could Fabius have given if we had put the following question to him? "What better chance or opportunity could the Carthaginians have had of combining justice and interest? According to your own account they disliked the proceeding of Hannibal: why did they not submit to the demands of Rome by surrendering the author of the injury; and thus get rid of the common enemy of the state without the odium of doing it themselves, and secure the safety of their territory by ridding themselves of the threatened war—all of which they could have effected by merely passing a decree?" If this question were put, I say, it would admit of no answer. The fact is that, so far from doing anything of the sort, they maintained the war in accordance with Hannibal's policy for seventeen years; and refused to make terms until, at the end of a most determined struggle, they found their own city and persons in imminent danger of destruction.

I do not allude to Fabius and his annals from any fear of their wearing such an air of probability in themselves as to gain any credit,—for the fact is that his assertions are so contrary to reason, that it does not need any argument of mine to help his readers to perceive it,—but I wished to warn those who take up his books not to be misled by the authority of his name, but to be guided by facts. For there is a certain class of readers in whose eyes the personality of the writer is of more account than what he says. They look to the fact that Fabius was a contemporary and a member of the Senate, and assume without more ado that everything he says may be trusted. My view, however, is that we ought not to hold the authority of this writer lightly: yet at the same time that we should not regard it as all-sufficient; but in reading his writings should test them by a reference to the facts themselves.

This is a digression from my immediate subject, which is the war between Carthage and Rome. The cause of this war we must reckon to be the exasperation of Hamilcar, surnamed Barcas, the father of Hannibal. The result of the war in Sicily had not broken the spirit of that commander. He regarded himself as unconquered; for the troops at Eryx which he commanded were still sound and undismayed: and though he yielded so far as to make a treaty, it was a concession to the exigencies of the times brought on by the defeat of the Carthaginians at sea. But he never relaxed in his determined purpose of revenge; and, had it not been for the mutiny of the mercenaries at Carthage, he would at once have sought and made another occasion for bringing about a war, as far as he was able to do so: as it was, he was preoccupied by the domestic war, and had to give his attention entirely to that.

When the Romans, at the conclusion of this mercenary war, proclaimed war with Carthage, the latter at first was inclined to resist to all hazards, because the goodness of her cause gave her hopes of victory,—as I have shown in my former book, without which it would be impossible to understand adequately either this or what is to follow. The Romans, however, would not listen to anything: and the Carthaginians therefore yielded to the force of circumstances; and though feeling bitterly aggrieved, yet being quite unable to do anything, evacuated Sardinia, and consented to pay a sum of twelve hundred talents, in addition to the former indemnity paid them, on condition of avoiding the war at that time. This is the second and the most important cause of the subsequent war. For Hamilcar, having this public grievance in addition to his private feelings of anger, as soon as he had secured his country's safety by reducing the rebellious mercenaries, set at once about securing the Carthaginian power in Iberia with the intention of using it as a base of operations against Rome. So that I record as a third cause of the war the Carthaginian success in Iberia: for it was the confidence inspired by their forces there which encouraged them to embark upon it. It would be easy to adduce other facts to show that Hamilcar, though he had been dead ten years at its commencement, largely contributed to bring about the second Punic war, but what I am about to say will be sufficient to establish the fact.

When, after his final defeat by the Romans, Hannibal had at last quitted his country and was staying at the court of Antiochus, the warlike attitude of the Aetolian league induced the Romans to send ambassadors to Antiochus, that they might be informed of the king's intentions. These ambassadors found that Antiochus was inclined to the Aetolian alliance, and was eager for war with Rome; they accordingly paid great court to Hannibal with a view of bringing him into suspicion with the king. And in this they entirely succeeded. As time went on, the king became ever more and more suspicious of Hannibal, until at length an opportunity occurred for an explanation of the alienation that had been thus secretly growing up between them. Hannibal then defended himself at great length, but without success, until at last he made the following statement: "When my father was about to go on his Iberian expedition, I was nine years old: and as he was offering the sacrifice to Zeus I stood near the altar. The sacrifice successfully performed, my father poured the libation and went through the usual ritual. He then bade all the other worshippers stand a little back, and calling me to him asked me affectionately whether I wished to go with him on his expedition. Upon my eagerly assenting, and begging with boyish enthusiasm to be allowed to go, he took me by the right hand and led me up to the altar, and bade me lay my hand upon the victim and swear that I would never be friends with Rome. So long, then, Antiochus, as your policy is one of hostility to Rome, you may feel quite secure of having in me a most thorough-going supporter. But if ever you make terms or friendship with her, then you need not wait for any slander to make you distrust me and be on your guard against me; for there is nothing in my power that I would not do against her."

Antiochus listened to this story, and being convinced that it was told with genuine feeling and sincerity, gave up all his suspicions. And we, too, must regard this as an unquestionable proof of the animosity of Hamilcar and of the aim of his general policy; which, indeed, is also proved by facts. For he inspired his son-in-law Hasdrubal and his son Hannibal with a bitterness of resentment against Rome which nothing could surpass. Hasdrubal, indeed, was prevented by death from showing the full extent of his purpose; but time gave Hannibal abundant opportunity to manifest the hatred of Rome which he had inherited from his father.

B. POLYBIUS ON THE ROMAN CONSTITUTION AND MORALS

As for the Roman constitution, it had three elements, each of them possessing sovereign powers: and their respective share of power in the whole state had been regulated with such a scrupulous regard to equality and equilibrium, that no one could say for certain, not even a native, whether the constitution as a whole were an aristocracy or democracy or despotism. And no wonder: for if we confine our observation to the power of the Consuls we should be inclined to regard it as despotic; if on that of the Senate, as aristocratic; and if finally one looks at the power possessed by the people it would seem a clear case of a democracy. What the exact powers of these several parts were, and still, with slight modifications, are, I will now state.

The Consuls, before leading out the legions, remain in Rome and are supreme masters of the administration. All other magistrates, except the Tribunes, are under them and take their orders. They introduce foreign ambassadors to the Senate; bring matters requiring deliberation before it; and see to the execution of its decrees. If, again, there are any matters of state which require the authorisation of the people, it is their businesss to see to them, to summon the popular meetings, to bring the proposals before them, and to carry out the decrees of the majority. In the preparations for war also, and in a word in the entire administration of a campaign, they have all but absolute power. It is competent to them to impose on the allies such levies as they think good, to appoint the Military Tribunes, to make up the roll for soldiers and select those that are suitable. Besides, they have absolute power of inflicting punishment on all who are under their command while on active service: and they have authority to expend as much of the public money as they choose, being accompanied by a Quaestor who is entirely at their orders. A survey of these powers would in fact justify our describing the constitution as despotic,—a clear case of royal government. Nor will it affect the truth of my description, if any of the institutions I have described are changed in our time, or in that of our posterity: and the same remarks apply to what follows.

The Senate has first of all the control of the treasury, and regulates the receipts and disbursements alike. For the Quaestors cannot issue any public money for the various departments of the state without a decree of the Senate, except for the service of the Consuls. The Senate controls also what is by far the largest and most important expenditure, that, namely, which is made by the censors every *lustrum* for the repair or construction of public buildings; this money cannot be obtained by the censors except by the grant of the Senate. Similarly all crimes committed in Italy requiring a public investigation, such as treason, conspiracy, poisoning, or wilful murder, are in the hands of the Senate. Besides, if any individual or state among the Italian allies requires a controversy to be settled, a penalty to be assessed, help or protection to be afforded,—all this is the province of the Senate. Or again, outside Italy, if it is necessary to send an embassy to reconcile warring communities, or to remind them of their duty, or sometimes to impose requisitions upon them, or to receive their submission, or finally to proclaim war against them,—this too is the business of the Senate. In like manner the reception to be given to foreign ambassadors in Rome, and the answers to be returned to them, are decided by the Senate. With such business the people have nothing to do. Consequently, if one were staying at Rome when the Consuls were not in town, one would imagine the constitution to be a complete aristocracy: and this has been the idea entertained by many Greeks, and by many kings as well, from the fact that nearly all the business they had with Rome was settled by the Senate.

After this one would naturally be inclined to ask what part is left for the people in the constitution, when the Senate has these various functions, especially the control of the receipts and expenditure of the exchequer; and when the Consuls again have absolute power over the details of military preparation and an absolute authority in the field? There is, however, a part left the people, and it is a most important one. For the people is the sole fountain of honour and of punishment; and it is by these two things and these alone that dynasties and constitutions and, in a word, human society, are held together; for where the distinction between them is not sharply drawn both in theory and practice, there no undertaking can be properly administered,—as indeed we might expect when good and bad are held in exactly the same honour. The people then are the only court to decide matters of life and death; and even in cases where the penalty is money, if the sum to be assessed is sufficiently serious, and especially when the accused have held the higher magistracies. And in regard to this arrangement there is one point deserving especial commendation and record. Men who are on trial for their lives at Rome, while sentence is in process of being voted,—if even only one of the tribes whose votes are needed to ratify the sentence has not voted,—have the privilege at Rome of openly departing and condemning themselves to a voluntary exile. Such men are safe at Naples or Praeneste or at Tibur, and at other towns with which this arrangement has been duly ratified on oath.

Again, it is the people who bestow offices on the deserving, which are the most honourable rewards of virtue. It has also the absolute power of passing or repealing laws; and, most important of all, it is the people who deliberate on the question of peace or war. And when provisional terms are made for alliance, suspension of hostilities, or treaties, it is the people who ratify them or the reverse.

These considerations again would lead one to say that the chief power in the state was the people's, and that the constitution was a democracy.

Such, then, is the distribution of power between the several parts of the state. I must now show how each of these several parts can, when they choose, oppose or support each other.

The Consul, then, when he has started on an expedition with the powers I have described, is to all appearance absolute in the administration of the business in hand; still he has need of the support both of people and Senate, and, without them, is quite unable to bring the matter to a successful conclusion. For it is plain that he must have supplies sent to his legions from time to time; but without a decree of the Senate they can be supplied neither with corn, nor clothes, nor pay, so that all the plans of a commander must be futile, if the Senate is resolved either to shrink from danger or hamper his plans. And again, whether a Consul shall bring any undertaking to a conclusion or no depends entirely upon the Senate: for it has absolute authority at the end of a year to send another Consul to supersede him, or to continue the existing one in his command. Again, even to the success of the generals the Senate has the power to add distinction and glory, and on the other hand to obscure their merits and lower their credit. For these high achievements are brought in tangible form before the eyes of the citizens by what are called "triumphs." But these triumphs the commanders cannot celebrate with proper pomp, or in some cases celebrate at all, unless the Senate concurs and grants the necessary money. As for the people, the Consuls are pre-eminently obliged to court their favour, however distant from home may be the field of their operations; for it is the people, as I have said before, that ratifies, or refuses to ratify, terms of peace and treaties; but most of all because when laying down their office they have to give an account of their administration before it. Therefore in no case is it safe for the Consuls to neglect either the Senate or the good-will of the people.

As for the Senate, which possesses the immense power I have described, in the first place it is obliged in public affairs to take the multitude into account, and respect the wishes of the people; and it cannot put into execution the penalty for offences against the republic, which are punishable with death, unless the people first ratify its decrees. Similarly even in matters which directly affect the senators,—for instance, in the case of a law diminishing the Senate's traditional authority, or depriving senators of certain dignities and offices, or even actually cutting down their property,—even in such cases the people have the sole power of passing or rejecting the law. But most important of all is the fact that, if the Tribunes interpose their veto, the Senate not only are unable to pass a decree, but cannot even hold a meeting at all, whether formal or informal. Now, the Tribunes are always bound to carry out the decree of the people, and above all things to have regard to their wishes: therefore, for all these reasons the Senate stands in awe of the multitude, and cannot neglect the feelings of the people.

In like manner the people on its part is far from being independent of the Senate, and is bound to take its wishes into account both collectively and individually. For contracts, too numerous to count, are given out by the censors in all parts of Italy for the repairs or construction of public buildings; there is also the collection of revenue from many rivers, harbours, gardens, mines, and land—everything in a word that comes under the control of the Roman government; and in all these the people at large are engaged; so that there is scarcely a man, so to speak, who is not interested either as a contractor or as being employed in the works. For some purchase the contracts from the censors for themselves; and others go partners with them; while others again go security for these contractors, or actually pledge their property to the treasury for them. Now over all these transactions the Senate has absolute control. It can grant an extension of time; and in case of unforeseen accident can relieve the contractors from a portion of their obligation, or release them from it altogether, if they are absolutely unable to fulfil it. And there are many details in which the Senate can inflict great hardships, or, on the other hand, grant great indulgences to the contractors; for in every case the appeal is to it. But the most important point of all is that the judges are taken from its members in the majority of trials, whether public or private, in which the charges are heavy. Consequently, all citizens are much at its mercy; and being alarmed at the uncertainty as to when they may need its aid, are cautious about resisting or actively opposing its will. And for a similar reason men do not rashly resist the wishes of the Consuls, because one and all may become subject to their absolute authority on a campaign.

The result of this power of the several estates for mutual help or harm is a union sufficiently firm for all emergencies, and a constitution than which it is impossible to find a better. For whenever any danger from without compels them to unite and work together, the strength which is developed by the State is so extraordinary, that everything required is unfailingly carried out by the eager rivalry shown by all classes to devote their whole minds to the need of the hour, and to secure that any determination come to should not fail for want of promptitude; while each individual works, privately and publicly alike, for the accomplishment of the business in hand. Accordingly, the peculiar constitution of the State makes it irresistible, and certain of obtaining whatever it determines to attempt. Nay, even when these external alarms are past, and the people are enjoying their good fortune and the fruits of their victories, and, as usually happens, growing corrupted by flattery and idleness, show a tendency to violence and arrogance,—it is in these circumstances, more than ever, that the constitution is seen to possess within itself the power of correcting abuses. For when any one of the three classes becomes puffed up, and manifests an inclination to be contentious and unduly encroaching, the mutual interdependency of all the three, and the possibility of the pretensions of any one being checked and thwarted by the others, must plainly check this tendency; and so the proper equilibrium is maintained by the impulsiveness of the one part being checked by its fear of the other.

[Polybius continues with a long section on the Roman army and its discipline. He then compares the Roman constitution with those of Thebes, Athens, Sparta, Crete, and Carthage.]

Now the Carthaginian constitution seems to me originally to have been well contrived in these most distinctively important particulars. For they had kings, and the Gerusia had the powers of an aristocracy, and the multitude were supreme in such things as affected them; and on the whole the adjustment of its several parts was very like that of Rome and Sparta. But about the period of its entering on the Hannibalian war the political state of Carthage was on the decline, that of Rome improving. For whereas there is in every body, or polity, or business a natural stage of growth, zenith, and decay; and whereas everything in them is at its best at the zenith; we may thereby judge of the difference between these two constitutions as they existed at that period. For exactly so far as the strength and prosperity of Carthage preceded that of Rome in point of time, by so much was Carthage then past its prime, while Rome was exactly at its zenith, as far as its political constitution was concerned. In Carthage therefore the influence of the people in the policy of the state had already risen to be supreme, while at Rome the Senate was at the height of its power: and so, as in the one measures were deliberated upon by the many, in the other by the best men, the policy of the Romans in all public undertakings proved the stronger; on which account, though they met with capital disasters, by force of prudent counsels they finally conquered the Carthaginians in the war.

If we look however at separate details, for instance at the provisions for carrying on a war, we shall find that whereas for a naval expedition the Carthaginians are the better trained and prepared,—as it is only natural with a people with whom it has been hereditary for many generations to practise this craft, and to follow the seaman's trade above all nations in the world,—yet, in regard to military service on land, the Romans train themselves to a much higher pitch than the Carthaginians. The former bestow their whole attention upon this department: whereas the Carthaginians wholly neglect their infantry, though they do take some slight interest in the cavalry. The reason of this is that they employ foreign mercenaries, the Romans native and citizen levies. It is in this point that the latter polity is preferable to the former. They have their hopes of freedom ever resting on the courage of mercenary troops: the Romans on the valour of their own citizens and the aid of their allies. The result is that even if the Romans have suffered a defeat at first, they renew the war with undiminished forces, which the Carthaginians cannot do. For, as the Romans are fighting for country and children, it is impossible for them to relax the fury of their struggle; but they persist with obstinate resolution until they have overcome their enemies. What has happened in regard to their navy is an instance in point. In skill the Romans are much behind the Carthaginians, as I have already said; yet the upshot of the whole naval war has been a decided triumph for the Romans, owing to the valour of their men. For although nautical science contributes largely to success in sea-fights, still it is the courage of the marines that turns the scale most decisively in favour of victory. The fact is that Italians as a nation are by nature superior to Phoenicians and Libyans both in physical strength and courage; but still their habits also do much to inspire the youth with enthusiasm for such exploits. One example will be sufficient of the pains taken by the Roman state to turn out men ready to endure anything to win a reputation in their country for valour.

Whenever one of their illustrious men dies, in the course of his funeral, the body with all its paraphernalia is carried into the forum to the Rostra, as a raised platform there is called, and sometimes is propped upright upon it so as to be conspicuous, or, more rarely, is laid upon it. Then with all the people standing round, his son, if he has left one of full age and he is there, or, failing him, one of his relations, mounts the Rostra and delivers a speech concerning the virtues of the deceased, and the successful exploits performed by him in his lifetime. By these means the people are reminded of what has been done, and made to see it with their own eyes,—not only such as were engaged in the actual transactions but those also who were not,—and their sympathies are so deeply moved, that the loss appears not to be confined to the actual mourners, but to be a public one affecting the whole people. After the burial and all the usual ceremonies have been performed, they place the likeness of the deceased in the most conspicuous spot in his house, surmounted by a wooden canopy or shrine. This likeness consists of a mask made to represent the deceased with extraordinary fidelity both in shape and colour. These likenesses they display at public sacrifices adorned with much care. And when any illustrous member of the family dies, they carry these masks to the funeral, putting them on men whom they thought as like the originals as possible in height and other personal peculiarities. And these substitutes assume clothes according to the rank of the person represented: if he was a consul or praetor, a toga with purple stripes; if a censor, whole purple; if he had also celebrated a triumph or performed any exploit of that kind, a toga embroidered with gold. These representatives also ride themselves in chariots, while the fasces and axes, and all the other customary insignia of the particular offices, lead the way, according to the dignity of the rank in the state enjoyed by the deceased in his lifetime; and on arriving at the Rostra they all take their seats on ivory chairs in their order. There could not easily be a more inspiring spectacle than this for a young man of noble ambitions and virtuous aspirations. For can we conceive any one to be unmoved at the sight of all the kindnesses collected together of the men who have earned glory, all as it were living and breathing? Or what could be a more glorious spectacle?

Besides the speaker over the body about to be buried, after having finished the panegyric of this particular person, starts upon the others whose representatives are present, beginning with the most ancient, and recounts the successes and achievements of each. By this means the glorious memory of brave men is continually renewed; the fame of those who have performed any noble deed is never allowed to die; and the renown of those who have done good service to their country becomes a matter of common knowledge to the multitude, and part of the heritage of posterity. But the chief benefit of the ceremony is that it inspires young men to shrink from no exertion for the general welfare, in the hope of obtaining the glory which awaits the brave. And what I say is confirmed by this fact. Many Romans have volunteered to decide a whole battle by single combat; not a few have deliberately accepted certain death, some in time of war to secure the safety of the rest, some in time of peace to preserve the safety of the commonwealth. There have also been instances of men in office putting their own sons to death, in defiance of every custom and law, because they rated the interests of their country higher than those of natural ties even with their nearest and dearest. . . .

Again the Roman customs and principles regarding money transactions are better than those of the Carthaginians. In the view of the latter nothing is disgraceful that makes for gain; with the former nothing is more disgraceful than to receive bribes and to make profit by improper means. For they regard wealth obtained from unlawful transactions to be as much a subject of reproach, as a fair profit from the most unquestioned source is of commendation. A proof of the fact is this. The Carthaginians obtain office by open bribery, but among the Romans the penalty for it is death. With such a radical difference, therefore, between the rewards offered to virtue among the two peoples, it is natural that the ways adopted for obtaining them should be different also.

But the most important difference for the better which the Roman commonwealth appears to me to display is in their religious beliefs. For I conceive that what in other nations is looked upon as a reproach, I mean a scrupulous fear of the gods, is the very thing which keeps the Roman commonwealth together. To such an extraordinary height is this carried among them, both in private and public business, that nothing could exceed it. Many people might think this unaccountable; but in my opinion their object is to use it as a check upon the common people. If it were possible to form a state wholly of philosophers, such a custom would perhaps be unnecessary. But seeing that every multitude is fickle, and full of lawless desires, unreasoning anger, and violent passion, the only resource is to keep them in check by mysterious terrors and scenic effects of this sort. Wherefore, to my mind, the ancients were not acting without purpose or at random, when they brought in among the vulgar those opinions about the gods, and the belief in the punishments in Hades; much rather do I think that men nowadays are acting rashly and foolishly in rejecting them. This is the reason why, apart from anything else, Greek statesmen, if entrusted with a single talent, though protected by ten checking-clerks, as many seals, and twice as many witnesses, yet cannot be induced to keep faith: whereas among the Romans, in their magistracies and embassies, men have the handling of a great amount of money, and yet from pure respect to their oath keep their faith intact. And, again, in other nations it is a rare thing to find a man who keeps his hands out of the public purse, and is entirely pure in such matters: but among the Romans it is a rare thing to detect a man in the act of committing such a crime.

63 / FREEDOM FOR GREECE

The peace terms granted to King Philip V of Macedon at the end of the Second Macedonian War (200–197 B.C.*) were drawn up by the Roman Senate, and important details were settled by Roman envoys despatched to Greece in collaboration with Flamininus, the victorious Roman commander. The Roman decisions* *were announced in dramatic fashion at the Isthmian Games held at Corinth in 196* B.C.[3]

The expectation of what would happen there [Corinth] drew the men of highest rank from nearly every quarter of the world; and there was a great deal of talk on the subject from one end of the assembled multitude to the other, and expressed in varied language. Some said that from certain of the places and towns it was impossible that the Romans could withdraw; while others asserted that they would withdraw from those considered most important, but would retain others that were less prominent, though capable of being quite as serviceable. And such persons even took upon themselves in their ingenuity to designate the precise places which would be thus treated. While people were still in this state of uncertainty, all the world being assembled on the stadium to watch the games, the herald came forward, and having proclaimed silence by the sound of a trumpet delivered the following proclamation: "The Senate of Rome and Titus Quintus [Flamininus], proconsul and imperator, having conquered King Philip and the Macedonians in war, declare the following peoples free, without garrison, or tribute, in full enjoyment of the laws of their respective countries: namely, Corinthians, Phocians, Locrians, Euboeans, Achaeans of Phiotis, Magnesians, Thessalians, Perrhaebians."

Now as the first words of the proclamation were the signal for a tremendous outburst of clapping, some of the people could not hear it at all, and some wanted to hear it again; but the majority feeling incredulous, and thinking that they heard the words in a kind of dream, so utterly unexpected was it, another impulse induced every one to shout to the herald and the trumpeter to come into the middle of the stadium and repeat the words: I suppose because the people wished not only to hear but to see the speaker, in their inability to credit the announcement. But when the herald, having advanced into the middle of the crowd, once more, by his trumpeter, hushed the clamour, and repeated exactly the same proclamation as before, there was such an outbreak of clapping as is difficult to convey to the imagination of my readers at this time. When at length the clapping ceased, no one paid any attention whatever to the athletes, but all were talking to themselves or each other, and seemed like people bereft of their senses. Nay, after the games were over, in the extravagance of their joy, they nearly killed Flamininus by the exhibition of their

[3] Evelyn S. Shuckburgh, *The Histories of Polybius,* Vol. II (London: Macmillan, 1889), pp. 241–3.

gratitude. Some wanted to look him in the face and call him their preserver; others were eager to touch his hand; most threw garlands and fillets upon him; until between them they nearly crushed him to death. But though this expression of popular gratitude was thought to have been extravagant, one might say with confidence that it fell short of the importance of the actual event. For that the Romans and their leader Flamininus should have deliberately incurred unlimited expense and danger, for the sole purpose of freeing Greece, deserved their admiration; and it was also a great thing that their power was equal to their intention. But the greatest thing of all is that Fortune foiled their attempt by none of her usual caprices, but that every single thing came to a successful issue at the same time; so that all Greeks, Asiatic and European alike, were by a single proclamation become "free, without garrison or tribute, and enjoying their own laws."

64 / THE NEW IMPERIALISM

Rome's war against Macedonia led her to further military involvements with other Hellenistic states, notably with the Seleucids and Ptolemies. King Antiochus IV Epiphanes attempted to recoup, by an attack on Egypt, the losses suffered by his father Antiochus III at the hands of the Romans. As long as the Third Macedonian War (171–167 B.C.*) was undecided, the Romans did not interfere. Immediately after the Roman victory at Pydna (167* B.C.*), however, the Senate dispatched an envoy to Egypt. C. Popilius Laenas' treatment (A) of the great Hellenistic king is symbolic of Rome's new imperialism, and should be compared with Flamininus' attitude toward Philip V and Greece a generation earlier (No. 63).*[4]

Rome's wars in the second century B.C. *were profitable enterprises, both for the state and for individuals. The second excerpt (B) illustrates how Rome plundered defeated enemies and how foreign wealth flowed into the imperial city. Lucius Aemilius Paullus' sack of Illyria and Epirus and his triumph occurred on*

[4] Evelyn S. Shuckburgh, *The Histories of Polybius,* Vol. II (London: Macmillan, 1889), pp. 405–6.

his homeward march from the Third Macedonian War (167 B.C.*). Note especially the capture of 150,000 prisoners who were subsequently sold into slavery. At the end of the selection there is a description of Paullus' triumph at Rome. It is based on the work on an annalist of the early first century* B.C.*, Valerius Antias, who wrote a Roman history in seventy-five books reaching down to at least 91* B.C.[5]

A. THE CIRCLE OF POPILIUS

When Antiochus had advanced to attack Ptolemy in order to possess himself of Pelusium, he was met by the Roman commander Gaius Popilius Laenas. Upon the king greeting him from some distance, and holding out his right hand to him, Popilius answered by holding out the tablets which contained the decree of the Senate, and bade Antiochus read that first: not thinking it right, I suppose, to give the usual sign of friendship until he knew the mind of the recipient, whether he were to be regarded as a friend or foe. On the king, after reading the despatch, saying that he desired to consult with his friends on the situation, Popilius did a thing which was looked upon as exceedingly overbearing and insolent. Happening to have a vine stick in his hand, he drew a circle round Antiochus with it, and ordered him to give his answer to the letter before he stepped out of that circumference. The king was taken aback by this haughty proceeding. After a brief interval of embarrassed silence, he replied that he would do whatever the Romans demanded. Then Popilius and his colleagues shook him by the hand, and one and all greeted him with warmth. The contents of the despatch was an order to put an end to the war with Ptolemy at once. Accordingly a stated number of days was allowed him, within which he withdrew his army into Syria, in high dudgeon indeed, and groaning in spirit, but yielding to the necessities of the time.

B. PLUNDER AND TRIUMPH

He [Lucius Aemilius Paullus] detached his son Quintus Maximus and Publius Nasica with half of the troops to lay waste the country of the Illyrians, who had assisted Perseus in the war, ordering them to meet him at Oricum; then taking the road to Epirus, on the evening of the fifteenth day he reached the city of Passaro.

[5] George Baker, *The History of Rome by Titus Livius,* Vol. VI (New York: Peter Mesier et al., 1823), pp. 282–3, 293–4.

Not far from hence was the camp of Anicius, to whom he sent a letter desiring him not to be alarmed at any thing that should happen, for the Senate had granted to his soldiers the plunder of those cities in Epirus which had revolted to Perseus. He despatched centurions who were to give out that they came to bring away the garrisons, in order that the Epirotes might be free, as well as the Macedonians; and summoning before him ten of the principal men of each city, he gave them strict injunctions that all their gold and silver should be brought into the public street. He then sent cohorts to the several states, ordering those who had the greater distance to go to set out sooner than the others, that they might all arrive at the places of their destination on the same day. The tribunes and centurions were instructed how to act. Early in the morning all the treasure was collected; at the fourth hour the signal was given to the soldiers to plunder, and so ample was the booty acquired that the shares distributed were four hundred denarii to a horseman and two hundred to a footman. One hundred and fifty thousand persons were led away captive. Then the walls of the plundered cities, in number about seventy, were razed, the effects sold, and the soldiers' shares paid out of the price. Paullus then marched down to the sea to Oricum; he found that, contrary to his opinion, he had by no means satisfied the wishes of his men, who were enraged at being excluded from sharing in the spoil of the King as if they had not waged any war in Macedonia. . . .

Valerius Antias tells us that the total of the captured gold and silver carried in the [triumphal] procession [at Rome] was one hundred and twenty millions of sesterces; but from the number of Philippics and the weights of the gold and silver specifically set down by himself the amount is unquestionably made much greater. An equal sum, it is said, had been either expended on the late war or dissipated during the King's flight on his way to Samothrace. It is wonderful that so large a quantity of money should have been amassed within the space of thirty years, since Philip's war with the Romans, out of the produce of the mines and the other branches of revenue Philip began war against the Romans with his treasury very poorly supplied; Perseus, on the contrary, with his immensely rich.

Last came Paullus in his chariot, making a very majestic appearance both from the dignity of his person and of his age. He was accompanied, among other illustrious personages, by his two sons, Quintus Maximus and Publius Scipio; then followed the cavalry, troop by troop, and the cohorts of infantry, each in its order. The donative distributed among them was one hundred denarii to each footman, double to a centurion, and triple to a horseman; and it is believed that he would have given double to each, had they not objected to his attaining the present honour or had answered with thankful acclamations when that sum was announced as their reward. Perseus, led through the city in chains before the chariot of the general, his conqueror, was not the only instance at the time of the misfortunes incident to mankind; another appeared even in the victorious Paullus, though glittering in gold and purple. For, of two sons, who, as he had given away two others on adoption, were the only remaining heirs of his name, the younger, about twelve years old, died five days before the triumph and the elder, fourteen years of age, three days after it; children who might have been expected a short time before to be carried in the chariot with their father, dressed in the praetexta, and anticipating in their hopes the like kind of honours for themselves.

65 / SOCIAL AND ECONOMIC CHANGES IN THE SECOND CENTURY B.C.

Early in the Second Punic War (215 B.C.*) the cost of protracted warfare exhausted the public treasury. To finance the war in Spain, the Roman government appealed to rich citizens to supply the armies (A). This system of financing the war was used frequently from that time on, and the class of financiers developed gradually into the "equestrian order."* [6]

Marcus Porcius Cato the Elder (234–149 B.C.*) fought valiantly to preserve the ancient virtues that had characterized the early Roman state. He came of Latin peasant stock, was a soldier in the later stages of the Second Punic War, and began his rise to high public office at the end of the war. As a "new man" he held the consulship in 195* B.C. *and the censorship in 184* B.C. *As praetor in Sardinia (198* B.C.*) he expelled usurers. He initiated legislation against luxury. He opposed the influx of Greek civilization, especially medicine and philosophy, into the Roman body politic,*

[6] George Baker, *The History of Rome by Titus Livius,* Vol. III (New York: Peter Mesier et al., 1823), pp. 165–7.

yet he was not anti-intellectual. He published many of his speeches and wrote a book on agriculture and another on Roman history. The second excerpt (B) from Plutarch's biography illustrates Roman conservatism in intellectual matters and the economic effects of world empire on a Roman arch-conservative.[7]

The third selection (C) relates to the year 171 B.C., *when Rome was making unusually elaborate preparations for the Third Macedonian War against King Perseus. One of the extraordinary features of that year's draft was that veteran centurions could be called back to service up to the age of fifty. Twenty-three centurions thus drafted appealed to the tribunes of the people, who in turn submitted the matter to the popular assembly. Their plea was that they should not be assigned to posts inferior to those which they had formerly held. In the end most of the centurions dropped their appeal and enlisted, but one of their group, Spurius Ligustinus, delivered the speech printed here and on the strength of it was given the highest noncommissioned rank. He was born prior to 221* B.C., *but somehow escaped service during the Second Punic War. He first enlisted in 200* B.C. *for the Second Macedonian War and in the course of it became a centurion under Flamininus (No. 63). Immediately after that war he served under Cato in Spain, then in the war against King Antiochus III, and subsequently he fought in several campaigns in Spain. Altogether he spent twenty-two years in the Roman army. It is easy to realize that many an Italian farmer with a career similar to that of Spurius Ligustinus must have lost his farm during his absence on military duty.*[8]

A. THE CONTRACTORS

Towards the close of that summer in which happened those events which we have related [215 B.C.], letters arrived from the Scipios, Publius and Cneius, setting forth the great importance and successful issue of their operations in Spain; but that they were in want of everything, pay, clothing, and corn for the army and the crews of

[7] A. H. Clough, *Plutarch's Lives,* Vol. II (Boston: Little, Brown and Co., 1875), pp. 343–7.

[8] George Baker, *The History of Rome by Titus Livius,* Vol. VI (New York: Peter Mesier et al., 1823), pp. 89–90.

the ships. With regard to the pay, they observed that if the treasury were low, they would themselves devise some method of procuring it from the Spaniards; but that the other articles must at all events be sent from Rome, otherwise neither the army nor the province could be preserved. When the letters were read, both the truth of the facts represented and the reasonableness of the demands were universally acknowledged; but they were struck by the following considerations: what numerous forces on land and sea they were obliged to maintain; and what a large additional fleet must soon be provided in case of a war with Macedonia breaking out; that Sicily and Sardinia, which before had yielded a revenue, now scarcely maintained the troops employed in their own defence; that the public expenses were supplied by a tax; but as the number of those who contributed to this tax had been diminished by the great slaughter of the troops at Trasimenus and at Cannae, so the surviving few, if loaded with multiplied impositions, must perish likewise, only by a different malady. It was therefore concluded that if the state did not find support in credit, it could find none in money; and it was judged proper that the praetor, Fulvius, should go out to the assembly of the commons and lay before the people the necessitous situation of the country, exhorting them that such as had increased their estates by farming the public revenues should now assist that government to which they owed their prosperity, with indulgence in respect of time; and that they should engage to furnish by contract the supplies necessary for the army in Spain, on condition, when money should come into the treasury, of being the first paid. These matters the praetor explained in the assembly and gave public notice of the day on which he would contract for the supplying of clothing and corn for the army in Spain and such other things as were necessary for the men on board the fleet.

When the time came, three companies consisting of nineteen men attended in order to engage in the contract. Their demands were twofold; first, that they should be exempted from military service as long as they might be concerned in this business of the state; the other, that when they had sent goods on shipboard, any damage afterwards sustained either through the means of storms or of the enemy should be at the public loss. Both being complied with, they concluded the contract, and with the money of private persons; such were the habits of thinking, such the love of their country which, with uniform influence, pervaded all ranks of men. As all engagements were entered into with great spirit, so were they fulfilled with the most faithful punctuality and exactly in the same manner as the supplies were drawn as formerly, out of an opulent treasury.

B. SLAVE PLANTATIONS AND THE HELLENIZATION OF ROME

He [Cato] purchased a great many slaves out of the captives taken in war, but chiefly bought up the young ones, who were capable to be, as it were, broken and taught like whelps and colts. None of these ever entered another man's house, except sent either by Cato himself or his wife. If any one of them were asked what Cato did, they answered merely that they did not know. When a servant was at home, he was obliged either to do some work or sleep; for indeed Cato loved those most who used to lie down often to sleep, accounting them more docile than those who were wakeful and more fit for anything when they were refreshed with a little slumber. Being also of opinion that the great cause of the laziness and misbehavior of slaves was their running after their pleasures, he fixed a certain price for them to pay for permission amongst themselves, but would suffer no connections out of the house. At first, when he was but a poor soldier, he would not be difficult in anything which related to his eating, but looked upon it as a pitiful thing to quarrel with a servant for the belly's sake; but afterwards, when he grew richer and made many feasts for his friends and colleagues in office, as soon as supper was over he used to go with a leather thong and scourge those who had waited or dressed the meat carelessly. He always contrived too, that his servants should have some difference one among another, always suspecting and fearing a good understanding between them. Those who had committed anything worthy of death be punished, if they were found guilty by the verdict of their fellow-servants. But being after all much given to the desire of gain, he looked upon agriculture rather as a pleasure than profit; resolving, therefore, to lay out his money in safe and solid things, he purchased ponds, hot baths, grounds full of fuller's earth, remunerative lands, pastures, and woods; from all which he drew large returns, nor could Jupiter himself, he used to say, do him much damage. He was also given to the form of usury which is considered most odious, in traffic by sea; and that thus: he desired that those whom he put out his money to, should have many partners, and when the number of them and their ships came to be fifty, he himself took one share through Quintio his freedman, who therefore was to sail with the adventurers and take a part in all their proceedings; so that thus there was no danger of losing his whole stock but only a little part, and that with a prospect of great profit. He likewise lent money to those of his slaves who wished to borrow, with which they bought also other young ones whom, when they had taught and bred up at his charges, they would sell again at the year's end; but some of them Cato would keep for himself, giving just as much for them as another had offered. To incline his son to be of this kind of temper, he used to tell him that it was not like a man, but rather like a widow woman, to lessen an estate. But the strongest indication of Cato's avaricious humor was when he took the boldness to affirm that he was a most wonderful, nay, a godlike man who left more behind him than he had received.

He was now grown old when Carneades the Academic and Diogenes the Stoic came as deputies from Athens to Rome, praying for release from a penalty of five hundred talents laid on the Athenians in a suit to which they did not appear, in which the Oropians were plaintiffs and Sicyonians judges. All the most studious youth immediately waited on these philosophers and frequently, with admiration, heard them speak. But the gracefulness of Carneades's oratory, whose ability was really greater and his reputation equal to it, gathered large and favorable audiences and erelong filled, like a wind, all the city with the sound of it. So that it soon began to be told that a Greek, famous even to admiration, winning and carrying all before him, had impressed so strange a love upon the young men that, quitting all their pleasures and pastimes, they ran mad, as it were, after philosophy; which indeed much pleased the Romans in general; nor could they but with much pleasure see the youth receive so welcomely the Greek literature and frequent the company of learned men. But Cato, on the other side, seeing this passion for words flowing into the city, from the beginning took it ill, fearing lest the youth should be diverted that way and so should prefer the glory of speaking well before that of arms and doing well. And when the fame of the philosophers increased in the city and Caius Acilius, a person of distinction, at his own request became their interpreter to the Senate at their first audience, Cato resolved under some specious pretence to have all philosophers cleared out of the city; and, coming into the Senate, blamed the magistrates for letting these deputies stay so long a time without being despatched, though they were persons that could easily persuade the people to what they pleased; that therefore in all haste something should be determined about their petition, that so they might go home again to their own schools and declaim to the Greek children and leave the Roman youth to be obedient as hitherto to their own laws and governors.

Yet he did this not out of any anger, as some think, to Carneades; but because he wholly despised philosophy and out of a kind of pride scoffed at the Greek studies and literature; as, for example, he would say that Socrates was a prating seditious fellow who did his best to tyrannize over his country, to undermine the ancient customs, and to entice and withdraw the citizens to opinions contrary to the laws. Ridiculing the school of Isocrates, he would add that his scholars grew old men before they had done learning with him, as if they were to use their art and plead causes in the court of Minos in the next world. And to frighten his son from any thing that was Greek, in a more vehement tone than became one of his age, he pronounced, as it were, with the voice of an oracle that the Romans would certainly be destroyed when they began once to be infected with Greek literature; though time indeed has shown the vanity of this his prophecy; as in truth the city of Rome has risen to its highest fortune while entertaining Grecian learning. Nor had he an aversion only against the Greek philosophers, but the physicians also; for having, it seems, heard how Hippocrates, when the king of Persia sent for him with offers of a fee of several talents, said that he would never assist barbarians who were enemies to the Greeks; he affirmed, that this was now become a common oath taken by all physicians and enjoined his son to have a care and avoid them; for that he himself had written a little book of prescriptions for curing those who were sick in his family; he never enjoined fasting to any one, but ordered them either vegetables or the meat of a duck, pigeon, or leveret; such kind of diet being of light digestion and fit for sick folks, only it made those who ate it dream a little too much; and by the use of this kind of physic, he said, he not only made himself and those about him well, but kept them so.

C. WAR AND THE ITALIAN YEOMAN FARMER

Spurius Ligustinus, one of those who had appealed to the plebeian tribunes, requested permission from the consul and tribunes to speak a few words to the people; and all having consented, he spoke, we are told, to this effect: "Romans, my name is Spurius Ligustinus; I am of the Crustuminian tribe and of a family originally Sabine. My father left me one acre of land and a small cottage, in which I was born and educated and where I now dwell. As soon as I came to man's estate, my father married me to his brother's daughter, who brought nothing with her but independence and modesty; except, indeed, a degree of fruitfulness that would have better suited a wealthier family. We have six sons and two daughters; the latter are both married; of our sons four are grown up to manhood, the other two are yet boys. I became a soldier in the consulate of Publius Sulpicius and Caius Aurelius [200 B.C.]. In the army which was sent over into Macedon I served as a common soldier against Philip two years;

and in the third year Titus Quintius Flamininus, in reward of my good conduct, gave me the command of the tenth company of spearmen. When Philip and the Macedonians were subdued and we were brought back to Italy and discharged, I immediately went a volunteer with the consul Marcus Porcius [Cato] into Spain. That no one commander living was a more accurate observer and judge of merit is well known to all who have had experience of him and of other generals in a long course of service. This commander judged me deserving of being set at the head of the first company of spearmen. A third time I entered a volunteer in the army which was sent against the Aetolians and King Antiochus; and Manius Acilius gave me the command of the first company of first-rank men. After Antiochus was driven out of the country and the Aetolians were reduced, we were brought home to Italy, where I served the two succeeding years in legions that were raised annually. I afterwards made two campaigns in Spain; one under Quintus Fulvius Flaccus, the other under Tiberius Sempronius Gracchus, praetors. Flaccus brought me with him, among others, to attend his triumph, out of regard to our good services. It was at the particular request of Tiberius Gracchus that I went with him to his province. Four times within a few years was I first centurion of my corps; thirty-four times I was honoured by my commanders with presents for good behaviour. I have received six civic crowns; I have fulfilled twenty-two years of service in the army, and I am upwards of fifty years of age. But if I had neither served out all my campaigns nor was entitled to exemption on account of my age, yet, Publius Licinius, as I can supply you with four soldiers instead of myself, I might reasonably expect to be discharged. But what I have said I wish you to consider merely as a state of my case; as to offering anything as an excuse from service, that is what I will never do, so long as any officer enlisting troops shall believe me fit for it. What rank the military tribunes may think I deserve they themselves can best determine. That no one in the army may surpass me in zealous discharge of duty, I shall use my best endeavours; and that I have always acted on that principle my commanders and my comrades can testify. And now, fellow-soldiers, you who assert your privilege of appeal, as you have never in your youthful days done any act contrary to the directions of the magistrates and the Senate, so will it be highly becoming in you to show yourselves obedient to their orders and to think every post honourable in which you can act for the defence of the commonwealth."

IX / THE ROMAN REVOLUTION

66 / THE GRACCHAN REFORM PROGRAM

The diminishing number of Italian farmers, the influx of slaves and foreign wealth, and the growth of large estates threatened to deprive Rome of her military manpower at the very time armies were needed to conquer the Hellenistic world. In the last third of the second century B.C. *a movement favoring economic reforms emerged, led by two Roman nobles, Tiberius and his brother Gaius Gracchus, grandsons of Scripo Africanus and brothers-in-law of Scipio Aemilianus.*

Tiberius Gracchus (A) had played an important role in the Roman siege of Numantia in Spain (143–134 B.C.*). He was elected tribune of the plebs for 133* B.C. *and during his tribuneship initiated his program of reform.*

Distribution of public lands continued after Tiberius' murder until 129 B.C. *In that year the questions of citizenship for Rome's Latin and Italian allies and that of the composition of criminal courts were raised for the first time, questions which were to poison Roman political life for many decades. Tiberius' younger brother Gaius was elected tribune for the year 123* B.C. *Excerpt B is Plutarch's account of the legislation passed on his initiative.*[1]

A. TIBERIUS' LAND LAW

His brother Caius has left it us in writing that when Tiberius went through Tuscany to Numantia and found the country almost depopulated, there being hardly any free husbandmen or shepherds, but for

[1] A. H. Clough, *Plutarch's Lives,* Vol. IV (Boston: Little, Brown and Company, 1875), pp. 514–28, 536 ff.

the most part only barbarian, imported slaves, he then first conceived the course of policy which in the sequel proved so fatal to his family. Though it is also most certain that the people themselves chiefly excited his zeal and determination in the prosecution of it, by setting up writings upon the porches, walls, and monuments, calling upon him to reinstate the poor citizens in their former possessions.

However, he did not draw up his law without the advice and assistance of those citizens that were then most eminent for their virtue and authority; amongst whom were Crassus, the high priest, Mucius Scaevola, the lawyer, who at that time was consul, and Claudius Appius, his father-in-law. Never did any law appear more moderate and gentle, especially being enacted against such great oppression and avarice. For they who ought to have been severely punished for transgressing the former laws and should at least have lost all their titles to such lands which they had unjustly usurped were notwithstanding to receive a price for quitting their unlawful claims and giving up their lands to those fit owners who stood in need of help. But though this reformation was managed with so much tenderness that, all the former transactions being passed over, the people were only thankful to prevent abuses of the like nature for the future, yet, on the other hand, the moneyed men and those of great estates were exasperated through their covetous feelings against the law itself, and against the lawgiver through anger and party spirit. They therefore endeavored to seduce the people, declaring that Tiberius was designing a general redivision of lands, to overthrow the government and put all things into confusion.

But they had no success. For Tiberius, maintaining an honorable and just cause and possessed of eloquence sufficient to have made a less creditable action appear plausible, was no safe or easy antagonist when, with the people crowding around the hustings, he took his place and spoke in behalf of the poor. "The savage beasts," said he, "in Italy, have their particular dens, they have their places of repose and refuge; but the men who bear arms and expose their lives for the safety of their country enjoy in the mean time nothing more in it but the air and light; and having no houses or settlements of their own, are constrained to wander from place to place with their wives and children." He told them that the commanders were guilty of a ridiculous error when, at the head of their armies, they exhorted the common soldiers to fight for their sepulchres and altars; when not any amongst so many Romans is possessed of either altar or monument, neither have they any houses of their own or hearths of their ancestors to defend. They fought, indeed, and were slain, but it was to maintain the luxury and the wealth of other men. They were styled the masters of the world, but in the mean time had not one foot of ground which they could call their own. An harangue of this nature, spoken to an enthusiastic and sympathizing audience by a person of commanding spirit and genuine feeling, no adversaries at that time were competent to oppose. Forbearing, therefore, all discussion and debate, they addressed themselves to Marcus Octavius, his fellow-tribune, who, being a young man of a steady, orderly character and an intimate friend of Tiberius, upon this account declined at first the task of opposing him; but at length, overpersuaded with the repeated importunities of numerous considerable persons, he was prevailed upon to do so and hindered the passing of the law; it being the rule that any tribune has the power to hinder an act and that all the rest can effect nothing if only one of them dissents. . . .

When the day appointed was come and the people summoned to give their votes, the rich men seized upon the voting urns and carried them away by force; thus all things were in confusion. . . . When the senate assembled and could not bring the business to any result through the prevalence of the rich faction, he then was driven to a course neither legal nor fair and proposed to deprive Octavius of his tribuneship, it being impossible for him in any other way to get the law brought to the vote. . . .

He referred the whole matter to the people, calling on them to vote at once whether Octavius should be deposed or not; and when seventeen of the thirty-five tribes had already voted against him and there wanted only the votes of one tribe more for his final deprivation, Tiberius put a short stop to the proceedings and once more renewed his importunities; he embraced and kissed him before all the assembly, begging with all the earnestness imaginable that he would neither suffer himself to incur the dishonor nor him to be reputed the author and promoter of so odious a measure. Octavius, we are told, did seem a little softened and moved with these entreaties; his eyes filled with tears, and he continued silent for a considerable time. But presently, looking towards the rich men and proprietors of estates, who stood gathered in a body together, partly for shame and partly for fear of disgracing himself with them, he boldly bade Tiberius use any severity he pleased. The law for his deprivation being thus voted, Tiberius ordered one of his servants whom he had made a freeman, to remove Octavius from the rostra, employing his own domestic freed servants in the stead of public officers. And it made the action seem all the sadder that Octavius was dragged out in such an ignominious manner. The people immediately assaulted him, whilst the rich men ran in to his assistance. Octavius, with some difficulty, was snatched away and safely conveyed out of the crowd; though a trusty servant of his, who had placed himself in front of his master that he might assist his escape, in keeping off the multitude had his eyes struck out, much to the displeasure of Tiberius, who ran with all haste, when he perceived the disturbance, to appease the rioters.

This being done, the laws concerning the lands were ratified and confirmed, and three commissioners were appointed to make a survey of the grounds and see the same equally divided. These were Tiberius himself, Claudius Appius, his father-in-law, and his brother Caius Gracchus, who at this time was not at Rome, but in the army under the command of Scipio Africanus before Numantia. These things were transacted by Tiberius without any disturbance, none daring to offer any resistance to him. . . .

About this time, king Attalus [of Pergamum], surnamed Philometor, died, and Eudemus, a Pergamenian, brought his last will to Rome, by which he had made the Roman people his heirs. Tiberius, to please the people, immediately proposed making a law that all the money which Attalus left should be distributed amongst such poor citizens as were to be the sharers of the public lands for the better enabling them to proceed in stocking and cultivating their ground; and as for the cities that were in the territories of Attalus, he declared that the disposal of them did not at all belong to the Senate, but to the people, and that he himself would ask their pleasure herein. By this he offended the Senate more than he had ever done before. . . .

[In the midst of the revolutionary situation at Rome, Tiberius and three hundred of his followers were killed by a posse organized by a Roman senator. Plutarch continues as follows:]

This, we are told, was the first sedition amongst the Romans, since the abrogation of kingly government, that ended in the effusion of blood. All former quarrels which were neither small nor about trivial matters were always amicably composed by mutual concessions on either side, the Senate yielding for fear of the commons, and the commons out of respect to the Senate. And it is probable indeed that Tiberius himself might then have been easily induced by mere persuasion to give way, and certainly, if attacked at all, must have yielded without any recourse to violence and bloodshed, as he had not at that time above three thousand men to support him. But it is evident that this conspiracy was fomented against him more out of the hatred and malice which the rich men had to his person than for the reasons which they commonly pretended against him.

B. GAIUS GRACCHUS' LEGISLATION

Of the laws which he now proposed with the object of gratifying the people and abridging the power of the Senate, the first was concerning the public lands which were to be divided amongst the poor citizens; another was concerning the common soldiers, that they should be clothed at the public charge without any diminution of their pay and that none should be obliged to serve in the army who was not full seventeen years old; another gave the same right to all the Italians in general of voting at elections as was enjoyed by the citizens of Rome; a fourth related to the price of corn, which was to be sold at a lower rate than formerly to the poor; and a fifth regulated the courts of justice, greatly reducing the power of the senators. For hitherto in all causes senators only sat as judges and were therefore much dreaded by the Roman knights and the people. But Caius joined three hundred ordinary citizens of equestrian rank with the senators, who were three hundred likewise in number, and ordained that the judicial authority should be equally invested in the six hundred. While he was arguing for the ratification of this law, his behavior was observed to show in many respects unusual earnestness, and whereas other popular leaders had always hitherto, when speaking, turned their faces towards the senate house and the place called the comitium, he on the contrary was the first man that in his harangue to the people turned himself the other way, towards them, and continued after that time to do so. An insignificant movement and change of posture, yet it marked no small revolution in state affairs, the conversion, in a manner, of the whole government from an aristocracy to a democracy; his action intimating that public speakers should address themselves to the people, not the Senate.

When the commonalty ratified this law and give him power to select those of the knights whom he approved of to be judges, he was invested with a sort of kingly power, and the Senate itself submitted to receive his advice in matters of difficulty.

67 / THE MISMANAGEMENT OF THE PROVINCES

The Gracchan disorders had been followed by wars in North Africa (against King Jugurtha), in Gaul (against the Germanic Cimbri and Teutones), and in Italy (against Rome's allies demanding Roman citizenship). In 88 B.C. *the rivalry of two experienced generals, Sulla and Marius, for a command against King Mithridates of Pontus led to Rome's first seizure by a revolutionary army commanded by Sulla. The next year saw the capture of Rome by Marius' party and the execution of leading members of the aristocracy. After Sulla's return from the first Mithridatic war (83* B.C.*) civil war was renewed, and Sulla's opponents, especially those of the equestrian order, were massacred in the course of systematic "proscriptions." Sulla, as dictator (82–79* B.C.*), re-established the senatorial government at Rome. The offices of tribune of the plebs, on which the popular party had principally relied to carry through its program, was deprived of much of its power. The jury courts, on which since the days of the Gracchi both senators and equestrians had served (No. 66B), were now reserved once more for senators. After Sulla's resignation Rome's leading statesman was Pompey. He had begun his public career as a supporter of Sulla. Later he distinguished himself in a war against Sertorius, an adherent of Marius in Spain (77–72* B.C.*). Upon his return at the head of his army to Rome (71* B.C.*) he forced the Senate to accept him as a candidate for the consulship of 70* B.C.*, although he did not meet the legal requirements. As consul he supported a law initiated by the praetor L. Aurelius Cotta which provided that the jury courts should be manned by senators, equestrians, and* tribuni aerarii.

One of the factors contributing to the dissatisfaction with the Sullan jury courts was the trial of C. Verres, who had governed Sicily from 78–70 B.C. *Verres was charged with having plundered his province before a jury still consisting (according to Sulla's legislation) exclusively of senators. The province entrusted its case to a young equestrian, Marcus Tullius Cicero of Arpinum (106–43* B.C.*), who had demonstrated his ability as a lawyer and was to become a leading statesman, orator, and writer on philo-*

sophical matters. Verres had much political influence and attempted to ruin the chances of the prosecution by having selected as his prosecutor one of his supporters, Quintus Caecilius Niger. In the first speech before the court Cicero, therefore, had to prove that he was better equipped to present the case than Caecilius. The court agreed. Cicero then pleaded his case so successfully that Verres went into self-imposed exile at Marseilles. After the trial Cicero published in book form the Verrine orations, both those actually delivered and those planned by Cicero prior to Verres' departure. The following excerpt is taken from the fourth book of Cicero's second pleading against Verres.[2]

I will mention the sacking of one city, also, and that the most beautiful and highly decorated of all, the city of Syracuse. And I will produce my proofs of that, O judges, in order at length to conclude and bring to an end the whole history of offences of this sort. There is scarcely any one of you who has not often heard how Syracuse was taken by Marcus Marcellus [in 211 B.C.], and who has not sometimes also read the account in our annals. Compare this peace with that war; the visit of this praetor [Verres] with the victory of that general [Marcellus]; the debauched retinue of the one with the invincible army of the other; the lust of Verres with the continence of Marcellus;—and you will say that Syracuse was built by the man who took it; was taken by the man who received it well established and flourishing. And for the present I omit those things which will be mentioned and have already been mentioned by me in an irregular manner in different parts of my speech—that the market-place of the Syracusans, which at the entrance of Marcellus was preserved unpolluted by slaughter, on the arrival of Verres overflowed with the blood of innocent Sicilians; that the harbour of the Syracusans, which at that time was shut against both our fleets and those of the Carthaginians, was, while Verres was praetor, open to Cilician pirates or even to a single piratical galley. I say nothing of the violence offered to people of noble birth, of the ravishment of matrons, atrocities which then, when the city was taken, were not committed, neither through the hatred of enemies nor through military licence nor through the customs of war or the rights of victory. I pass over, I say, all these things which were done by that man for three whole years. Listen rather to acts which are connected with those matters of which I have hitherto been speak-

[2] C. D. Yonge, *The Orations of Marcus Tullius Cicero,* Vol. I (London: George Bell and Sons, 1878), pp. 452–6.

ing. You have often heard that the city of Syracuse is the greatest of the Greek cities and the most beautiful of all. It is so, O judges, as it is said to be; for it is so by its situation, which is strongly fortified and which is, on every side by which you can approach it, whether by sea or land, very beautiful to behold. And it has harbours almost enclosed within the walls and in the sight of the whole city; harbours which have different entrances, but which meet together and are connected at the other end. By their union a part of the town, which is called the island, being separated from the rest by a narrow arm of the sea, is again joined to and connected with the other by a bridge. . . .

Now I will return to Marcellus, that I may not appear to have entered into this statement without any reason. He, when with his powerful army he had taken this splendid city, did not think it for the credit of the Roman people to destroy and extinguish this splendour, especially as no danger could possibly arise from it, and therefore he spared all the buildings, public as well as private, sacred as well as ordinary, as if he had come with his army for the purpose of defending them, not of taking them by storm. With respect to the decorations of the city, he had a regard to his own victory and a regard to humanity; he thought it was due to his victory to transport many things to Rome which might be an ornament to this city and due to humanity not utterly to strip the city, especially as it was one which he was anxious to preserve. In this division of the ornaments, the victory of Marcellus did not covet more for the Roman people than his humanity reserved to the Syracusans. The things transported to Rome we see before temples of Honour and Virtue and also in other places. He put nothing in his own house, nothing in his gardens, nothing in his suburban villa; he thought that his house could only be an ornament to the city if he abstained from carrying the ornaments which belonged to the city to his own house. But he left many things of extraordinary beauty at Syracuse; he violated not the respect due to any god; he laid hands on none. Compare Verres with him; not to compare the man with the man,—no such injury must be done to such a man as that, dead though he be; but to compare a state of peace with one of war, a state of law and order and regular jurisdiction with one of violence and martial law and the supremacy of arms; to compare the arrival and retinue of the one with the victory and army of the other.

There is a temple of Minerva in the island, of which I have already spoken, which Marcellus did not touch, which he left full of its treasures and ornaments, but which was so stripped and plundered by Verres that it seems to have been in the hands not of any enemy,—for enemies, even in war, respect the rites of religion and the customs of the country—but of some barbarian pirates. There was a cavalry battle of their king Agathocles exquisitely painted in a series of pictures, and with these pictures the inside walls of the temple were covered. Nothing could be more noble than those paintings; there was nothing at Syracuse that was thought more worthy going to see. These pictures Marcus Marcellus, though by that victory of his he had divested everything of its sacred inviolability of character, still, out of respect for religion, never touched; Verres, though, in consequence of the long peace and the loyalty of the Syracusan people, he had received them as sacred and under the protection of religion, took away all those pictures and left naked and unsightly those walls whose decorations had remained inviolate for so many ages and had escaped so many wars: Marcellus, who had vowed that if he took Syracuse he would erect two temples at Rome, was unwilling to adorn the temple which he was going to build with these treasures, which were his by right of capture; Verres, who was bound by no vows to Honour and Virtue as Marcellus was, but only to Venus and to Cupid, attempting to plunder the temple of Minerva. The one was unwilling to adorn gods in the spoil taken from gods, the other transferred the decorations of the virgin Minerva to the house of a prostitute. Besides this he took away out of the same temple twenty-seven more pictures beautifully painted; among which were likenesses of the kings and tyrants of Sicily, which delighted one not only by the skill of the painter, but also by reminding us of the men and by enabling us to recognise their persons. And see now how much worse a tyrant this man proved to the Syracusans than any of the old ones, as they, cruel as they were, still adorned the temples of the immortal gods, while this man took away the monuments and ornaments from the gods.

68 / THE CONSPIRACY OF CATILINE

In the years following his first consulship, Pompey defeated Mithridates, established Roman suzerainty over Asia Minor, and formed a new Roman province out of the remnants of the Seleucid kingdom and parts of Judaea (63 B.C.*). While Pompey was away in the East, another general, Crassus, attempted to gain power in Rome. One of his supporters was L. Sergius Catilina. He had been charged with extortion (66* B.C.*) and with conspiracy to murder the consuls of 65, but in 64* B.C. *he offered* *himself as a candidate for the consulship. His program consisted in the general cancellation of debts and appealed to farmers, financiers, and especially to impoverished nobles. Cicero, who had become a staunch supporter of Pompey and who was solidly backed by the equestrian order, was another candidate. Cicero was elected; Catiline failed. In 63* B.C. *a young patrician, C. Julius Caesar, was elected* pontifex maximus *and* praetor. *During Cicero's consular year Catiline formed a conspiracy, organizing a military force in Northern Etruria which was to seize Rome in the fall of 63* B.C. *This plot was thwarted by the vigilance and eloquence of Cicero; the effect of his first Catilinarian oration was that Catiline was forced to leave the city and thereby confess his guilt. A few days later Cicero delivered a speech before the popular assembly informing the Romans of the conspiracy; Catiline was declared by the Senate a public enemy. Cicero had obtained irrefutable evidence of the conspiracy and had laid it before the Senate. A great debate ensued in which the consul-elect Silanus, Cicero, and the Younger Cato argued for the death penalty, but Caesar for life imprisonment. In the end Catiline's followers at Rome were executed, and Catiline himself was killed in a great battle at Pistoria, fighting at the head of the rebel troops.*[3]

At length, O Romans, we have dismissed from the city, or driven out or, when he was departing of his own accord, we have pursued with words, Lucius Catiline, mad with audacity, breathing wickedness, impiously planning mischief to his country, threatening fire and sword to you and to this city. He is gone, he has departed, he has disappeared, he has rushed out. No injury will now be prepared against these walls within the walls themselves by that monster and prodigy of wickedness. And we have without controversy defeated him, the sole general of this domestic war. For now that danger will no longer hover about our sides; we shall not be afraid in the campus, in the forum, in the senate-house—, ay and within our private walls. He was moved from his place when he was driven from the city. Now we shall openly carry on a regular war with an enemy without hinderance. Beyond all question we ruin the man; we have defeated him splendidly when we have driven him from secret treachery into open warfare.

[3] C. D. Yonge, *Select Orations of Cicero* (New York: Harper and Brothers, 1860), pp. 15–21.

But that he has not taken with him his sword red with blood as he intended—that he has left us alive—that we wrested the weapon from his hands—that he has left the citizens safe and the city standing, what great and overwhelming grief must you think that this is to him! Now he lies prostrate, O Romans, and feels himself stricken down and abject, and often casts back his eyes towards this city, which he mourns over as snatched from his jaws, but which seems to me to rejoice at having vomited forth such a pest and cast it out of doors. . . .

Therefore, with our Gallic legions, and with the levies which Quintus Metellus has raised in the Picenian and Gallic territory and with these troops which are every day being got ready by us, I thoroughly despise that army composed of desperate old men, of clownish profligates, and uneducated spendthrifts; of those who have preferred to desert their bail rather than that army, and which will fall to pieces if I show them not the battle array of our army but an edict of the praetor. I wish he had taken with him those soldiers of his whom I see hovering about the forum, standing about the senatehouse, even coming into the senate, who shine with ointment, who glitter in purple; and if they remain here, remember that that army is not so much to be feared by us as these men who deserted the army. And they are the more to be feared because they are aware that I know what they are thinking of and yet they are not influenced by it.

I know to whom Apulia has been allotted, who has Etruria, who the Picenian territory, who the Gallic district, who has begged for himself the office of spreading fire and sword by night through the city. They know that all the plans of the preceding night are brought to me. I laid them before the senate yesterday. Catiline himself was alarmed and fled. Why do these men wait? Verily, they are greatly mistaken if they think that former lenity of mine will last forever. . . .

But I am confident that some fate is hanging over these men; and that the punishment long since due to their iniquity and worthlessness and wickedness and lust is either visibly at hand or at least rapidly approaching. And if my consulship shall have removed, since it can not cure them, it will have added not some brief span but many ages of existence to the republic. For there is no nation for us to fear—no king who can make war on the Roman people. All foreign affairs are tranquilized, both by land and sea, by the valor of one man. Domestic war alone remains. The only plots against us are within our own walls—the danger is within—the enemy is within. We must war with luxury, with madness, with wickedness. For this war, O citizens, I offer myself as the general. I take on myself the enmity of profligate men. What can be cured I will cure by whatever means it may be possible. What must be cut away, I will not suffer to spread to the ruin of the republic.

Let them depart, or let them stay quiet; or if they remain in the city and in the same disposition as at present, let them expect what they deserve. . . .

For I will tell you, O Romans, of what classes of men those forces are made up and then, if I can, I will apply to each the medicine of my advice and persuasion.

There is one class of them who with enormous debts have still greater possessions and who can by no means be detached from their affection to them. Of these men the appearance is most respectable, for they are wealthy, but their intention and their cause are most shameless. Will you be rich in lands, in houses, in money, in slaves, in all things and yet hesitate to diminish your possessions to add to your credit? What are you expecting? War? What! In the devastation of all things, do you believe that your own possessions will be held sacred? Do you expect an abolition of debts? They are mistaken who expect that from Catiline. There may be schedules made out, owing to my exertions, but they will be only catalogues of sale. Nor can those who have possessions be safe by any other means; and if they had been willing to adopt this plan earlier, and not, as is very foolish, to struggle on against usury with the profits of their farms, we should have them now richer and better citizens. But I think these men are the least of all to be dreaded, because they can either be persuaded to abandon their opinions, or if they cling to them, they seem to me more likely to form wishes against the republic than to bear arms against it.

There is another class of them, who, although they are harassed by debt, yet are expecting supreme power; they wish to become masters. They think that when the republic is in confusion they may gain those honors which they despair of when it is in tranquillity. And they must, I think, be told the same as every one else—to despair of obtaining what they are aiming at; that in the first place, I myself am watchful for, am present to, am providing for the republic. Besides that, there is a high spirit in the virtuous citizens, great unanimity, great numbers, and also a large body of troops. Above all that, the immortal gods will stand by and bring aid to this invincible nation, this most illustrious empire, this more beautiful city, against such wicked violence. And if they had already got that which they with the greatest madness wish for, do they think that in the ashes of the city and blood of the citizens, which in their wicked and infamous hearts they desire, they will become consuls and dictators, and even kings? Do they not see that they are wishing for that which, if they were to obtain it, must be given up to some fugitive slave, or to some gladiator?

There is a third class, already touched by age, but still vigorous from constant exercise; of which class is Manlius himself, whom Catiline is now succeeding. These are men of those colonies which Sulla established at Fæsulæ, which I know to be composed, on the whole, of excellent citizens and brave men; but yet these are colonists, who, from becoming possessed of unexpected and sudden wealth, boast themselves extravagantly and insolently; these men, while they build like rich men, while they delight in farms, in litters, in vast families of slaves, in luxurious banquets, have incurred such great debt, that, if they would be saved, they must raise Sulla from the dead; and they have even excited some countrymen, poor and needy men, to entertain the same hopes of plunder as themselves. And all these men, O Romans, I place in the same class of robbers and banditti. But, I warn them, let them cease to be mad, and to think of proscriptions and dictatorships; for such a horror of these times is ingrained into the city, that not even men, but it seems to me that even the very cattle would refuse to bear them again.

There is a fourth class, various, promiscuous, and turbulent; who indeed are now overwhelmed; who will never recover themselves; who, partly from indolence, partly from managing their affairs badly, partly from extravagance, are embarrassed by old debts; and worn out with bail-bonds, and judgments, and seizures of their goods, are said to be betaking themselves in numbers to that camp both from the city and the country. These men I think not so much active soldiers as lazy insolvents; who, if they cannot stand at first, may fall, but fall so, that not only the city but even their nearest neighbors know nothing of it. For I do not understand why, if they cannot live with honor, they should wish to die shamefully; or why they think they shall perish with less pain in a crowd, than if they perish by themselves.

There is a fifth class, of parricides, assassins, in short of all infamous characters, whom I do not wish to recall from Catiline, and indeed they cannot be separated from him. Let them perish in their wicked war, since they are so numerous that a prison cannot contain them.

There is a last class, last not only in number but in the sort of men and in their way of life; the especial body-guard of Catiline, of his levying; ay, the friends of his embraces and of his bosom; whom you see with carefully combed hair, glossy, beardless, or with well-trimmed beards; with tunics with sleeves, or reaching to the ankles; clothed with veils, not with robes; all the industry of whose life, all the labor of whose watchfulness, is expended in suppers lasting till daybreak.

69 / CICERO'S CORRESPONDENCE

Cicero, one of the principal statesmen of the first century B.C., *left an enormous body of correspondence (almost one thousand letters) covering the years 68 to 44* B.C. *These letters contain a day-by-day commentary on the private affairs of the man and his friends, as well as on the progress of the Roman Revolution. They are personal documents of first importance, as most of them were written without any thought of publication.*

Relations among the triumvirs (Pompey, Caesar, Crassus) deteriorated after the death in 54 B.C. *of Julia, Pompey's wife and Caesar's daughter. Caesar's conquest of Gaul provoked Pompey's jealousy, and Caesar's enemies within the Senate schemed to break up the triumvirate and to ruin him politically. Their principal objective was to force Caesar to lay down his Gallic command and return to Rome as a private citizen to become the center of political trials and chicanery. Cicero had just completed his term as governor of Cilicia and tried in vain to patch up a compromise. On January 7, 49* B.C., *the Senate passed the "Last Decree," urging consuls and proconsuls (i.e., Pompey) "to take care lest the Republic be harmed." On January 10 Caesar crossed the river Rubicon, the frontier between Cisalpine Gaul and Italy, and thus the civil war began. Cicero wrote the following letter (A) on January 12, 49, to his secretary Tiro, at a time when he had not yet been informed of Caesar's crossing the Rubicon.*

In the first two months of the Civil War Caesar captured all of Italy and forced Pompey to cross the Adriatic with five legions. Before this had happened, and a month after he had written the letter comprising excerpt A, Cicero faced a most difficult decision —whether to join Pompey or Caesar. He discussed this problem in a letter (B) written on February 18, 49, and addressed to Atticus.[4]

[4] Evelyn S. Shuckburgh, *The Letters of Cicero*, Vol. II (London: George Bell and Sons, 1899), pp. 234 ff., 280–83.

A. THE BEGINNINGS OF CIVIL WAR

Cicero and his son, Terentia, Tullia, Quintus and his son, send warm greetings to Tiro. Though I miss your ever ready help at every turn, yet it is not for my sake so much as for yours that I grieve at your illness. But now that the violence of your disease has abated so far as to become a quartan fever—for so Curius writes me word—I hope that with care you will soon become stronger. Only be sure—as becomes a man of your good sense—to think of nothing for the present except how to get well in the best possible way. I know how your regret at being absent worries you, but all difficulties will disappear, if you get well. I would not have you hurry, for fear of your suffering from sea-sickness in your weak state and finding a winter voyage dangerous. I arrived at the city walls on the 4th of January. Nothing could be more complimentary than the procession that came out to meet me; but I found things in a blaze of civil discord, or rather civil war. I desire to find a cure for this and, as I think, could have done so; but I was hindered by the passions of particular persons, for on both sides there are those who desire to fight. The long and short of it is that Caesar himself—once our friend—has sent the senate a menacing and offensive despatch and is so insolent as to retain his army and province in spite of the senate, and my old friend Curio is backing him up. Furthermore, our friend Antonius and Q. Cassius, having been expelled from the house, though without any violence, left town with Curio to join Caesar directly the senate had passed the decree ordering "consuls, praetors, tribunes, and us proconsuls to see that the Republic received no damage." Never has the state been in greater danger: never have disloyal citizens had a better prepared leader. On the whole, however, preparations are being pushed on with very great activity on our side also. This is being done by the influence and energy of our friend Pompey, who now, when it is too late, begins to fear Caesar. In spite of these exciting incidents, a full meeting of the senate clamoured for a triumph being granted me: but the consul Lentulus, on order to enhance his service to me, said that as soon as he had taken the measures necessary for the public safety, he would bring forward a motion on the subject. I do nothing in a spirit of selfish ambition, and consequently my influence is all the greater. Italy has been marked out into districts, showing for what part each of us is to be responsible. I have taken Capua. That is all I wanted to tell you. Again and again I urge you to take care of your health, and to write to me as often as you have anyone to whom to give a letter. Good-bye, good-bye.

B. POMPEY OR CAESAR?

A prey to the gravest and most depressing anxieties, though I am precluded from discussing the question with you personally, I have, nevertheless, resolved to seek your advice. The whole question in debate is this: if Pompey quits Italy, which I suspect that he is about to do, what do you think I ought to do? To assist you in giving me advice, I will state briefly what occurs to my mind on either side. Pompey's very great services in securing my restoration and the intimacy existing between us, as well as the interests of the Republic themselves, lead me to the conclusion that my policy or, if you choose, my fortune must be united with his. Then there is this: if I stay here and desert that company of most loyal and illustrious citizens, I must come under the power of one man: and although he shows by many instances that he is well disposed to me—and you yourself know what precautions I took in that direction because I suspected the storm that was hanging over our heads—yet I must look at the matter in two lights: first, how far I can trust him; and, secondly, however certain I may be that he will be my friend, whether it is the action of a brave man and a good citizen to remain in a city in which, after having enjoyed the highest offices and commands, after having performed the most important services and been invested with the most august priesthood, he is to become a mere name and to incur danger, not perchance unaccompanied by some disgrace, if Pompey ever restores the constitution. So much for that side. Now for the other. Our friend Pompey has shown neither wisdom nor courage in anything that he has done: I may add that he has acted in every case against my counsel and advice. I put out of the question the old scores: how he fostered Caesar against the Republic, promoted, armed him; assisted him in the passing of laws by violence and against the auspices; supported the addition of farther Gaul to his provinces; married his daughter; acted as augur at the adoption of Publius Clodius; showed greater zeal in effecting my recall than in preventing my exile; supported the extension of Caesar's provincial government; championed his cause at every point in his absence; actually in his third consulship, when he started being a defender of the constitution, yet urged the ten tribunes to propose the bill allowing Caesar's candidature in his absence; confirmed the same privilege in a certain law of his own and resisted the consul Marcus Marcellus when he proposed to fix the end of Caesar's government on the 1st of March. Well, to pass over all this, what could be more discreditable, more ill-considered, than this departure from the city, or I should rather call it his most shameful, most unprincipled flight?

What terms could there be that were not preferable to the abandonment of one's country? The terms offered were bad. I confess it: but could anything be worse than this? But (you say) he will recover the Republic. When? What preparation has been made for realizing that hope? Is not Picenum lost? Is not the road to the city open to his opponent? In fact, there is no cause to support, no forces to support it, no rallying point for those who wish the constitution maintained. Apulia has been selected, the most sparsely peopled district of Italy and the most widely removed from the point of attack in this war: it is evident that from sheer desperation the object in view is flight and the facilities of a sea-coast. . . . For what can possibly be done else? Don't think me more inclined to remain, because I have used more words on that side. It may very well be, as happens in many investigations, that one side has the superiority in words, the other in truth. Wherefore please give me your advice on the understanding that I am considering a most important matter with impartiality. There is a vessel at Caieta ready for me, and another at Brundisium. . . .

70 / CAESAR'S AVENGERS

Following the murder of Caesar there was a period of confusion. The leaders of the Caesarean party, his former aides Marc Antony and Marcus Aurelius Lepidus, as well as his young heir Octavius, quarrelled among each other and made various short-term agreements with the senatorial party, but in the end they patched up their differences and decided to punish the tyrannicides. Their revolutionary pact is known as the Second Triumvirate (43 B.C.*). Its terms, as well as the proscriptions which followed it, are described in the following selection from Appian of Alexandria (second century* A.D.*), author of a history of Rome's foreign and civil wars. The execution of Rome's distinguished statesman and philosopher Cicero may serve as an illustration of the horrors of the Roman civil war.*[5]

Octavius and Antony composed their differences on a small, gradually sloping islet in the river Lavinius near the city of Mutina. Each had

[5] Horace White, *The Roman History of Appian of Alexandria,* Vol. II (New York: The Macmillan Company, 1899), pp. 292–305.

five legions of soldiers whom they stationed opposite each other, after which each proceeded with 300 men to the bridges over the river. Lepidus himself went before them, searched the island, and shook his military cloak as a signal to them to come. Then each left his three hundred in charge of friends on the bridges and advanced to the middle of the island in plain sight, and there the three sat together in council, Octavius in the centre because he was consul. They were in conference from morning till night for two days and came to these decisions: That Octavius should resign the consulship and that Ventidius should take it for the remainder of the year; that a new magistracy for quieting the civil dissensions should be created by law, which Lepidus, Antony, and Octavius should hold for five years with consular power (for this name seemed preferable to that of dictator, perhaps because of Antony's decree abolishing the dictatorship); that these three should at once designate the yearly magistrates of the city for the five years, that a distribution of the provinces should be made, giving to Antony the whole of Gaul except the part bordering the Pyrenees Mountains, which was called Old Gaul. The latter, together with Spain, was assigned to Lepidus, while Octavius was to have Africa, Sardinia, and Sicily, and the other islands in the vicinity thereof.

Thus was dominion of the Romans divided by the triumvirate among themselves. The assignment of the parts beyond the Adriatic only was postponed, since these were still under the control of Brutus and Cassius, against whom Antony and Octavius were to wage war. Lepidus was to be consul the following year and to remain in the city to do what was needful there, meanwhile governing Spain by proxy. He was to retain three of his legions to guard the city and to divide the other seven between Octavius and Antony, three to the former and four to the latter, so that each of them might lead twenty legions to the war. To encourage the army with the expectation of booty they promised them, besides other gifts, eighteen cities of Italy as colonies—cities which excelled in wealth, in the fertility of their territory, and in handsome houses and which were to be divided among them (land, buildings, and all), just as though they had been captured from an enemy in war. The most renowned among these were Capua, Rhegium, Venusia, Beneventum, Nuceria, Ariminum, and Vibo. Thus were the most beautiful parts of Italy marked out for the soldiers. But they decided to destroy their personal enemies beforehand, so that the latter should not interfere with their arrangements while they were carrying on war abroad. Having come to these decisions, they reduced them to writing, and Octavius, as consul, communicated them to the soldiers, all except the proscriptions. When the soldiers heard them, they applauded and embraced each other in token of mutual reconciliation. . . .

As soon as the triumvirs were by themselves, they joined in making a list of those who were to be put to death. They put on the list those whom they suspected because of their power and also their personal enemies, and they swapped their own relatives and friends with each other for death, both then and later. For they made additions to the catalogue from time to time, some on the ground of enmity, others for a grudge merely, or because the victims were friends of their enemies or enemies of their friends. Some were proscribed on account of their wealth, for the triumvirs needed a great deal of money to carry on the war, since the revenue from Asia had been paid to Brutus and Cassius, who were still collecting it, and the kings and satraps were cooperating with them. So the triumvirs were short of money because Europe, and especially Italy, was exhausted by wars and exactions; for which reason they levied very heavy contributions from the plebeians and finally even from women and contemplated taxes on sales and rents. Some were proscribed because they had handsome villas or city residences. The number of senators who were sentenced to death and confiscation was about 300, and of the so-called knights about 2000. There were brothers and uncles of the triumvirs in the list of the proscribed, and also some of the lieutenants serving under them who had some difficulty with the leaders or with their fellow-lieutenants.

As they left the conference to proceed to Rome, they postponed the proscription of the greater number of victims, but they decided to send executioners in advance and without warning to kill twelve, or, as some say, seventeen, of the most important ones, among whom was Cicero. Four of these were slain immediately, either at banquets or as they were met on the streets. Search was made for the others in temples and houses. There was a sudden panic which lasted through the night, and a running to and fro with cries and lamentation as in a captured city. When it was known that men had been seized and massacred, although nobody had been previously sentenced by proscription, every man thought that he was the one whom the pursuers were in search of. In despair some were on the point of burning their own houses, and others the public buildings, or of committing some terrible deed in their frenzied state before the blow should fall upon them; and they would have done so had not the consul Pedius hurried around with heralds and encouraged them, telling them to wait till daylight and get more accurate information. When morning came, Pedius, contrary to the intention of the triumvirs, published the list of seventeen as deemed the sole authors of the civil strife and the only ones condemned. To the rest he pledged the public faith, being ignorant of the determinations of the triumvirs. Pedius died in consequence of fatigue the following night. . . .

[There follows a detailed account of proscriptions and executions.]

Cicero, who had held supreme power after Caesar's death as much as a public speaker could, was proscribed, together with his son, his brother, and his brother's son and all of his household, his faction, and his friends. He fled in a small boat, but as he could not endure the seasickness, he landed and went to a country place of his own near Caieta, a town of Italy, which I visited to gain knowledge of this lamentable affair, and here he remained quiet. While the searchers were approaching (for of all others Antony sought for him most eagerly, and the rest did so for Antony's sake), crows flew into his chamber and awakened him from sleep by their croaking and pulled off his bed-covering until his servants, perceiving that this was a warning from one of the gods, put him in a litter and again conveyed him toward the sea, going cautiously through a dense thicket. Many soldiers were hurrying around in squads inquiring if Cicero had been seen anywhere. Some people, moved by goodwill and pity, said that he had already put to sea; but a shoemaker, a client of Clodius, who had been a most bitter enemy of Cicero, pointed out the path to Laena, the centurion, who was pursuing with a small force. The latter ran after him and, seeing slaves mustering for the defense in much larger number than the force under his own command, he called out by way of stratagem, "Come on, you centurions in the rear, this is the place"; whereupon the slaves, thinking that more soldiers were coming, were terror-stricken.

Laena, although he had been once saved by Cicero when under trial, drew his head out of the litter and cut it off, striking it three times, or rather sawing it off by reason of his inexperience. He also cut off the hand with which Cicero had written the speeches against the tyranny of Antony and which he had entitled Philippics in imitation of those of Demosthenes. Then some of the soldiers hastened on horseback and others on shipboard to convey the good news quickly to Antony. The latter was sitting in front of the tribunal in the forum when Laena, a long distance off, showed him the head and hand by lifting them up and shaking them. Antony was delighted beyond measure. He crowned the centurion and gave him 250,000 Attic drachmas in addition to the stipulated reward for killing the man who had been his greatest and most bitter enemy. The head and hand of Cicero were suspended for a long time from the rostra in the forum where formerly he had been accustomed to make public speeches, and more people came together to behold this spectacle than had previously come to listen to him. It is said that even at his meals Antony placed the head of Cicero before his table, until he became satiated with the horrid sight. Thus was Cicero, a man famous even yet for his eloquence and one who had rendered the greatest service to his country when he held the office of consul, slain and insulted after his death.

71 / THE DEEDS OF AUGUSTUS

The first Roman princeps, *Octavian Augustus, had begun to prepare, probably as early at 2* B.C., *a written account of his public activities. The latest version of this account, completed in the year of his death (14* A.D.*), he deposited with the Vestal Virgins. Following Augustus' wish, his successor, Tiberius, had this text inscribed on two bronze pillars standing in front of Augustus' mausoleum on the Campus Martius in Rome. This inscription is lost, but faithful copies survived in the provinces of the Roman Empire. The most important of these was found in the temple of Rome and Augustus at Ancyra (modern Ankara, capital of Turkey), and the inscription, the queen of Latin inscriptions, is therefore often referred to as* Monumentum Ancyranum, *or the* Res Gestae Divi Augusti *(because it appears under this heading in the inscription at Ancyra). Throughout the document Augustus speaks in the first person singular. The first part of the document lists the honors bestowed on him by Senate and people. There follows a list of gifts to the armed forces and commoners and of his building activities and other liberalities (here omitted). The last part contains a general account of Augustus' military and domestic accomplishments. Most interesting are the last two sections, in which Augustus summarizes his constitutional position. This is a sober and highly official document. The information contained therein is correct so far as it goes, but it is obvious that the revolutionary origins of Augustus' power, as well as the seamier aspects of his reign, are minimized.*[6]

[6] E. S. Shuckburgh, *Augustus* (London: T. Fisher Unwin, n.d.), pp. 293–301.

When I was nineteen I collected an army on my own account and at my own expense, by the help of which I restored the republic to liberty, which had been enslaved by the tyranny of a faction; for which services the Senate, in complimentary decrees, added my name to the roll of their House in the counsulship of Gaius Pansa and Aulus Hirtius [43 B.C.], giving me at the same time consular precedence in voting; and gave me imperium. It ordered me as propraetor "to see along with the consuls that the republic suffered no damage." Moreover, in the same year, both consuls having fallen, the people elected me consul and a triumvir for revising the constitution.

Those who killed my father [C. Julius Caesar] I drove into exile after a legal trial in punishment of their crime, and afterwards, when these same men rose in arms against the republic, I conquered them twice in a pitched battle.

I had to undertake wars by land and sea, civil and foreign, all over the world, and when victorious, I spared surviving citizens. Those foreign nations who could safely be pardoned I preferred to preserve rather than exterminate. About 500,000 Roman citizens took the military oath to me. Of these I settled out in colonies or sent back to their own towns, after their terms of service were over, considerably more than 300,000, and to them all I assigned lands purchased by myself or money in lieu of lands. I captured 600 ships, not counting those below the rating of triremes.

I twice celebrated an ovation, three times curule triumphs, and was twenty-one times greeted as imperator. Though the Senate afterwards voted me several triumphs, I declined them. I frequently also deposited laurels in the Capitol after performing the vows which I had taken in each war. For successful operations performed by myself or by my legates under my auspices by land and sea, the Senate fifty-three times decreed a supplication to the immortal gods. The number of days during which, in accordance with a decree of the Senate, supplication was offered amounted to 890. In my triumphs there were led before my chariot nine kings or sons of kings. I had been consul thirteen times at the writing of this, and am in the course of the thirty-seventh year of my tribunician power [A.D. 13–14].

The Dictatorship offered me in my presence and absence by the Senate and people in the consulship of Marcus Marcellus and Lucius Arruntius [22 B.C.] I declined to accept. I did not refuse at a time of very great scarcity of corn the commissionership of corn supply, which I administered in such a way that within a few days I freed the whole people from fear and danger. The consulship—either yearly or for life—then offered to me I declined to accept.

In the consulship of M. Vinicius and Q. Lucretius [19 B.C.], of P. and Cn. Lentulus [18 B.C.], and of Paullus Fabius Maximus and Q. Tubero [11 B.C.], when the Senate and people of Rome unanimously agreed that I should be elected overseer of the laws and morals with unlimited powers without a colleague, I refused every office offered me which was contrary to the customs of our ancestors. But what the Senate at that time wished me to manage I carried out in virtue of my tribunician power, and in this office I five times received at my own request a colleague from the Senate.

I was one of the triumvirate for the re-establishment of the constitution for ten consecutive years. I have been *princeps senatus*, up to the day on which I write this, for forty years. I am Pontifex Maximus, Augur, one of the fifteen commissioners for religion, one of the seven for sacred feasts, an Arval brother, a *sodalis Titius*, a fetial.

In my fifth consulship [29 B.C.] I increased the number of the patricians by order of people and Senate. I three times made up the roll of the Senate, and in my sixth consulship [28 B.C.] I took a census of the people with M. Agrippa as my colleague. I performed the *lustrum* after an interval of forty-one years, in which the number of Roman citizens entered on the census roll was 4,063,000. A second time with consular imperium, I took the census by myself in the consulship of Gaius Censorinus and Gaius Asinius [8 B.C.], in which the number of Roman citizens entered on the roll was 4,223,000. I took a third census with consular imperium, my son Tiberius Caesar acting as my colleague, in the consulship of Sextus Pompeius and Sextus Appuleius [A.D. 14], in which the number of Roman citizens entered on the census roll was 4,937,000. By new laws passed I recalled numerous customs of our ancestors that were falling into desuetude in our time, and myself set precedents in many particulars for the imitation of posterity.

The Senate decreed that vows should be offered for my health by consuls and priests every fifth year. In fulfilment of these vows the four chief colleges of priests or the consuls often gave games in my lifetime. Also, individually and by townships, the people at large always offered sacrifices at all the temples for my health.

By a decree of the Senate my name was included in the ritual of the Salii; and it was ordained by a law that my person should be sacred and that I should have the tribunician power for the term of my natural life. I refused to become Pontifex Maximus in succession to my colleague [Lepidus] during his life, though the people offered me that sacred office formerly held by my father. Some years later I accepted that sacred office on the death of the man who had availed himself of the civil disturbance to secure it, such a multitude flocking to my election from all parts of Italy as is never recorded to have come to Rome before, in the consularship of P. Sulpicius and C. Valgius [6 March, 12 B.C.].

The Senate consecrated an altar to Fortuna Redux, near the temple of Honour and Virtue, by the Porta Capena, for my return, on which it ordered the Vestal Virgins to offer a yearly sacrifice on the day on which, in the consulship of Q. Lucretius and M. Vinucius [19 B.C.], I returned to the city from Syria, and gave that day the name *Augustalia* from my cognomen [15 Dec.].

By a decree of the Senate at the same time part of the praetors and tribunes of the plebs, along with the consul Q. Lucretius and leading nobles, were despatched into Campania to meet me—an honour that up to this time has been decreed to no one else. When I returned to Rome from Spain and Gaul after successful operations in those provinces, in the consulship of Tiberius Nero and Publius Quintilius [13 B.C.], the Senate voted that an altar to Pax Augusta should be consecrated for my return on the Campus Martius, upon which it ordered the magistrates and priests and Vestal Virgins to offer an annual sacrifice [30 Jan.].

Whereas the Ianus Quirinus, which our ancestors ordered to be closed when peace throughout the whole dominions of the Roman people by land and sea had been obtained by victories, is recorded to have been only twice shut before my birth since the foundation of the city, the Senate voted its closure during my principate.

My sons Caius and Lucius Caesar, whom fortune snatched from me in their early manhood, in compliment to me the Senate and Roman people designated consuls in their fifteenth year with a proviso that they should enter on that office after an interval of five years. From the day of their assuming the *toga virilis* the Senate decreed that they should take part in public business. Moreover, the Roman equities in a body gave each of them the title of *Princeps Iuventutis* and presented them with silver shields and spears. . . .

I cleared the sea of pirates. In that war I captured about 30,000 slaves who had run away from their masters and had borne arms against the republic, and handed them back to their owners to be punished. The whole of Italy took the oath to me spontaneously and demanded that I should be the leader in the war in which I won the victory off Actium. The provinces of the Gauls, the Spains, Africa, Sicily, Sardinia, took the same oath. Among those who fought under my standards were more than seven hundred Senators, eighty-three of whom had been, or have since been, consuls up to the time of my writing this, 170 members of the sacred colleges.

I extended the frontiers of all the provinces of the Roman people which were bordered by tribes that had not submitted to our Empire. The provinces of the Gauls and Spains and Germany, bounded by the Ocean from Gades to the mouth of the river Elbe, I reduced to a peaceful state. The Alps, from the district near the Adriatic to the Tuscan sea, I forced to remain peaceful without waging unprovoked war with any tribe. My fleet sailed through the Ocean from the mouth of the Rhine towards the rising sun, up to the territories of the Cimbri, to which point no Roman had penetrated up to that time either by land or sea. The Cimbri, and Charydes, and Semnones and other peoples of the Germans, belonging to the same tract of country, sent ambassadors to ask for the friendship of myself and the Roman people. By my command and under my auspices two armies were marched into Aethiopia and Arabia, called Felix, nearly simultaneously, and large hostile forces of both these nations were cut to pieces in battle, and a large number of towns were captured. Aethiopia was penetrated as far as the town Nabata, next to Meroe. Into Arabia the army advanced into the territories of the Sabaei as far as the town Mariba.

I added Egypt to the Empire of the Roman people. When I might have made the Greater Armenia a province after the assassination of its king Artaxes, I preferred, on the precedent of our ancestors, to hand over that kingdom to Tigranes, son of King Artavasdes, grandson of King Tigranes, by the hands of Tiberius Nero, who was then my stepson. The same nation being afterwards in a state of revolt and rebellion, I handed over to the government of King Ariobarzanes, son Artabazus, king of the Medes, after it had been reduced by my son Gaius; and after his death to his son Artavasdes, upon whose assassination I sent Tigranes, a member of the royal family of the Armenians, into that kingdom. I recovered all the provinces on the other side of the Adriatic towards the East and Cyrenae, which were by this time for the most part held by various kings, and before them Sicily and Sardinia, which had been overrun by an army of slaves.

I settled colonies of soldiers in Africa, Sicily, Macedonia, both the Spains, Achaia, Asia, Syria, Gallia Narbonensis, Pisidia. Italy has twenty-eight colonies established under my auspices, which have in my lifetime become very densely inhabited and places of great resort.

A large number of military standards, which had been lost under other commanders, I recovered, after defeating the enemy, from Spain and Gaul and the Dalmatians. I compelled the Parthians to restore the spoils and standards of three Roman armies and to seek as suppliants the friendship of the Roman people. These standards I laid up in the inner shrine belonging to the temple of Mars Ultor.

The tribes of the Pannonii, which before I was *princeps* an army of the Roman people never reached, having been subdued by Tiberius

Nero, who was then my stepson and legate [11 B.C.], I added to the Empire of the Roman people, and I extended the frontier of Illyricum to the bank of the river Danube. And when an army of the Daci crossed to the south of that river, it was conquered and put to flight under my auspices; and subsequently my army, being led across the Danube, forced the tribes of the Daci to submit to the orders of the Roman people.

To me there were often sent embassies of kings from India, who had never before been seen in the camp of any Roman general. By ambassadors the Bastarnae and the Scythians and the kings of the Sarmatians, who live on both sides of the river Don, and the king of the Albani and of the Hiberi and of the Medes sought our friendship.

Kings of the Parthians—Tiridates, and afterwards Phrates, son of King Phrates—fled to me for refuge; of the Medes Artavasdes; of the Adiabeni Artaxares; of the Britons Dumnobellaunus and Tim. . . . ; of the Marcomanni and Suebi. . . . Phrates, king of the Parthians, son of Orodes, sent all his sons and grandsons to me in Italy, not because he had been overcome in war, but seeking our friendship by means of his own sons as pledges. And a very large number of other nations experienced the good faith of the Roman people while I was *princeps*, with whom before that time there had been no diplomatic or friendly intercourse.

The nations of the Parthians and the chief men of the Medes, by means of embassies, sought and accepted from me kings of those peoples—the Parthians Vonones, son of King Phrates, grandson of King Orodes; the Medes Ariobarzanes, son of King Artavasdes, grandson of King Ariobarzanes.

In my sixth and seventh consulships [28–27 B.C.], when I had extinguished the flames of civil war, having by universal consent become possessed of the sole direction of affairs, I transferred the republic from my power to the will of the Senate and people of Rome. For which good service on my part I was by decree of the Senate called by the name of Augustus, and the door-posts of my house were covered with laurels in the name of the state, and a civic crown was fixed up over my door, and a golden shield was placed in the Curia Iulia, which, it was declared by its inscription, the Senate and people of Rome gave me in recognition of valour, clemency, justice, piety. After that time I took precedence of all in authority, but of power I had nothing more than those who were my colleagues in the several magistracies.

While I was administering my thirteenth consulship [2 B.C.], the Senate and equestrian order and the Roman people with one consent greeted me as FATHER OF MY COUNTRY, and decreed that it should be inscribed in the vestibule of my house and in the Senate house and in the Forum Augustum and under the chariot which was there placed in my honour in accordance with a senatorial decree.

When I wrote this I was in my seventy-sixth year [A.D. 13–14].

72 / LATIN POETRY

The age of the Roman Revolution, down to the death of Augustus, was the golden age of Roman literature. Among prose writers Caesar, Cicero, and Livy have been referred to before. Here selections will be given from the Roman poets Virgil and Horace. Both reveal the profound influence of Greek or Hellenistic writers, as Roman poets were the first to admit—Virgil that of Homer, and Horace that of the Greek lyric poets. Yet Roman poets adapted their Greek models to the Roman world view and the requirements of a different historical situation. Latin literature in general sustains a more pronounced historical consciousness and moralism than does Greek literature.

Rome's great epic poem was Virgil's Aeneid. *Virgil (70–19* B.C.*) had lost his farm, located in northern Italy, after the battle of Philippi (42* B.C.*), when Antony and Octavian distributed land to their veterans. In later years both he and Horace befriended one of Octavian's principal lieutenants, Maecenas, and through Maecenas gained the protection of Octavian himself. Virgil composed the* Aeneid *during the last ten years of his life, a work in which the* princeps *took great personal interest. The* Aeneid *describes the flight of Prince Aeneas from Troy after it was conquered by the Greeks under Agamemnon. It is made explicit from the beginning of the poem that Aeneas will establish a new realm in Italy and that his descendants will found a powerful empire. In the course of his wanderings Aeneas visits the underworld, where his father Anchises points out to him the souls of future Romans waiting to be born (A). This "Vision of Heroes" constitutes a preview of Roman history from Romulus to Augustus. Anchises' vision contains a famous and profound analysis of the Roman achievement as compared with that of the Greeks. The young Marcellus mentioned at the end of the selection was*

Augustus' nephew, Marcus Claudius Marcellus, whom Augustus had chosen as his heir and successor. He died prematurely in 23 B.C.[7]

Horace (65–8 B.C.*) was the great lyric poet of the Augustan Age. He fought in Brutus' army at Philippi (42* B.C.*), but later became a friend of Maecenas and enjoyed Augustus' favor. His lyric poems deal with both personal and public matters. In the first of his odes printed below (B) the poet celebrates Octavian's victory over Antony and Cleopatra at Actium (31* B.C.*) and reveals the Roman fear of Cleopatra. In the second ode the poet states his anticipation of the fact that Augustus will carry out Caesar's plan for a war against Parthia to avenge the shame of Crassus' defeat at Carrhae (53* B.C.*). In fact, Augustus never undertook that war, but arrived instead at a peaceful arrangement with Parthia. In the poem Horace contrasts with the Republic's indolent acceptance of the Parthian defeat the attitude of Marcus Atilius Regulus, one of Rome's commanders during the First Punic War. In 255* B.C. *Regulus and two thousand Roman soldiers were captured by the Carthaginians. Sent from Carthage to Rome several years later to arrange for the release of the Roman prisoners, he warned the Roman Senate against a "deal" of this kind. He returned to Cathage and, according to Roman legend, died there under torture.*[8]

A. VIRGIL

"Survey (pursued the sire) this airy throng,
As, offered to the view, they pass along.
These are the Italian names, which Fate will join
With ours, and graff upon the Trojan line.
Observe the youth who first appears in sight,
And holds the nearest station to the light,
Already seems to snuff the vital air,
And leans just forward on a shining spear:
Silvius is he, thy last begotten race,
But first in order sent, to fill thy place—

[7] John Dryden, *The Works of Virgil* (New York: American Book Exchange, 1881), pp. 261–5.

[8] A. Hamilton Bryce, *The Poems of Horace* (London: George Bell and Sons, 1897), pp. 27 ff., 51 ff.

An Alban name, but mixed with Dardan blood:
Born in the covert of a shady wood,
Him fair Lavinia, thy surviving wife,
Shall breed in groves, to lead a solitary life.
In Alba he shall fix his royal seat,
And, born a king, a race of kings beget;—
Then Procas, honor of the Trojan name,
Capys, and Numitor, of endless fame.
A second Silvius after these appears—
Silvius Æneas, for thy name he bears—
For arms and justice equally renowned;
Who, late restor'd, in Alba shall be crown'd.
How great they look! how vigorously they wield
Their weighty lances, and sustain the shield!
But they, who crowned with oaken wreaths appear,
Shall Gabian walls and strong Fidæne rear;
Nomentum, Bola, with Pometia, found;
And raise Collatian towers on rocky ground.
All these shall then be towns of mighty fame,
Though now they lie obscure, and lands without a name,
See Romulus the great, born to restore
The crown that once his injured grandsire wore.
This prince a priestess of our blood shall bear;
And like his sire in arms he shall appear.
Two rising crests his royal head adorn:
Born from a god, himself to godhead born,
His sire already signs him for the skies,
And marks his seat amidst the deities.
Auspicious chief! thy race, in times to come,
Shall spread the conquests of imperial Rome—
Rome whose ascending towers shall heaven invade,
Involving earth and heaven into her shade;
High as the mother of the gods in place,
And proud, like her, of an immortal race,
Then, when in pomp she makes the Phrygian round,
With golden turrets on her temples crowned:
A hundred gods her sweeping train supply,
Her offspring all; and all command the sky.
Now fix your sight, and stand intent, to see
Your Roman race, and Julian progeny.
There mighty Cæsar waits his vital hour,
Impatient for the world, and grasps his promised power.
But next behold the youth of form divine—

Cæsar himself, exalted in his line—
Augustus, promised oft, and long foretold,
Sent to the realm that Saturn ruled of old;
Born to restore a better age of gold.
Africa and India shall his power obey;
He shall extend his propagated sway
Beyond the solar year, without the starry way.
Where Atlas turns the rolling heavens around,
And his broad shoulders with their lights are crowned.
At his foreseen approach, already quake
The Caspian kingdoms and Mæotian lake.
Their seers behold the tempest from afar;
And threatening oracles denounce the war.
Nile hears him knocking at his sevenfold gates,
And seeks his hidden spring, and fears his nephew's fates.
Nor Hercules more lands or labors knew,
Not though the brazen-footed hind he slew,
Freed Erymanthus from the foaming boar,
And dipped his arrows in Lernæan gore;
Nor Bacchus, turning from his Indian war,
By tigers drawn triumphant in his car,
From Nysa's top descending on the plains,
With curling vines around his purple reins.
And doubt we yet through dangers to pursue
The paths of honor, and a crown in view?—
But what's the man, who from afar appears,
His head with olive crown'd, his hand a censer bears?
His hoary beard and holy vestments bring
His lost idea back. I know the Roman king.
He shall to peaceful Rome new laws ordain,
Called from his mean abode, a sceptre to sustain.
Him Tullus next in dignity succeeds,
An active prince, and prone to martial deeds.
He shall his troops for fighting fields prepare,
Disused to toils and triumphs of the war.
By dint of sword, his crown he shall increase,
And scour his armor from the rust of peace.
Whom Ancus follows with a fawning air,
But vain within, and proudly popular.
Next view the Tarquin kings, the avenging sword
Of Brutus, justly drawn, and Rome restored.
He first renews the rods and axe severe,
And gives the consuls royal robes to wear.

His sons, who seek the tyrant to sustain,
And long for arbitrary lords again,
With ignominy scourged in open sight,
He dooms to death deserved, asserting public right,
Unhappy man! to break the pious laws
Of nature, pleading in his children's cause!
Howe'er the doubtful fact is understood,
'Tis love of honor, and his country's good;
The consul, not the father, sheds the blood.
Behold Torquatus the same track pursue;
And next the two devoted Decii view—
The Drusian line, Camillus loaded home
With standards well redeemed, and foreign foes to come.
The pair you see, in equal armor shine,
Now, friends below, in close embraces join:
But, when they leave the shady realms of night,
And, clothed in bodies, breathe your upper light,
With mortal hate each other shall pursue:
What wars, what wounds, what slaughter, shall ensue!
From Alpine heights the father first descends;
His daughter's husband in the plain attends:
His daughter's husband arms his eastern friends.
Embrace again, my sons! be foes no more;
Nor stain your country with her children's gore!
And thou, the first, lay down thy lawless claim,
Thou, of my blood, who bear'st the Julian name!
Another comes, who shall in triumph ride,
And to the Capitol his chariot guide,
From conquered Corinth, rich with Grecian spoils.
And yet another, famed for warlike toils,
On Argos shall impose the Roman laws,
And on the Greeks, revenge the Trojan cause;
Shall drag in chains their Achillean race;
Shall vindicate his ancestors' disgrace,
And Pallas, for her violated place.
Great Cato there, for gravity renowned,
And conquering Cossus goes with laurels crowned.
Who can omit the Gracchi? who declare
The Scipio's worth, those thunderbolts of war,
The double bane of Carthage? Who can see,
Without esteem for virtuous poverty,
Severe Fabricius, or can cease to admire
The ploughman consul in his coarse attire?

Tired as I am, my praise the Fabii claim;
And thou, great hero, greatest of thy name,
Ordain'd in war to save the sinking state,
And, by delays, to put a stop to Fate!
Let others better mould the running mass
Of metals, and inform the breathing brass,
And soften into flesh, a marble face;
Plead better at the bar; describe the skies,
And when the stars descend, and when they rise.
But Rome! 'tis thine alone, with awful sway,
To rule mankind, and make the world obey,
Disposing peace and war, thy own majestic way:
To tame the proud, the fettered slave to free:—
These are imperial arts, and worthy thee."
He paused—and, while with wondering eyes they viewed
The passing spirits, thus his speech renewed:
"See great Marcellus! how, untired in toils,
He moves with manly grace, how rich with regal spoils.
He, when his country (threatened with alarms)
Requires his courage, and his conquering arms,
Shall more than once the Punic bands affright;
Shall kill the Gaulish king in single fight;
Then to the Capitol in triumph move:
And the third spoils shall grace Feretrian Jove."
Æneas here beheld, of form divine,
A godlike youth, in glittering armor shine,
With great Marcellus keeping equal pace:
But gloomy were his eyes, dejected was his face.
He saw, and wondering, asked his airy guide,
What and of whence was he, who pressed the hero's side?
"His son, or one of his illustrious name?
How like the former, and almost the same?
Observe the crowds that compass him around:
All gaze, and all admire, and raise a shouting sound:
But hovering mists around his brows are spread;
And night with sable shades involves his head."
"Seek not to know (the ghost replied with tears)
The sorrows of thy sons in future years.
This youth (the blissful vision of a day)
Shall just be shown on earth, then snatched away.
The gods too high had raised the Roman state,
Were but their gifts as permanent as great.

What groans of men shall fill the Martian Field!
How fierce a blaze his flaming pile shall yield!
What funeral pomp shall floating Tiber see,
When, rising from his bed, he views the sad solemnity!
No youth shall equal hopes of glory give,
No youth afford so great a cause to grieve.
The Trojan honor, and the Roman boast,
Admired when living, and adored when lost!
Mirror of ancient faith in early youth!
Undaunted worth, inviolable truth!
No foe, unpunished, in the fighting field
Shall dare thee, foot to foot, with sword and shield,
Much less in arms oppose thy matchless force,
When thy sharp spurs shall urge thy foaming horse.
Ah! couldst thou break through Fate's severe decree,
A new Marcellus shall arise in thee!
Full canisters of fragrant lilies bring,
Mixed with the purple roses of the spring:
Let me with funeral flowers his body strow,
This gift, which parents to their children owe,
This unavailing gift, at least I may bestow!"

B. HORACE

Cleopatra

Now must we drink, now must we beat the floor with tripping foot; this was the time, my comrades, to load the temples of the gods with sumptuous repasts. Before, it was an impious act to bring from our ancestral bins the good old Caecuban, while yet a foreign queen devised mad schemes to ruin for the city, and death to our sovereign sway, with a vile herd of followers, loathsome with disease, (she) wild enough to hope for anything, and drunken with sweet Fortune's draught. But one ship only from the flames preserved her frenzy tamed, and Caesar brought to real fear her mind by wine of Marea distraught, pursuing her in ships while far from Italy she fled (as hawk pursues the timid dove, as nimble hunter tracks the hare in snowy plains of Thrace), that to chains he might commit the fatal monster. But seeking by a nobler death to die she neither feared the sword, as woman might, nor made in rapid sail for coasts remote. She even dared with countenance unmoved to see again her ruined halls and boldly handle angry snakes that in her frame she might imbibe fell poison's draught, emboldened by a stern resolve to die, disdaining to be led "unqueened" in haughty triumph in Liburnian ships—a woman she of no mean dignity.

War Against Parthia!

From his thunder we believe that Jupiter in heaven is king. Augustus shall be deemed a Deity on earth when Britons and dread Parthians are added to his sway. What! have Crassus' soldiers deigned to live degraded husbands of barbarian wives? and,—shame on the Senate and our altered ways!—has Marsian or Apulian brave, forgetting sacred shields and Roman name and dress, and Vesta's never-dying flame, grown old in pay of marriage kin under a Persian king, while Rome is safe, and Jove's great temple too? This had the wary mind of Regulus foreseen when he refused the proffered terms, vile in themselves and fraught with mischief for the time to come, unless the captive youth, with none to pity, died. I've seen, he said, the Roman eagles hung in Punic shrines, and weapons from our soldiers wrung without a blow: I've seen the arms of citizen bound fast behind a freeman's back, and gates thrown open wide, and fields our arms once spoiled now tilled again!

A soldier ransomed by gold will return, forsooth, a braver man! You only add the loss of money to the foul disgrace: as wool when stained with dye will ne'er regain the colour lost, so sterling worth when ousted once cares not to take its place in baser breast. When stags set free from tangled nets show fight, then he'll be brave who once has yielded to the treacherous foe, and in a second war that man shall crush the Punic hosts, who on his pinioned arms has felt the thongs, the coward! and has feared to die. He, knowing not how life to win, has mixed up peace with war. Oh, shame! O Carthage! higher raised by Italy's base fall!

'Tis said he [Regulus] put aside his wife's chaste kiss and little sons' good-bye, as being a Roman citizen no more, and with his purpose stern, fixed on the ground a hero's gaze, while striving to confirm the Senate's wavering mind by counsel never given before, and hasting forth to noble exile from the midst of weeping friends. And yet he knew full well what cruelties the torturer prepared: but still he moved aside opposing kin and throngs who barred his going, just as if he'd judged a case and leaving clients' weary suits were hurrying off to Venafrum, or to Tarentum, that Laconian town.

X / THE ROMAN EMPIRE

73 / THE FIRST SUCCESSION TO THE PRINCIPATE

The most important narrative source for the first century A.D. *are the works of Cornelius Tacitus (about* A.D. *55–after 115). He first appeared in public life under the Emperor Vespasian, held a praetorship in 88 under Domitian, and was a member of the senatorial order during the latter's regime of terror. He held a consulship in 97 and was proconsul of Asia in* A.D. *112–113. Among Tacitus' works represented in this volume the earliest was the biography of his father-in-law, Julius Agricola, written in* A.D. *98. The* Histories *covered the period from 69–96, but only the beginning of this work is preserved. The* Annals, *also incomplete, begin with the death of Augustus in* A.D. *14 and end in* A.D. *66. Tacitus was interested primarily in events at Rome, at the court of the* princeps *and in the senate house, but foreign wars were also discussed at length, and the development of the provinces and provincial administration were frequently touched upon, especially where these matters affected the capital. Tacitus longed for the days of the Republic and took a dim view of the principate, the peace it brought, and the efficiency of its administration. Senate and magistrates, according to Tacitus, had become pliant tools in the hands of the rulers, who wielded all power with the help of their creatures, wives, freedmen, and informers. The somber and often cruel picture which Tacitus painted of the Roman empire under the principate in the first century* A.D. *is on the whole justified, although his portraits of individuals (e.g., Tiberius) were sometimes distorted.*

The following passage describes the political atmosphere in Rome immediately following Augustus' death (A.D. 14). It was a momentous occasion, for this was the first test of the permanence of Augustus' settlement. Tiberius needed the consent of the Senate, of the army (especially of the praetorian guard organized by Augustus, the only military force in Italy), and of the people for his accession to power.[1]

Meanwhile at Rome people plunged into slavery—consuls, senators, knights. The higher a man's rank, the more eager his hypocrisy, and his looks the more carefully studied, so as to betray neither joy at the decease of one emperor nor sorrow at the rise of another while he mingled delight and lamentations with his flattery. Sextus Pompeius and Sextus Apuleius, the consuls, were the first to swear allegiance to Tiberius Caesar, and in their presence the oath was taken by Seius Strabo and Caius Turranius, respectively the commander of the praetorian cohorts and the superintendent of the corn supplies. Then the Senate, the soldiers, and the people did the same. For Tiberius would inaugurate everything with the consuls, as though the ancient constitution remained, and he hesitated about being emperor. Even the proclamation by which he summoned the senators to their chamber he issued merely with the title of Tribune, which he had received under Augustus. The wording of the proclamation was brief and in a very modest tone. "He would," it said, provide for the honours due to his father and not leave the lifeless body, and this was the only public duty he now claimed."

As soon, however, as Augustus was dead, he had given the watchword to the praetorian cohorts as commander-in-chief. He had the guard under arms, with all other adjuncts of a court; soldiers attended him to the forum; soldiers went with him to the Senate House. He sent letters to the different armies, as though supreme power was now his, and showed hesitation only when he spoke in the Senate. His chief motive was fear that Germanicus, who had at his disposal so many legions, such vast auxiliary forces of the allies, and such wonderful popularity, might prefer the possession to the expectation of empire. He looked also at public opinion, wishing to have the credit of having been called and elected by the State rather than of having crept into power through the intrigues of a wife and a dotard's adoption. It was

[1] A. J. Church and W. J. Brodribb, *Annals of Tacitus* (London: Macmillan and Co., 1895), p. 4 ff.

subsequently understood that he assumed a wavering attitude, to test likewise the temper of the nobles. For he would twist a word or a look into a crime and treasure it up in his memory.

74 / TIBERIUS AND EMPEROR WORSHIP

In the Hellenistic world it had been a not infrequent occurrence that outstanding statesmen and generals were honored by the establishment of a religious cult. When Rome conquered the Hellenistic East, the peoples of the East established cult centers for the goddess Roma *or for individual Roman generals. Augustus permitted the construction of a temple at Pergamun, the capital of the Roman province of Asia, and this temple was dedicated to the worship of the goddess* Roma *and Augustus. Later similar cult centers were established spontaneously in other Eastern provinces. In the West they were founded on the* princeps' *initiative, and provincial councils were entrusted with the duties of this imperial cult. In promoting the imperial cult, Augustus had a political motive: to create a common loyalty in the various parts of the empire. Tiberius' speech shows this emperor's desire to continue his predecessor's policies and his awareness that the imperial cult, if applied automatically to later emperors, might become mere flattery and its political value thus be vitiated.*[2]

About the same time Further Spain sent a deputation to the Senate with a request to be allowed, after the example of Asia, to erect a temple to Tiberius and his mother. On this occasion the emperor, who had generally a strong contempt for honours and now thought it right to reply to the rumour which reproached him with having yielded to vanity, delivered the following speech:—

"I am aware, Senators, that many deplore my want of firmness in not having opposed a similar recent petition from the cities of Asia.

[2] A. J. Church and W. J. Brodribb, *Annals of Tacitus* (London: Macmillan and Co., 1895), p. 130 ff.

I will therefore both explain the grounds of my previous silence and my intentions for the future. Inasmuch as the Divine Augustus did not forbid the founding of a temple at Pergamos to himself and to the city of Rome, I who respect as law all his actions and sayings have the more readily followed a precedent once approved, seeing that with the worship of myself was linked an expression of reverence towards the Senate. But though it may be pardonable to have allowed this once, it would be a vain and arrogant thing to receive the sacred honour of images representing the divine throughout all the provinces, and the homage paid to Augustus will disappear if it is vulgarised by indiscriminate flattery.

"For myself, Senators, I am mortal and limited to the functions of humanity, content if I can adequately fill the highest place; of this I solemnly assure you and would have posterity remember it. They will more than sufficiently honour my memory by believing me to have been worthy of my ancestry, watchful over your interests, courageous in danger, fearless of enmity when the State required it. These sentiments of your hearts are my temples, these my most glorious and abiding monuments. Those built of stone are despised as mere tombs if the judgment of posterity passes into hatred. And therefore this is my prayer to our allies, our citizens, and to heaven itself; to the last, that to my life's close it grant me a tranquil mind, which can discern alike human and divine claims; to the first, that when I die, they honour my career and the reputation of my name with praise and kindly remembrance."

Henceforth Tiberius, even in private conversations, persisted in showing contempt for such homage to himself. Some attributed this to modesty; many to self-distrust; a few to a mean spirit. "The noblest men," it is said, "have the loftiest aspirations, and so Hercules and Bacchus among the Greeks and Quirinus among us were enrolled in the number of the gods. Augustus did better, seeing that he had aspired. All other things princes have as a matter of course; one thing they ought insatiably to pursue, that their memory may be glorious. For to despise fame is to despise merit."

75 / THE ACCESSION OF CLAUDIUS

In A.D. *41 C. Caesar Caligula was murdered by a tribune of the Praetorian Guard, and the Praetorian Guard then proclaimed Caligula's uncle, Tiberius Claudius Nero, emperor. Augustus and Tiberius had thought him disqualified for the succession because he was a cripple. Claudius consolidated his power with the help of the Praetorian Guard, whose support he was the first emperor to buy with the promise of a huge donative.*[3]

Having spent the greater part of his life under these and the like circumstances, he [Claudius] came at last to the empire in the fiftieth year of his age by a very surprising turn of fortune. Being, as well as the rest, prevented from approaching Caius by the conspirators, who dispersed the crowd under the pretext of desiring to be private, he retired into an apartment called the Hermaeum; and soon afterwards, terrified by the report of Caius being slain, he crept into an adjoining balcony, where he hid himself behind the hangings of the door. A common soldier who happened to pass that way, spying his feet and desirous to discover who he was, pulled him out; when immediately recognizing him, he threw himself in a great fright at his feet and saluted him by the title of emperor. He then conducted him to his fellow-soldiers, who were all in a great rage and irresolute what they should do. They put him into a litter and, as the slaves of the palace had all fled, took their turns in carrying him on their shoulders and brought him into the camp sad and trembling; the people who met him lamenting his situation as if the poor innocent was being carried to execution. Being received within the ramparts, he continued all night with sentries on guard, recovered somewhat from his fright, but in no great hopes of the succession. For the consuls, with the Senate and civic troops, had possessed themselves of the Forum and Capitol, with the determination to assert the public liberty; and he, being sent for likewise by a tribune of the people to the Senate-house to give his advice upon the present juncture of affairs, returned answer, "I am under constraint and cannot possibly come." The day afterwards, the

[3] *The Lives of the Twelve Caesars by C. Suetonius Tranquillus,* tr. by Alexander Thomson, rev. by T. Forester (London: George Bell and Sons, 1914), p. 301 ff.

Senate being dilatory in their proceedings and worn out by divisions amongst themselves, while the people who surrounded the Senate-house shouted that they would have one master, naming Claudius, he suffered the soldiers assembled under arms to swear allegiance to him, promising them fifteen thousand sesterces a man; he being the first of the Caesars who purchased the submission of the soldiers with money.

76 / THE INVASION OF BRITAIN

The conquest of Britain, attempted by C. Julius Caesar, abandoned by Augustus, and taken up again unsuccessfully by Caligula, was accomplished by Claudius (A.D. 44). Under him the Romans pushed northward to the river Trent and westward into Wales. The process of conquest continued for many decades after Claudius' death.[4]

He [Claudius] undertook only one expedition, and that was of short duration. The triumphal ornaments decreed him by the Senate he considered as beneath the imperial dignity and was therefore resolved to have the honour of a real triumph. For this purpose he selected Britain which had never been attempted by any one since Julius Caesar and was then chafing with rage because the Romans would not give up some deserters. Accordingly he set sail from Ostia, but was twice very near being wrecked by the boisterous wind called Circius upon the coast of Liguria and near the islands called Stoechades. Having marched by land from Marseilles to Gessoriacum [now Boulogne], he thence passed over to Britain, and part of the island submitting to him within a few days after his arrival without battle or bloodshed he returned to Rome in less than six months from the time of his departure and triumphed in the most solemn manner; to witness which he not only gave leave to governors of provinces to come to Rome, but even to some of the exiles. Among the spoils taken from the enemy he fixed upon the pediment of his house in the Palatium a naval crown, in token of his having passed and, as it were, conquered the Ocean, and had it

[4] *The Lives of the Twelve Caesars by C. Suetonius Tranquillus*, tr. by Alexander Thomson, rev. by T. Forester (London: George Bell and Sons, 1914), pp. 308–310.

suspended near the civic crown which was there before. Messalina, his wife, followed his chariot in a covered litter. Those who had attained the honour of triumphal ornaments in the same war rode behind; the rest followed on foot, wearing the robe with the broad stripes. Crassus Frugi was mounted upon a horse richly caparisoned in a robe embroidered with palm leaves, because this was the second time of his obtaining that honour.

77 / PROVINCIALS IN THE ROMAN SENATE

Augustus and his immediate successors were parsimonious in granting Roman citizenship to provincials. Furthermore, the Roman magistracies and, consequently, membership in the Roman Senate were normally reserved for Italians. In A.D. *48 the Emperor Claudius wished to admit some prominent Gauls to the Roman Senate. He ran into opposition from some of the senators, who wished to keep Senate membership accessible only to Italians. Claudius successfully argued against them, and the Gauls were admitted. This precedent established, provincials were admitted to the Senate in greater number until, in the third century* A.D., *the Senate became a cross section of the empire's population. Claudius' speech was modified slightly by Tacitus in accordance with the principles of ancient historiography established by Thucydides (No. 39 and introduction), but the original text has survived in an inscription on bronze set up at Lyons.*[5]

In the consulship of Aulus Vitellius and Lucius Vipstanus [A.D. 48] the question of filling up the Senate was discussed, and the chief men of Gallia Comata, as it was called, who had long possessed the rights of allies and of Roman citizens, sought the privilege of obtaining public offices at Rome. There was much talk of every kind on the subject, and it was argued before the emperor with vehement opposition. "Italy," it was asserted, "is not so feeble as to be unable to furnish its own capital with a Senate. Once our native-born citizens sufficed for peoples

[5] A. J. Church and W. J. Brodribb, *Annals of Tacitus* (London: Macmillan and Co., 1895), pp. 191–3.

of our own kin, and we are by no means dissatisfied with the Rome of the past. To this day we cite examples which under our old customs the Roman character exhibited as to valour and renown. Is it a small thing that Veneti and Insubres have already burst into the Senate-house, unless a mob of foreigners, a troop of captives, so to say, is now forced upon us? What distinctions will be left for the remnants of our noble houses or for any impoverished senators from Latium? Every place will be crowded with these millionaires, whose ancestors of the second and third generations, at the head of hostile tribes, destroyed our armies with fire and sword and actually besieged the divine Julius [Caesar] at Alesia. These are recent memories. What if there were to rise up the remembrance of those who fell in Rome's citadel and at her altar by the hands of these same barbarians! Let them enjoy indeed the title of citizens, but let them not vulgarise the distinctions of the Senate and the honours of office."

These and like arguments failed to impress the Emperor. He at once addressed himself to answer them and thus harangued the assembled Senate. "My ancestors, the most ancient of whom was made at once a citizen and a noble of Rome, encourage me to govern by the same policy of transferring to this city all conspicuous merit, wherever found. And indeed I know as facts that the Julii came from Alba, the Coruncanii from Camerium, the Porcii from Tusculum, and not to inquire too minutely into the past, that new members have been brought into the Senate from Etruria and Lucania and the whole of Italy, that Italy itself was at last extended to the Alps, to the end that not only single persons but entire countries and tribes might be united under our name. We had unshaken peace at home; we prospered in all our foreign relations in the days when Italy beyond the Po was admitted to share our citizenship and when, enrolling in our ranks the most vigorous of the provincials under colour of settling our legions throughout the world, we recruited our exhausted empire. Are we sorry that the Balbi came to us from Spain and other men not less illustrious from Narbon Gaul? Their descendants are still among us and do not yield to us in patriotism.

"What was the ruin of Sparta and Athens but this, that mighty as they were in war, they spurned from them as aliens those whom they had conquered? Our founder Romulus, on the other hand, was so wise that he fought as enemies and then hailed as fellow-citizens several nations on the very same day. Strangers have reigned over us. That freedmen's sons should be intrusted with public office is not, as many wrongly think, a sudden innovation, but was a common practice in the old commonwealth. But, it will be said, we have fought with the Senones. I suppose then that the Volsci and Aequi never stood in array against us. Our city was taken by Gauls. Well, we also gave hostages to the Etruscans and passed under the yoke of the Samnites. On the whole, if you review all our wars, never has one been finished in a shorter time than that with the Gauls. Thenceforth they have preserved an unbroken and loyal peace. United as they now are with us by manners, education, and intermarriage, let them bring us their gold and their wealth rather than enjoy it in isolation. Everything, Senators, which we now hold to be of the highest antiquity was once new. Plebeian magistrates came after patrician; Latin magistrates after plebeian; magistrates of other Italian peoples after Latin. This practice too will establish itself, and what we are this day justifying by precedents will be itself a precedent."

The Emperor's speech was followed by a decree of the Senate, and the Aedui were the first to obtain the right of becoming Senators at Rome. This compliment was paid to their ancient alliance and to the fact that they alone of the Gauls cling to the name of brothers of the Roman people.

78 / THE HISTORICAL JESUS AND HIS TEACHING

In A.D. *33 the Roman procurator in Judea, Pontius Pilatus, sentenced to death a Jew, Jesus of Nazareth. Jesus' death, however, proved to be the beginning of a new era in world history because of what Jesus' followers told about him, about the events following his death and about his teachings. His disciples considered him the Messiah, or Christ, that is, the anointed king of Israel. This may have been Jesus' view, for he referred to himself as the Son of Man, a term which, whatever it may have meant originally (see introduction to No. 19), was understood in a Messianic sense. A novel aspect of his teaching was his view that he as the Messiah must suffer and die, but that he also expected to be resurrected after three days—a prophecy borne out by the events (A). The gospel, or "good news," that Jesus preached was very simple: "The time is fulfilled and the Kingdom of God is at hand: repent ye and believe in the gospel." Jesus never tired of explaining in parables what he meant by the term "Kingdom of God," or "Kingdom of Heaven." According to Jesus, membership in the Kingdom of God was not a reward earned by good behavior, but a free gift of God, an act of grace for which God owed no accounting and which could be given to high and low, rich and poor, pious and sinners (B). Yet, paradoxically, this did not mean that Jesus had come to abolish the law, i.e., the commands of the Old Testament. In fact, Jesus interpreted the Ten Commandments (No. 13) to regulate not so much man's external behavior as, above all, his inward being (C). One of the most important elements in the spread of Christianity in the Roman world was the account of his crucifixion and resurrection (D).*

Information on the life and death of Jesus derives primarily from the Gospels of Matthew, Mark, and Luke. The Gospel of Mark, as well as the common written source underlying the other two "synoptic" gospels, were composed shortly after A.D. *70. They embody the tradition current among Jesus' disciples during the generation after his crucifixion.*[6]

A. JESUS THE MESSIAH

And Jesus went forth, and his disciples, into the villages of Caesarea Philippi: and on the way he asked his disciples, saying unto them, Who do men say that I am? And they told him, saying, John the Baptist; and others; Elijah; but others, One of the prophets. And he asked them, But who say ye that I am? Peter answereth and saith unto him, Thou are the Christ. And he charged them that they should tell no man of him.

And he began to teach them, that the Son of man must suffer many things, and be rejected by the elders, and the chief priests, and the scribes, and be killed, and after three days rise again.

B. THE KINGDOM OF HEAVEN

The Kingdom of heaven is like unto a man that was a householder, who went out early in the morning to hire laborers into his vineyard. And he went out about the third hour, and saw others standing in the marketplace idle; and to them he said, Go ye also into the vineyard, and whatsoever is right I will give you. And they went their way. Again he went out about the sixth and the ninth hour, and did likewise. And

[6] *The New Testament*, Standard Edition, American Revision Committee (New York: Thomas Nelson and Sons, 1900), pp. 44, 22, 4 ff., 54 ff.

about the eleventh hour he went out, and found others standing; and he saith unto them, Why stand ye here all the day idle? They say unto him, Because no man hath hired us. He saith unto them, Go ye also into the vineyard. And when even was come, the lord of the vineyard saith unto his steward, Call the laborers, and pay them their hire, beginning from the last unto the first. And when they came that were hired about the eleventh hour, they received every man a shilling. And when they received it, they murmured against the householder, saying, These last have spent but one hour, and thou hast made them equal unto us, who have borne the burden of the day and the scorching heat. But he answered and said to one of them, Friend, I do thee no wrong: didst not thou agree with me for a shilling? Take up that which is thine, and go they way; it is my will to give unto this last, even as unto thee. Is it not lawful for me to do what I will with mine own? or is thine eye evil because I am good? So the last shall be first, and the first last.

C. THE SERMON FROM THE MOUNT

"Think not that I came to destroy the law or the prophets; I came not to destroy but to fulfill. For verily I say unto you, Till heaven and earth pass away, one jot or one tittle shall in no wise pass away from the law, till all things be accomplished. Whosoever therefore shall break one of these least commandments, and shall teach men so, shall be called least in the kingdom of heaven: but whosoever shall do and teach them, he shall be called great in the kingdom of heaven. For I say unto you, that except your righteousness shall exceed the righteousness of the scribes and Pharisees, ye shall in no wise enter into the kingdom of heaven.

"Ye have heard that it was said to them of old time, Thou shalt not kill, and whosoever shall kill shall be in danger of the judgment: but I say unto you that every one who is angry with his brother shall be in danger of the judgment: and whosoever shall say to his brother, Raca, shall be in danger of the council; and whosoever shall say, Thou fool, shall be in danger of the hell of fire. If therefore thou art offering thy gift at the altar, and there rememberest that thy brother hath aught against thee, leave there thy gift before the altar and go thy way, first be reconciled to thy brother, and then come and offer thy gift. Agree with thine adversary quickly, while thou are with him in the way; lest haply the adversary deliver thee to the judge, and the judge deliver thee to the officer, and thou be cast into prison. Verily I say unto thee, Thou shalt by no means come out thence, till you have paid the last farthing.

"Ye have heard that it was said, Thou shalt not commit adultery; but I say unto you, that every one that looketh on a woman to lust after her hath committed adultery with her already in his heart. And if thy right eye causeth thee to stumble, cut it off, and cast it from thee: for it is profitable for thee that one of thy members should perish, and not thy whole body be cast into hell. And if thy right hand causeth thee to stumble, cut it off, and cast it from thee: for it is profitable for thee that one of thy members should perish, and not thy whole body go into hell. It was said also, Whosoever shall put away his wife, let him give her a writing of divorcement: but I say unto you, that every one that putteth away his wife, saving for the cause of fornication, maketh her an adulteress; and whosoever shall marry her when she is put away committeth adultery.

"Again ye have heard that it was said to them of old time, Thou shalt not forswear thyself, but shalt perform unto the Lord thine oaths: but I say unto you, Swear not at all; neither by the heaven, for it is the throne of God; nor by the earth, for it is the footstool of his feet; nor by Jerusalem, for it is the city of the great King. Neither shalt thou swear by thy head, for thou canst not make one hair white or black. But let your speech be, Yea, yea; Nay, nay; and whatsoever is more than these is of the evil one.

"Ye have heard that it was said, An eye for an eye, and a tooth for a tooth: but I say unto you, Resist not him that is evil, but whosoever smiteth thee on thy right cheek, turn to him the other also. And if any man would go to law with thee and take away they coat, let him have thy cloak also. And whosoever shall compel thee to go one mile, go with him two. Give to him that asketh thee, and from him that would borrow of thee turn not thou away.

"Ye have heard that it was said, Thou shalt love they neighbor and hate thine enemy; but I say unto you, Love your enemies and pray for them that persecute you; that ye may be sons of your Father who is in heaven; for he maketh his sun to rise on the evil and the good and sendeth rain on the just and the unjust. For if ye love them that love you, what reward have ye? do not even the the publicans the same? And if ye salute your brethren only, what do ye more than others? do not even the Gentiles the same? We therefore shall be perfect as your heavenly father is perfect."

D. CRUCIFIXION AND RESURRECTION

And they [the soldiers] bring him unto the place Golgotha, which is, being interpreted, The place of a skull. And they offered him wine mingled with myrrh: but he received it not. And they crucify him, and part his garments among them, casting lots upon them, what each should take. And it was the third hour, and they crucified him. And the superscription of his accusation was written over, THE KING OF THE JEWS. And with him they crucify two robbers; one on his right hand, and one on his left. And they that passed by railed on him, wagging their heads, and saying, Ha!, thou that destroyest the temple, and buildest it in three days, save thyself and come down from the cross. In like manner also the chief priests mocking him among themselves with the scribes said, He saved others, himself he cannot save. Let the Christ, the king of Israel, now come down from the cross, that we may see and believe. And they that were crucified with him reproached him.

And when the sixth hour was come, there was darkness over the whole land until the ninth hour. And at the ninth hour Jesus cried with a loud voice, Eloi, Eloi, lama sabachthani?, which is, being interpreted, My God, my God, why hast thou forsaken me? And some of them that stood by, when they heard it, said, Behold, he calleth Elijah. And one ran, and filling a sponge full of vinegar, put it on a reed, and gave him to drink, saying, Let be; let us see whether Elijah cometh to take him down. And Jesus uttered a loud voice, and gave up the ghost. And the veil of the temple was rent in two from the top to the bottom. And when the centurion, who stood by over against him, saw that he so gave up the ghost, he said, Truly this man was the Son of God. And there were also women beholding from afar: among whom were both Mary Magdalene, and Mary the mother of James the less and of Joses, and Salome; who, when he was in Galilee followed him, and ministered unto him; and many other women that came up with him unto Jerusalem. . . .

And when the sabbath was past, Mary Magdalene, and Mary the mother of James, and Salome, bought spices, that they might come and anoint him. And very early on the first day of the week, they come to the tomb when the sun was risen. And they were saying among themselves, Who shall roll us away the stone from the door of the tomb? and looking up, they see that the stone is rolled back: for it was exceeding great. And entering into the tomb, they saw a young man sitting on the right side, arrayed in a white robe; and they were amazed. And he saith unto them, Be not amazed: ye seek Jesus, the Nazarene, who has been crucified: he is risen; he is not here: behold, the place where they laid him. But go, tell his disciples and Peter, He goes before you into Galilee: there ye shall see him as he said unto you. And they went out, and fled from the tomb; for trembling and astonishment had come upon them: and they said nothing to any one; for they were afraid.

[What follows is omitted in two of the oldest Greek manuscripts. In some texts the Gospel of Mark has a different ending.]

Now when he was risen early on the first day of the week, he appeared first to Mary Magdalene, from whom he had cast out seven demons. She went and told them that had been with him, as they mourned and wept. And they, when they heard that he was alive, and had been seen of her, disbelieved.

And after these things he was manifested in another form unto two of them as they walked on their way into the country. And they went away and told it unto the rest: neither believed they them.

And afterward he was manifested unto the eleven themselves as they sat at meat; and he upbraided them with their unbelief and hardness of heart, because they believed not them that had seen him after he was risen. And he said unto them, Go ye into all the world, and preach the gospel to the whole creation. He that believeth and is baptized shall be saved; but he that disbelieveth shall be condemned. And these signs shall accompany them that believe: in my name shall they cast out demons; they shall speak with new tongues; they shall take up serpents, and if they drink any deadly thing, it shall in no wise hurt them; they shall lay hands on the sick, and they shall recover.

So then the Lord Jesus, after he had spoken unto them was received up into heaven, and sat down at the right hand of God. And they went forth, and preached everywhere, the Lord working with them, and confirming the word by the signs that followed. Amen.

79 / PAUL OF TARSUS

The personality and teachings of Jesus of Nazareth did not make a great impression upon the Jewish masses, but in the non-Jewish world, among the Gentiles, Christianity was actively spread by Jewish missionaries sent out by Jesus during his lifetime. The most successful missionary, however, the Jew, Paul of Tarsus, had never known Jesus in the flesh. In his youth he had persecuted the Christian sect, but en route to Damascus he had seen Jesus in a vision and accepted from him the mission to the Gentiles. He spent the rest of his life traveling in Syria, Asia

Minor, Greece, and Italy and died a martyr's death during the Neronian persecution (A.D. 65). He also wrote a great number of letters to Christian congregations founded by himself and other missionaries.

The following excerpt is taken from his epistle to the Galatians (in Asia Minor). The principal problem of the mission to the Gentiles was a definition of the attitude to be taken toward the Law, especially toward the ritual law, the dietary laws, and the divine command of circumcision as laid down in the Old Testament. Was the Law binding on Gentile converts to the Christian faith? On this question opinions clashed sharply in the generation after Jesus' death, but Paul claimed that in A.D. 48 the "pillars" of the church at Jerusalem, among them James the brother of Jesus and Cephas (or Peter), authorized him to waive the requirements of the Law in the case of Gentile converts. Paul adhered to this agreement, although, according to him, Peter later repudiated it. Paul taught that man was justified not by the Law, but by faith in Jesus Christ. The "liberty" from the Law proclaimed by Paul vastly facilitated the mission to the Gentiles, and explains at least partially the historic success of the Pauline mission.[7]

Then after the space of fourteen years I went up again to Jerusalem with Barnabas taking Titus also with me. And I went up by revelation, and I laid before them the gospel which I preach among the Gentiles but privately before them who were of repute; lest by any means I should be running or had run in vain. But not even Titus who was with me being a Greek was compelled to be circumcised; and that because of the false brethren privily brought in, who came in privily to spy out our liberty which we have in Christ Jesus, that they might bring us into bondage; to whom we gave place in the way of subjection, no, not for an hour; that the truth of the gospel might continue with you. But from those who were reputed to be somewhat (whatsoever they were, it maketh no matter to me: God accepteth not man's person)—they, I say, who were of repute imparted nothing to me: but contrariwise when they saw that I had been intrusted with the gospel of the uncircumcision, even as Peter with the gospel of the circumcision (for he that wrought for Peter unto the apostleship of the

[7] *The New Testament,* Standard Edition, American Revision Committee (New York: Thomas Nelson and Sons, 1900), p. 198 ff.

circumcision wrought for me also unto the Gentiles); and when they perceived the grace that was given unto me, James and Cephas and John, they who were reputed to be pillars, gave to me and Barnabas the right hands of fellowship, that we should go unto the Gentiles and they unto the circumcision; only they would that we should remember the poor; which very thing I was also zealous to do.

But when Cephas came to Antioch, I resisted him to the face because he stood condemned. For before that certain came from James, he ate with the Gentiles; but when they came he drew back and separated himself, fearing them that were of the circumcision. And the rest of the Jews dissembled likewise with him; insomuch that even Barnabas was carried away with their dissimulation. But when I saw that they walked not uprightly according to the truth of the gospel, I said unto Cephas before them all, If thou, being a Jew, livest as do the Gentiles and not as do the Jews, how compellest thou the Gentiles to live as do the Jews? We being Jews by nature and not sinners of the Gentiles, yet knowing that a man is not justified by the works of the law but through faith in Jesus Christ, even we believed on Christ Jesus, that we might be justified by faith in Christ, and not by the works of the law: because by the works of the law shall no flesh be justified. But, if while we sought to be justified in Christ, we ourselves also were found sinners, is Christ a minister of sin? God forbid. For if I build up again those things that I destroyed, I prove myself a transgressor. For I through the law died unto the law, that I might live unto God. I have been crucified with Christ; and it is no longer I that live but Christ liveth in me; and that life which I now live in the flesh, I live in faith, the faith which is in the Son of God who loved me and gave himself up for me. I do not make void the grace of God: for if righteousness is through the law, then Christ died for nought.

80 / THE WAR OF THE LEGIONS

After Nero's suicide in A.D. *68 the legions discovered "that secret of empire that emperors could be made elsewhere than at Rome." Three short-lived emperors, Galba, Otho, and Vitellius, made their bid for supreme power before Vespasian (*A.D. *69–79) was able to establish the power of the principate on secure* *foundations once more. In* A.D. *69 the forces of Vespasian advanced upon Rome, captured the city, and killed Vitellius. Tacitus' account of the Flavianists' entrance into the capital is a masterpiece.*[8]

Antonius, however, summoned the legions to an assembly and endeavoured to calm them, proposing that they should encamp near the Mulvian bridge and enter the capital on the following day. His reason for delay was the fear that the soldiers, once exasperated by conflict, would respect neither the people nor the Senate nor even the shrines and temples of the Gods. They, however, looked with dislike on all procrastination as inimical to victory. At the same time the colours that glittered among the hills, though followed by an unwarlike population, presented the appearance of a hostile array. They advanced in three divisions, one column straight from where they had halted along the Via Flaminia, another along the bank of the Tiber, a third moved on the Colline Gate by the Via Salaria. The mob was routed by a charge of the calvary. Then the Vitellianist troops, themselves also drawn up in three columns of defence, met the foe. Numerous engagements with various issue took place before the walls, but they generally ended in favour of the Flavianists, who had the advantage of more skillful generalship. Only that division suffered which had wound its way along narrow and slippery roads to the left quarter of the city as far as the gardens of Sallust. The Vitellianists, taking their stand on the garden-walls, kept off the assailants with stones and javelins till late in the day, when they were taken in the rear by the cavalry, which had then forced an entrance by the Colline Gate. In the Campus Martius also the hostile armies met, the Flavianists with all the prestige of fortune and repeated victory, the Vitellianists rushing on in sheer despair. Though defeated, they rallied again in the city.

The populace stood by and watched the combatants; and, as though it had been a mimic conflict, encouraged first one party and then the other by their shouts and plaudits. Whenever either side gave way, they cried out that those who concealed themselves in the shops or took refuge in any private house should be dragged out and butchered, and they secured the larger share of the booty; for while the soldiers were busy with bloodshed and massacre, the spoils fell to the crowd. It was a terrible and hideous sight that presented itself throughout the

[8] A. J. Church and W. J. Brodribb, *The History of Tacitus* (London: Macmillan and Co., 1894), p. 137 ff.

city. Here raged battle and death; there the bath and the tavern were crowded. In one spot were pools of blood and heaps of corpses, and close by prostitutes and men of character as infamous; there were all the debaucheries of luxurious peace, all the horrors of a city most cruelly sacked, till one was ready to believe the country to be mad at once with rage and lust. It was not indeed the first time that armed troops had fought within the city; they had done so twice when Sulla, once when Cinna, triumphed. The bloodshed then had not been less, but now there was an unnatural recklessness, and men's pleasures were not interrupted even for a moment. As if it were a new delight added to their holidays, they exulted in and enjoyed the scene, indifferent to parties and rejoicing over the sufferings of the commonwealth.

81 / ROMAN IMPERIALISM

*As a result of the civil war (*A.D. *68–69) a rebellion broke out on the Rhine frontier in which both Gallic and Germanic tribes participated. Vespasian's lieutenants finally suppressed the revolt. The commander of Vespasian's army, Q. Petilius Cerialis, entered the city of Trèves (Trier), a rebel stronghold, and attempted to explain in a speech (A) to a Gallic audience the benefits bestowed upon the provinces by the Roman empire.*[9]

The Roman conquest of Britain, begun under Claudius (No. 76), continued under the Flavian emperors. Tacitus' father-in-law, Gn. Julius Agricola, was appointed governor of Britain in A.D. *77. He waged war in Wales and invaded Scotland. In excerpt (B) Tacitus describes the effects of the conquest on the natives during the winter 79–80. The Romanization of the western provinces of the Roman Empire is one of the most important developments of the first three centuries of our era.*

In A.D. *83 or 84 Agricola again invaded Scotland and faced a formidable army of 30,000 Britons at the Graupian Mountains. Tacitus placed into the mouth of a British chieftain, Calgacus, a terrifying indictment (C) of Roman rule.*[10]

[9] A. J. Church and W. J. Brodribb, *The History of Tacitus* (London: Macmillan and Co., 1894), p. 184 ff.

[10] *The Works of Tacitus,* The Oxford Translation, Revised, Vol. II (London: George Bell and Sons, 1887), pp. 366, 372–3.

A. A FAVORABLE JUDGMENT

"I have never cultivated eloquence; it is by my sword that I have asserted the excellence of the Roman people. Since, however, words have very great weight with you, since you estimate good and evil not according to their real value, but according to the representations of seditious men, I have resolved to say a few words which, as the war is at an end, it may be useful for you to have heard rather than for me to have spoken. Roman generals and emperors entered your territory, as they did the rest of Gaul, with no ambitious purposes, but at the solicitation of your ancestors, who were wearied to the last extremity by intestine strife, while the Germans, whom they had summoned to their help, had imposed their yoke alike on friend and foe. How many battles we have fought against the Cimbri and Teutones, at the cost of what hardships to our armies, and with what result we have waged our German wars is perfectly well known. It was not to defend Italy that we occupied the borders of the Rhine, but to insure that no second Ariovistus should seize the empire of Gaul. Do you fancy yourselves to be dearer in the eyes of Civilis and the Batavi and the Transrhenane tribes than your fathers and grandfathers were to their ancestors? There have ever been the same causes at work to make the Germans cross over into Gaul, lust, avarice, and the longing for a new home, prompting them to leave their own marshes and deserts and to possess themselves of this most fertile soil and of you its inhabitants. Liberty, indeed, and the like specious names are their pretexts; but never did any man seek to enslave his fellows and secure dominion for himself without using the very same words.

"Gaul always had its petty kingdoms and intestine wars till you submitted to our authority. We, though so often provoked, have used the right of conquest to burden you only with the cost of maintaining peace. For the tranquillity of nations cannot be preserved without armies; armies cannot exist without pay; pay cannot be furnished without tribute; all else is common between us. You often command our legions. You rule these and other provinces. There is no privilege, no exclusion. From worthy emperors you derive equal advantage, though you dwell so far away, while cruel rulers are most formidable to their neighbours. Endure the passion and rapacity of your masters, just as you bear barren seasons and excessive rains and other natural evils. There will be vices as long as there are men. But they are not perpetual, and they are compensated by the occurrence of better things. Perhaps, however, you expect a milder rule under Tutor and Classicus, and fancy that armies to repel the Germans and the Britons will be furnished by less tribute than you now pay. Should the Romans be driven out (which God forbid), what can result but wars between all these nations? By the prosperity and order of eight hundred years has this fabric of empire been consolidated, nor can it be overthrown without destroying those who overthrow it. Yours will be the worst peril, for you have gold and wealth, and these are the chief incentives to war. Give, therefore, your love and respect to the cause of peace and to that capital in which we, conquerors and conquered, claim an equal right. Let the lessons of fortune in both its forms teach you not to prefer rebellion and ruin to submission and safety."

B. THE ROMANIZATION OF THE PROVINCIALS

The succeeding winter was employed in the most salutary measures. In order, by a taste of pleasures, to reclaim the natives from that rude and unsettled state which prompted them to war and reconcile them to quiet and tranquillity, he incited them by private instigations and public encouragements to erect temples, courts of justice, and dwelling-houses. He bestowed commendations upon those who were prompt in complying with his intentions and reprimanded such as were dilatory; thus promoting a spirit of emulation which had all the force of necessity. He was also attentive to provide a liberal education for the sons of their chieftains, preferring the natural genius of the Britons to the attainments of the Gauls; and his attempts were attended with such success that they who lately disdained to make use of the Roman language were now ambitious of becoming eloquent. Hence the Roman habit began to be held in honour, and the toga was frequently worn. At length they gradually deviated into a taste for those luxuries which stimulate to vice: porticos and baths and the elegances of the table; and this, from their inexperience, they termed politeness, whilst in reality it constituted a part of their slavery.

C. ROMAN IMPERIALISM ACCUSED

"When I reflect on the causes of the war and the circumstances of our situation, I feel a strong persuasion that our united efforts on the present day will prove the beginning of universal liberty to Britain. For we are all undebased by slavery; and there is no land behind us, nor does even the sea afford a refuge, whilst the Roman fleet hovers around. Thus the use of arms, which is at all times honourable to the brave, now offers the only safety even to cowards. In all the battles which have yet been fought with various success against the Romans, our countrymen may be deemed to have reposed their final hopes and resources in us: for we, the noblest sons of Britain, and therefore stationed in its last recesses far from the view of servile shores, have preserved even our eyes unpolluted by the contact of subjection. We, at the furthest limits both of land and liberty, have been defended to this day by the remoteness of our situation and of our fame. The extremity of Britain is now disclosed; and whatever is unknown becomes an object of magnitude. But there is no nation beyond us; nothing but waves and rocks and still more hostile Romans, whose arrogance we cannot escape by obsequiousness and submission. These plunderers of the world, after exhausting the land by their devastations, are rifling the ocean: stimulated by avarice if their enemy be rich; by ambition if poor: unsatiated by the East and by the West: the only people who behold wealth and indigence with equal avidity. To ravage, to slaughter, to usurp under false titles they call empire; and where they make a desert, they call it peace."

"Our children and relations are by the appointment of nature the dearest of all things to us. These are torn away by levies to serve in foreign lands. Our wives and sisters, though they should escape the violation of hostile force, are polluted under names of friendship and hospitality. Our estates and possessions are consumed in tributes; our grain in contributions. Even our bodies are worn down amidst stripes and insults in clearing woods and draining marshes. Wretches born to slavery are once bought and afterwards maintained by their masters. Britain every day buys, every day feeds, her own servitude. And as among domestic slaves every newcomer serves for the scorn and derision of his fellows; so, in this ancient household of the world, we, as the newest and vilest, are sought out to destruction. For we have neither cultivated lands nor mines nor harbours which can induce them to preserve us for our labours. The valour, too, and unsubmitting spirit of subjects only render them more obnoxious to their masters; while remoteness and secrecy of situation itself, in proportion as it conduces to security, tends to inspire suspicion. Since then all hopes of mercy are vain, at length assume courage, both you to whom safety and you to whom glory is dear. The Trinobantes, even under a female leader, had force enough to burn a colony, to storm camps, and, if success had not damped their vigour, would have been able entirely to throw off the yoke; and shall not we, untouched, unsubdued, and struggling not for the acquisition but the security of liberty, show at the very first onset what men Caledonia has reserved for her defense? . . ."

82 / LATIFUNDIA AND COLONI

In spite of the prosperity of the cities in the Roman empire, the vast majority of its inhabitants made their living from agriculture. The Julio-Claudian emperors had attempted to check the growth of latifundia, *or large estates, but their measures had not been successful. The Elder Pliny had remarked in his* Natural History *(XVIII, VII, 35), "the* latifundia *have ruined Italy and soon will ruin the provinces as well. Six owners were in possession of one half of the province of Africa at the time when the Emperor Nero put them to death." On medium-size and large estates slave labor was supplanted by* coloni, *or tenant farmers. The following letter was written by the Younger Pliny (*A.D. *61–before 114), a nephew of the Elder Pliny. He held important offices of state under the emperors Domitian, Nerva, and Trajan.*[11]

As you are not of a disposition to expect from your friends the common ceremonies of the world when they cannot observe them without inconvenience to themselves, so I too warmly love you to be apprehensive you will take otherwise than I wish you should my not waiting upon you on the first day of your entrance upon the consular office, especially as I am detained here by the necessity of letting my farms upon long leases. I am obliged to enter upon an entire new method with my tenants; for under the former leases, though I made them very considerable abatements, they have run greatly in arrears. For this reason several of them have not only taken no sort of care to lessen a debt which they found themselves incapable of wholly discharging; but even seized and consumed all the produce of the lands in the belief that it would now be no advantage to themselves to spare it. I must therefore obviate this increasing evil and endeavor to find out some remedy against it. The only one I can think of is not to reserve my rent in money but in kind, and so place some of my servants to overlook the tillage and guard the stock; as indeed there is no sort of revenue more agreeable to reason than what arises from the bounty of the soil, the seasons and the climate. 'Tis true, this method will

[11] William Melmoth, *The Letters of Pliny,* Vol. II (London: R. Dodsley, 1747), p. 569 ff.

require great integrity and diligent attendance in the person I appoint my bailiff and put me to the expense of employing many hands. However, I must hazard the experiment, and, as in an inveterate distemper, try every change of remedy. You see, it is not any pleasurable indulgence that prevents my attending you on the first day of your consulship. I shall celebrate it, nevertheless, as much as if I were present, and pay my vows for you here with all the warmest sentiments of joy and congratulation. Farewell.

83 / THE CITIES OF THE EMPIRE: IMPERIAL INTERVENTION

The Greek cities were accustomed to run their own governments long before they became part of the Roman Empire. Under the principate, however, the emperors were often forced to intervene in the domestic affairs of these cities because the local governments failed to discharge their functions properly. The cities' difficulties were frequently financial. Around A.D. *112 Trajan despatched the Younger Pliny to Bithynia in Asia Minor as imperial legate with extraordinary powers. From Bithynia Pliny addressed a number of enquiries concerning the cities of Bithynia to his imperial master and received his replies.*[12]

PLINY TO TRAJAN:

The city of Nicomedia, Sir, has expended three million three hundred and twenty-nine sesterces in building an aqueduct; but not being able to finish it, the works are entirely falling to ruin. They made a second attempt in another place, where they laid out two millions. But this likewise is discontinued; so that after having been at an immense charge to no purpose, they must still be at a further expense in order to be accommodated with water. I have examined a fine

[12] William Melmoth, *The Letters of Pliny*, Vol. II (London: R. Dodsley, 1747), p. 623 ff.

spring from whence the water may be conveyed over arches (as was done in their first design) in such a manner that the higher as well as level and low parts of the city may be supplied. There are but very few of the old arches remaining; the square stones, however, employed in the former building, may be used in turning the new ones. I am of the opinion that part should be raised with brick, as that will be the easier and cheaper method. But that this work may not be carried on with the same ill success as the former, it will be necessary to send hither an architect and an engineer. And I will venture to say, from the beauty and usefulness of the design, it will be a work well worthy the splendor of your times.

TRAJAN TO PLINY:

Care must be taken to supply the city of Nicomedia with water; and you will do so, I am well persuaded, with all the diligence you ought. But it is most certainly no less incumbent upon you to examine by whose misconduct it has happened that such large sums have been thrown away upon this work; lest by applying the money to private purposes this aqueduct should likewise be left unfinished. You will let me know the result of your enquiry.

84 / THE EMPEROR TRAJAN AND THE CHRISTIANS

In the tenth book of the Younger Pliny's letters (introduction to No. 82) one of Pliny's enquiries and a reply from Trajan dealt with Christians in Bithynia. In this province Christianity apparently made a great number of converts; this situation was peculiar to Asia Minor and did not prevail in most other parts of the Roman Empire. Pliny was clearly puzzled by the strangeness of the new religion (note his information concerning the Christian cult) and the fanaticism of its adherents, but he seemed to have come to the realization that in fact the new religion was not subversive. Note that on one occasion he felt that participation in the imperial cult was the criterion of guilt or innocence. In his reply Trajan established the rule that persons accused of being Christians must be punished, but that the Roman authorities should not search for Christians or act upon anonymous denunciations.[13]

PLINY TO TRAJAN:

It is a rule, Sir, which I inviolably observe, to refer myself to you in all my doubts; for who is more capable of removing my scruples or informing my ignorance? Having never been present at any trials concerning those who profess Christianity, I am unacquainted not only with the nature of their crimes or the measure of their puishment, but how far it is proper to enter into an examination concerning them. Whether therefore any difference is usually made with respect to the ages of the guilty, or no distinction is to be observed between the young and the adult; whether a repentance entitles them to a pardon; or if a man has once been a Christian, it avails nothing to desist from his error; whether the very profession of Christianity, unattended with any criminal act, or only the crimes themselves inherent in the profession are punishable; in all these points I am greatly doubtful. In the meanwhile the method I have observed towards those who have been brought before me as Christians is this: If they confessed, I repeated the question twice again, adding threats at the same time; when, if they still persevered, I ordered them to be immediately punished: for I was persuaded, whatever the nature of their opinions might be, a contumacious and flexible obstinacy certainly deserved correction. There were others also brought before me possessed with the same infatuation, but being citizens of Rome, I directed them to be carried thither. But this crime spreading (as is usually the case) while it was actually under prosecution, several instances of the same nature occurred. An information was presented to me without any name subscribed, containing a charge against several persons who upon examination denied they were Christians or had ever been so. They repeated after me an invocation to the gods and offered religious rites with wine and frankincense before your statue (which for this purpose I had ordered to be brought, together with those of the gods) and even reviled the name of Christ: whereas there is no forcing, it is said, those who are really Christians into a compliance with any of these articles: I thought proper therefore to discharge them. Some among those who were accused by a witness in person at first confessed themselves Christians, but immediately after denied it; while the rest owned indeed that they had been of that number formerly, but had now

[13] William Melmoth, *The Letters of Pliny*, Vol. II (London: R. Dodsley, 1747), pp. 671–7.

(some above three, others more, and a few above twenty years ago) forsaken that error. They all worshipped your statue and the images of the gods, throwing out imprecations at the same time against the name of Christ. They affirmed the whole of their guilt or their error was that they met on a certain stated day before it was light and addressed themselves in a form of prayer to Christ as to some God, binding themselves by a solemn oath, not for the purposes of any wicked design, but never to commit any fraud, theft, or adultery, never to falsify their word, nor deny a trust when they should be called upon to deliver it up; after which it was their custom to separate and then reassemble to eat in common a harmless meal. From this custom, however, they desisted after the publication of my edict, by which, according to your orders, I forbade the meeting of any assemblies. After receiving this account, I judged it so much the more necessary to endeavor to extort the real truth by putting two female slaves to the torture who were said to administer in their religious functions: but I could discover nothing more than an absurd and excessive superstition. I thought proper therefore to adjourn all farther proceedings in this affair in order to consult with you. For it appears to be a matter highly deserving your consideration, more especially as great numbers must be involved in the danger of these prosecutions, this enquiry having already extended and being still likely to extend to persons of all ranks and ages and even of both sexes. For this contagious superstition is not confined to the cities only, but has spread its infection among the country villages. Nevertheless, it still seems possible to remedy this evil and restrain its progress. The temples, at least, which were once almost deserted, begin now to be frequented; and the sacred solemnities, after a long intermission, are again revived, while there is a general demand for the victims, which for some time past have met with but few purchasers. From hence it is easy to imagine what numbers might be reclaimed from this error if a pardon were granted to those who shall repent.

TRAJAN TO PLINY:

The method you have pursued, my dear Pliny, in the proceedings against those Christians which were brought before you is extremely proper; as it is not possible to lay down any fixed plan by which to act in all cases of this nature. But I would not have you officiously enter into any enquiries concerning them. If indeed they should be brought before you and the crime is proved, they must be punished; with this restriction, however, that where the party denies himself to be a Christian and shall make it evident that he is not by invoking our gods, let him (notwithstanding any former suspicion) be pardoned upon his repentance. Informations without the accuser's name subscribed ought not to be received in prosecutions of any sort; as it is introducing a very dangerous precedent, and by no means agreeable to the equity of my government.

85 / THE MILITARY MONARCHY AND THE PROBLEM OF ROMAN CITIZENSHIP

*The Severan dynasty came to power in the course of a second War of the Legions, or Civil War (*A.D. *193–197; for the first War of the Legions see No. 80). The military basis of the principate, carefully disguised by Augustus and almost forgotten during the reign of the "Five Good Emperors" in the second century* A.D.*, was thus once more brought into the open. Consequently the Emperor Caracalla (*A.D. *211–217)—or Antoninus, as he is called in the following selection because Septimius Severus had declared himself adopted into the Antonine family—favored the armed forces over the civilian population. His grant of Roman citizenship to all inhabitants of the Roman Empire mentioned in the following selection is confirmed by a papyrus; according to it a group of people, the* dediticii *(meaning uncertain), were excluded from the grant (which occurred probably in 213). The fiscal motive for Caracalla's measure, mentioned in the excerpt below, is, however, doubtful. Whatever the reason for its promulgation, the* Constitutio Antoniniana *was the climax of a long development during which Roman citizenship was gradually extended to provincials. The excerpt is taken from the* Roman History *of Dio Cassius, which covered the entire period from Rome's beginnings to* A.D. *229. The author held the consulship twice, once in 193 and again in 229.*[14]

[14] Reprinted by permission of the publishers from the Loeb Classical Library, translated by E. Cary, *Dio Cassius, Roman History,* Vol. IX (Cambridge, Mass.: Harvard University Press; London: William Heinemann; New York: G. P. Putnam's Sons, 1927), pp. 295–301.

Antoninus was fond of spending money upon the soldiers, great numbers of whom he kept in attendance upon him, alleging one excuse after another and one war after another; but he made it his business to strip, despoil, and grind down all the rest of mankind, and the senators by no means least. In the first place, there were the gold crowns that he was repeatedly demanding, on the constant pretext that he had conquered some enemy or other; and I am not referring, either, to the actual manufacture of the crowns—for what does that amount to?—but to the vast amount of money constantly being given under that name by the cities for the customary "crowning," as it is called, of the emperors. Then there were the provisions that we were required to furnish in great quantities on all occasions, and this without receiving any remuneration and sometimes actually at additional cost to ourselves—all of which supplies he either bestowed upon the soldiers or else peddled out; and there were the gifts which he demanded from the wealthy citizens and from the various communities; and the taxes, both the new ones which he promulgated and the ten per cent tax that he instituted in place of the five per cent tax applying to the emancipation of slaves, to bequests, and to all legacies; for he abolished the right of succession and exemption from taxes which had been granted in such cases to those who were closely related to the deceased. This was the reason why he made all the people in his empire Roman citizens; nominally he was honouring them, but his real purpose was to increase his revenues by this means, inasmuch as aliens did not have to pay most of these taxes. . . .

To such an extent was the entire world, so far as it owned his sway, devastated throughout his whole reign, that on one occasion the Romans at a horse-race shouted in unison this, among other things: "We shall do the living to death, that we may bury the dead." Indeed, he often used to say: "Nobody in the world shall have money but me; and I want it to bestow upon the soldiers." Once when Julia chided him for spending vast sums upon them and said, "There is no longer any source of revenue, either just or unjust, left to us," he replied, exhibiting his sword, "Be of good cheer, mother: for as long as we have this, we shall not run short of money."

86 / ROMAN LAW: HISTORY AND NATURE

Roman law reached the climax of its development in the second and third centuries A.D. *Its sources were of several kinds. In addition to "laws" technically so called, of which the most ancient had been collected in the Twelve Tables (No. 58), there were the ancient plebiscites, or decisions of the plebs, which since the* Lex Hortensia *of 287* B.C. *had the force of law; the* senatus consulta, *or decisions of the Senate, which strictly speaking had an advisory function only; the yearly edicts of the praetor, in which this chief judicial officer of the Roman state announced under what conditions he would allow parties to avail themselves of various legal remedies; and the legislation* (constitutiones) *of the* princeps. *A most important and peculiar source of law were the legal opinions of the jurisprudents, who were often consulted on difficult problems of law and whose "replies" to these questions enjoyed great authority.*

In the second century A.D. *the Roman jurist Pomponius wrote, among numerous other works, a short treatise (A) on the history of Roman law.*

Excerpt B may illustrate further several sources of Roman law, as well as its nature. Early Roman law had been extremely formal. Contracts enjoyed full legal protection by the magistrates and law courts, provided that the prescribed forms were observed. Under this formal administration of the law, it could occur that the courts would protect one party who, by a contract, had deceived another party. As Roman law developed, the tendency grew for the courts to look behind the form and to grant to a party deceived by a contract a measure of protection. In excerpt B there is a quotation from the praetor's edict, which by this time had become standardized and which under certain conditions granted a legal remedy against dolus malus, *or deceit. The excerpt derives from a commentary on the praetor's Edict, written by one of the greatest of Roman jurisprudents, Ulpian (+*A.D. *228). In it he cites several earlier jurisprudents. He dis-*

cusses the definition of dolus malus, *as well as cases where there is no room for the special remedy.*[15]

A. A BRIEF HISTORY OF ROMAN LAW

Now at the time of the origin of our state the citizens at large (*populus*) undertook at first to proceed without fixed statutes or any fixed law at all, and everything was regulated by the direct control of the kings. After that, the state being more or less enlarged, the tradition is that Romulus himself divided the body of the citizens into thirty parts, which parts he called *curiae*, for the reason that he exercised his care (*cura*) of the commonwealth in accordance with the opinions of the parts referred to. Accordingly he himself proposed to the people certain curiate statutes, and the kings that succeeded him did the same thing; all which statutes exist in writing in the book of Sextus Papirius, who was contemporary with Superbus the son of Demaratus of Corinth, and was one of the leading men. That book, as above mentioned, is called the Papirian civil law; not that Papirius inserted anything in it of his own composition, but because statutes which had been passed in an unsystematic way were (therein) reduced by him to a single body of law. The kings being subsequently expelled by a tribunician statute, the above statutes all went out of use, and the Roman people came once more to live by loosely ascertained law or by mere custom rather than by any formal statute, to which condition it submitted for about twenty years. Afterwards, in order to put an end to this state of things, it was determined that ten men should be appointed by the authority of the state through whom application should be made for statutes to Greek cities and the Roman state should be put on a statutable foundation. The laws so obtained they wrote on ivory tablets and set them up before the rostra, to the end that they might be the more clearly perceptible, and supreme authority in the state was given for that year to the officers mentioned, their duty being to amend the statutes where necessary and also to expound their meaning, and there was to be no appeal from their decisions as there was from those of magistrates in general. They, however, themselves took note of certain deficiencies in the original statutes just referred to, and accordingly, in the course of the ensuing year, they added two more tables to those already existing; hence the statutes taken all together were called the statutes of the Twelve Tables. It has been stated by some writers that the passing of these laws was suggested to the Tenmen

15 Charles Henry Monro, *The Digest of Justinian*, Vol. I (Cambridge: Cambridge Univeristy Press, 1904), pp. 6–9, 215 ff.

by one Hermodorus, an Ephesian, who was living as an exile in Italy. These statutes being enacted, it thereupon followed that discussion in the forum (*disputatio fori*) became a necessity, as in fact it naturally must be the case that correct interpretation requires the guidance of those learned in the law. (The results of) such discussion and the rules of that particular law, which is composed by the learned and established without the use of writing, are not called by any special name like the other parts of the law which have their respective designations; they are both comprised under the general appellation of civil law. After this there were at about the same time various forms of actions devised, founded on the above statutes, by which people in general might carry on litigation; and in order to prevent the citizens from bringing their actions in any way they pleased, the Tenmen required that they should be in set and solemn form. This branch of the law is called that of statute-actions (*legis actiones*), in other words, statutable action (*legitimae actiones*). Accordingly, these three branches of law arose at about the same time, that is to say, the statute of the Twelve Tables was first passed, these tables gave rise to the civil law, and in accordance with the same were devised the statute-actions. . . . Hereupon, there being in public use the statute of the Twelve Tables and the civil law and also the statute-actions, it came to pass that discord arose between the plebs and the fathers, whereupon the former seceded and established laws for itself, which laws are called plebiscites. Soon after, on the plebs being induced to return, a great deal of disagreement arose in connexion with these plebiscites, in consequence of which it was enacted by the *lex Hortensia* that they should be observed as if they were regular statutes. The result of this was that the difference between a plebiscite and a statute consisted thereafter in the formal method of enactment, but the force of the two was the same. Next, seeing that the plebs found in course of time that it was difficult for them to meet together, and the general body of the citizens no doubt found it much more difficult still, considering the vast increase of their numbers, the very necessity of the case caused the administration of the commonwealth to be put in the hands of the senate; hence that body came to take a new part in the management of affairs, and whatever it enacted was observed as law, the enactment being called a senatus-consultum. At this time, besides the above, there were magistrates who administered justice, and in order that the citizens might be aware what kind of pronouncement the officer would make in any given case and take their measures accordingly, the magistrates published edicts. The edicts of the praetor constituted the honorary law, the name "honorary" being derived from the public office (*honos*) of the praetor. Lastly, in accordance with the growing uniformity in the methods of creating law which (the state) was found to have already adopted bit by bit, as the occasion required, it came to be a matter of necessity that the business of providing for the public welfare should be in the hands of one man, as it was impossible for the senate to carry on with the same diligence every department of the administration; accordingly a head of the state was established, and he was entrusted with power to the effect that whatever he laid down should be held valid.

B. THE LEGAL REMEDY FOR DECEIT

In this Edict the praetor gives assistance against shifty and deceitful people who use some kind of craft to the prejudices of other persons, his object being to secure that the former shall not profit by their cunning and the latter shall not be losers by their simplicity. The words of the Edict are as follows:—"where acts are alleged to be done with *dolus malus,* then, if there is no other action available in the case, and there appears to be sufficient cause, I will grant a trial." *Dolus malus* is defined by Servius as follows:—a contrivance for the purpose of deceiving someone else in which one thing is pretended and another thing is aimed at. Labeo, however, says that it is possible, even without any pretence, for a man to aim at circumventing his neighbour; and it is possible, he thinks, even without *dolus malus,* for one thing to be aimed at and another pretended, as is done by such as seek to promote or protect their own or other people's interests by the use of this sort of concealment. Accordingly his own definition of *dolus malus* is that it is any craft, deceit, or contrivance, employed with a view to circumvent, deceive, or ensnare other persons. Labeo's definition is correct. The praetor was not content merely to say *dolus,* he added the word *malus* (bad), because the old lawyers used to speak of good *dolus* as well as bad, applying this expression as equivalent to that of "ingenious device," especially where anything was contrived against an enemy or a brigand. The praetor's words are:—"if there is no other action available in the case." The praetor does well to offer this action where no other is open, as an action involving infamy ought not to be lightly ordered by the praetor if a civil or praetorian one is available by way of which the party might proceed; so true is this that Pedius himself says that even where there is an Interdict given which a man can sue for, or there is some *exceptio* by which he can protect himself, this Edict will not apply. Pomponius says the same thing, and he adds this:—even where a man is secured by means of a stipulation, he cannot have the action of *dolus;* suppose, for example, there were a stipulation against *dolus.* The same writer says further that where no action at all can be granted against a man, for example, where he has been induced by *dolus malus* to promise on stipulation under circumstances so dishonouring to the promisee that no magistrate would allow an action in pursuance of the stipulation, the promisor need not trouble himself to ask for an action on *dolus malus,* because no magistrate would allow an action against him.

87 / THE PERSECUTIONS OF THE CHRISTIANS

Both the Jewish and the Christian religions were unpopular in the pagan world. Unlike their pagan contemporaries, Jews and Christians were unwilling to worship their neighbors' gods or to participate in the imperial cult. During the first two centuries and the first half of the third century persecutions of Christians were sporadic and local. On the whole, however, Christians lived unmolested and the imperial government refrained from concerning itself with them. The first empire-wide persecution of Christians occurred in 250 under Decius, and the second in 257–8 under Valerian. The latter persecution is described in the following letter by the bishop Cyprian of Carthage, a great churchman and author of the third century A.D. *Note that Xistus, mentioned in the text, was the bishop of Rome. The persecutions under Decius and Valerian, as well as the last and most cruel general persecution under Diocletian (303–311), bore out the dictum of another father of the early church, Tertullian: "The blood of the martyrs is the seed of the church."* [16]

Cyprian to his brother Successus, greeting. The reason why I could not write to you immediately, dearest brother, was that all the clergy, being placed in the very heat of the contest, were unable in any way to depart hence, all of them being prepared in accordance with the devotion of their mind for divine and heavenly glory. But know that those have come whom I had sent to the City for this purpose, that

[16] Robert E. Wallis, "The Writings of Cyprian Bishop of Carthage," in *Ante-Nicene Christian Library,* ed. by A. Roberts and James Donaldson, Vol. VIII (Edinburgh: 1868), p. 329 ff.

they might find out and bring back to us the truth, in whatever manner it had been decreed respecting us. For many various and uncertain things are current in men's opinions. But the truth concerning them is as follows, that Valerian had sent a rescript to the Senate to the effect that bishops and presbyters and deacons should immediately be punished; but that senators and men of importance and Roman knights should lose their dignity and moreover be deprived of their property; and if, when their means were taken away, they should persist in being Christians, then they should also lose their heads; but that matrons should be deprived of their property and sent into banishment. Moreover, people of Caesar's household, whoever of them had either confessed before or should now confess, should have their property confiscated, and should be sent in chains by assignment to Caesar's estates. The Emperor Valerian also added to this address a copy of the letters which he sent to the presidents of the provinces concerning us; which letters we are daily hoping will come, waiting according to the strength of our faith for the endurance of suffering, and expecting from the help and mercy of the Lord the crown of eternal life. But know that Xistus was martyred in the cemetery on the eighth day of the Ides of August and with him four deacons. Moreover, the prefects in the city are daily urging on this persecution; so that if any are presented to them, they are martyred and their property claimed by the treasury.

I beg that these things may be made known by your means to the rest of our colleagues, that everywhere, by their exhortation, the brotherhood may be strengthened and prepared for the spiritual conflict, that every one of us may think less of death than of immortality; and, dedicated to the Lord, with full faith and entire courage, may rejoice rather than fear in this confession, wherein they know that the soldiers of God and Christ are not slain, but crowned. I bid you, dearest brother, ever heartily farewell in the Lord.

88 / THE REGULATED ECONOMY

Military anarchy succeeded the rule of the Severan dynasty (235–284). The armed forces had been strengthened and pampered by the policy of the Severan house, and they made themselves the masters of the Roman Empire. Army units in the various provinces proclaimed their commanders emperors and on many occasions attempted to seize power by means of civil war. As a result, the defensive system as well as the economy of the empire collapsed. The frontiers of the empire were overrun by Germans and Persians; parts of the empire, both in the East and West, seceded; economic activity was greatly reduced, and inflation was rampant. Several attempts were made to restore the Roman Empire, and this restoration was finally carried out by Diocletian (284–305). This emperor reorganized the imperial office by appointing three colleagues to share with him the imperial authority. He enlarged and reorganized the army, defeated the usurpers, and consolidated once more the system of military defense. He built a large bureaucracy, tried to put an end to inflation, and reformed the system of taxation. Diocletian saved the Roman Empire, but the empire thus saved differed radically from the one ruled by the Julio-Claudian or Antonine emperors. The emperor was an autocrat, no longer the princeps, *or first citizen. The machinery of state—armed forces and civilian administration—had become huge. The economy was no longer free, but regulated in the interest of the needs of the state (army and bureaucracy). By an edict in* A.D. *301, of which the prologue is printed here, Diocletian tried to dictate maximum prices for all commodities and services: 100* denarii *for a measure of wheat, 4* denarii *for a* sextarius *of Gallic or Pannonian beer, 25* denarii *as the daily wages of a farm laborer, etc. The attempt to establish maximum prices was unprecedented and failed in the end, but the measure is characteristic of the new policy of regulation which, from the time of Diocletian, replaced the* laissez-faire *attitude of the principate toward society and economy.*[17]

That the fortune of our state—to which, after the immortal gods, as we recall the wars which we have successfully fought, we must be grateful for a world that is tranquil and reclining in the embrace of the most profound calm, and for the blessings of a peace that was won with great effort—be faithfully disposed and suitably adorned, is the demand of public opinion and the dignity and majesty of Rome; therefore, we, who by the gracious favor of the gods have repressed the

[17] Tenney Frank, *An Economic Survey of Ancient Rome,* Vol. V (Baltimore: The Johns Hopkins Press, 1940), pp. 311–17. Reprinted by permission of The Johns Hopkins Press.

former tide of ravages of barbarian nations by destroying them, must guard by the due defenses of justice a peace which was established for eternity. If, indeed, any self-restraint might check the excesses with which limitless and furious avarice rages—avarice which with no thought for mankind hastens to its own gain and increase, not by years or months or days but by hours and even minutes—; or, if the general welfare could endure undisturbed the riotous license by which it, in its misfortune, is from day to day most grievously injured, there would perhaps be left some room for dissimulation and silence, since human forbearance might alleviate the detestable cruelty of a pitiable situation. Since, however, it is the sole desire of unrestrained madness to have no thought for the common need and since it is considered among the unscrupulous and immoderate almost the creed of avarice, swelling and rising with fiery passions, to desist from ravaging the wealth of all through necessity rather than its own wish; and since those whom extremes of need have brought to an appreciation of their most unfortunate situation can no longer close their eyes to it, we—the protectors of the human race—viewing the situation, have agreed that justice should intervene as arbiter, so that the long-hoped-for solution which mankind itself could not supply might, by the remedies of our foresight, be applied to the general betterment of all. Common knowledge recognizes and the facts themselves proclaim how nearly too late our provision for this situation is, while we were laying plans or reserving remedies already devised, in the hope that—as was to be expected through the laws of nature—mankind, apprehended in the most serious offenses, might reform itself, for we think it far better that the stains of intolerable depredation be removed from men's minds by the feeling and decision of the same men whom, as they daily plunged into more and more serious offenses and turned, in their blindness, to crimes against the state, their grievous iniquity had charged with most cruel inhumanity, the enemies of individual and state. We, therefore, hasten to apply the remedies long demanded by the situation, satisfied that there can be no complaints that the intervention of our remedy may be considered untimely or unnecessary, or trivial or unimportant among the unscrupulous who, in spite of perceiving in our silence of so many years a lesson in restraint, have been unwilling to copy it. For who is so insensitive and so devoid of human feeling that he cannot know, or rather, has not perceived, that in the commerce carried on in the markets or involved in the daily life of cities immoderate prices are so widespread that the uncurbed passion for gain is lessened neither by abundant supplies nor by fruitful years; so that without a doubt men who are busied in these affairs constantly plan actually to control the very winds and weather from the movements of the stars, and, evil as they are, they cannot endure the watering of the fertile fields by the rains from above which bring the hope of future harvests, since they reckon it their own loss if abundance comes through the moderation of the weather. And the men whose aim it always is to profit even from the generosity of the gods, to restrain general prosperity, and furthermore to use a poor year to traffic in harvest (?) losses and agents' services—men who, individually abounding in great riches which could completely satisfy whole nations, try to capture smaller fortunes and strive after ruinous percentages—concern for humanity in general persuades us to set a limit, our subjects, to the avarice of such men. But even now we must detail the facts whose urgency after long delay has finally driven our tolerance to action, in order that—although it is difficult for the avarice which rages throughout the whole world to be described by a specific illustration or, rather, fact—nevertheless, the establishment of a remedy may be considered more just when utterly unrestrained men are forced by some sign and token to recognize the untamed desires of their own minds. Who, therefore, does not know that insolence, covertly attacking the public welfare—wherever the public safety demands that our armies be directed, not in villages or towns only, but on every road—comes to the mind of the profiteer to extort prices for merchandise, not fourfold or eightfold, but such that human speech is incapable of describing either the price or the act; and finally that sometimes in a single purchase a soldier is deprived of his bonus and salary, and that the contribution of the whole world to support the armies falls to the abominable profits of thieves, so that our soldiers seem with their own hands to offer the hopes of their service and their completed labors to the profiteers, with the result that the pillagers of the nation constantly seize more than they know how to hold. Aroused justly and rightfully by all the facts which are detailed above, and with mankind itself now appearing to be praying for release, we have decreed that there be established, not the prices of articles for sale—for such an act would be unjust when many provinces occasionally rejoice in the good fortune of wished-for low prices and, so to speak, the privilege of prosperity—, but a maximum, so that when the violence of high prices appears anywhere—may the gods avert such a calamity!—avarice which, as if in immense open areas, could not be restrained, might be checked by the limits of our statute or by the boundaries of a regulatory law. It is our pleasure, therefore, that the prices listed in the subjoined summary be observed in the whole of our empire in such fashion that every man know that while permission to exceed them has been forbidden him, the blessing of low prices has in no case been restricted in those places where supplies are seen to abound, since special provision is made for these when avarice is definitely quieted. Moreover, among buyers and sellers who customarily visit ports and foreign provinces this universal decree should be a check so that, when they too know that in the time of high prices there is no possibility of transcending the determined prices for commodities, such a reckoning of places, transportation, and the whole business may be made at the time of sale that the justice of our decree forbidding those who transport merchandise to sell anywhere at higher prices may be evident. Since, therefore, it is agreed that even in the time of our ancestors it was customary in passing laws to restrain insolence by attaching a proscribed penalty—since it is indeed rare for a situation tending to the good of humanity to be embraced spontaneously, and since, as a guide, fear is always found the most influential preceptor in the performance of duty—it is our pleasure that anyone who shall have resisted the form of this statute shall for his daring be subject to a capital penalty. And let no one consider the penalty harsh since there is at hand a means of avoiding the danger by the observance of moderation. To the same penalty, moreover, is he subject who in the desire to buy shall have conspired against the statute with the greed of the seller. Nor is he exempt from the same penalty who, although possessing necessities of life and business, believes that subsequent to this regulation he must withdraw them from the general market, since a penalty should be even more severe for him who introduces poverty than for him who harasses it against the law. We, therefore, urge upon the loyalty of all our people that a law constituted for the public good may be observed with willing obedience and due care; especially since in such a statute provision has been made, not for single states and peoples and provinces, but for the whole world, to whose ruin very few are known to have raged excessively, whose avarice neither fullness of time nor the riches for which they strive could lessen or satisfy.